RURAL
COMMUNITIES

RURAL

COMMUNITIES

LEGACY AND CHANGE

THIRD EDITION

CORNELIA BUTLER FLORA AND JAN L. FLORA

Iowa State University

Westview
PRESS

A Member of the Perseus Books Group

Find us on the World Wide Web at www.westviewpress.com.

Westview Press books are available at special discounts for bulk purchases in the United States by corporations, institutions, and other organizations. For more information, please contact the Special Markets Department at the Perseus Books Group, 2300 Chestnut Street, Suite 200, Philadelphia, PA 19103, or call (800) 255-1514, or e-mail special.markets@perseusbooks.com.

Designed by Trish Wilkinson
Set in 11 point Adobe Garamond

Library of Congress Cataloging-in-Publication Data
Flora, Cornelia Butler, 1943–
    Rural communities : legacy and change. — 3rd ed. / Cornelia Butler Flora and Jan L. Flora.
        p.   cm.
    Includes bibliographical references and index.
    ISBN-13: 978-0-8133-4377-8
    ISBN-10: 0-8133-4377-1
    1. United States—Rural conditions. 2. Sociology, Rural. I. Flora, Jan L., 1941– II. Title.
HN65R85 2008
307.720973—dc22   2007034345

10 9 8 7 6 5 4 3 2

Table of Contents

PART 1

COMPONENTS OF RURAL COMMUNITY: COMMUNITY CAPITALS

PART 2

THE TRANSFORMATION OF COMMUNITY
CAPITALS IN A CHANGING WORLD

Tables and Illustrations

Boxes

PREFACE

When we first conceived the *Rural Communities: Legacy and Change* project, we wanted to provide a textbook that would allow those using it to better understand rural communities and empower them to act to make them better places to live, work, and play. We were convinced that basic sociological concepts could build that understanding.

The first edition of *Rural Communities: Legacy and Change* was written to accompany a video series (see Appendix) by the same name for PBS. We used that edition for many years in conjunction with the video series and found that as the field of community studies advanced, we needed to update it. This led to a substantial reorganization in the second edition, where we brought in the community capitals. We found this version helpful, but again, the field progressed and the situation facing rural communities continued to change.

In the third edition, we have applied our experiences using the book with classes and with communities, reorganizing to show the relationships between material and social elements of community in the community capitals framework. We redirected our emphasis to an assets-based approach to community, focusing on what was already present in each community to address local issues of class, race, gender, and other types of exclusion. This edition focuses much more on community agency in response to structure than our previous editions.

We have updated tables, figures, cases, and data in the text when reliable new data were available, and we increased our emphasis on immigration and climate change. Chapter 11, Governance, now provides an alternative to looking solely at governments in addressing change in rural communities.

Other major changes include the introduction of the concepts of market, state, and civil society in Chapter 1, which we then used throughout the book. Chapter 2, Natural Capital, focuses more on how communities can confront global warming and invasive species, and Chapter 3, Cultural Capital and Legacy, continues its focus on stratification, domination, and resistance. Chapter 4, Human Capital, increases the focus on rural poverty and its implications. Chapter 5, Social Capital and Community, emphasizes the implications of different combinations of community bridging and bonding social capital, while Chapter 6, Political Capital, adds the smart-growth movement with relation to the growth machine and antigrowth forces in the discussion of the processes and structures of community power. Chapter 7, Financial Capital, introduces new financial instruments utilized in favor of excluded groups in rural areas. In Chapter 8, Built Capital, we introduce ways that rural communities have mobilized political capital to provide their own telecommunications services. We also focus more on the way waste from built capital contributes to both global warming and environmental degradation. Chapter 9, The Global Economy, now includes immigration as an important part of globalization not anticipated by international trade agreements. Chapter 10, Consumption in Rural America, brings in global warming and its implications for cultural change in terms of how we think of ourselves as consumers. Chapter 11 has been reformulated from governments to Governance, showing the importance of coalitions of market, state, and civil society actors at various levels to provide services and generate economic viability. Chapter 12, Generating Community Change, adds appreciative inquiry and assets-based analysis as an approach to community change, showing the importance for rural areas of shifting from a deficit to a strategy for systemic change that builds from rural community capitals.

Our goal is to engage readers—both in the classroom and outside it—in the dynamic process of community change, and the diverse legacies and global forces that influence that change.

PART I

COMPONENTS OF RURAL COMMUNITY

Community Capitals

1

The Rural Landscape and the Importance of Place

Christine Walden grew up in paradise. Christine, the daughter of schoolteachers, spent her childhood in Mammoth Lakes, California, surrounded by the majestic peaks, lush forests, and crystal-clear lakes of the Sierra Nevada range. The town, population two thousand, provided a nurturing environment. Changes began occurring in 1954 when an all-weather road and a double chair lift opened, beckoning skiers to the north face of Mammoth Mountain. By 2000, the town's population was more than three times what it had been in 1970, the year Christine was born. Golf courses replaced horse pastures, as befit a major tourism destination. Christine now teaches in the same school district that her parents did, but she no longer lives in Mammoth Lakes. Land development and speculation have driven housing costs beyond what a local teacher's salary can support. So Christine lives in Bishop and commutes forty miles each way to work. As gas prices have increased, even with carpooling and a hybrid SUV, she finds it more and more difficult to continue in her chosen profession in the place she loves.

Wade Skidmore grew up working in the mines. Part of the fifth generation of Skidmores to live in McDowell County, West Virginia, Wade had a childhood that was shaped by what was underground rather than by the slopes of the rugged Appalachian Mountains. He attended school only through the tenth grade; working in the mines did not require a high level of education and offered him a chance to work at his own pace. For a time, the work was steady and the pay was good. Then coal-loading machines came along—machines that could do the work of fifty men. Then some veins started giving out. The coal company changed first to long-wall and then to open-pit mining, cutting off the tops of mountains with huge machines. Wade was laid off, and the company left the town where he lived, which it had built. The company no longer maintained the water system, and the house was expensive to maintain. McDowell County, which lost more than 22 percent of its population between 1990 and 2000, and Wade Skidmore represent a region and a people trapped in persistent poverty. To make things worse, devastating floods swept the county in 2002, seriously damaging the Skidmore home, built along the banks of the Tug Fork of the Big Sandy River—the only flat land around. Most of the communities in McDowell County were destroyed, and the recovery effort is projected to continue until 2012. Wade's son just completed high school, and his daughter is in her junior year. He knows that they must go to college if they are to be able to make a living with dignity. He just hopes that it can be in McDowell County.

Maurice and Mae Thompson face a life-changing decision. Their farm near Irwin, Iowa, inherited from Mae's parents, may lead them deep into debt because they need new equipment to replace their combination harvester and planters, which are nearly forty years old and constantly break down. When hog prices were low in the late 1990s, the Thompsons regretfully closed their hog-raising operation. They fed their hogs on corn and soybeans that they raised themselves and sold the finished pigs to the stockyard in Sioux City, Iowa. But that stockyard has since closed, and the Thompsons are raising only corn and soybeans. Unfortunately, the amount of land they own is not enough to convince the local banker to lend them money to buy new equipment. To get the loan, they would have to buy or rent land from their neighbors.

The Thompsons have a few other options to consider as well. Some of their neighbors have contracts to raise feeder pigs with Murphy Farms, a subsidiary of Smithfield Foods, a large conglomerate. That method of raising feeder pigs also requires a large investment in hog houses and manure pits. However, the local bank readily lends money to these enterprises because they have ten-year contracts with the conglomerate. Such a contract would relieve the Thompsons of the risks of the fluctuating hog prices but would carry alternate risks, involving possible manure spills or increasing energy costs. Additionally, with such a contract, they would no longer purchase their feed additives, seed, fertilizers, and herbicides at the Farm

Services Cooperative in Irwin; Murphy Farms would deliver their feed on a regular basis. If they decided to expand their farm operation, they would buy their new equipment from Robinson Implement Inc., in Irwin.

Another alternative was presented to them by a friend they met through Practical Farmers of Iowa, a group interested in sustainable agriculture. Their friend raises hogs in hoop houses and sells them to Neiman Farms, which markets to high-end restaurants and mail-order consumers. This takes less capital, but it requires a lot of skill and learning—and if the hogs are not the right quality, they will not be purchased. This kind of contract also has its risks. Mae holds a job in the office of the local consolidated school, which gives her summers off and, most important, health insurance. Maurice feels as if he "just has to farm." All of these options leave the Thompsons with more questions: Should they go into debt to get more land and equipment or to construct the infrastructure to raise contract hogs? Should they risk an innovative way of producing "happy hogs" for a specialty market? Or should they sell their equipment and rent out their land or find a farm management company so someone else will farm it? (Mae's siblings would never agree to sell the land.) In any of those cases, the new operators probably would not buy locally. Or should the Thompsons replace aging machinery, rent land from retired farmers, and reduce their off-farm employment during planting and harvest seasons?

Billie Jo Davis Williams and her husband, Clayton Williams, are moving to Atlanta. Raised in Eatonton, Georgia, they grew up enjoying the gentle hills and dense stands of loblolly pine in Putnam County. Eatonton is home—both the Williams and Davis families go back to plantation days. But Billie Jo cannot find a job. She just finished a degree in business administration at Fort Valley State College, and Putnam County is growing rapidly—it grew by more than 33 percent between 1990 and 2000. But there are few jobs for African American women in Eatonton, since the textile factories moved overseas, other than domestic workers for the rich families who have built retirement homes on the lake. Clayton settled into a factory job at Horton Homes right out of high school, but he figures he can find work in Atlanta. It seems strange. Eatonton has been more successful than most communities in adapting to change—shifting from cotton farming to dairying to manufacturing and now to recreation/retirement economies. However, most African Americans have a hard time finding jobs offering more than the minimum wage.

Which is the real rural America: ski slopes of California, mines of West Virginia, farms in Iowa, or exurban resort and manufacturing communities in Georgia? Family farms and small farming communities dominate our images of rural America, in part because politicians, lobbyists, and the media cultivate those rural icons, supporting the myth that agricultural policy is rural policy. In fact, rural areas embrace ski slopes, mines, manufacturing, farms, retirement communities, American Indian reservations, bedroom communities, and much, much more. On average, in the twenty-first century, rural communities differ more from each other than they do from urban areas.

The diversity found among rural communities extends to the issues that emerge as each responds to the social and economic changes under way. Some communities that are rural and remote share the concerns of Irwin, wondering if their population will become too small to support a community business. The *amenity-based* community of Mammoth Lakes faces rapid growth. Its citizens are grappling with how to protect both the environment and the small-town character they value. In Eatonton, Georgia, which is a long commute from several large urban centers, the growth has been substantial because of the expansion of the resort economy and manufacturing, but Eatonton's black citizens have not shared equally in its success. Eatonton's population is highly transient, and its poverty rate remains higher than that of the state of Georgia as a whole. Those living in McDowell County face poverty and high out-migration, despite the wealth that the mines produced. Nearly one-third of the population falls below the poverty level, and median income is nearly $13,000 less than in the rest of West Virginia.

Despite the stereotype that life in the country is simpler, rural people face many of the same issues and concerns urban residents do, plus issues related to dispersion and distance. Indeed, rural and urban areas are linked. The garbage produced in New York City may find its way into landfills in West Virginia. Italian sausage served in Chicago could be made from hogs fattened on Iowa corn, grown with fertilizers that increase productivity but that may endanger rural water supplies. A housing boom in San Francisco creates jobs in the lumber industry in Oregon. However, the jobs last only as long as the forests. Air-quality concerns in Boston could shut down coal mines in West Virginia.

This book examines the diversity of rural America: its communities, the social issues they face in the twenty-first century, and the histories that explain those issues. It also addresses ways rural communities use their history and their increasing connectedness to creatively address those issues.

DEFINING RURAL

Giving a place a particular characteristic by naming it suggests how people and institutions act toward it. Researchers and policy makers depend on two federal systems when defining urban and rural. One, designed by the U.S. Census Bureau, separates the territory of the nation into urban and rural. Its intent is to differentiate urban and rural. The other, designed under the leadership of the Office of Management and Budget (OMB), focuses on the integration of urban and rural within *metropolitan* and micropolitan areas. Government-established labels for places are generally for administrative purposes: determining which places are eligible for specific government programs. Federal programs currently use more than fifteen definitions of rural. Thirty million Census Bureau–defined rural people live in OMB-defined metropolitan areas. Twenty million Census Bureau–defined urban people live in OMB-defined *nonmetropolitan* areas.

Economist Andrew Isserman focuses on the important distinction between separation and integration. At stake is the misunderstanding of rural conditions, the misdirection of federal programs and funds, and a breakdown of communication that confuses people. He suggests two alternatives that can strengthen the foundations of research and policy. The ideal solution is for the federal government to make available the same data for urban and rural areas that are available for counties. The pragmatic alternative, on hand immediately, is to use existing county data in a different way that recognizes that most counties are combinations of urban and rural areas. The new rural-urban density county typology seeks to separate urban and rural to the extent possible within a county framework (Isserman 2005).

When scholars establish labels, it is generally for analytic purposes, but because governments collect data, scholars often use government-established categories. Box 1.1 suggests how to evaluate different definitions of rural. Media and advertisers use place labels such as rural to evoke particular images. In the past, small size and isolation combined to produce relatively homogeneous rural cultures, economies based on natural resources, and a strong sense of local identity. But globalization, connectivity, and lifestyle changes accompanying shifting income distributions have altered the character of rural communities. They are neither as isolated nor as homogeneous as they once were.

Box 1.1   Definitions of Rural

There is no single, universally preferred definition of rural that serves all policy purposes. The choice of definition affects who benefits from a policy and who does not. Key considerations for understanding the policy implications of different rural definitions include the following:

- Rural definitions can be built on different units of geography, each of which has distinct advantages and disadvantages.
- The two most commonly used classification systems, those of the Census Bureau and the Office of Management and Budget, result in very different sets of places defined as rural. Sample population-size cutoffs for qualifying for USDA-based rural programs (definitions fixed by statute made by Congress or regulation made by the administration):
  - rural housing: 20,000 or fewer
  - telecom loans: 5,000 or fewer
  - water and waste grants: 10,000 or fewer
  - intermediary relending loans: 25,000 or fewer
  - rural business programs: 50,000 or fewer outside a metropolitan area
  - electric, prior to 2000: 1,500 or fewer in 1993; as of 2000: 2,500 or fewer
- Policies and programs can be targeted when rural definitions are combined with key demographic, economic, or service provider characteristics, such as size of hospital or school.
- Rural designations can change with shifts in population distribution or commuting patterns, or as a result of changes in geographic boundaries.
- Data availability is essential to support the application of the rural definition.

Metro and nonmetro areas are defined by the Office of Management and Budget (OMB). In 2003, OMB defined metro areas as (1) central counties with one or more urbanized areas, and (2) outlying counties that are economically tied to the core counties as measured by work commuting. Outlying counties are included if 25 percent of workers

continues

living in the county commute to the central counties, or if 25 percent of the employment in the county consists of workers coming out from the central counties—the so-called reverse commuting pattern. Nonmetro counties are outside the boundaries of metro areas and are further subdivided into two types: micropolitan areas, centered on urban clusters of 10,000 or more people, and all remaining noncore counties.

Many resources are available to help with understanding the complexities of rural definitions. The Rural Assistance Center in partnership with the Community Informatics Center (www.raconline.org/maps) and the Economic Research Service (http://ers.usda.gov/Briefing/Rurality/Whatis Rural/) look at counties. The U.S. Department of Education examines school districts and recently devised a procedure to determine the degree of rurality using geographic information systems and distance and density criteria (http://nces.ed.gov/pubs2007/ruraled/measuring.asp).

SOURCES

Adapted from Coburn, Andrew F., A. Clinton MacKinney, Timothy D. McBride, Keith J. Mueller, Rebecca T. Slifkin, and Mary K. Wakefield. 2007. "Choosing Rural Definitions." Issue Brief No. 2, March. Rural Policy Research Institute Health Panel. Also online; available: www.cdktest .com/rupri/Forms/RuralDefinitionsBrief.pdf; accessed September 8, 2007.
U.S. Department of Agriculture. Economic Research Service. "Measuring Rurality: What is Rural?" *Briefing Rooms*, updated March 22, 2007. Online; available: www.ers.usda.gov/Briefing/Rurality/WhatIsRural/; accessed September 8, 2007.

Isolation

Isolation is part of the rural image. There is a belief that rural people live out their entire lives in the town in which they were born, with some people going no further than a regional trade center or the state capital throughout their lifetime, but in actuality this was never true. Loggers, miners, farmers, and a host of others routinely moved to wherever they could find work or land. Other rural people were, in fact, isolated. In parts of McDowell County, mountain men and women lived in "hollows" in the hills, living on wild game and part-time construction work or cutting and selling wood. They created a rich culture of self-sufficiency. Canals, railroads, highways, and airways have altered much of rural isolation. Improved road systems have also changed the occupations and

Figure 1.1   The Rural-Urban Density Typology

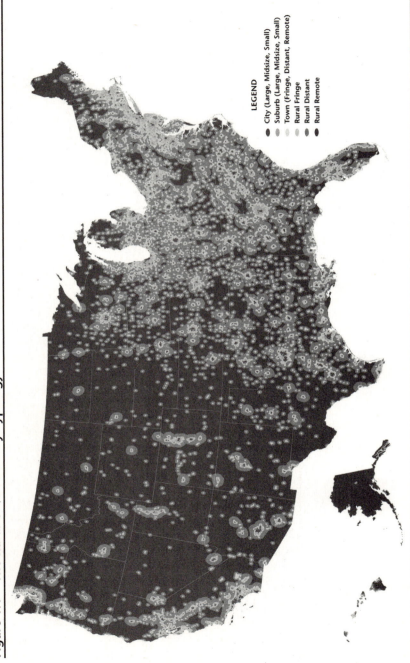

LEGEND

● City (Large, Midsize, Small)
● Suburb (Large, Midsize, Small)
● Town (Fringe, Distant, Remote)
● Rural Fringe
● Rural Distant
● Rural Remote

SOURCE: U.S. Department of Education. 2007. *Status of Rural Education.* Online; available: http://nces.ed.gov/pubs2007/ruraled/exhibit_c.asp; accessed September 9, 2007.

spending patterns of rural people. Those living near urban areas often commute to work, living in one town and working in another. They purchase many of their material goods in suburban malls.

Communication technologies have had an even greater effect in reducing isolation. Electronic chat rooms link rural residents with people from around the world who share their interests. Rural people now watch opera from New York, football games from San Francisco, ballet from Houston, and congressional deliberations from Washington, D.C., over satellite dishes. Rural people have become as literate, informed, and enriched as their urban counterparts. However, a rural-urban connectivity divide still exists. Many residents on reservations in the Great Plains do not have phone service, much less broadband Internet connectivity. Wireless strategies based on satellites still present problems in mountainous areas. Although the isolation that distance imposes is much less than it once was, communities that are rural and remote and those that are persistently poor are much more isolated than rural residents in areas of urban sprawl and high rural amenities. The map in Figure 1.1 shows the degree of ruralness based on distance from urban areas, as suggested by Isserman. It is not based on counties, avoiding what Isserman calls "the county trap" (Isserman 2005, 472), but is based on geographic locations.

Ethnicity and Change in Rural America

Ioway Sioux Indians were some of the original settlers along the rich river bottoms of the Nishnabotna River in Shelby County, Iowa. In Mono County, California, the Northern and Owens Valley Paiute walked through what is now Mammoth Lakes as part of their sacred rituals to ensure success in their hunting and gathering. Shawnee and Delaware occasionally hunted in what is now McDowell County, West Virginia. Creek Indians occupied mid-Georgia, including Putnam County, prior to being forced west, first by the Cherokee and then by the Europeans. The U.S. government then forcibly removed the Cherokee to Oklahoma, where many lost their lives on the Trail of Tears (Nunna daul Tsuny).

First commercial and then industrial interests brought Europeans, Africans, and Asians to rural America; national interests encouraged Europeans, in particular, to settle land. Fur trappers for British, Spanish, French, and then American trading companies, spurred by the Lewis and Clark expedition, pushed westward across Canada and the United States. Fur trading was only a prelude to the development of settled agriculture.

African Americans were critical to the land-extensive, labor-intensive agricultural system of the South. Prior to the Civil War, African Americans escaping slavery from Missouri and Arkansas crossed over Shelby County, Iowa, on their way to freedom. African Americans who had worked in the coal mines in Birmingham, Alabama, moved to McDowell County to open those mines, even though their children attended segregated schools until the late 1950s. Asians, particularly Chinese, who helped build the western half of the intercontinental railroad, participated in the mining boom in Mammoth Lakes in the 1880s and 1890s. When they were barred from mining, they provided essential services, such as cooking and washing, to the miners.

Spanish and Native American cultures occupied much of the West long before U.S. expansion. The abolition of slavery left African American families scattered throughout a rural South extending from the Atlantic Ocean to central Texas and as far north as Kansas and Missouri. Migrant workers from the Deep South and Mexico followed the harvest as far north as Maine in the East and Washington State in the West. More recently, as a result of the war in Southeast Asia, refugees from Vietnam, Laos, and Cambodia, including very distinct cultures such as the Hmong, have moved to rural areas. Like the Mexicans, they also took jobs that U.S.-born rural residents were unwilling or unable to fill, such as in meatpacking plants in rural areas with aging populations. Immigrants saved money by having many workers per household and by keeping their consumption low. Although some stayed in the rural Midwest, other Asian refugees used their modest savings to move to urban or coastal areas, excelling both in fishing on the Gulf of Mexico and in raising vegetables around large cities.

As other international conflicts create refugees, migrants from the Sudan, Bosnia, and now Afghanistan settle in rural communities as well as in large cities. (Unlike in other conflicts, Iraqis displaced by wars in their country have not been granted refugee status in the United States as of September 2007.) This influx changes the religious as well as the racial composition of areas that once were extremely homogeneous.

DEFINING COMMUNITY

Many functional definitions and descriptions of rural areas utilize counties as the smallest geographic unit for which data are readily available and comparable. Yet people typically act through communities. As of the 2000 census, nearly five million rural people lived in communities of fewer than

2,500 residents. Demographers can count communities, but sociologists have a much harder time defining just what a community is. In this section, we look at the concept of community, the definition used in this book, and the extent to which our study of rural communities relates to urban communities.

The Concept of Community

Sociologists use the term *community* in several ways, all of which focus on groups of people. In one use of the term, community refers to a place, a location in which members of a group interact with one another. A second use of the term looks at the social system itself, the organization or set of organizations through which a group of people meets its needs. Finally, sociologists also use the word community to describe a shared sense of identity held by a group of people who may or may not share the same geographic space.

The concept of community often is based on a shared sense of place. This sense of place involves relationships with the people, cultures, and environments, both natural and built, associated with a particular area. For many rural residents, the area associated with a particular place may be very different from any area defined by the political boundaries of a town or even county. Stereotypes of rural communities conjure up images of isolated, relatively self-sufficient, sometimes backward or unsophisticated cultures. The stereotype may never have been entirely accurate, but at one time rural people turned to their communities for nearly everything. People lived, worked, worshipped, shopped, banked, sent their children to school, and socialized all in the same place. When the community's economy rested on a single resource, such as mining or farming, people even had a shared sense of what it took to make a living and run a household.

These three elements of community—location, social system, and common identity—are increasingly separate. In the past, a community offered a place that housed a set of social institutions (schools, churches, governments, businesses) through which people's daily needs could be met, and a place where people could share a sense of identity. However, improved transportation has made us more mobile, and telecommunications now put us in touch with a wider circle of acquaintances. Some people feel a sense of community with those who do similar things or share common values, not with those living in the same town. Thus, we consider both communities of place and communities of interest. A group of high-energy physicists, for example, might be a community of interest. These people share a common identity—they interact through meetings, journals, e-mail, or telephone—yet they are dispersed throughout the world.

The rural landscape may not have changed as much over the past century as has the social organization of rural communities. Cars enable people to live in one town, work in another, and shop in yet a third. Better roads have allowed schools to consolidate, which has led to social institutions that may be less attached to their communities, both physically and socially. As rural communities broaden their economic activity, people's work roles become very different from one another and much less publicly visible. Thus, rural people, like urbanites, are known less by what they do than by what they consume.

Our definition of community applies to both rural and urban areas. Communities may have political boundaries, or they may simply have social ones. Communities may be recognized politically, through local governments and the power to tax their residents. They may also be informal groupings of households—neighborhoods—within the larger city. Issues can cause neighborhoods to band together to demand better services from the city just as they inspire rural communities to take control over their economic future. Although the focus in this book is on rural communities, many of the topics are immediately relevant to communities within urban settings as well.

Institutional Community Actors

Communities of place have three sets of institutional actors: the market, the state, and civil society. An individual is a part of all three sectors, but most community firms, agencies, and organizations are more functionally discrete.

Markets.   The market sector includes the many firms and institutions that exchange goods and services at a profit. When there is competition and free flow of information, they are incredibly efficient at distributing goods and services to those who can pay. They are not particularly efficient at distributing goods and services to those who cannot pay or at protecting the environment. Local communities often absorb the burden of these "market failures" and externalities.

Markets are highly dynamic, with much competition and the constant entrance and exit of firms. Market institutions are present at the local, state, national, and transnational levels. These institutions sometimes compete, sometimes collaborate, and are integrated forward and backward to differing degrees. The purpose of market institutions is to make a profit for their owners. Sometimes the owners are individuals or families. Sometimes owners are stockholders. Stockholders tend to evaluate firms on two factors: how much profit they have generated in the past quarter and their market value. When either of these is viewed as unsatisfactory, owners seek to change the hired managers. Consolidation, competition, and cooperation among market firms suggest a very dynamic sphere. Farms, cooperatives, and transnational firms are all part of the market sector. Max Weber points out that a modern economy requires a separation of management from ownership for market firms. This separation is increasingly occurring in rural areas. Although such separation definitely can increase short-term profits and the net worth of firms, absentee owners can more easily ignore the voices of those who wish to increase their own economic participation. However, absentee owners also are less likely to intervene in local actions that do not directly affect their firm (Trounstine and Christensen 1982).

States. The *state* (or government) makes markets possible. Markets need fairly stable conditions in which to operate. Weber (1978, 161–166) presents a convincing argument for the necessity of a strong state for the effective functioning of what he refers to as "the modern economy." Markets need contracts that are enforceable through an effective administrative and judiciary system. They need a reliable money supply. They need to know that the legislative system will put rules into place. And they need to know that the rules will be administered in a universalistic way—the same rules are applied to everyone. Thus the state, which is government from international levels down to the national, state, and local levels, is critical to the market in that, in a universalistic way, it sets and enforces the rules within which the market operates, an example of formal rationality. But the state has the additional responsibility of providing for the public welfare. Only by attention to both formal and substantive rationality (Weber 1978, 85) can states maintain legitimacy.

Regulatory policies determine what markets exist and how they can function. Regulation is both positive and negative for firms. On the one hand, it limits what they can do and how they do it. On the other, it limits what their competition can do and how they do it, creating a more level playing field. Different entities (firms, organizations, associations) of market and civil society struggle over what the state will regulate and for what ends.

State agencies often are at odds with each other—local with state, state with national, and national with international. The state, like the market, is a dynamic, contested sector. In the United States, governors and legislators disagree. Very often, local levels of government, particularly counties and small cities, feel imposed upon by the state or federal governments, particularly as they deal with unfunded mandates. Thus, within the state sphere, which sets the rules and conditions for the market and the safety net for its citizens, the terrain is very contested.

In the United States, the state includes the three branches of government: the legislative (which makes the laws and allocates resources), the administrative (which implements the laws through administrative rules and regulations and distributes the resources), and the judicial (which interprets laws and sanctions those who do not follow the laws). In many countries that come from the European tradition, a much closer relationship exists between the legislative and the administrative functions than in the United States, where strict separation of powers—which greatly increases the transaction costs of governing—were installed in the constitution of "the first new nation" (Lipset 1963; Browne 2001). The state provides the rules under which the market operates in order that the common good be served at the same time firms are profitable, thus serving one of its functions, accumulation. And the state provides a safety net for people and protects natural resources deemed to be in the common good. By doing this—paying attention to substantive rationality—the state remains legitimate. The state is a highly contentious sphere. Even within state agencies, different branches of the same bureaucracy seek to gain or maintain hegemony, influence, and budget.

A major purpose of the state under capitalism not only is to ensure conditions under which firms can make a profit but also to be sure that making a profit also serves the common good. Elected officials often are judged by the degree to which they serve the common good. However, definition of the common good is almost always contested, by market players who claim that what is good for the stock market is good for the country, and by civil society, which may be more concerned with climate change, war, or poverty.

Civil Society.   *Civil society* can define the common good. When civil society is absent, either bureaucrats or firms define the common good, usually in ways that enhance their own sphere of influence (Perlmutter 1991). These groups, formal and informal, join together around common interests or values. Through their organized activity, they impact the market and the state. The faith community, including churches, synagogues, and mosques; the National Rifle Association; and gun-control groups are all part of civil society. So are Friends of the Earth, Oxfam, the Sierra Club, and Ducks Forever, as are parent-teacher organizations and Rotary clubs. These organizations articulate their shared interests and values in a variety of ways as they interact with the market and the state.

Civil society influences the market through forming consumer groups that can engage in boycotts and information campaigns.

Civil society influences the state by bringing lawsuits (influencing the judicial branch of government), by forging legislation (influencing the legislative part of government), and by urging that particular laws be enforced (influencing the administrative part of government).

Civil society generally exerts influence based on deeply held values or desired future conditions. Groups in civil society, both formal and informal, form around those shared future conditions and their mental/causal models of how the world works. Individuals relate to civil society when they become participants or members. Groups in civil society also are in hot dispute with one another. Since the definition of the collective conscience is negotiated here, groups struggle to gain participants and to co-opt other groups. The dynamism of this sector influences both the market and the state.

Community Capitals

Every community, however rural, isolated, or poor, has resources within it. When those resources, or assets, are invested to create new resources, they become *capital.* We have found it useful when looking at communities to focus on seven types of capital in the following order: natural, cultural, human, social, political, financial, and built. These capitals can either enhance or detract from one another. Furthermore, resources can be transformed from one form of capital to another. When one type of capital is emphasized over all others, the other resources are *decapitalized,* and the economy, environment, or social equity thus can be compromised. These community capitals form the basic organization of the book.

Natural capital is the base on which all other capitals depend. It is the landscape, climate, air, water, soil, and biodiversity of both plants and animals. It can be consumed or extracted for immediate profit, or it can be a continuing resource for communities of place.

Cultural capital includes values and approaches to life that have both economic and noneconomic implications. Cultural capital can be thought of as the filter through which people live their lives, the daily or seasonal rituals they observe, and the way they regard the world around them. The socialization process serves to transmit values and cultural capital from a group to its members. Elites use cultural capital to gain strategic class-based ties for their children, thereby excluding the children of others who lack those resources and the necessary strategic vision to move their children up the social ladder (Bourdieu 1986).

Human capital is the skills and abilities of each individual within a community. It includes potentials, like a good ear for music, and acquired skills, such as playing the trumpet. Formal and informal education and life experience contribute to human capital. One's health and leadership skills are also part of human capital.

Social capital includes the networks, norms of reciprocity, and mutual trust that exist among and within groups and communities. It contributes to a sense of a common identity and shared future. Community social capital facilitates groups' working together. Both bonding (multiple linkages to enforce norms and encourage trust) and bridging (single-purpose linkages) forms of social capital are important for community prosperity and sustainability.

Political capital is the ability of a group to influence the standards of the market, state, or civil society; the codification of those standards in laws and contracts; and the enforcement of those standards. This in turn influences the distribution of resources within a social unit, including helping set the agenda for what resources are available and who is eligible to receive them. Political capital includes organization, connections, voice, and power. Rural communities have relatively little political capital at the federal level. The ability of a *commodity organization,* such as the National Corn Growers or National Pork Producers, to channel government funds to large producers is not the same as political capital for rural communities.

Financial capital consists of money that is used for investment rather than consumption. Investment means using a purchase or a financial instrument to create additional value. Communities can utilize the financial capital of state, market, and civil society.

Built capital is the infrastructure that supports other community capitals: factories, schools, roads, restored habitat, community centers, and

Figure 1.2 Community Capitals Framework

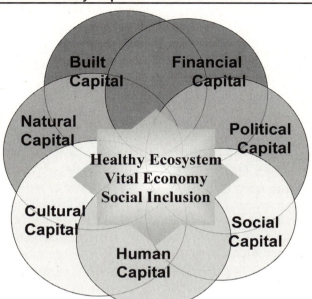

SOURCE: Flora, C. B. 2004. "Social Aspects of Small Water Systems." *Journal of Contemporary Water Research and Education* 128: 6–12.

the like. Built capital can be appropriated by special interests or be widely available to all community residents.

The Community Capitals Framework provides fuzzy boundaries for the capitals, which all overlap with each other (Figure 1.2). They can come together to create sustainable communities with healthy ecosystems, vital economies, and social inclusion. Or one capital can be favored to the extent that the others are consumed to maximize the single capital. The destruction of natural capital to produce financial capital in McDowell not only left the area highly vulnerable to extreme climate events, which have increased in frequency as a result of global warming, but had negative effects on human capital, social capital, built capital, and local financial capital.

RURAL COMMUNITIES AND CHANGE

Rural communities have never been insulated from the social and economic change under way in the broader society. The interstate highway system, started by President Dwight D. Eisenhower in the 1950s as a national security measure, had a profound effect on rural communities. For example, people can live in Eatonton and work in Atlanta.

Telecommunications have broken the isolation experienced in remote regions. Irwin has several businesses that engage in e-commerce, for example. Increased competition with foreign products led manufacturers to abandon urban labor markets for rural ones during the 1970s, only to abandon those for even cheaper labor overseas a decade later. With the North American Free Trade Agreement (NAFTA) and the World Trade Organization (WTO), the twenty-first century is seeing even greater movement of low-wage manufacturing to less developed countries. Mexico, the low-wage country in NAFTA, is experiencing an exodus of jobs to China, where wages are considerably lower than in Mexico. Thus, for example, nothing easily replaces mining in McDowell County. Increasing affluence has led to more decisions on where to live being based on lifestyle than on jobs alone. As the affluent choose their lifestyle, the less affluent move in behind them to support that lifestyle, as in the case of Mammoth Lakes.

The rural profiles that opened this chapter illustrate some of these differences among rural communities and the impact of those differences on people's lives. The problems Christine Walden faces arise from the rapid amenity-based growth occurring in Mammoth Lakes. Growth in the exurban town of Eatonton has not greatly benefited African American citizens such as Billie Jo Davis Williams. Wade Skidmore, the miner from McDowell County, finds his family falling into poverty now that the mines have closed. Maurice and Mae Thompson see their options to farm decreased through increased land prices, farm concentration, and international competition. These four patterns—*rapid growth* based on natural amenities, rapid growth based on nearness to urban areas, persistent poverty, and rural and remote location—provide a useful structure with which to compare communities, the capitals they have, and the impact that changes in market, state, and civil society have on them.

Amenity-Based Rapid Growth

Mammoth Lakes has always revolved around its natural capital, though its population varied as the region's economic activity shifted from mining to timber to hiking and fishing and finally to skiing. Today, Mammoth Lakes is one of many rural communities in high-amenity areas struggling with the problems of rapid growth: high in-migration, high housing costs, increasing taxes that force long-term residents out of the community, and a growing immigrant population attracted by jobs in the service economy.

Rapid development affects natural capital as well. Water used for commercial development lowers lakes and decreases the flow of area streams, threatening the very wildlife that beckons hunters and fishers each summer. Forests and meadows are disappearing under condominiums and parking lots, and sewage has become a serious problem. Increased use of the land also contributes to soil erosion and to a general degradation of nearby wilderness areas.

Depending on the specific character of the amenities, such areas may attract younger adults interested in active sports, as in the case of Mammoth Lakes, or they may primarily attract retirees. The two patterns sometimes shade into each other when people regularly visit a particular place for recreation and decide to retire there. Communities such as Mammoth Lakes are growing because of the natural amenities they provide.

Persistent-Poverty Communities

McDowell County is one of many rural counties struggling with low incomes and the problems of persistent poverty. As the mining companies pulled out, they left families who had known nothing but mining for generations. Illiteracy is high, as is infant mortality. Doctors, dentists, and other professionals are hard to find. Young people see little reason to invest effort in school because there are no jobs to prepare for. Communities find it hard to attract businesses; there is no tax base with which to build the needed roads, bridges, and schools. Those who can leave do. Those who can't leave simply make do.

McDowell County is among the 363 nonmetropolitan counties classified as *persistently poor.* Ninety percent of these counties are found in sixteen Southern states. Nearly 13.4 percent of rural people in these counties had income levels below the 2000 poverty level, established as $20,550 for a family of three. Many of these counties have been successful in attracting and creating jobs. In some cases, they have experienced population increases. Although poverty decreased in these counties during the 1990s, particularly in Appalachia and the Mississippi Delta, a substantial proportion of the population still has low income.

Rural and Remote

The term *rural and remote* refers to counties that have small populations and are far from metropolitan centers. Often they are losing population. They are home to a little more than one-fourth of the nation's nonmetropolitan population. For the most part, these populations are well educated and have enjoyed relatively high average incomes in the past. Jobs have not grown fast enough, however, to replace those lost. The population of these counties is aging because young people are leaving. Some ask whether the residents of this region will become the new poor.

Rapid-Growth Exurban

Communities within commuting distance of large metropolitan areas, such as Eatonton, face a different set of problems. These counties are often referred to as *exurban*. Urban sprawl threatens their natural, financial, and social capital. As farmland gives way to development, new services are required. The tax base does not expand as fast as the needs of the growing population. Although developers make money, local governments struggle to keep basic services in place for community residents. Residents often disagree as to what constitutes adequate services. Newcomers and long-term residents often have different expectations for schools, the role of local government, and appropriate neighborly behavior. These groups also have different tolerances for barnyard or feedlot smells, slow-moving vehicles on the roads, and the accumulation of old vehicles and machinery around rural farmsteads.

ABOUT THIS BOOK

In this book, we talk primarily about communities of place, although they are crosscut by communities of interest. A geographic community may or may not provide the social system through which its members' needs are met. It may or may not provide a sense of identity for its members. A geographic community does provide what some sociologists now call locality, a geographically defined place where people interact. How people interact shapes the structures and institutions of the locality. Those structures and institutions in turn shape the activities of the people who interact. Consider your sense of community. Where do you go to college? Where did you grow up? Where does your family live? Where do you vacation? These communities of place relate you to people and the environment, both natural and built. Or is your main community one of interest? Your sports team, your fraternity or sorority, your political party, or your church, synagogue, or mosque may provide you with a sense of belonging and of purpose. Your identity can arise from a place and its ethnic roots, or from your market, state, or civil society affiliations.

Communities differ in the degree to which they agree on the meaning and value of the various capitals and on the degree to which they see the market, state, or civil society as the proper entity to invest in each capital. And a great deal of diversity surrounds these issues within rural communities as well. In this book, we will learn more about the sources of inter- and intracommunity diversity.

Assumptions

The most basic assumption we make here is that the rural perspective is worth exploring. Our society has become so deeply urbanized that we almost assume urbanization to be a natural law. Urbanization was important to industrialization, but many people now argue that the economic reasons for urbanization no longer are as compelling as they once were. Others point to the limits of growth, arguing that the social costs of overcrowding have exceeded whatever economies of scale made urbanization preferable. Still others point to the contributions rural areas make to the nation: (1) food security, (2) a sense of land stewardship that protects natural resources, (3) a value system connected to both the land and human relationships, and (4) protection of biodiversity.

The reality is that more than one-fourth of the nation's people have chosen to live in rural areas. As we make the transition to the digital age, it seems appropriate to reexamine rural areas—asking why people have stayed, how federal and state policies have contributed to current conditions in rural areas, and what role individual choice can play in dealing with current social issues.

Given the choice to focus on rural communities, these assumptions guided the selection of topics and organization used for this book. First, we have assumed that trends are not destiny. Individuals, groups, and communities can modify trends through appropriate actions. Our understanding of the drivers of those trends becomes part of the reality in which we live, affecting the choices we make as individuals and as a society.

Second, we have assumed that what occurs in rural areas is the result of history, especially the changing relationship between urban and rural society. Although it is simpler to think about rural and urban communities as separate worlds, in reality they are connected. Georgia was established as a colony because of London's problems with debtors. Much of the rural West was settled to provide the resources needed to fuel industrial growth in the East. Timber in Washington State was cleared to build the houses in Los Angeles. McDowell County was populated because industry needed coal to operate its factories. Irwin was settled because the railroads needed grain to haul and Eastern cities needed a dependable food supply. The connections continue today. To understand what is occurring in rural areas, we must continually look to both past and present rural-urban linkages.

Social issues involve human relationships and thus social capital, but much of what leads to these problems is related to access and control over the other capitals. For example, a 4-H leader in the Florida Panhandle points out that he cannot separate the problems of child abuse from the problems of persistent poverty. Efforts to build an economy capable of alleviating poverty are as important to him as programs on effective parenting. Our third assumption is that it is necessary to look at the seven capitals as highly interrelated. Increasing only one capital without attention to the others can lead to many unintended—and unpleasant—consequences.

The fourth and fifth assumptions simply describe the tension between public policy and individual choice. The fourth assumption states that political decisions at the state and national level influence where and how economic and social change takes place. Problems of rural poverty, ethnic conflicts, or climate change can be understood partly in terms of public policy, that is, in terms of the political choices, made by state, market, and civil society actors. Thus, the differential access to political capital influences rural realities.

The fifth assumption adds that the rural experience is the sum of group responses to both political constraints and individual choice. People can make a difference, either by influencing the broader policy agenda that constrains them or by making choices within the policy framework. We are not just victims of society or passive consumers of broader national change. The choices rural people make affect the direction change takes in their communities.

Simply stated, these assumptions argue that rural issues can be examined in terms of change. Change can be explained in terms of history and in terms of the interplay among the different types of capital in the context of global trends and local conditions. Change involves both individual and institutional choices related to market, state, and civil society.

Organization of This Book

We first introduce the seven capitals, based on how we see them as building on one another in place. Each chapter opens with one or more rural profiles. These profiles are fictional in the sense that they are not always descriptions of actual individuals. The circumstances are real, however. Historical documents, site visits, research journals, taped telephone and video interviews, newspaper articles, and a variety of other sources were used to collect information about real rural communities. The issues identified also are real, expressed by people living in rural communities throughout the country.

Individual experiences often have causes embedded in the institutions and conventions of society. Understanding how this happens is a part of what sociologists undertake as they study human society and social behavior. Each chapter is structured to help the reader move from an issue voiced by rural people to the sociological issue suggested by the concepts and theories of the social sciences. Seen from this broader perspective, social problems experienced by rural people become societal problems capable of being solved through collective action.

Part 1 looks at each capital individually and how it interacts with other capitals. Part 2 examines how the community capitals interact with and are transformed by globalization (Chapter 9), consumption (Chapter 10), governance (Chapter 11), and purposive community change (Chapter 12).

Chapter 12 describes models for effective community change and describes situations where those models have been successful. The focus is on how rural communities can identify and combine community capitals for change that addresses the triple bottom line: equity, economics, and environment.

CHAPTER SUMMARY

Many people imagine a rural America characterized by farming, homogeneous cultures, and close-knit communities. In reality, rural communities differ more among themselves than they do, on average, from urban areas. Four major circumstances predominate in rural America: sprawl in areas near cities, rapid growth near natural amenities, persistent poverty, and rural and remote areas.

What is defined to be a rural community has changed over time. In general, definitions of rural include descriptions of both size and location. Some current definitions use the distinction between nonmetropolitan and metropolitan counties, equating nonmetropolitan with rural. Definitions of community also have changed. This text defines community as a place or location in which people interact for mutual benefit. The community need not provide all the services individuals require and may not necessarily offer community members a common sense of identity.

Rural communities differ in terms of ethnicity and in terms of the realities that most affect their options. Rural communities are among the most ethnically diverse as well as the most ethnically homogeneous, depending on the region of the country in which they are located. Yet, because the counties that were the most ethnically homogeneous are also the ones aging most quickly, a subset of these also has the highest rate of recent immigration from other countries.

This book assumes that social issues can be explained in terms of a community's history and the resulting capitals that are available to that community. Economic and policy choices made at the state and federal levels and individual choices made by the communities themselves mean that, even for poor, remote rural communities, trend is not destiny.

Key Terms

Amenity-based communities are those located near natural resources that are viewed as a source of beauty and recreation by the larger population. They include counties by bodies of water and mountains.

Built capital is capital that is transformed from financial capital and includes factories, schools, roads, habitat restoration, and community centers, all of which contribute to building other capitals for communities.

Capital is a resource invested to create new resources.

Civil society is made of groups of people organized around beliefs or interests who do not seek to make a profit through those groups. Civil society is made up of both formal associations and informal groups.

The *collective conscience* is composed of the shared beliefs and moral attitudes that operate as a unifying force within society.

A *commodity organization* is a group with market interest in commodities (general categories of goods marketed in bulk). Its constituents join together to achieve political and market goals.

A *community* is a place or location where groups of people interact for mutual support.

Decapitalized resources lose value when one type of capital is emphasized over all others, and the economy, environment, or social equity is thus compromised.

E-commerce is the process of conducting business (obtaining inputs or marketing one's products or services) via the Internet.

Exurban areas are those that are just beyond the suburbs. Previously agricultural, they are characterized by mixed agricultural-residential usage. The residential lots are larger than urban or suburban lots and often exist cheek-to-jowl with farms whose use is often intensifying due to the rising price of land. Exurban counties are those on the metropolitan fringe.

Financial capital consists of money that is used for investment rather than for consumption.

Human capital consists of the skills and abilities of each individual within a community.

The *market* is made of profit-oriented firms and individuals when they buy or sell goods or services.

Metropolitan areas consist of one or more adjacent counties containing at least one city of 50,000 or more inhabitants.

Natural capital is the landscape, air, water, soil, and biodiversity of both plants and animals.

Nonmetropolitan counties are those counties that lie outside a standard metropolitan area and do not include a city of 50,000 or more inhabitants.

Persistently poor counties are those whose per capita family income was in the lowest 20 percent of counties in 1960, 1970, 1980, 1990, and 2000.

Political capital is the ability of a group to influence the distribution of resources within a social unit, including helping to determine what resources are available and who is eligible to receive them.

The term *rapid growth* applies to rural counties that experienced population increases greater than the national average. Rapid-growth exurban counties owe their growth to the adjacent metropolitan areas.

Rural and remote counties are those that are not adjacent to urban areas and that themselves have no town of substantial size.

Social capital includes the networks, norms of reciprocity, and mutual trust that exist among and within groups and communities.

The term *state* refers to all governments at all levels: local, county, state, national, and international. These governments have specific territorial responsibilities that may overlap with those of other state entities.

REFERENCES

Bourdieu, Pierre. 1986. "The Forms of Capital." In *Handbook of Theory and Research for the Sociology of Education,* ed. John C. Richardson, 241–258. New York: Greenwood Press.

Browne, W. P. 2001. *The Failure of National Rural Policy: Institutions and Interests.* Washington, D.C.: Georgetown University Press.

Isserman, Andrew M. 2005. "Defining Rural and Urban Correctly in Research and Public Policy." *International Regional Science Review* 28: 465–499.

Lipset, S. M. 1963. *The First New Nation: The United States in Historical and Comparative Perspective.* New York: Basic Books.

Perlmutter, T. 1991. "Italy: Why No Voluntary Sector?" In *Between States and Markets: The Voluntary Sector in Comparative Perspective,* ed. R. Wuthnow, 157–188. Princeton, N.J.: Princeton University Press.

Trounstine, P. J., and T. Christensen. 1982. *Movers and Shakers: The Study of Community Power.* New York: St. Martin's Press.

Weber, Max. 1978. *Economy and Society,* eds. G. Roth and C. Wittich. Berkeley: University of California Press.

2

Natural Capital

Eric Ritter was frustrated. It was the third time he had called the Colorado Division of Wildlife (DOW) about the elk tearing down his fences. He wanted to organize a group of guys to shoot the herds of elk that were competing with his cattle for grass and ruining his fences. But the laws were clear. Instead he requested financial assistance to fix his fences. He always got the money, but he still had to rebuild the fence. Something had to change.

About a month later, Eric got a call from the Colorado Cattlemen's Association to meet with the DOW and others to come up with alternatives. The meeting included hunters, outfitters who took people on hunting trips in the mountains where Eric ranched, and people from various environmental organizations. Eric felt uncomfortable with the last group, folks he viewed as "tree huggers," especially Sue Graves, who was always stopping everything in the name of environmental protection. He privately called her "Mother Earth." But he stuck with the new program, called the Habitat Partnership Program. He learned that similar groups were meeting in other districts in Colorado—all with the same concern about the conflicting use of natural capital in the mountain valleys.

After getting together for meals and field visits, the environmentalists and the livestock producers realized they shared some concerns. Since fires had been suppressed, trees were invading the meadows and pastures, limiting the grass available for both the game animals and the cattle. If there was more grass available higher up, the deer and elk might not come down to the cattle areas. And if more grass grew in the valleys, the occasional presence of the deer and elk would not be such a problem. Furthermore, as they talked, Eric learned about a new kind of fencing that had a shiny white strip along the top wire. When the deer and elk saw the strip, they just jumped over the fence, which still served as a barrier that kept the cattle in their proper location. Working together, the environmentalists and the livestock producers wrote a plan for burning and restoring pastures and meadows, and they even had a good time putting the plan into action. Now Eric knows the environmentalists by name—and he even drops in for coffee with Sue Graves. He learned that she used to call him "That Redneck." And as he enters her shop in town, he shouts out, "Mother Earth, do you have the coffee on? This Redneck is mighty thirsty."

For more information: http://wildlife.state.co.us/LandWater/Private LandProgram/HPP/.

When the Europeans came to North America, the landscape was already managed by indigenous peoples in ways to ensure that grass was available for wild ruminants, such as buffalo, deer, elk, and moose, and crop production (identification and protection of areas where berries, edible roots, and reeds grew, and where they could plant corn, beans, and other plants that they domesticated and trees for constructing tools and homes, and irrigation in more arid regions of the continent). That management favored some species over others, changing the biodiversity of the area over time. However, to European eyes, the land looked wild and untamed. In Europe, most land had been privatized, fenced, and cultivated. The natural capital of the New World—plants, animals, soil, and water—seemed abundant. All that was needed was to tame the wild lands in order to produce financial and built capital.

Whereas most Native American tribes used the land to develop a subsistence economy, with a strong focus on converting natural capital to social and cultural capital, most Europeans came to the Americas to transform natural capital to financial capital. Fur trappers, timber companies, and miners used the resources until they were depleted and then moved on. European governments often financed explorations of the New World and expected new wealth in return. A number of English companies actually sold stock to finance early settlements. Once established, these settlements were expected to become self-sufficient and then to begin exporting products to pay off their debts and dividends to their stockholders.

The hope of the conversion of natural capital to financial capital motivated the U.S. government to finance such expeditions as Meriwether Lewis and William Clark's Corps of Discovery and other westward exploration. The explorers and those who accompanied them expected to receive land as a result of their work, which would then be translated into financial wealth (Ambrose 1996). Although the expeditions generated cultural capital in terms of new knowledge about the people and the lands, the explorers' goal was to beat the English, French, and Spanish to claim the territory and the wealth of its natural resources.

LAND USE

Land-settlement policies played an important role in the economic character of early rural communities. In New England, the English Crown gave land to trading companies that, in turn, gave land to groups of settlers. These groups established central villages surrounded by farmland. Farmers worked their fields by day but returned to the village at night. A village-style settlement created an environment capable of eventually supporting other economic functions, such as manufacturing and domestic crafts.

In the South, however, the English Crown gave land directly to individuals. The landowners then settled large, relatively self-sufficient plantations that depended upon slave labor. Few villages or towns were created.

Although a few hardy adventurers were always willing to push westward, efforts to settle land west of the Appalachian Mountains were slow to develop. When forests in the Northeast had been exhausted in the 1840s, logging companies pushed into the Great Lakes region in search of new timber. The discovery of gold and silver in the late 1840s brought waves of prospectors westward.

Despite these early migrations, it was not until Abraham Lincoln signed the Homestead Act in 1862 that European Americans began to settle in the West. The Homestead Act gave settlers 160 acres of land each if they would establish a home on the land and work to increase its productivity for at least five years. Railroads also received land grants. They then sold tracts of land to raise funds to construct the rail lines. Because the Homestead Act required settlers to live on the land, people remained dispersed across the countryside.

In some states, such as West Virginia and Kentucky, mining companies bought up huge tracts of land. When they did not own the land itself, they bought the mineral rights, which allowed them to mine underneath homes and farms, an activity that was often followed by the collapse of the land itself and the destruction of homes and livelihoods. Mining companies also sought timber rights, because wood cut from nearby hillsides shored up the mines. Control over natural resources by those companies generally benefited growing urban areas. The transformation of natural capital to financial capital drained both resources from rural communities.

Urban sprawl and the development of remote areas are often a result of the use of political capital (see the discussion of the growth machine in Chapter 6). The resulting paving-over of farmland and filling-in of natural areas such as wetlands have led to declines in water quality, decreased sequestration of carbon, increased greenhouse gases, global warming, greater tendencies toward flooding, loss of biodiversity and the habitat that supports it, loss of open space, and increased traffic congestion, which is accompanied by a decline in air quality, with serious health impacts. More and more communities are seeing these outcomes as undesirable. A variety of mechanisms is available for local communities to address these issues (see Chapter 11 on the powers some local governments have over land use through zoning, property taxes, and tax abatements) (see Box 2.1).

Conflicts over land use have increased, and local governments often attempt to protect the natural capital in their area and thus their human capital. For example, in Iowa, those who stand to benefit from large *confined-animal feeding operations* frequently have sued rural counties that have attempted to limit confinement operations. Those companies have very deep pockets (that is, abundant financial capital) compared to cash-strapped county governments. Investment in lawyers and court fees is a legitimate capital investment and is tax deductible, whereas for rural governments and local nonprofit organizations, defense against lawsuits requires drawing on already limited resources.

Although some say that changes in land use are a natural result of market forces, others point to the role that political capital and government subsidies play in the creation of urban sprawl and the exploitation of natural resources on public lands. Ultimately, negotiation of alternative uses of natural capital that are sustainable depends on such groups as the Habitat Partnership Program to establish places of common ground and sustainable alternatives.

Box 2.1 Working Together to Combat Sprawl

In Steamboat Springs, Colorado, "progress" is a loaded term. This small community, located in Routt County, has a popular ski resort, great shopping, beautiful mountainous views, and many, many tourists. Steamboat Ski and Resort Corporation, the third-largest ski resort in Colorado, has more than a million skier-days annually in good years, contributing $500,000 to the community by way of fees, services, and cash and donations. Although the community welcomed the financial revenue, some residents felt that the growth in this resort area was spiraling out of control. In the early 1990s, when another new ski resort wanted to move in six miles from the existing one, people responded. Ranchers in nearby small communities began to see their access to land for grazing cut off. Other residents were concerned about traffic congestion and increasing real estate prices. Still others were worried about land conservation and pollution. Bumper stickers appeared saying STOP THE BRUTAL MARKETING OF STEAMBOAT. Many groups wanted the growth to slow down or cease altogether, but they were somewhat unaware of one another. That soon would change.

When Dean Rossi, head of the local cattlemen's association, met with Holly Richter, a scientist from the Nature Conservancy, they may not have known what mutual goals they had. However, it was not long before they realized they had made an important and necessary connection. Richter's goal was to build a sustainable plant community; Rossi wanted to make sure establishing plant communities did not impinge upon his land use, but he felt that more plant growth could help his cattle. These sorts of coalitions have helped save more than ten thousand acres around Steamboat for ranching; needless to say, the new ski resort was not built in Routt County. A project named Vision 2020, which included a diverse group of citizens, encouraged discussions about what residents wanted to protect and enhance around Steamboat. What everyone began to realize was that being confrontational and shrill did not work. Everyone had to collaborate to improve the community; offering rational alternatives made the difference. This sort of mentality spread as a group called Environment 2000 began sponsoring annual "nonconfrontational" conferences to discuss topics surrounding community development. People began to listen to others' ideas, and respect among groups became apparent.

A strong connection was formed among ranchers, conservationists, and local government officials. Saving ranching in the area was something

continues

Box 2.1 *continued*

the groups agreed upon. They all wanted to protect their water and air from pollution caused by high-density resort development, particularly in places such as the Yampa Valley, a lush and unique landscape. Instead of fighting the land-preservation mentality, Gary Mielke, the president of Steamboat Ski and Resort Corporation, got on board, recognizing the heritage of the area: "We're committed to preserving the area's open lands and developing only where it's appropriate. . . . Our ranching heritage is as important to this company as snow" ("Routt County . . ." 1997).

In 1996, the Yampa River System Legacy Project was invited to submit a grant proposal to Great Outdoors Colorado, a foundation with a lottery-financed coffer of $10 million to $20 million per year. Representatives from all parts of Steamboat, including private businesses, landowners, educators, and government officials, came together to form a committee. They wrote a 150-page proposal that included forty-three letters of support from the region's most important leaders. The project's theme, "to protect and enhance the ecological health of the Yampa River and the productive agricultural lands it supports while providing for appropriate recreational opportunities," accompanied five goals. The overriding objective was to protect and conserve the river and the area surrounding it. It was soon apparent that the project was well received. Great Outdoors Colorado awarded the project $6 million, its second-largest grant in the state and its largest per capita.

Coalition-forming between diverse community leaders and residents is vital to community development, but as Routt County Commissioner Ben Beall pointed out, it takes learning and listening to people who live and work on the land: "My advice to other county officials is to look at your culture and figure out how that fits in with your vision and how the preservation of land fits with your culture. If it doesn't, then it's not going to work" ("Routt County . . ." 1997).

In 2005, funding for the Yampa River System Legacy Project ran out and the group disbanded, but many successes were made while the project was in place. As evidenced in and around Steamboat, remarkable things can happen when people work together toward a common goal, but collaboration takes shared passion and mutual respect among all players.

Source

1997. "Routt County, CO: Holding the Reins." Washington, D.C.: Joint Center for Sustainable Communities. Yampa River System Legacy Project. 2005. Online; available: www.redlodgeclearinghouse.org/stories/yampa .html; accessed September 9, 2007.

In the course of American history, land has been viewed as valuable in terms of:

- provision of natural resources to be turned into financial capital (logging, mining, trapping)
- production of natural resources to be transformed into financial capital (farming and some timber production)
- consumption to enhance cultural, built, and social capital (those with wealth purchasing land on which to build elegant homes and large estates to entertain their friends)
- speculation to directly increase financial capital (land bought with the expectation that its price will increase)
- creation of the foundation for built capital (housing developments, shopping malls, factories)
- provision of important ecosystem services (clean water, air, biodiversity, carbon sequestration), and
- preservation of cultural capital (land valued for its spiritual meaning)

These differing values given to land have led to struggles over its access and control. Does it matter that what I do on my land to produce financial capital (building a mall or a mine) affects what happens on your land (flooding, decreased air quality, or landslides)? How are different values for land negotiated in the market and in public policy? And how do our decisions about land use affect natural capital in general?

WATER CONCERNS

The availability of clean, potable water has been called the number one challenge facing the world and its people today. In the western United States, water has always been a scarce commodity. The first men and women recognized it as one of the fundamental elements of the universe, and husbanded it accordingly. The control of water literally shaped the history of the West. . . . [F]or years, Albuquerque's approach to managing water resources was simple and relatively inexpensive. The city just extracted all the water it needed from its underground aquifer, assuming the river was replacing it. We carved Midwestern landscapes into the desert and were among the highest water users in the southwest—with

about the lowest water rates. However, times have changed. (City of
Albuquerque, Albuquerque Municipal Utilities, Water Resources Division 2000)

Water—its quantity and quality—is an increasingly scarce natural resource as one moves from east to west across the North American continent. Whereas in the East, the current water issues in rural communities
revolve around water quality, in the West, they involve access to water.
The old Western adage "Whiskey is for drinking, water is for fighting"
holds true now as much as it did during the settlement period and has international implications.

To grow, communities must acquire new sources of water. Los Angeles,
for example, could not have grown to its present size had it not been able
to divert water from the north down into the arid southern California
lands (see Box 2.2). The land initially was so dry that land values were determined by the quantity and certainty of the water supply. "Sell the water
and throw the land in free" became the slogan of real estate brokers subdi-
viding the rolling hills of southern California. Recognizing the tremendous
importance of water for all phases of residential and industrial development, public officials and private entrepreneurs struggled over whether it
should be public or private. The classic movie *Chinatown* presents a somewhat fictionalized account of the intrigues involved in that fight.

Providing water to one community can mean depriving another. Thus,
conflicts and public debates have emerged over who gets water from
where and who pays for it. Although these issues are important throughout the country, they are gaining increasing attention in the Southwest
and on the western plains. For example, the people of Caliente, Nevada, a
remote rural community, became concerned about the efforts of Las Vegas
to buy up water rights. Under the *appropriation doctrine,* Las Vegas can
purchase the rights to water and divert it to support its own rapidly growing population, even if this usage diminishes the water available to the
people of Caliente. Denver is seeking access to the aquifer in the San Luis
Valley in south-central Colorado, much to the dismay of rural communities and landowners. This situation has caused much discord between urban dwellers and rural farmers. Urban dwellers and lobbyists believe that
they are the engine that keeps the state running and that they deserve access to the water. Rural farmers who do not want to give up any of the
water supply have been targeted as being "selfish." However, the farmers'
position is that people living in the city do not understand how much

Box 2.2 Water and Urban-Rural Connections?

Control of Owens River and Owens Lake has been contested since the turn of the twentieth century as local citizens and communities of interest battled to reestablish its flow after the City of Los Angeles had control of the water.

That control began as powerful Los Angeles interests realized that the city must have water to grow and that the eastern Sierra Nevada provided the most accessible water source. To gain access to that water, the city had to do two things: First it had to buy the water rights from the local farmers, the right of way for an aqueduct, and land for a reservoir. Initial visits to Owens Valley by representatives of the city were disguised as tourism. Later, city officials obscured their goal of obtaining water rights by disguising land purchases that included water rights. Once the water rights were obtained, city officials had to change the uses approved for that water. Should water from Owens Lake be used to support residential use in Los Angeles or agricultural use in the Sierra Nevada?

Next they had to transport the water from Owens Lake down to Los Angeles. Would that system be controlled by the market or the state? Los Angeles Mayor Frederick Eaton conferred with investors, who envisioned large profits in building the aqueduct and controlling the water rights. William Mulholland, head of the Los Angeles Department of Water, sought public funds to develop the infrastructure as a public trust and pressured Eaton to give up a private role in the Owens Valley project, from which Eaton would have gained financially. Los Angeles was well on its way to gaining control of the Owens Valley aqueduct project.

Los Angeles quickly won the right to have the water system in public hands, in part because the high construction costs made it unattractive to the market sector. The privately held Pacific Light and Power Company pressured the city to use the flow of the water to generate electricity, causing the city to consider becoming a public utility to provide energy as well as water. The Los Angeles Department of Water then became the Department of Water and Power, headed by Mulholland.

When Owens Valley residents realized what Los Angeles planned to do with the water, the battle over who would control the water began. Owens Valley newspapers defended local water rights, while Los Angeles newspapers declared that the well-being of Owens Valley communities must be sacrificed for the greater good and the greater profit of Los Angeles.

continues

Box 2.2 *continued*

The fight to stop construction of the aqueduct illustrates the role that different levels of government play in providing built capital. The aqueduct, ultimately paid for by the taxpayers of Los Angeles, had to pass over public land. The people of Owens Valley tried to block the city's access to public land as one means of stopping the project. Not only was the aqueduct allowed to cross public lands, but the U.S. Forest Service, by presidential proclamation, claimed the Owens Valley as part of the Sierra Forest Reserve, a move that eliminated private claims on the land.

Despite the investment by Los Angeles and the diverse support for the project, Owens Valley residents continued to fight it. In 1913, the first water from Owens Valley arrived in Los Angeles. The aqueduct went into operation in the late 1920s and was fully completed in 1941. During those twenty years, resistance to the aqueduct included physical attacks on it. Explosions would rock the valley as people, angry as they watched lush vegetation and agricultural production wither for lack of water, attempted to blow holes in the aqueduct. The growth of Los Angeles was accompanied by the decline of the towns, ranches, and farms along the river valley.

In September 2006, a California Court of Appeals panel made a decision that was a true victory for Owens Valley: Los Angeles was pushed to restore a sixty-two-mile stretch of the Owens River and was banned from using the aqueduct. This ruling also affects Owens Lake, which was nearly dry from the exporting of water. Now, with the "rewetting" of Owens Lake, lush vegetation and animals have returned.

SOURCE

National Public Radio. 2006. "L.A. Returns Water to the Owens Valley." December 6. Online; available: www.npr.org/templates/story/story.php?storyId=6590362; accessed September 9, 2007.

---

farmers rely on the water supply to farm their land. The water crisis in the West is real, and decisions regarding the use of rural water supplies are difficult and multifaceted.

Large-scale agricultural users have also been drawn into conflict with traditional dryland farmers. The withdrawal of water from the Ogallala aquifer to irrigate fields and support feedlots and packing plants in Garden City, Kansas, is lowering the water table. As global warming increases, dryland farmers and rural communities in the area must dig deeper wells simply to get water for livestock and for residential and commercial use. Because the Ogallala aquifer is essentially not replenishable, residents fear that the future of any economic activity is being compromised. The current rush to produce biofuels also uses a great deal of water and adds to the problem.

Water for human use comes from two sources: surface water (lakes, streams, and in some cases—such as in Tampa, Florida, with its desalinization plant—oceans) and groundwater, which is pumped from underground aquifers. Water's mobility and its relatively tenuous relation to land has resulted in the need to set rules around access and control of water. In the United States, these primarily are state laws. However, the federal government has heavily subsidized the provision of water, particularly in the West. During the Era of Reclamation, from about 1880 to 1980, the American people, through their legislative leaders, saw augmenting the water supply for multiple users as an appropriate role for governments. In the twenty-first century, environmental concerns about irrigation-induced water and soil quality problems also have united political and natural capital.

As water supplies become more erratic due to climate change, the laws that govern access to and control of water become points of hot contention. We have moved to an era of reallocation and improved management (National Research Council 1992). The current conflict involves not only the market transfer of water (based on who will pay the most) but also the third-party effects—who will suffer or benefit from water loss or gain. Because urban areas generally have more market power, there is concern that such water transfers will disadvantage rural areas in terms of water quantity. How the rural lands are managed also has an enormous impact on water quality. New rural-urban partnerships are based on recognition of what is needed if rural land managers are to enhance water quality (see Box 2.3).

Who has rights to use water and who has the responsibility of improving poor water quality remain contentious issues. The role of rural people in resolving these issues nationwide increasingly is recognized. Because water is seasonally and geographically limited in the West, encouraging its productive use has always been a key policy objective, from the days of the Ancestral Pueblo people (referred to by some as the Anasazi) to the present.

Box 2.3 Rural-Urban Collaborations for Safe Drinking Water: New York City and the Catskills

Nine million residents of New York City and surrounding suburbs rely for the source of their drinking water on a series of reservoirs located many miles away in the Catskill and Delaware watersheds in upstate New York. New York City owns less than 10 percent of the watershed, which covers roughly 1,900 square miles. The Catskill/Delaware watershed has a year-round population of around 77,000, as well as a significant number of summer residents. Dairy farms comprise a majority of the 350 farms there.

For many decades, relations between New York City and the watershed areas have been marked by controversy and conflict, focusing on the City's past acquisitions of reservoir lands and the use of regulatory and management authority in the watershed. In 1989, the EPA's Surface Water Treatment Rule (SWTR), issued under the federal Safe Drinking Water Act, required filtration of all surface water supplies (rivers and lakes) to protect against microbial contamination of drinking water. This requirement can be waived if a water system's treatment processes and natural conditions provide safe water and if the watershed is actively protected to ensure that safety in the future. For New York City, the new regulation meant they had to get cooperation from those who managed the land in these two watersheds if they were not to spend tens of billions of dollars building complex filtration systems.

The Stresses

Although New York City residents have enjoyed superior drinking water for 150 years because of its high quality upland supplies, the potential for microbial contamination has become an increasing concern as evidenced by a series of boil water alerts since 1993. Wastewater discharges from treatment plants (some operated by New York City) and runoff from urban and agricultural sources, which contribute both microbial pathogens as well as phosphorus, are the primary pollution sources.

The Strategy

In 1993, the EPA issued New York City a waiver of the filtration requirement on condition that the City would take numerous steps to maintain and protect the Catskill/Delaware's drinking water quality. The EPA

continues

then urged the Governor to convene a group representing New York City, New York State, watershed communities, the U.S. EPA, and environmental groups to negotiate an effective and equitable watershed program. It was hoped that such a program would enable the City to meet the waiver conditions, protect the City's water supply while avoiding the multi-billion dollar cost of a filtration plant for Catskill/Delaware water supplies, and address the concerns and goals of residents in the upstate counties.

The negotiations produced a landmark agreement that successfully resolved long-standing controversies and set forth responsibilities and benefits for all major parties. The City finalized its regulations for watershed land uses, acquired sensitive lands to protect key reservoirs and waterways, conducts more extensive water quality testing in the watershed, and supports upstate/downstate partnership programs (including major investments in wastewater treatment facility upgrades, a fund for compatible economic development in the watershed, and a regional watershed partnership council). . . . [U]pstate community representatives participate in the regional watershed partnership council, which includes representatives of the State, City, and downstate consumers.

[In reviewing the implementation, which began in 1997, the National Research Council stressed the intersection between technical solutions and community involvement and priority setting. Without urban investment in sustainable rural development, rural areas could not invest in decreasing non–point source pollution for urban water consumers.]

SOURCE

EPA. 1996. "Watershed Progress: New York City Watershed Agreement." EPA840-F–96–005. December. Online; available: www.epa.gov/owow/watershed/ny/nycityfi.html; accessed September 9, 2007.

In the Middle Rio Grande Valley (MRG), where Albuquerque, New Mexico, is located, many groups claim the water. First, the Pueblo Indians of the MRG have the longest historic claim to water. Because they were practicing irrigated farming when the Spanish arrived, the king of Spain granted them Mercedes del Aqua (water rights) as part of the treaty following the Pueblo uprising in the late 1600s. The Mexican and then the U.S. governments each have in turn honored those rights. The Pueblo rights, spelled out in treaties, involve water quality as well as quantity. Rituals, key to maintaining cultural capital, demand very high quality water.

The second claim is by farmers, who claim historic water rights dating back to the Spanish era under the collective acequia system. These ditch canals are operated and managed locally but operate under a deed from the government that guarantees land users rights to a given amount of water from the general system. The term acequia is also used to mean a collectivity of irrigation farmers who live along the ditch network and distribute water among themselves. The acequia ditches are under the management and distribution authority of the elected regional conservancy district, which monitors water distribution for a fee. Landowners with holdings along the irrigation ditch network, whether or not they are farmers, have voting rights in conservancy district elections.

The most recent holders of water rights are the various municipalities, which have purchased or been granted water rights over time. Specifically, Albuquerque claims the Rio Grande's water for drinking water and uses the San Juan/Chama Diversion to divert the San Juan River upstream into the Rio Grande.

None of these claims factor in the downstream rights of the state of Texas and the nation of Mexico. Texas has guaranteed its claims to Rio Grande water through the Rio Grande Compact, signed by Texas, New Mexico, and Colorado in 1957 to guarantee access to water for each state. Mexico maintains some rights to Rio Grande waters under the "First in time, first in rights" laws that were applied under Spanish rule and then adopted by Mexico and codified in the treaty between the United States and Mexico following the Mexican-American War.

Water Rights

Legal doctrines govern appropriate or fair use of surface water. The *riparian doctrine* governs water use primarily in states east of the Mississippi River. Water rights are given to those whose lands are adjacent to streams. Landowners do not own the water, but they can make reasonable use of the water flowing over their lands, as long as such use does not severely diminish the flow of streams or levels in lakes. The appropriation doctrine, sometimes called the California Doctrine, is used throughout the more arid states of the West. This policy allows users to divert water from its original channel as long as the water is used for beneficial purposes and the amount of water withdrawn does not exceed what the user is entitled to under the permit.

Laws governing groundwater are even more complex. Early in the twentieth century, laws allowed landowners to use groundwater on their own land even if it depleted the groundwater available to adjacent landowners, but these same landowners could not deplete groundwater resources by removing water from their land and using it elsewhere. More recently, some states have modified this doctrine to protect neighboring landowners and waterways that are supplied by the groundwater. Landowners are allowed to withdraw groundwater, but they may not exceed their fair share of water resources or harm neighboring uses of groundwater.

With increasing population, global warming, and development, less unappropriated water is reliably available. Consequently, the acquisition and transfer of established water rights frequently satisfy new water demands. For example, the city of Las Vegas, Nevada, has acquired the water rights of many of the surrounding valleys, which has negative implications for the future of those rural areas.

Cultural Capital and Natural Capital

A part of the problem of water scarcity is a result of cultural capital. Immigrants from the East and the Midwest, where rain was abundant, sought to re-create the green lawns and colorful gardens that had been brought to the North American continent from England. As a result, the expectation of water abundance was implicit in the planning of cities. Yet as many Western cities built in deserts rose to be important urban centers—Las Vegas, Los Angeles, San Diego, Albuquerque, and Denver, among others—the water had to come from somewhere. That "somewhere" was rural areas, often hundreds of miles away.

Rural citizens east of the Sierra Nevada in California, who settled the land to farm, were astounded when they found that Los Angeles had acquired rights to their water and was building an aqueduct to ship it to the ever-expanding city to the south at the beginning of the twentieth century. The Los Angeles Department of Water and Power (LADWP) took water first from the once-verdant Owens Valley, in spite of legal fights and sabotage of the aqueduct by local community groups (see Box 2.2). By 1941, Los Angeles's growth meant expanding the water supply. The LADWP diverted Mono Lake's tributary streams 350 miles south to meet the growing water demands of Los Angeles. Deprived of its freshwater sources, Mono Lake saw its volume halved while its salinity doubled. Unable to adapt to these changing conditions within such a short period of time, the ecosystem began to collapse. Islands in the lake, previously important nesting sites, became peninsulas where birds were vulnerable to mammalian and reptilian predation, reducing biodiversity. Photosynthetic rates of algae, the base of the food chain, were reduced, and the reproductive abilities of brine shrimp became impaired. Stream ecosystems unraveled due to lack of water. Air quality grew poor as the exposed lake bed became the source of airborne particulate matter, violating the Clean Air Act. If something was not done, Mono Lake was certain to become a lifeless chemical sump. In 1978, the citizens of Mono County and others from across California formed the Mono Lake Committee (MLC) and began talking to conservation clubs, schools, service organizations, legislators, lawyers, and anyone who would listen about the value of this high-desert lake. The MLC grew to twenty thousand members and gained legal and legislative recognition for Mono Lake. They organized around seeking a solution that would "meet the real water needs of Los Angeles and leave our children a living, healthy, and beautiful lake" (Mono Lake Committee 1978). After several years in the court system, L.A. was pushed to restore the Owens River and stop using the aqueduct that was exporting water from the area. Now the river and lake have water, and vegetation has returned, as has the wildlife.

The MLC, mobilizing around natural capital, created alliances (political capital) with organizations that shared its cultural capital regarding appropriate biodiversity, water quality, and air quality. Although the MLC was not obligated to meet the water needs of Los Angeles, it found ways of doing so through cooperative solutions, without transferring environmental problems to other areas. Today the lake is "rising and healthy" (Kay 2006).

IMPORTANCE OF BIODIVERSITY

Biodiversity is defined as the variety of life in all its forms, levels, and combinations. It includes ecosystem diversity, species diversity, and genetic diversity. Maintaining biodiversity at all three levels allows for greater resilience in the face of change. Those concerned about biodiversity generally understand that ecosystem diversity is necessary for species diversity.

For example, rural interests have been greatly conflicted over the definition and function of wetlands and over the degree to which they should be protected. To some, protecting the prairie potholes in rural, remote areas of North Dakota, which held water only part of the year, seemed like a foolish waste of perfectly good farmland; some farmers thought the potholes should just be leveled to maximize productivity. Their political capital was manifested through a variety of traditional farm groups, such as the Farm Bureau. For others in the rural communities and their urban allies, the prairie potholes, with water in the spring, were critical habitats for migrating waterfowl, bringing hunters and bird-watchers who helped diversify the local economy and maintain worldwide biodiversity. Local chapters of the Audubon Society worked with their national organization to mobilize political capital and negotiate with the farm groups. The 2002 Farm Bill (Farm Security and Rural Investment Act) contains language that allows farmers to be paid to protect biodiversity (and water quality, because wetlands also filter chemicals from water) at the same time they receive a variety of supports (loan deficiency payments, *countercyclical payments,* and direct payments) for the agricultural commodities they produce (which decreases biodiversity). Like many programs, the Farm Bill contains both perverse and positive incentives regarding protection of natural capital in rural areas.

Rural areas have suffered in the past from lack of genetic diversity in the crops and animals they produce. Although genetic similarity can yield a standard crop or animal, it can also make that crop or animal extremely vulnerable to disease and pests. Pathogens spread more easily and epidemics are more severe when hosts (corn plants, hogs, or chickens) are more uniform and abundant. Outbreaks of avian flu (a fatal chicken disease) occur regularly in the Chesapeake Bay area, where large numbers of chickens of the same genetic stock are raised in close confinement. In Hong Kong in 1998, an outbreak of a new avian flu strain to which humans seemed susceptible led to the death or destruction of hundreds of millions of chickens. The Great Potato Famine of 1845–1849 in Ireland and the southern corn leaf blight in 1970 in the United States, which wiped out the corn crop, were both caused by insufficient biodiversity in the affected crops (Council of Agricultural Sciences and Technology 1999).

Invasive Species

Another threat to biodiversity is *invasive species.* These are species of plants and animals (including insects) that are introduced, either accidentally or on purpose, from another area of the country or the world and that, removed from their natural enemies, outcompete native species and become a monoculture. For example, in order to control soil erosion in "cottoned out" areas of the South, the Soil Conservation Service introduced kudzu from Japan. Although the soil has stabilized, kudzu covers everything in its path, crowding out native plants that were habitats for many indigenous species of wildlife.

Rural (and urban) streets and neighborhoods in the Eastern United States were changed drastically in the 1910s by chestnut blight, brought in through chestnut trees imported from China and Japan that then were sold by mail order all over the United States. By 1950, the huge, majestic American chestnut trees were gone, taking out 25 percent of the trees in the Appalachian Mountains. Detection and identification were slow, as was response by officials, without community-based education and organization of the public. The U.S. Department of Agriculture (USDA) quarantine came too late.

In the twenty-first century, another landscape-changing pest is attacking U.S. forests and urban and small-town landscapes. The emerald ash borer (EAB) was discovered in southeastern Michigan near Detroit in the summer of 2002. The EAB probably arrived in the United States on solid wood packing material carried in cargo ships or airplanes originating in its native Asia. The pest also is established in Windsor, Ontario, and was found in Ohio in 2003, northern Indiana in 2004, and northern Illinois in 2006. Since its discovery, the EAB has:

- killed more than twenty million ash trees in Michigan, Ohio, and Indiana. Most of the devastation is in southeastern Michigan.
- caused regulatory agencies and the USDA to enforce quarantines (Ohio, Indiana, Michigan, Illinois, Maryland) and fines to prevent potentially infested ash trees, logs, or firewood from moving out of areas where EAB occurs.
- cost municipalities, property owners, nursery operators, and forest products industries tens of millions of dollars.

In contrast to the response to chestnut blight, communities are now organizing educational campaigns to stop the EAB's movement across the Midwest. A coalition of state and federal agencies (Michigan departments of Natural Resources and of Agriculture, in cooperation with the Southeast Michigan Resource Conservation & Development Council, Michigan State University, Michigan Urban and Community Forestry Council, USDA Animal and Plant Health Inspection Service, and USDA Forest Service) developed to provide an Emerald Ash Borer Community Preparedness Plan. That community-based plan is being shared with other states to contain infestations and prevent them from spreading. Because the spread is mainly through firewood and wood products—which often are cut and marketed from one county to another—community awareness and mobilization are particularly important. Without mobilizing social capital and political capital, protection of natural and financial capital cannot occur.

CLIMATE CHANGE

Global climate change will have major impacts on natural capital as changes in water regimes and humidity increase pests. It will affect human capital through health threats brought about by changes in food production, access to freshwater, exposure to vector- and water-borne diseases, sea-level rise and coastal flooding, and extreme weather events. Such extreme weather events as longer and more severe droughts and more intense rain and snow have implications for soil erosion and water quality.

Although we know of actions that can slow global warming, such as decreasing greenhouse gases and increasing the amount of carbon sequestered, the United States has been slow to respond. The facts that climate is an open-access good (see the discussion in Chapter 8) and that those who act to reduce global warming do not receive any immediate personal benefit (except perhaps in enhancing social or cultural capital) make it difficult to justify the *transaction costs* of moving to new ways of doing things. In the United States, we have made decreasing pollution a market good by creating a market for pollution trading as a way to comply with U.S. environmental laws. But the reluctance of the U.S. government to acknowledge human agency as a cause of climate change has kept the United States from making carbon sequestration a similar tradable good. Although some farm groups want the federal government to pay them for sequestering carbon through such means as no-till agriculture, they are unwilling to tax carbon emissions as a way of supporting the carbon sequestration payments. They are encouraged in this stand by oil companies and some industries that also are hesitant to change the way they do business.

Alternative Energy

What can communities do? Some communities have moved to reduce carbon emissions through a variety of measures that also reduce their expenditures. For example, a number of small communities have purchased hybrid cars (powered by both batteries and internal combustion engines), such as the Toyota Prius and Honda Civic Hybrid, for city employees, including police on routine business. Others put their police on bicycles in good weather. Small cities use smart-growth strategies to encourage use of public transportation, recycling, and dense neighborhoods where stores and housing are within walking distance of each other. Yet others have moved to renewable energy sources, combining with private-sector firms to generate wind power. It is not just the increasing price of oil that helps make wind energy competitive. The Wind Energy Production Tax Credit, extended in 2000, gives a credit of 1.5 cents per kilowatt-hour to users of wind energy, thus effectively cutting its price.

On February 27, 2003, the first utility-scale Native American 750-kilowatt NEG MICON wind turbine was installed on the Rosebud Sioux Indian Reservation in South Dakota. Its installation marked the end of an eight-year preparation, begun in 1995 when the Rosebud Tribe, the Tribal Utility Commission, and the Rosebud Casino began measuring the wind resources.

In 1998, the tribe applied to the Department of Energy (DOE) for a cooperative grant (50/50) to build a commercial utility turbine. The tribe had compiled eighteen months of wind data to present to the DOE, and that preparation helped them obtain the grant. Working closely with the Intertribal Council on Utility Policy (ICOUP) and Distributed Generation, Inc., the Rosebud Tribe also negotiated the first USDA Rural Utilities Service loan to a tribe for a commercial wind energy project, which was used to match the DOE grant.

Electricity generated by the turbine provides power to the Rosebud Casino and motel and to surrounding areas. The tribe sells the excess clean renewable energy that it generates to Basin Electric for local use, with a multiyear sale of "green power" to Ellsworth Air Force Base, near Rapid City, delivered through a cooperative effort with Basin, Nebraska Public Power, and the Western Area Power Administration.

The tribe also negotiated the first tribal sale of Green Tags—renewable energy certificates that replace traditional polluting sources of electricity with clean, secure, and sustainable renewable sources of energy that come from solar and wind power from across North America—generated by this turbine to NativeEnergy of Vermont. The company has marketed the tags to thousands of individual green-power supporters, including Ben & Jerry's Ice Cream, the Dave Matthews Band, the Natural Resources Defense Council for its Rolling Stones climate change awareness benefit concert, and other parties interested in the development of renewable energy on American Indian lands.

The Rosebud turbine installation is the first phase of a long-term plan for multi-megawatt wind development on Indian reservations across the Great Plains, the world's richest wind regime. Through collaboration with the Tribal Resource Development Office, Tribal Utilities Commission, and Tribal Planner, the Rosebud Tribe has negotiated for the construction of a thirty-megawatt wind farm on the reservation and has submitted a request for proposal for two other sites. The tribe is working with wind developers and will earn a percentage of the gross profits, plus lease money for the turbines.

Inspired by the success of its clean energy efforts, the tribe is leveraging the Low Income Home Energy Assistance Program (a source of federal dollars to help low-income householders pay for utilities or to weatherize their dwellings) in partnership with the Pine Ridge Reservation to install solar heating systems for tribal employees through payroll deductions. The Tribal Utilities Commission and the Tribal Housing Department have constructed a pilot home with solar heating, a small wind turbine to provide electricity, and windbreak trees. Working with Denver-based Trees, Water & People (www.treeswaterpeople.org) and a grant from the Bush Foundation, the tribe is retrofitting existing homes to be more energy efficient.

A video, *Wind Powering Native America,* showing the turbine installation is available at www.eere.energy.gov/windandhydro/windpoweringamerica/filter_detail.asp?itemid=749.

Not only can the energy choices communities make save money, but they also can help ensure a healthy planet for their children's children.

CHAPTER SUMMARY

Humans often have sought to use natural capital to build other forms of capital. Native Americans used—and continue to use—natural capital in the strengthening of cultural and social capital; European settlers converted it into financial capital, moving westward when they depleted natural capital in settled areas. Today, urban sprawl places stress on natural capital in ways that more compact settlement patterns would not. Land and water are forms of natural capital central in European Americans' closing of the frontier. Village-centered settlement stimulated industrial and commercial development in nonmetropolitan parts of the Northeast, whereas plantation settlement retarded such developments in the South. In the arid West, human-directed organization of water gave value to the land during the settlement period and today. Property law regarding water developed differently west of the Mississippi than east of it. In the West, where one did not have to own the land through which a watercourse ran, water was overappropriated by the time the frontier closed. This overappropriation of a scarce commodity generated conflict that continues to this day. As cities grow, rural-urban conflicts grow as well. Agricultural, environmental, and urban interests vie to control water for purposes each values highly. As water increasingly is recognized as a public good, legal patterns change and negotiated solutions such as that between residents of the Catskills region and New York City occasionally can generate a win-win situation. Too often, parties still view the situation as a zero-sum game.

As globalization proceeds apace, interdependence among different groups, regions, and nations becomes more evident. Global warming, introduction of exotic species, and other issues related to natural capital increasingly will require greater recognition that it is in the long-term interest of the well-to-do (whether individuals or nations) to provide monetary and other incentives to those who are less well-off to "do the right thing" by the environment. This presupposes that the wealthy themselves are concerned about the environment. If greed can be curbed and creativity given its head with the objective of lightening humans' footprint on the earth, perhaps we can pass a planet on to our children that is indeed better than what we inherited.

Key Terms

Appropriation doctrine allows water rights to be established by the first claimant even if that user does not own land adjacent to the watercourse. The user is limited to a specified amount of water that can be withdrawn.

Biodiversity is the variety of life in all its forms, levels, and combinations.

Confined-animal feeding operations involve raising livestock and poultry in an industrial fashion. The animals are confined in large buildings where the conditions are controlled so as to produce a uniform product. A huge amount of manure is a by-product. To the degree possible, the production system is rationalized to increase output per unit of labor, much as occurs on the industrial assembly line. Also, holding the animals in a confined space promotes efficient conversion of feed to meat or eggs, since the animals expend very little energy in exercise.

Countercyclical payments are available for covered commodities whenever the effective (market) price is less than the target price.

Ecosystem services—critical services such as water purification, biodiversity maintenance, and climate stabilization—are generated spontaneously by healthy ecosystems. Because these services are chronically undervalued in the marketplace, they are highly vulnerable to degradation.

An *invasive species* is one (1) that is nonnative (or alien) to the ecosystem under consideration and (2) whose introduction causes or is likely to cause economic or environmental harm or harm to human health.

Riparian doctrine limits water rights to landowners whose lands are contiguous to streams. They can make reasonable use of the water but cannot severely diminish its flow.

Transaction costs are incurred when making an exchange. These costs can be direct monetary costs, such as fees, or indirectly monetized, as with the time or social interactions necessary to use to make things happen.

REFERENCES

Ambrose, Stephen E. 1996. *Undaunted Courage: Meriwether Lewis, Thomas Jefferson, and the Opening of the American West.* New York: Simon and Schuster.

City of Albuquerque Public Works Department. Water Resources Division. 2000. In "Water and Our Future," advertising supplement, *Albuquerque Journal,* December 10.

Council of Agricultural Sciences and Technology (CAST). 1999. "Benefits of Biodiversity." Task Force Report No. 133.

Kay, Jane. 2006. "It's Rising and Healthy." *San Francisco Chronicle,* July 29.

Mono Lake Committee. 1978. Online; available: www.monolake.org/committee/history.htm; accessed September 8, 2007.

National Research Council. 1992. *Water Transfers in the West: Efficiency, Equity, and the Environment.* Washington, D.C.: National Academies Press.

3

CULTURAL CAPITAL AND LEGACY

Dave and Rosemary glared at each other. There had been some heated discussions around the dinner table recently. Dave opposes the local school bond. He is trying to save money to buy more land, so he doesn't want property taxes to increase. Rosemary believes that the school's quality must be maintained, so she wants the bond to pass.

Dave Stitz and Rosemary Turner met while attending college. He majored in general agriculture, and she majored in botany. Dave was a fourth-generation farmer, the first in his family to go to college. Rosemary's father was a county extension agent and her mother was a schoolteacher. Dave and Rosemary married soon after graduation and moved to the Stitz family farm. Dave works the fields with his father, and Rosemary runs the heirloom seed business they started with Dave's mother, an avid gardener. In order to understand their different positions on the school bond issue, it helps to know something about each of their personal histories.

Ever since Dave could remember, he knew he was going to be a farmer. He came from a long line of farmers. His great-great-grandparents came to western Kansas in the 1890s by covered wagon. Their granddaughter, Dave's grandmother, married the son of a local farmer, and they began farming as soon as they were married. Over time, his grandparents expanded their farm and acquired enough land for their four children. Upon their death, they left an equal part of their land to each of their children. Dave's father was left with one-fourth of the family farm, which would not be enough land to pass on to his future children. Therefore, once Dave's parents were married, acquiring more land became a high priority.

Dave's parents bought more land during the expansive times of the 1970s, even though the land was priced higher than it could ever yield in crops. Because they anticipated having a family, they knew they needed more land. They postponed their family when land prices suddenly dropped, and they struggled to make their loan payments. Dave's father got a job driving a truck across the country while he continued to farm and negotiate with local bankers to refinance the farm. With sacrifices, they were able to keep the farm and start their family, and they had one son, Dave. Land payments absorbed much of their income, although Dave's father was able to give up cross-country trucking. Dave came home from school each day to help with the farming, leaving no time for extracurricular activities outside of church. Dinner conversations were subdued, for everyone was exhausted and the television was on. Dave graduated from high school and chose to go to college, paying his own way. He attended only in the spring semester so he could be home during winter wheat planting and milo harvesting in the fall. When he started farming, first with his father and later on his own, his parents' friends were impressed. At first they asked him to custom plant or custom harvest their wheat, and he brought his machinery to the land they indicated for that particular operation. Once he had proven the quality of his work on their land, they asked him to rent their land or work it for a share of the crop.

Despite their struggle, the effort was worth it to Dave's parents. The farm was their legacy to their child, and they believed they had provided him with an excellent set of tools for a happy and productive life: access to land and the willingness to work hard to make that land productive.

Rosemary was the daughter of a county extension agent and a school-teacher, so she was no stranger to farming. Her parents did not earn a large income, but it was secure. From the day Rosemary was born, however, they regularly put aside money for her college fund. Her parents felt that a college education was the most important thing they could give their daughter. They encouraged her to get into organizations in the community and in school, and they constantly encouraged her to talk to professionals in the county about how they had chosen their careers. Dinner conversations were structured around current events. Rosemary's parents, too, were thinking of legacy. A college education and knowing people and politics would enable Rosemary to support herself and maintain a comfortable lifestyle.

Given this background, it is less surprising that Dave and Rosemary are on different sides of the school bond issue. Dave's parents saw how education, particularly vocational agriculture, could be useful on the farm. When hard choices had to be made, however, they emphasized the need to acquire land. By contrast, Rosemary's parents put obtaining a college education and cultivating skills for her future career above everything else. In their reactions to the school bond issue, Dave and Rosemary are simply reflecting and continuing the legacies bequeathed to them. Their ways of seeing the world show differences in cultural capital.

Both Dave's and Rosemary's parents gave them what they valued most: land and education. Like most parents, they wanted their children to be able to earn a good living and have a good life. As the example illustrates, however, what parents believe they should pass on varies from one family to another. This chapter examines cultural capital, the social and economic factors that contribute to the legacy young people receive from their family and community, and how cultural capital is affected by gender, race, and ethnicity.

WHAT IS LEGACY?

We normally think of legacy as the money or property left to someone through a will, typically what parents leave their children. But parents leave more than just material goods to their children. They pass on an understanding of society and their role in it, speech, dress, and ways of being—cultural capital—that in turn affect the choices their children make. *Legacy* is what families, communities, groups, and nations pass on to the next generation.

There are many cultural capitals even within North America, although one cultural capital is more highly valued than others and is thought to be the right way to know, act, and understand. Cultural capital determines what constitutes knowledge, how knowledge is to be achieved, and how knowledge is validated. Those with power are able to define these key issues according to their own values, and they provide their children with cultural advantages that translate into social and economic advantages.

Cultural capital includes the values and symbols reflected in clothing, music, machines, art, language, and customs. Cultural capital can be thought of as the filter through which people live their lives, the daily or seasonal rituals they observe, the way they regard the world around them, and what they think is possible to change. The socialization process serves to transmit values via various forms of communication, both verbal and nonverbal. Whether people learn to share money or save it, whether they trust people in authority or fear them, what career they choose to pursue, or simply what they consider important are all products of cultural capital.

From the parents' perspective, legacy provides the tools needed for survival. Dave's parents saw land ownership as a key to his future. Consequently, they were willing to risk nearly everything to ensure that Dave had that tool for survival. Rosemary's parents had never owned land—at least not beyond the property on which their house was located—and both had made a living based on their college degrees. Rosemary's parents scrimped and saved to ensure that she left home equipped with the tool that had been most valuable to them, education.

Communities also impart legacies in terms of aspirations. In the dominant U.S. society—middle-class, suburban, or small-town European Americans—the norm is to succeed educationally and to achieve a higher status than one's parents. These shared aspirations of parents and children unite them during the end of their high school years to prepare to leave the community and enter college life. These aspirations tie them more closely to their parents and to their parents' lifestyle. But in Appalachia, on American Indian reservations, and in the Mississippi Delta, as well as in many inner-city neighborhoods, educational aspirations separate young people from their community and their parents. It is obvious to all in the community, to peers and to parents, that some young people are "learning to leave." Local folks no longer want to have much to do with these youth, figuring that they already feel superior to their community. The community, observing that such young people are "opting out" by spending time studying instead of reinforcing local ties, may even become hostile toward them.

CONFLICTING CULTURAL CAPITALS AND CULTURAL DOMINATION

What happens when one group is technologically and militarily superior and attempts to impose its cultural capital on another group with a very different legacy? This is illustrated by the cultural clash between Native American and European American cultures. For the Owens Valley Paiute People of California, their language was critical, for its words conveyed important meaning about survival techniques: how to find food in different places throughout the year, how to find and process material for baskets, what ceremonies to perform to ensure that food and materials were available, and how to watch the weather to decide when to plant and when to hunt. Their cultural capital allowed them to live in a wide territory during different seasons and through both dry and wet years. Social advantage was determined by the degree to which one shared what one had and how one adhered to the religious rituals and rules. Children were taught carefully what their elders thought was critical for survival, and they learned through watching and practicing.

The Dawes Act of 1887 was aimed specifically at substituting the cultural capital of the dominant U.S. society for the "unproductive" cultural capital of Native Americans. The goal was to make the Native Americans become like white people—and to take their land. Congressman Henry Dawes, author of the act, once expressed his faith in the civilizing power of private property with the claim that to be civilized was to "wear civilized clothes . . . cultivate the ground, live in houses, ride in Studebaker wagons, send children to school, drink whiskey [and] own property" (quoted in *Archives of the West* 2007). The act allotted 160 acres of land to individual tribal members, giving the "excess" land to the U.S. government to dispose of among white settlers. The reduction of land area was supposed to force Native Americans to become farmers. The privatized land, in many cases, was lost quickly to European Americans who took advantage of the fact that private land ownership was an absolutely foreign concept to most Native American bands and tribes. The cultural capital of those in control completely negated the ability of Native Americans to use their local cultural capital to maintain their social and economic well-being.

However, land loss was not enough to convince many Native Americans to give up their own cultural capital to adopt "the white man's ways." Other mechanisms to remove Native American cultural capital (assuming that it automatically would be replaced by the dominant cultural capital, making the hearts and minds of Native Americans identical to those of European Americans, even if their skin color was not) included forced attendance at boarding schools, where European hairstyles and dress were enforced, despite the religious significance of long hair for many Native American males. Native Americans' names were changed to "sound" English. These last names often were similar to the names of those allocating the land, who then slipped the names of their own European relatives into the land rolls, making them owners of Native American land and decreasing the land available to indigenous people. Native American children were punished for speaking their native language. Because Native Americans' religion was seen as the basis for their unwillingness to adopt a more materialistic approach to life that would allow them to properly conform to the values of the European Americans, the U.S. government supported Christian missionaries from different denominations (specifically excluding Catholics and Mormons), putting them in charge of different parts of Indian Country. And since religion was tied to specific sacred places, many tribes were moved long distances to more barren lands, which conveniently left their fertile lands and forests to European Americans.

Paiutes throughout the West sought to maintain and re-create cultural capital in many ways. A Paiute Indian, Wavoka (who had been given the English name Jack Wilson), had a revelation during a total eclipse of the sun. This revelation was the genesis of a religious movement, the Ghost Dance. To participate in the dance, Native Americans of different tribes gave up alcohol, farming, and other practices of the European Americans in order to restore the past. The movement spread eastward from tribe to tribe. Desperate Native Americans began dancing and singing the songs that would cause the world to open up and swallow all other people, leaving the Native Americans and their friends on the land, which would return to its beautiful and natural state. The unity and fervor that the Ghost Dance movement inspired among tribes, however, only spurred fear and hysteria among white settlers, which ultimately contributed to the events ending in the U.S. Army's massacre of Lakota women and children at Wounded Knee, South Dakota, in 1890. Violence was a final tool used to eliminate a conflicting cultural capital.

Although the Dawes Act was repealed by the Indian Reorganization Act in 1934, Native American land loss continued. The 1934 act had a number of provisions that seemingly would benefit Native Americans; however, they were never funded or put into place. Additionally, this act ended traditional tribal government, and the system that replaced it took the form of the federal government, with constitutions, elections, short-term offices, and governmental branches. Systems that were far more integrated and beneficial to the tribe's health and well-being were uprooted and replaced. The idea of lifetime service and leadership within a tribe was eradicated when this new governmental system was implemented. Consequently, Native Americans lost their form of tribal leadership and their land. The natural, political, and financial capitals that these represented had dramatic impacts on cultural capital.

Relocating Native Americans in the United States continued well into the twentieth century. In 1952, Native Americans began to be moved to urban areas, and by 2003, two-thirds of the Native American population lived in urban areas. This effort was presented as a way to find jobs, make money, and attain affordable housing. Many of the relocated Native Americans were single men who, after much convincing, "voluntarily" moved into cities. These efforts appeared to benefit Native Americans by providing them with jobs and housing; however, their cultural ties diminished. Additionally, in the cities, Native Americans were treated as outsiders and were alienated through obvious forms of discrimination. People did not understand Native American culture, and Native Americans did not easily embrace big-city culture. Consequently, many Native Americans felt as if they did not fit in anywhere, and living in the city was overwhelming and uncomfortable. In some instances, returning to the reservation was an option; however, their cultural and spiritual connections to their tribes had been compromised by their having lived in the city. When men returned to their tribes from the city and became tribal leaders, their commitment to preserving some of the very fundamental parts of cultural capital—leadership, language, and religion—was decreased. As a result, cultural capital was diminished because of their urban experience.

By 2007, few Paiute language speakers were left among the Owens Valley Paiutes, despite attempts on the part of elders to teach young people to "talk Indian." Their young people have lost their traditional cultural capital. And they have not received the cultural capital of working- and middle-class European Americans. Their access to the natural resources they traditionally used for survival was lost, with the U.S. government substituting Treaty Rights, which stated that the U.S. government would take care of them since they were giving up their ability to care for themselves. Removal and denigration of cultural capital combined with economic dependence on the federal government left a legacy of a lack of identity and many social problems, including substance abuse on the reservation. Many tribal leaders are working hard to re-instill tribal cultural capital to help improve the other capitals on the reservations.

SOCIAL CLASS, STRATIFICATION, AND DOMINATION

Societies and most social groups, including communities, rank households and household members hierarchically. Some individuals and families have more prestige, power, or wealth than others. Sociologists disagree on how this ranking takes place. Some sociologists argue that it occurs because of differences in functional importance: What some people do is more important to society than what other people do. Thus, they argue, it makes perfect sense for the chief executive officer (CEO) of a corporation to receive a salary more than five hundred times that of the average worker in the firm. (This ratio does not take into consideration stock options, year-end bonuses, and loans forgiven that are part of CEO privileges not available to ordinary workers.) Other sociologists argue that it is not functional importance but differential power that gives some people more resources than others. They say that certain groups have more power than others and use that power to maintain a higher position in a group or society. Both sets of sociologists agree that in American society, those on top tend to have more income, wealth, power, and prestige. Other characteristics, such as age, sex, ethnicity, race, and religion are associated with different positions in the hierarchy. Furthermore, there is a strong relationship between the position of parents and of their children in that hierarchy.

Sociologists have explored inequality and social class from a variety of perspectives. Marxist approaches focus on material relations; Weberian approaches focus on social groups; and Bourdieu and his followers look at the intersection of financial and cultural capital.

Marxian Perspectives

Writing during the industrial revolution of the nineteenth century, Karl Marx defined social class in terms of the economy. To understand his perspective, however, we first need to look at how a business functions and how individuals within that business accumulate wealth.

The goal of any business is to make money. Profit essentially represents the difference between the price of the product sold and the cost of producing it, including the costs of materials, labor, land, and capital (interest paid on debt). Business owners receive the profits, either directly as proprietors or indirectly through dividends paid to them as investors. Those who own the business, then, accumulate wealth through business profits over which they have some control and through the increase in the value of their business, as indicated by the daily value of its stock.

Those who sell their labor to the company, who work for the company, receive wages in return. Only rarely do they receive part of the profits, as in a cooperative or in an employee stock ownership plan. Consequently, they accumulate wealth through their labor and any saving that can be generated from their wages after paying to maintain themselves and their families. Their bargaining power with business owners is based on their ability to make their labor scarce, either by acquiring skills and knowledge that are in demand or by collectively threatening to withhold their labor through unions or employee associations.

Given this difference in the capacity to accumulate wealth, Marx identified two social classes: capitalists and proletarians. Those who own the means of production, the factories or offices, make up the *capitalist class.* Those who sell their labor for wages form the working class, or *proletarians.* Marx also identified a part of the capitalist class that he called the *petty bourgeoisie,* which included small shopkeepers and farmers. These individuals own the means of production, manage the firms themselves, and often use family labor alone or combined with hired labor. Marx saw the petty bourgeoisie as a remnant of the preindustrial economy. Consequently, he expected the class to disappear entirely once the transition to the industrial age was complete.

We have moved through the industrial age and beyond, leading some sociologists to revise Marx's early theory. As corporations grew increasingly larger, sociologists saw a class of people emerge that fit somewhere between the capitalist and proletariat classes, the *managerial and professional class.* This group includes managers or professionals within businesses or who serve businesses as well as public-sector managers. These individuals do not own the means of production, yet they enjoy more autonomy and control over the work environment than do members of the proletariat.

A second modification is needed because the petty bourgeoisie class has not disappeared. Although the number of small-business owners and farmers declined substantially in most industrialized nations, the number of self-employed people (now reported in government statistics as "proprietors") has increased since the 1960s. In the United States, for example, self-employment fell from nearly 42 percent of the workforce in 1880 to 13 percent in 1969. By 1998 proprietors had increased modestly to 16.6 percent of the total workforce. They represent an even higher proportion of the labor force in rural areas, in part because people are adding new sources of income as real wage rates decline, thus increasing the number of jobs and the number of business endeavors per person. More important is the changing structure of the labor market. As industrial firms downsize, they subcontract work out to smaller businesses, and employment shifts to the service sector, which consists primarily of smaller businesses. Sociologists have concluded that the petty bourgeoisie (made up of small-business owners) is an integral part of the class system in this postindustrial age. Many governmental and private-sector programs are aimed at encouraging entrepreneurship (see Chapter 7, Financial Capital).

Weberian Perspectives

Whereas Marx defined class in terms of material relationships, including the intergenerational transfer of wealth and property, sociologists have argued that other factors are equally important in defining social class. Writing during the late nineteenth and early twentieth centuries, Max Weber argued that people also are stratified by prestige and power, which combine in a hierarchy of status groups. These groups have their own status culture, which controls access to rewards and privileges. Stratification is based on cultural capital as well as on financial and built capital. *Socialization,* the process of learning the cultural expectations of one's group, and association (social capital) reinforce it.

From the Weberian perspective, then, *social stratification* describes the hierarchy of status groups. Social stratification seems to be a feature of all societies. What differs is the extent to which the stratification system is open or closed. Closed systems are those in which members are not free to move from one class to another. Open systems allow individuals and families to move across layers. *Social mobility* is the term used to describe the movement of an individual from one status group to another, either up or down.

Bourdieu and Social Domination

Pierre Bourdieu linked Marx's materialism and Weber's notion of society composed of status groups to examine the social and mental structures of domination. Families, through kinship ties, and communities, through their educational systems, contribute to inequality. These are major mechanisms through which cultural capital is transmitted. Like other capitals, cultural capital can be thought of as what Bourdieu called "congealed and convertible social energy." Cultural capital determines how we see the world, what we take for granted, what we value, and what things we think can be changed. *Hegemony* allows one social group to impose its symbols and reward system on other groups.

Bourdieu, observing the rigid class structure in France, saw that the wealthy provided personal and symbolic connections for their children. They automatically knew how to behave in formal situations and could chat easily with others of their class. That shared behavior and knowledge of symbols gave the children of the upper classes power beyond their material situation when dealing with those in authority, from government bureaucracies to corporations to civic organizations. Richard Sennet and Jonathan Cobb (1972) saw different kinds of cultural capital contributing to the "hidden injuries of class." People in positions of power feel uncomfortable and threatened when entering communities composed of excluded groups, because the excluded groups may resent power symbols they do not have, such as cars, dress, and language. Powerful people in such situations do not comprehend the symbols that give the situation meaning to the powerless, and that failure to comprehend contributes to the powerless group's feelings of discomfort.

Class and ethnic cultures—and the cultural capital they represent— develop out of each group's experience with the social world. Cultural capital that is helpful in one setting is often a disadvantage in another, as was shown when a streetwise city boy from Chicago, Emmett Till, came to a small Mississippi town. His inability to judge correctly the dominant symbolic signals—and the violent power they implied—was fatal. Till was an African American teenager who in August 1955, on a dare, spoke to a white woman in Mississippi as he would to white women he knew in Chicago, leaving her store saying, "Bye, baby." In response, the outraged husband and a white male friend beat, murdered, and mutilated Emmett Till. Despite their clear responsibility for the crime, the all-white jury acquitted them. In his closing statement, the defense attorney for the two men called upon the importance of defending Southern white symbols in the face of northern pressure: "Your fathers will turn over in their graves if [J. W. Milam and Roy Bryant are found guilty] and I'm sure that every last Anglo-Saxon one of you has the courage to free these men in the face of that [outside] pressure" (Williams 1987).

LEGACY AND THE FAMILY

In preparing for their children's future, parents typically work toward three goals: enabling their children to have a place to live, providing a means by which to earn a living (sometimes viewed as standard of living), and encouraging personal fulfillment (sometimes viewed as quality of life). In one sense, legacy stands at the intersection of what parents have achieved in their own lives relative to these goals and what parents see as possible and desirable for their children to achieve.

Survey researchers have shown that middle-class parents have very different values and childrearing styles than do working-class and poor parents. (Michèle Lamont [2000] points out that steadily employed men in what scholars refer to as working-class occupations refer to themselves as "lower-middle-class.") Parents' behaviors in socializing their children are strongly influenced by their awareness of the traits they consider necessary for survival and success. Because environmental and economic risk increases as social class position declines, working-class and, in particular, poor parents focus more on survival than on success. Middle-class parents value creativity, reasoning, and autonomy, whereas working-class parents favor obedience and conformity. Middle-class parents tend to encourage exploration, whereas poor parents focus on setting limits. These are rational responses to different levels of experienced environmental risk, which is then related to the job rewards that young people seek. Young people concerned with having a predictable, secure future that includes not moving from place to place are less likely to continue in school. They also are more likely to come from poor or working-class homes. Those interested in intrinsic rewards (interesting jobs that use all of one's skills and abilities, the learning of new skills, the chance to be creative) and in influence (participating in challenging work and decision making) are more likely to continue their education and to have middle-class backgrounds. As a result, initial cultural capital that came from socialization is increased by acquiring the dominant cultural capital through formal schooling.

Annette Lareau (2003) has done systematic ethnographic work to show how parental values translate into cultural capital. Middle-class parents engage in *concerted cultivation* of their children. They feel that what they do will have an enormous impact on their children's future, so they actively assess and foster each child's talents, options, and skills. To do this, they actively organize their children's lives, ensuring participation in leisure activities orchestrated by adults. This requires that the parents' own work generate a high enough income to pay for their child's participation (from sporting gear to music lessons) and has enough flexibility to allow them to provide transportation and to attend school programs when needed. Middle-class parents are particularly concerned about language use. They use reasoning, even when offering directives: "Put on your cap and coat before we go out. It is very cold today and you know how unhappy you are when your ears are cold." Children are allowed, even encouraged, to contest adult statements: "It's not really that cold; can't I wear a sweater?" which may result in extended negotiations between parent and child: "Let's look at the thermometer outside your room to see what the temperature is. Is the wind blowing? You know that makes it feel even colder. Let's look at the trees to see if we can tell." Middle-class families have weak extended family ties. Because of their low concern for roots and security within the extended family, they are likely to live apart from relatives. And when they do live near relatives, scheduled children's events (such as starring in the school play) take precedence over family events (such as Grandma's birthday). Middle-class children therefore are more likely to spend time in homogeneous age groupings, for that is the way most of their activities are organized.

Middle-class parents feel comfortable intervening when their children experience problems, and they encourage their children to do the same: "You got a 'C' on the math test. Did you talk to your teacher to help you understand long division better?" That pattern of concerted cultivation encourages an emerging sense of entitlement in the children.

In contrast, poor and working-class parents believe that as long as they provide love, food, and safety, their children will grow and thrive. Lareau calls this the *accomplishment of natural growth* approach to childrearing. These parents do not have the resources or do not believe it necessary to engage their children in a multitude of free-time activities to encourage their particular talents. These children have more leisure time and hang out a lot, particularly with kin. Parent-child interactions are often in terms of directives: "Put on your jacket and cap." A child who responds that it doesn't seem that cold out is admonished to "Put on your jacket and cap NOW." If the child resists, physical punishment is more likely to result. However, it is rare for young poor or working-class children to question or directly challenge adults (although they may not actually wear the cap and jacket to school). There are strong extended-family ties, and most older adults feel very comfortable giving directives to their younger relatives. Children spend much of their time in mixed-age groups.

Working-class and poor adults feel much less comfortable around authority figures. Their experience with police, teachers, doctors, and social workers generally has resulted in having things—including their children—taken away from them. Thus, they are hesitant to share information with authority figures, for they are unsure how the information might be used against them. Working-class and poor adults and children are deferential and outwardly accepting in their interactions with professionals, but they are very distrustful of them. Lareau found that the accomplishment of natural growth encourages an emerging sense of constraints. (Table 3.1 summarizes the differences between these two approaches.)

Table 3.1 Summary of Differences in Childrearing Approaches

	Childrearing Approaches	
Dimensions Observed	Concerted Cultivation	Accomplishment of Natural Growth
Key elements of each approach	Parent actively fosters and assesses child's talents, opinions, and skills.	Parent cares for child and allows child to grow.
Organization of daily life	Multiple leisure activities are orchestrated by adults for child.	Child "hangs out," particularly with kin.
Language use	Reasoning/directives Child contestation of adult statements Extended negotiations between parents and child	Directives Rare questioning or challenging of adults by child General acceptance by child of directives
Social connections	Weak extended-family ties Child often in homogeneous age groupings	Strong extended-family ties Child often in heterogeneous age groupings
Interventions in institutions	Criticisms and interventions on behalf of child Training of child to intervene on his or her own behalf	Dependence on institutions Sense of powerlessness and frustration Conflict between childrearing practices at home and at school
Consequences	Emerging sense of entitlement on the part of the child	Emerging sense of constraint on the part of the child

SOURCE: Lareau, Annette. 2002. "Invisible Inequality: Social Class and Childrearing in Black Families and White Families." *American Sociological Review* 67:753.

Differences in family life lie not only in the advantages parents obtain for their children but also in the skills they transmit to children for negotiating their own life paths (Lareau 2002).

Independent Entrepreneurs

People who expected to run their own business, what we now call independent entrepreneurs, settled many rural communities, particularly in the Northeast and the Midwest. These businesses are often family businesses, and self-employed businesspeople make up a higher percentage of the workforce in rural communities than in metropolitan areas.

Independent entrepreneurs are the backbone of the Jeffersonian view of the ideal society, which the Dawes Act sought to promote among Native Americans, ironically, by taking away most of their access to land. That ideology promotes attitudes of industriousness, self-improvement, and optimism. Following slavery, African Americans became independent farmers and entrepreneurs, generally in their own towns or on the "black" side of the tracks. Unfortunately, after Reconstruction, their successes were reversed by illegal and violent actions against them, and they lost their land and businesses to European Americans.

The rural myth, best expressed in *Small Town in Mass Society* (Vidich and Bensman 1968), describes the ideal rural entrepreneur. That individual has the right attitudes and works hard. As a result of good attitudes and hard work, that individual accumulates wealth over his or her lifetime. Those who do not accumulate wealth are viewed as lazy ("They don't work hard") and as having the wrong attitudes ("They don't value what we value"). Work is pursued with great personal sacrifice and is oriented toward the improvement of self and family and to the accumulation of wealth. However, wealth generally is not sought for its own sake or for the consumption of luxury goods and services. Instead, wealth is needed to acquire or develop an independent business. As a result, attitudes of industriousness, self-improvement, and optimism lead to behavior conducive to economic activity, which in turn generates wealth.

The legacy such parents have for their children is influenced directly by the resources they have accumulated. Parents work hard to invest in farms or businesses. These investments then provide employment and housing for their children as well as a source of social status within the community. All of this hard work is considered an investment in their children's future as well as in their own. Because Dave Stitz's father had acquired land for his son, it seems only natural that Dave is now acquiring land for a son yet to be born.

For those who farm or operate small businesses in rural communities, the three legacy goals combine in a single place. A place to live is often part of the means by which a family makes its living. Consequently, houses are valued for their use, and they are worth maintaining for long-term use by the family and community. Personal fulfillment comes from the family business and involvement in the local community, which makes the connection between legacy and place enormously strong. When that legacy is blocked, as it was for many farm families during the farm crisis of the 1980s, the loss can be especially difficult to accept.

Values such as industriousness, self-improvement, and optimism certainly are important to any business. But so are social connections, and as a result, legacy for this social class is place-specific. Parents develop a set of skills crucial to running their business and being accepted within a community. Although some of the knowledge needed to run a successful business may transfer from one community to another, understanding how to run a business in any particular town may be specific to that town's culture. Consequently, knowledge and connections important to economic survival in a given community transfer from parent to child. For Dave Stitz, the connections he inherited from his parents that gave him access to more than his own farmland allowed him to continue farming.

Managers and Professionals

The managerial and professional class includes those who sell their labor but retain some autonomy in their work. Rural communities have always collectively purchased the labor of certain professionals, such as ministers and teachers. Although these individuals do not necessarily earn a large income, they enjoy the respect of the community and are critical in reproducing the area's cultural capital.

Manufacturing plants and service industries now require managers and administrators to regulate the labor of workers and clerks. For the most part, these salaried managers and professionals are relatively well paid and share some characteristics with those who own the means of production. They have a high degree of autonomy on the job. In addition to determining the schedule and content of their own work, they often make decisions that affect others. Conversely, this autonomy reinforces self-esteem and enhances the value of independence and decision-making ability. Consequently, the most important legacy that middle-class parents impart to their children is the ability to command a high price for their labor, based on the credentials they earn through formal education.

For Rosemary Turner's parents, who are themselves salaried professionals, education substitutes for the transmission of material wealth. Like many others in this social class, they encouraged Rosemary and her siblings to do well in school, helping them with their homework and challenging them to question and discuss issues with teachers. Independent thought is valued as part of the education process, and it is a trait that is important in making management decisions. Like many of their counterparts, the Turners believe that their success is directly related to their education; likewise, they believe that their children's hope for satisfaction is linked to their higher education, and they struggle to save money for their children to attend college.

Families like the Turners expect that their children will become part of a regional or national labor force. To an extent, this legacy is location-free. Parents will be committed to and actively involved in the local school system to ensure that their children receive the preparation they need for college. Buying a home becomes an investment made for its exchange value. In contrast to the independent entrepreneur, however, the three legacy goals are not linked together by a place.

Working Class

Mining, timber, manufacturing, and service industries in rural areas all create a working class, those who sell their labor but have little autonomy or control over their work. Throughout history in the United States, textile mills in the South, garment and shoe factories in New England, lumber camps in the Northwest and the upper Great Lakes, and mines in various parts of the country all have employed large numbers of workers. Many went to work in these industries with the hope of saving enough to open their own business. Some eventually succeeded. Others, however, found that the low wages and high expenses involved in living in mill towns, mining towns, or lumber camps made saving difficult. A strong labor movement later increased wages in some of these industries, especially mining and timber. Wages rose to the point that workers could not afford to quit and start their own businesses. Many settled into depending on wages for their livelihood. Their children have continued that tradition. But as these sectors of the economy are restructured due both to technologies that substitute capital for labor and to globalization, which moves labor-intensive production to nations where labor is cheaper, the options of the rural working class become more limited.

In most cases, working-class jobs require skills that are learned on the job rather than through formal education. In some industries, such as mining or logging, workers receive substantially higher wages than do some people whose jobs require a college education, such as teachers. Consequently, there is little incentive to invest in education. This was the case in mining areas, such as McDowell County, West Virginia. Eager to earn money for personal use or to help the family with debts, young people go to work at an early age. Homes are purchased not for their resale value but as a secure place to live. Seasonal layoffs or changing patterns in national and international markets often make employment unstable, so families seek security through home ownership.

For workers whose jobs depend on natural resources, legacy is often tied to a sense of place. In the early days, those in logging or fishing simply moved on when they tired of a particular job. Other jobs were always waiting, sometimes for better wages. The introduction of unions substantially increased the wages paid in these jobs, but at a cost to worker mobility. Those in McDowell County have become second- or third-generation mineworkers. Their investments—in homes, for example—are tied to a place. When the local economy declines, the value of their homes go down, making it impossible to recover the cash needed to relocate. Consequently, most workers try to weather periodic economic downturns and layoffs. Like independent entrepreneurs, those in the rural working class often see legacy and place as strongly connected. The loss of an industry can mean the loss of all three legacy goals.

The Poor

Some working-class jobs in rural areas pay very poorly, and their employers, whose cultural capital prevails, describe these jobs as requiring few skills. These jobs are unstable, low paying, part time, or seasonal, and they sometimes require migration. The wage earned depends not on a worker's skills but rather on the supply of workers willing to take jobs and on the cultural assessment of what the work is worth. The supply of workers almost always exceeds demand, so the state's minimum wage becomes the maximum wage for this group. In many cases, these individuals see little chance of accumulating enough money to buy their own business or home. These individuals move often, because they live in low-quality housing or in undesirable areas or cannot pay that month's rent. A few months of staying with relatives or friends, a few months of living independently, moving to a new town hoping to find better work, or even sleeping in the car means that children attend school irregularly and often change schools during an academic year.

Poor parents' aspirations for their children focus around physical safety and physical nurturing. Those in authority are viewed as threatening, as are the everyday conditions of life. Parents see inner discipline as less important, since keeping a job depends more on the labor supply or an employer's whim than on an individual's behavior. Those who are poor often feel that they have little control over their environment. They perceive, often correctly, that hard work does not lead to wealth or high self-esteem. People often are pessimistic about their children's prospects for the future, and they may feel unable to influence them positively. The legacies they want to give their children are modest: stay safe, find steady work, and stay out of trouble.

In contradiction to the stereotype that poor people are lazy and do not want to work, a substantial number of the rural poor are among the working poor. More than two-thirds of the rural poor who are not ill, disabled, or retired work all or part of the year. In many respects, the legacy passed on by the working poor accurately represents the society they have experienced.

Transmitting Legacy through the Community

Like culture, legacy is transmitted from one generation to another through social institutions. Institutions that control the means of production, provide education, reinforce values, or support personal connections all influence the legacy that is handed down. This section looks briefly at two of the institutions, the family and the schools.

Family Influence on Legacy

Families are, of course, the primary means by which legacies are transmitted. Parents exert a great deal of influence over the values their children adopt, the sense of self-esteem and self-worth with which children face the tasks of growing to adulthood, and the opportunities available to them. As described earlier, these legacies link what parents have achieved and what they see as possible for their children. To some extent, however, these legacies also depend on whether parents expect their children to remain in the community.

Rural families are deeply affected by the opportunity structure in their community. If parents expect or want their children to stay nearby, then they are very much aware of the local job opportunities and class structures. The legacies they pass on to their children often perpetuate existing class structures and certainly reflect parents' experience in the workplace.

If parents expect their children to leave, then the legacy they pass on may be very different. Middle-class parents, who are managers or professionals, emphasize education. Working-class families who are eager to see their children achieve a better life also emphasize education, realizing that job opportunities, class structures, or both will require their children to leave the community. Those in declining farm communities or in manufacturing communities such as Eatonton, Georgia, often encourage their children to leave. Families in expanding communities, such as Mammoth Lakes, California, may see vastly different opportunities. Latinos migrating to the town for seasonal work see the chance to make ends meet. Middle-class families see the opportunity for entrepreneurial activity.

Role of the School

The family is not the only institution that transmits legacy. Funded and staffed by community members, schools play an important role in orienting children toward their future position in society. In turn, the legacies parents have for their children influence the school's character.

In the rural Midwest, where small businesses are still somewhat prevalent, legacies reflect the sense of social equality that existed during the settlement period when most aspired to the same goal, owning a business. Class differences are ameliorated within the school. Parents expect their children to manage a business or become a salaried professional, so they want their children to develop independence and the work habits needed to make such a living. They also understand that both businesses and professions depend on connections with people who have power and authority, so they try to help their children feel comfortable around people with power in their community through informal interactions. Schools generally encourage participation by all students, regardless of class. Smaller schools in the Midwest and Northeast have higher rates of participation in extracurricular activities, a part of concerted cultivation on the part of the school. Education may also be oriented toward out-migration as parents acknowledge that few jobs are available locally, leading to disinvestments in community by both parents and children.

In communities in other parts of the country, particularly in low-income areas in the South and Appalachia, parents see limited job opportunities for their children. As discussed earlier, they also see little connection between hard work and success. Consequently, their investment in education is not nearly as great. Dropout rates are high, and teenage pregnancy is more prevalent. Parents and young people do not see any immediate advantage to remaining in school. Consequently, the sense of independence created by going to work, even at a low-paying job, or becoming a parent is not offset by what seems to be the remote chance that education will lead to higher earnings. Unfortunately, high school dropouts experience higher unemployment rates.

August Hollingshead's (1949) study of "Elmtown" (pseudonym for a Midwestern town) looked at the extent to which social class and legacy were passed from parent to child through community institutions such as the school. Hollingshead identified three mechanisms by which a rural community's social stratification was reproduced in the school: First, through cliques and recreational activities, the young people replicated the social structure of the adult world. Second, those adults who had a direct impact on the children, including teachers, school administrators, and community leaders, systematically discriminated against children from lower classes. Finally, children from the lower class learned patterns both at home and in school that hampered them in educational and occupational attainment.

As social institutions that transmit legacy and culture, schools are an enigma. Rural communities have fought long and hard to maintain local control of schools, in part to ensure that the values and attitudes of the local community are respected and transmitted through education. Tribal schools and tribal colleges were established by tribal governments to make sure that Native American cultural capital related to that tribe and that place are transmitted as well as the dominant cultural capital. State and federal courts informed by congressional and state civil rights legislation, however, see education as a social equalizer, enabling anyone willing to apply him- or herself in school to move into the middle and upper middle classes. Research such as that conducted by Hollingshead demonstrates the extent to which schools can block mobility, replicating the community's social class structure, so that those in the lower classes see no way to advance. Some rural communities are looking very carefully at who succeeds and does not succeed in school, asking themselves to what extent the school serves all students fairly.

Impact of Gender, Race, and Ethnicity

Although class and social status are important in shaping legacy, their impact differs depending on gender, race, and ethnicity. Parental aspirations vary greatly for their children, depending on the sex of the child and the family's race or ethnic heritage.

Any discussion of these issues carries some of the same risks as discussions of the relationship between social class and legacy: It is extremely difficult to generalize across populations without seeming to stereotype. Differences in legacy based on gender, race, and ethnicity do exist, although they are complex. This discussion reflects some of the current thinking as to how these differences occur. By no means, however, does it capture the full complexity of the issues involved or the diversity found across any given population.

Gender and Legacy

Traditionally, parents, schools, and communities expected different things of girls and boys. Through the 1950s, men and women assumed distinct roles in society, so parents expected male and female children to need different skills and values. Parents expected males to be able to earn a living that would support themselves and their families. Men were socialized to be independent, able to compete, and competent in a skill or profession. Women were socialized to make the best marriage possible, relying on men for financial security. Maintaining an attractive appearance and developing homemaking and social skills were the values and skills considered important to that future. To some extent, the social and homemaking skills women needed depended on their parents' assessment of the kind of men they would marry. A farm girl would learn a variety of production skills, such as gardening, home canning, and sewing. A town girl, whose parents felt her future rested on marrying a middle-class professional, would learn music, arts, and leisure sports as well as homemaking skills.

The Turners' commitment to Rosemary's education demonstrates how dramatically these expectations have changed since the 1970s. Women are entering the labor force in increasing numbers, partly to achieve self-sufficiency and self-satisfaction. Economic conditions also require that many women work to help support their families, sometimes because they are single parents. In 2002, women represented 57.5 percent of employed people ages sixteen and above.

Women's increased presence in the workforce has affected childrearing patterns. Increasingly, women choose to or are forced to return to the labor force soon after the birth of their children. They are no longer willing, or in some cases able, to stay out of the workforce to raise a family. Between 1999 and 2000, more than 55 percent of women ages fifteen to forty-four returned to work or actively sought a job within one year of having a baby, compared to the record high of 59 percent set in 1998 (U.S. Census 2000).

Legacy and Race

Despite advances in civil rights during the past three decades, race continues to exert a dramatic impact on legacy. African Americans made up the largest portion of the minorities in the United States until 2002, constituting nearly 13 percent of the population. Their history, shaped by periods of slavery, segregation, and the civil rights movement of the 1950s and 1960s, has left a variety of legacies, some positive and others negative.

Because of their roots in slavery and the persecution that followed emancipation, generations of blacks in the United States were not able to pass on significant material wealth to their children. Instead, many focused on providing children with a social and cultural heritage that allowed them to survive in an often-hostile environment. Legacy for rural blacks meant stressing the linkages within the family and to the larger black community, as well as the mutual obligations and supports such linkages provided. Black parents, regardless of class, stressed family relations, the value of family, and family links to the community and to church. Because of segregation, African Americans lived in multiclass communities, so children of sharecroppers were able to see schoolteachers, doctors, and preachers who looked like they did. In the face of segregated school systems, many African American communities in the South started, supported, and staffed their own schools, providing mobility within the community for youth with promise.

As it has become possible for African American professionals to move into areas from which they once were excluded, poor African American children in both rural and urban areas are less likely to interact with professionals they know socially. When schools were integrated, European Americans usually got the teaching positions, so the cultural capital once present in rural African American towns has shifted away from the cultural values that stress and demonstrate the importance of education and the possibilities of social mobility.

Dignity in the face of continued racism is an important part of legacy for blacks. Ways of responding to racism without resorting to violence or being attacked are important components of the skills parents foster in their children.

Legacy and Ethnicity

In addition to gender and racial differences, parents are influenced by their ethnic heritage in identifying suitable legacies for their children. An ethnic group is a population that shares an identity based on distinctive cultural patterns and shared ancestry. The United States is often referred to as a "melting pot," implying that migrants' diverse ethnic origins are blended. In reality, distinct ethnic subcultures continue to exist.

For example, about 2.4 million Native Americans live in the United States. Almost 22 percent live in rural areas or on reservations, mostly west of the Mississippi River. They represent the poorest ethnic minority in the country. Despite the rich history and culture of the various tribes, Native Americans today offer their children one of the bleakest legacies. In 2000, 26 percent of Native Americans lived below the poverty line, more than twice the national rate of 11.8 percent. The average length of schooling is only eight years, and the high school dropout rate is twice the national average. Alcoholism is a pervasive and persistent problem, with Native Americans experiencing a rate nearly five times that of the nation as a whole. Tribal elders stress the necessity to build and use tribal cultural capital to confront these forms of dependency, which mirror the dependency established by Treaty Rights, through which Native Americans gave up their ways of supporting themselves in response to a promise that the U.S. government would take care of them, directly and explicitly creating dependency.

Even in the face of such devastating statistics, Native Americans strive to maintain and convey pride in their heritage. Schools on some reservations, once used as a tool to eliminate the Native American cultures, now incorporate native and the dominant culture into their curricula. Efforts to stimulate economic development on native lands also are beginning to reflect native values and orientations toward the land. Increasingly, Native Americans seek to transfer a legacy that respects their own culture but equips young people to function more effectively in the white world.

One of the fastest growing ethnicities in the United States is Latino/a. Latino is used to refer to people of Spanish-speaking ancestry, but this clearly is not a homogeneous group. Of the approximately fifteen million Latinos living in the United States, about nine million are Mexican American, two million are Puerto Rican, close to one million are Cuban, and the remaining three million are drawn from many countries of Central and Latin America. Latinos are the fastest-growing ethnic minority in the United States and officially surpassed blacks as the dominant minority in 2002.

Although many Latinos in the West and Midwest can trace their residence in the United States back for generations, their ancestors having arrived earlier than those of immigrants from northern Europe, the vast majority of Latinos arrived after World War II. Significant migration continues today, particularly from Mexico and such Central American countries as El Salvador, Honduras, and Guatemala. As other newly arrived immigrants did in the past, Latinos tend to reside in national enclaves, to an extent resisting assimilation into the wider culture in order to survive. For many, there are limited job opportunities, a function in part of inadequate English-language skills. Many are drawn into low-paying manufacturing and service occupations in rapidly expanding rural communities. These typically offer few opportunities for advancement. Like the black community, Latinos value family loyalty, respect, obligation, and commitment to mutual support. Strong backlash against new immigrants has criminalized their status in states such as Georgia, even though no federal criminal law prohibits entering the United States or overstaying a visa. Coupled with the climate of fear associated with the raids on rural homes and businesses by Immigration and Customs Enforcement, assimilation is further delayed.

Asian migration began on a large scale during the late nineteenth century as the Chinese were recruited to serve as cheap labor for the developing industries of the West, such as mining and construction. Although Chinese immigration was legally suspended in 1882, a diminished but continuous stream of Asians made its way to the United States. Many settled in California or in large cities such as New York and Chicago. Changes in immigration laws in 1965 resulted in increased flows once again, particularly from war-torn areas of Vietnam, Laos, and Cambodia. Today, many Asian Americans reside in rural areas, settling in small towns in states such as Kansas, Minnesota, and Massachusetts.

Although the nationalities represented among Asian Americans value different characteristics and behaviors, there is a general appreciation for education, industriousness, and family cohesion. Until such time as material success is widely available to these ethnic groups, these qualities will define the principal legacy bequeathed to Asian American children by their parents.

INEQUALITY: WHOSE LEGACY?

Rosemary and Dave Stitz received different legacies from their parents, legacies that contributed to their different stands on the school bond issue. Heated discussions aside, both inherited a legacy capable of helping them maintain a stable lifestyle that encouraged them to contribute to the community.

Cultural capital gives individuals their sense of identity and their range of alternatives in a changing society. Throughout our history, dominant groups have tried to impose their cultural capital on others—including values that reinforce the current hierarchies and inequalities. At times the imposition of the values of cultural capital has been violent, as the dominant society sought to eliminate those who did not seem to incorporate the dominant values. Education once was aimed at getting every child to accept the dominant cultural values, to learn to advance if they had the ability, or to accept their place in life if they did not. However, scholars now understand that it is not that simple. Cultural capitals can coexist. The self-confidence to act positively toward oneself and others requires a pride in legacy rather than a complete rejection of it. Individual and social problems arise when cultural capital is given up, yet it is impossible to completely appropriate the cultural capital of the dominant group. Individuals who do try to replace their own cultural capital with that of the dominant group are vulnerable, marginal to both their group of origin and the dominant group.

CHAPTER SUMMARY

Cultural capital is a filter through which people regard the world around them, defining what is problematic and therefore can be changed. Cultural capital generally is expressed through families and other social institutions, and it varies by race, class, ethnicity, and gender. Legacy is the aspect of cultural capital that is transmitted or modified intergenerationally. From the parents' perspective, legacy provides the tools for the next generation to survive and/or prosper.

Legacy is what parents seek to pass on to their children, including both material possessions and values and norms. Legacy depends, to some extent, on current economic opportunities. Parents' social class also affects legacy. Sociologists define *social class* either in terms of how individuals relate to the means of production or in terms of their social status within the community. When social status differences are large and opportunities to improve one's status are small, a community or society is said to be highly stratified.

Membership in a given social class often affects the legacy passed on to children. Because parents who are small-business owners or entrepreneurs often pass on land or a business to their children, legacy is strongly linked to place. Although they want their children to take over the business or farm, other small-business owners or farmers realize that such a legacy may not be realistic in the current economy. Therefore, they encourage their children to get a good education.

Those in the middle class, particularly managers and professionals, typically invest in their children's education and value independent thinking and the capacity to make decisions. Limited to the manufacturing or natural-resource jobs available in the local rural community, working-class parents value discipline and want to ensure that their children can adapt to externally imposed rules. Some working-class parents find that their salary is not sufficient to keep the family out of poverty. Those who are persistently poor often feel they have little control over what happens to themselves and their family. Consequently, they see little connection between hard work or education and a better future. Thus, even when they have high levels of ability recognized by themselves and others, they underinvest in acquiring the dominant symbols and values and maintain local cultural capital.

Legacy is transferred from one generation to another through social institutions. Of course, the family serves as the primary social group through which legacy is transferred. Schools can either reinforce existing class structures or offer opportunities for social mobility.

Issues of gender, race, and ethnicity often modify the relationship between legacy and social class. In earlier times, men and women had distinct roles that affected the legacy bequeathed to each. Structural racial often blocks black parents from passing acquired social mobility on to their children. Native American people struggle with the legacy left by decades of oppression. Social inequalities continue to exist, limiting communities as well as individuals. Immigrants seek to have their children appreciate their culture of origin while acquiring the tools to succeed in a new culture, economy, and society.

Key Terms

Accomplishment of natural growth describes a situation where parents do not intervene in their children's activities or associations but provide for their basic needs, including love, food, and physical safety.

The *capitalist class* includes those who own the means of production.

Concerted cultivation describes a situation where parents work hard to determine how their children spend their time, how they think and speak, and with whom they associate.

Hegemony is the dominance of one social group over another, such that the ruling group acquires some degree of consent from the subordinate, as opposed to dominance purely by force.

Legacy is that which parents seek to pass on to their children, including material possessions, education, values, and behavioral patterns.

The *managerial and professional class* includes managers, professionals, and government officials, individuals who sell their labor but maintain considerable job autonomy.

The *petty bourgeoisie* includes those who own the means of production but rely primarily on their own labor rather than on the labor of others.

Proletarians or the *proletariat* include those who sell their labor for wages, also known as the working class.

Social class has two distinct meanings. It describes people with similar relationships to the means of production. Alternately, it refers to a particular layer, or stratum, in a social stratification system.

Social mobility is the process through which people move from one position in a stratification system to another.

Social stratification is the division of people into layers, or strata, based on a series of attributes related to social status.

Socialization is the process through which people learn to think, feel, evaluate, and behave as individuals in relation to others and to social systems.

REFERENCES

Bourdieu, Pierre. 1986. "The Forms of Capital." In *Handbook of Theory and Research for the Sociology of Education,* ed. John C. Richardson, 241–258. New York: Greenwood Press.

Hollingshead, August B. 1949. *Elmtown's Youth: The Impact of Social Classes on Adolescents.* New York: John Wiley and Sons.

Lamont, Michèle. 2000. *The Dignity of Working Men: Morality and the Boundaries of Race, Class, and Immigration.* Cambridge, Mass.: Harvard University Press.

Lareau, Annette. 2002. "Invisible Inequality: Social Class and Childrearing in Black Families and White Families." *American Sociological Review* 67:747–776.

———. 2003. *Unequal Childhoods.* Berkeley: University of California Press.

Public Broadcasting Service. 2001. *Archives of the West.* Online; available: www.pbs.org/weta/thewest/resources/archives/eight/dawes.htm; accessed September 9, 2007.

Sennett, Richard, and Jonathan Cobb. 1972. *The Hidden Injuries of Class.* New York: Vintage Books.

U.S. Census. 2000. Online; available: www.census.gov; accessed January 24, 2003.

Vidich, Arthur, and Joseph Bensman. 1968. *Small Town in Mass Society.* Princeton, N.J.: Princeton University Press.

Williams, Juan. 1987. *Eyes on the Prize: America's Civil Rights Years, 1954–1965.* New York: Penguin, Inc.

4

HUMAN CAPITAL

The Tennessee Overhill Heritage Association was at a critical stage in bringing together its ecotourism plan. Although the maps of its trails were good, the association needed more knowledge of the plants and animals that could be seen at various points on the trails. Its members had brought in a wildlife specialist from the Tennessee Department of Environment and Conservation, but she had gotten her Ph.D. by conducting research in another part of the state. She had general information to share based on her formal education and fieldwork in western Tennessee, but she could not give the association's members the local details they needed to put their plan into action.

The eight members of the ecotourism committee were stymied. Should they just go with something general? Or should they follow their principle of developing a unique cultural and environmental experience? One member of the committee, Andrew Finney, suddenly realized something. He turned to another member, Jean Littlefox, and said, "Your husband, Thad, grew up in these woods. His Cherokee grandmother taught him all about the plants and animals. He can whistle more birdsongs than anyone I know. Would he help with the ecotourism committee as we put our map together?"

Jean was embarrassed. She knew how uncomfortable Thad, a school custodian, felt around groups, especially college-educated people who tended to write everything down on flip charts. She said, "You know, Thad doesn't know how to read. He just never took to it, somehow."

Andrew stopped for a moment. Then he replied, "We have eight people on this committee who know how to read. We don't have anyone who knows as much as Thad does about nature around here."

Thad joined the committee. The project served not only tourists, who were impressed by the uniqueness of the places on the trail, but also schoolchildren, who were thrilled to accompany their custodian on hikes and learn the birdcalls from him.

———•———

Human capital consists of the assets each person possesses: health, formal education, skills, knowledge, leadership, and talents. Although the dominant cultural capital tends to define human capital in terms of formal learning, human capital is far more than educational attainment.

What Is Human Capital?

Gary Becker and his colleague Theodore Schultz, both Nobel Prize laureates, have done the most to ensure that human capital is a core concept in economics and in social sciences in general. Here is how Becker describes human capital:

> To most people capital means a bank account, a hundred shares of IBM stock, assembly lines, or steel plants in the Chicago area. These are all forms of capital in the sense that they are assets that yield income and other useful outputs over long periods of time.
>
> But these tangible forms of capital are not the only ones. Schooling, computer skills, a healthy lifestyle, and the virtues of punctuality and honesty also are capital. That is because they raise earnings, improve health, or add to a person's good habits over much of his lifetime. Therefore, economists regard expenditures on education, training, medical care, and so on as investments in human capital. They are called "human capital" because people cannot be separated from their knowledge, skills, health, or values in the way they can be separated from their financial and physical assets. (Becker 2002)

Human capital includes those attributes of individuals that contribute to their ability to earn a living, strengthen community, and otherwise contribute to community organizations, to their families, and to self-improvement. Thad Littlefox strengthened his community by using skills and knowledge he already had, such as bird calling and knowledge of nature. Although Becker defines human capital rather broadly, he categorically states education and training are the most important forms of human capital. But one also suspects that economists and sociologists have focused on formal education because level of education is easy to measure and the data are accessible. But equally important are learning skills and gaining knowledge through experience, as demonstrated by Thad Littlefox.

As Becker suggests, investment in the health care of people in the labor force and of the citizenry in general is an investment in human capital. In a rich country such as the United States, health is not often thought of as being an important component of human capital, but in poorer countries, illness and impoverishment limit the contributions of large parts of the population as members of the workforce, as community members, as contributing family members, and as citizens. Communicable diseases associated with poverty may also spread to those who are not poor, reducing the effectiveness of their human capital. If poor people are not vaccinated or treated for communicable diseases, others in the society may be at risk as well. To the degree that inequalities breed crime against property or persons, victims may find their own human capital diminished. The fact that in the United States mental illness is not covered by insurance at the same level as physical illnesses are may substantially reduce the effect of other investments in human capital.

Interpersonal skills, values, and leadership capacity are part of human capital. What values individuals hold and how they exercise leadership may determine the extent to which they contribute to production, family, and community. If an individual's values, interpersonal relations, and leadership styles are not appropriate for an occasion or for the organization or community of which he or she is a part, these components of human capital can actually have a negative effect on productive or other collective enterprises.

During an earlier era, human capital was also related to strength and tenacity in carrying out physical work. Strength and physical labor, although still important in many occupations, are not well rewarded. Frequently, employers turn to immigrants to supply the labor for jobs that require physical strength or that are dangerous, dirty, or otherwise unpleasant. The settlement of rural areas of the United States by Europeans (voluntarily), Africans (involuntary until recently), and Asians, Mexicans, and other Latin Americans (voluntarily but welcome only when there was a labor shortage) is largely a story of people with very little formal education but with an ability to innovate and the willingness to engage in hard physical labor.

Legacy of the Plantation Economy in the South

The legacy of the plantation South lives on. Rural poverty, which in the Mississippi Delta is primarily black poverty, is the greatest precisely in those counties where the modern cotton, rice, and soybean farms are located. The Southern Rural Development Initiative conducted a study that shows that those 107 nonmetro counties with a majority minority population (mostly African Americans) are also the ones whose farmers received more than $9 billion in agricultural subsidies from 2001 to 2003. At most, 5 percent of those government payments went to African American farmers. The rest went to large farms owned by a rather small number of white farmers. Jason Gray, the author of the 2007 study, examined eleven "deep Delta" counties in Arkansas, with poverty rates that ranged between 18 percent and 29 percent and population losses ranging up to 9 percent during the first five years of the twenty-first century. Only one of the eleven counties had a population increase (2 percent). The highly mechanized row-crop farms receiving the subsidies (more than $1 billion in three years) obviously do not generate direct or indirect employment for the African American population. Although these counties sorely need job opportunities, the U.S. Department of Agriculture provided rural development grants, loans, and loan guarantees amounting to about one-eighth of the farm subsidies. For every rural development grant dollar, the USDA provided $150 in agricultural subsidies to these eleven Delta counties. Because of the high rate of poverty, USDA nutrition and food stamp expenditures were $252 million, which reached only a portion of low-income households. Would it be a greater public good to invest a significant portion of the $1.25 billion (farm subsidies + nutrition programs) in better public schools, job training and creation, and economic development so that the other programs no longer would be necessary?

Great Plains Family Labor Farms

The "filling in" of the Great Plains and the West, to which European Americans turned their attention after the Civil War, involved removing Native Americans. Military incursions and Indian wars (up to the presidency of Ulysses S. Grant), movement to reservations (from 1870 to the 1930s), and assimilation (attempted through boarding schools, which were aimed to "get the red out," and through movement to urban areas) were the means of removal.

Although skeletal evidence from the 1600s on both continents suggests that Native Americans on the Great Plains and northern woodlands of North America probably were healthier than their European counterparts, the health status of Native Americans declined rapidly with European settlement as disease and removal from their food supply decimated their populations.

Railroads were key in European settlement of the Great Plains and the interior West of the United States from the 1860s to the 1890s. Government land grants to railroads and cheap government land prices for speculators with available cash led initially to large private landholdings. Labor scarcity and high risk, due mainly to unpredictable weather, came to define the production systems that developed. There was a shortage of human capital to work in agriculture. The rapid industrial growth and expanding demand for labor in the cities, the difficulty of recruiting a laboring "underclass" to the countryside, and a scattered and scarce population meant that more than wages was required to attract the people necessary to get agricultural work done. The promise of landownership brought yeoman farmers to the central and western grasslands and forests to raise grains and livestock, with their large families providing substantial but inexpensive labor.

The need for more settlers to generate railroad freight in the form of grain and livestock, the spectacular failure of a large-scale corporate grain farm experiment (called Bonanza Farms) on the western plains, and higher rates of return in urban economic activities led corporate landowners to divide and sell this land in the great Midwestern part of the nation to smallholders, that is, farmers who relied on family labor. U.S. railroads advertised widely in northern Europe and the eastern United States to sell land to people who wanted to improve their lot in life. The growing cities, such as New York, Chicago, and Boston, needed cheap food to feed the workers who fueled their industrial revolutions.

Although these new family farmers were diverse ethnically, they were homogeneous racially. The only groups or individuals with adequate capital to purchase land—or to buy passage from overseas—were Europeans or Americans of European descent. For example, in 1872 Emil Flushe began selling railroad land west of Irwin, Iowa, recruiting Catholics from

Germany to come to a town he named Westphalia (just as he had named Westphalia, Minnesota, and would name Westphalia, Kansas) as he followed the railroad west. Westphalia, Iowa, maintains its street signs in German and still has a strong collective orientation centered on the culture of its German Catholicism. A Norwegian American farmer who recently moved to the community worried about fitting in. He did, for with time and two world wars, the ethnic differences between and within most Midwestern and Western communities were covered by a durable varnish of U.S. culture. Today, the fact that grandparents or great-grandparents of the "native" (European) residents of those communities were immigrants who maintained their own language for several generations does not appear to contribute to rural acceptance of new waves of immigrants from Latin America, Asia, and Africa to certain communities of the Midwest. Iowa, for example, made English its official language in 2002.

Labor-Intensive Corporate Agriculture in the West

The West has a history of large landholdings, beginning with the Spanish (later Mexican) land grants. After the 1848 defeat of Mexico in the Mexican-American War, one-third of Mexico's territory was ceded to the United States. Long-term residents found it more difficult to access natural capital, such as land, water, and timber. Some land grants were sold intact to Anglos (non-Hispanic whites). In other cases, U.S. courts did not recognize legal ownership of the land grants. In northern New Mexico, Spanish communities settled in the 1600s lost their right to graze the common lands. This was in spite of the fact that they had title to land grants consisting of homesteads and of common grazing lands. Community common lands had been eliminated in England with the enclosure acts of the eighteenth century to "free" labor for industry, and the new nation of the United States did not recognize commonly held land. Common lands were not compatible with the U.S. approach to property rights, so these lands were ceded to the states or sold to entrepreneurs and logging companies, or they became federal lands. The Hispanic inhabitants, called españoles, or Spaniards, lacked adequate land for grazing their sheep and other livestock.

The need for labor—in mining, in building the transcontinental railroad, and in agriculture—brought waves of immigrants to rural areas of the West. First came the Chinese, then the Filipinos, Japanese, and Mexicans, to which have recently been added other Latin American peoples.

Asian groups, often pushed by difficult economic or political conditions in the sending country, were welcomed as a new source of cheap labor when there was a particular job to be done. Chinese workers cleared 88,000 acres of rich swampland in California in the San Joaquin–Sacramento delta area and built the western end of the transcontinental railroad that joined in Ogden, Utah, in 1869.

When a project was finished or when the economy contracted in the United States, these Asian immigrants then were excluded. The Chinese were prohibited from immigrating to the United States in 1882, the Japanese in 1908, and the Filipinos in 1934 (when Congress legislated the independence of the Philippines, although independence was actually granted in 1946). Asians in general were excluded from citizenship in 1924. California's Alien Land Law of 1913 forbade persons not eligible for citizenship to lease or own land.

Japanese Americans were the most productive truck farmers in California in 1941, producing half of the vegetables in the state. Their strong social capital and the credit system that it spawned helped them acquire property where other immigrant groups were not so successful. Following the bombing of Pearl Harbor, they were evacuated to concentration camps, even though there was scant evidence that they would be anything other than loyal to the United States. Most lost access to land and other possessions. Only in 1965 did the United States eliminate the anti-Asian bias in its immigration law. Given the greater opportunities in urban areas, it is not surprising that in 2000, 96 percent of Asian Americans lived in metropolitan areas.

HUMAN CAPITAL AS LABOR FORCE

A job meets several human needs. It provides income, regulates daily activity, establishes a sense of identity, and offers opportunities for social interactions and meaningful life experiences. As a result, the kinds of jobs available and the opportunities for creating jobs within communities have enormous implications for the individuals who live or come to work there.

Character of the Local Labor Force

Human capital attributes of the labor force include both the skills and training acquired and the level of schooling people in a community complete. Despite the lower status often accorded to natural-resource-based industries, most such industries required workers to develop skills for which they then were relatively well paid. Those skills were generally acquired from experience on the job and from family and friends.

Despite the importance of skills acquired through on-the-job training, level of schooling is becoming an important asset to a community. The industries that are growing, such as computer and information-processing activities, require more highly educated workers. Manufacturing plants planning to convert to new technology look carefully at the educational level of current workers. If those workers cannot be trained to handle the new equipment, companies will relocate. Math skills are critical to training success. Historically, rural areas have lagged behind urban areas in terms of the educational level of the labor force. This is one reason that routine manufacturing plants were more likely to locate in rural areas than in metropolitan areas and then to move offshore.

The wage gap between urban and rural workers reflects a rural workforce with less education and training than urban workers. In 2006, median weekly earnings for nonmetro workers ($509) were about 84 percent of the metro average ($607). In 2005, only 16.9 percent of rural adults age twenty-five and older had completed college, half the percentage of urban adults. Moreover, the rural-urban gap in college completion has widened since 1990. Employers are increasingly attracted to rural areas offering concentrations of well-educated and skilled workers. A labor force with low educational levels poses challenges for many rural counties seeking economic development. Rural areas with poorly funded public schools, few good universities or community colleges, very low educational attainment, and high levels of economic distress may find it hard to compete in the new economy. Recent USDA Economic Research Service–sponsored research documents the direct link between improved labor force quality and economic development outcomes, finding that increases in the number of adults with some college education resulted in higher per capita income and employment growth rates, although less so in nonmetro than metro counties. Efforts to reduce high school dropout rates, increase high school graduation rates, enhance student preparation for college, and increase college attendance are all critical to improving local labor quality (Whitener and Parker 2007).

The growth of high-tech firms and the decline of routine manufacturing in the United States is reflected in wage rates. Becker points out that, nationwide, the salary premium for completion of college had by the 1980s grown to its highest in history, whereas the average wage of people without a high school diploma had dropped by 25 percent since the early 1970s (Becker 2002). Unfortunately, in many parts of the rural Midwest and South, in response to the farm crisis and the recession of the early and middle 1980s, rural communities recruited low-wage firms in the belief that "any job is better than no job." Since the early 1990s, there has been much greater awareness of the importance of generating high-quality jobs, but it is not easy for a community to change an existing low-wage industrial profile.

The age structure of the community is another important aspect of the labor market. Is there an abundant labor force at the entry level? In many urban areas, a lack of young people willing to work for minimum wage and no benefits has driven up wages for jobs such as fast-food counter worker. In the Midwest, declining populations often result from the exodus of young people. The average age in rural farming communities is increasing, which leaves few workers at the entry level. Consequently, these communities are at a relative disadvantage in attracting manufacturing plants. A high proportion of elderly residents in a community influences both the types of jobs available and the types of workers available to fill them. Although recreation counties and counties that attract retirees are growing faster than any other category of rural counties, the jobs that are generated tend to be in the lower register of the service sector and are often seasonal.

One of the most significant changes in the nature of rural labor forces is the increasing participation of women. Rural women traditionally have participated less in the formal labor market than have urban women. This has been partly because of the importance of women's unpaid economic activities, including caring for livestock, helping with crops, or maintaining the financial records. Changes in the economy have decreased the opportunities for women to perform these traditional activities. Financial pressures have also increased the need for women to seek cash income. Farm women often will take off-farm jobs to ensure that the family has health insurance. Many of the industries that have located in rural areas, including the textile, electronics, and pharmaceutical industries, now employ mainly women. The urban-rural differential in female participation in the labor force has narrowed substantially.

Finally, increased mobility makes the description of a rural labor force somewhat complex. Improved transportation has increased the likelihood that a person can live in one town yet commute to work in another. But the high cost of fuel may provide a new limitation on commuting to low-wage jobs.

Any description of a labor force often has to be regional rather than local. To capture this activity, economists have introduced the concept of *labor market areas (LMAs),* which include both the residence and work destinations of local people. These areas are multicounty regions that encompass those places where relatively large numbers of people routinely move back and forth from home to work. Approximately half the nation's LMAs are rural. Most are very large, particularly those in the West. Rural people are very mobile in their pursuit of work.

The Dual Labor Market

The *labor force* consists of all employed persons plus all persons seeking employment. The labor market can be divided into two segments: the primary labor market, which seeks specific skills, and the secondary labor market, which seeks unskilled workers. Peripheral firms hire mostly from the secondary labor market. Core industries increasingly hire from both segments of the labor market (Parcel and Sickmeier 1988).

People are recruited into the *primary labor market* because of their educational and skill levels. Jobs in the primary labor market provide good wages, safe working conditions, opportunities for advancement within the firm, stability of employment, and due process in the enforcement of work rules. Jobs in the primary labor market can be either managerial/ professional or craft/skilled occupations.

Jobs in the *secondary labor market* generally have low status, low pay, poor benefits, and little or no chance for advancement. Working conditions can sometimes be less clean and less safe. Job security is often low. There is little movement from the secondary to the primary labor market, but much movement by an individual from one secondary labor market job to another. In addition, there is little correlation between education and income. For example, people with certain characteristics may be hired preferentially for the secondary labor market. Thus, in certain firms or industries, women may be hired into lower-wage positions with less opportunity for advancement than the positions men are hired into, regardless of formal qualifications such as education. Organizing job ladders within communities or regions that allow workers to advance from secondary to primary labor markets is a new rural development strategy.

Nearly one in four wage and salary workers age twenty-five and older living in the rural (nonmetro) United States in 2005 were low-wage workers (Economic Research Service 2007). More than 40 percent of these workers were the sole or principal wage earners in their households. Rural low-wage workers are more likely to be employed in service and retail trade industries, part of the secondary labor market.

In a given industry, low-wage workers tend to work in less-skilled occupations requiring less education. Although the share of white men in low-wage jobs has grown since 1979, low-wage rural workers continue to be overwhelmingly women and minorities. In the secondary labor market, *ascribed characteristics* related to human capital, such as race and gender, are much more important than *achieved characteristics,* such as education.

Most firms generate jobs that are regulated by laws specifying limits on number of hours worked, safety regulations, dismissal procedures, and so on. Records are kept that can document the exchange of work for wages and thus the number of individuals employed in a given industry. Firms that provide such employment and are subject to governmental oversight make up the *formal economy.* The *informal economy* includes firms unregulated by societal institutions. A handshake rather than a contractual relation between employer and employee is the basis for hiring in the informal economy. Individuals hired to do informal activities generally represent the lower part of the secondary labor force. They lack social benefits, are often paid less than minimum wage (often in cash), are subject to arbitrary dismissal, and often work under unapproved safety and health conditions.

The informal sector has existed for a long time. As Manuel Castells and Alejandro Portes (1989) point out, what is new is that it is growing at the expense of previously formalized positions, particularly in urban areas. In rural areas, one kind of informal activity is substituted for another. Informal relations are shifting from agriculture and natural-resource sectors to manufacturing, construction, and particularly to service sectors, such as tourism.

How a community's human capital is divided between the primary and secondary labor markets or between formal and informal activities affects the stability and well-being of a community. For the most part, employment in rural areas is more likely to be in the secondary labor market. Hanes Textiles was the second-largest employer in Eatonton, Georgia, but nearly all its local employees are in the secondary labor market. Those working at Hanes were paid minimum wage and saw limited opportunities for advancement. Most were women; African American women were overrepresented. Hanes has now left Georgia.

Ultimately, a dual labor market benefits firms more than the local community. Labor costs are kept low. However, those employed are working at jobs that may not fully use their skills, let alone their potential talents.

Incomes are limited, which makes it difficult for the local economy to flourish. The community suffers because much of its human capital is underutilized. Companies that rely heavily on the secondary labor market often make a relatively small contribution to the community.

Opportunity Structure and Human Capital

Just as the educational and skill levels of a community help determine the types of industries that locate in an area or the businesses that can be initiated, the types of jobs available in turn influence the educational level of the community. When coal mining and logging were profitable, young men often dropped out of high school to go to work in the mines or forests, assuming that within a relatively short time, they would be making more money than their teachers. Any further investment in education seemed foolish and unnecessary. Regions such as McDowell County, West Virginia, characteristically developed low commitments to schools, although support has increased in recent years.

Towns such as Irwin and Eatonton face a different dilemma. Much of the agricultural Midwest has historically had a strong commitment to education, and well-supported local schools enable most young people to pursue some type of postsecondary education. Once they finish college, however, Irwin's young people go elsewhere. Few local jobs require the skills or knowledge they have developed. In Eatonton, African American women work either for the tourist industry or as domestics. When Billie Jo Williams finished her degree in business administration, she found she could not use her education in Eatonton (see Chapter 1).

The interaction between educational level and type of jobs available has become a vicious cycle for many rural communities. The *opportunity structure* of the community—the types of jobs and investment opportunities available—affects the character of the local labor force. The local labor force in turn affects the community's success in attracting or supporting new business enterprises. Communities that invest heavily in education see the more educated young people leave because of the lack of opportunity, unless community leaders and citizens work collectively to generate jobs that they would like their own children to take. Those that do not invest in education rely on assembly plants for jobs—industries that depend upon the less educated workers who are willing to accept lower wages. These jobs offer young people little motivation to invest in education.

Communities, in their efforts to promote local economic development, need to focus both on creating high-quality jobs and on developing and sustaining a strong educational system.

BUILDING HUMAN CAPITAL

Rural Schools

One of the most dramatic changes in rural areas has been the decline in the number of public school districts since World War II. In 1942, there were about 108,000 school districts in the United States. By 1962, that number was down to just under 35,000. As of 1987, there were 14,721 school districts, and in 2002, the numbers showed a decrease again, with 13,522 school districts remaining. However, that number had increased to 14,199 by the 2005–2006 school year. Almost half of these districts were classified as rural by the U.S. Department of Education. The period of the most intense consolidation was between 1939 and 1973. The desire to reduce expenses and lower taxes is leading many states to push for further consolidation of school districts, despite evidence that suggests that smaller schools and districts cost less per graduate (Rural Policy Matters 2006).

School consolidation illustrates the tension that often exists between local and state governments. Professional education groups and state departments of education pushed school district mergers in the 1950s. Because professional educators were concerned about the quality of education in extremely small districts, they pushed for consolidation in an effort to standardize schools. States were beginning to assume more responsibility in funding education and were eager to increase the fiscal efficiency of school systems. Small schools were said to be inefficient; thus, most of the decrease in the number of school districts resulted from the consolidation of rural districts. The expected changes in efficiency, in terms of return to social and human capital, rarely were measured.

Before the move toward consolidation, each of the small, one-room elementary schools scattered throughout the country formed a single district. When students graduated from the elementary schools (K–8), they changed districts to attend high school in town. During the first phase of consolidation, these one-school districts were unified into districts of kindergarten through twelfth grade (K–12) based in villages and cities. Initially, these new school districts had multiple attendance centers, but gradually the centers in the countryside were closed, and all children attended school in town. A second wave of consolidation occurred in more sparsely populated areas. In that phase, some villages or towns lost their schools entirely. Often, when two or more towns could not reach agreement as to which one would have the new school, new high schools were built in wheat fields or cornfields, equidistant from all of them.

The consolidation of rural school districts has been accompanied by increased state control of education. The state of Vermont, for example, maintains firm control over nearly every aspect of the educational system, including the following matters:

- the licensing and qualification of all public school personnel
- attendance and records of attendance of all pupils
- standards for student performance
- adult basic education programs
- approval of independent schools
- disbursement of funds
- equal access by all Vermont students to a high-quality education

As the educational system has become more standardized, some critics argue that it has become less responsive to local needs and resources. Given the extent to which state funds are being used to support local schools, however, states may feel that they have little choice.

Losing schools in rural areas has a significant impact on the welfare of the community as a whole, as Thomas Lyson (2002) points out in his research on the loss of schools in rural communities. Lyson collected data from all 352 villages and towns with populations under 2,500 in New York State. He divided them into two groups based on the population size and made comparisons within groups. For the smaller group (population 500 or less), he found that only 46 percent of the communities without schools grew in population between 1990 and 2000, whereas 60 percent of those with schools saw population growth. (For the larger communities, the difference was only 4 percentage points, but in the same direction.) Communities with schools have higher home values and somewhat higher wages and per capita income. Lyson also established that communities with schools have more professional, managerial, and executive workers, along with more self-employed residents and fewer residents who commute outside the community to work. Lyson recognized that keeping schools close to the community should be a significant part of every state's rural development strategy.

Beyond research establishing that students have better attitudes and more involvement in extracurricular activities in smaller schools, the U.S. Department of Education (1998) report *Violence and Discipline Problems in the U.S. Public Schools: 1996–97* revealed that larger schools (1,000 students or more) have 825 percent more violent crime, 270 percent more vandalism, 378 percent more theft and larceny, 394 percent more physical fights or attacks, 3,200 percent more robberies, and 1,000 percent more weapons incidents. Fifty-two percent of principals of small schools (fewer than 300 students) report that they have either no or only minor discipline problems, and small schools' dropout rates are substantially lower. The report revealed that virtually none of the large-school problems were evident in the smaller schools. School consolidation, although a popular economic solution, may not always be the best one for a community's welfare. (See Box 4.1 for a comparison of rural, suburban, and urban schools.)

Investing in the Rural Poor

Hurricanes Katrina and Rita made the world aware of poverty in the United States. While the media focused on urban New Orleans, rural counties along the Gulf Coast suffered similar devastation and unequal recovery. Across rural America, use of food pantries, food stamps, and other welfare services is on the rise. Has human capital investment in low-income people been sufficient to ensure that they can be productive members of society and provide for their own needs?

There is ample evidence that poverty in an affluent society such as ours has negative effects on those who experience it, but how do we define poverty? Molly Orshansky, who worked in the Social Security Administration during Lyndon B. Johnson's War on Poverty, developed a means of measuring poverty that is used to this day. She set the poverty threshold at three times the cost of the "thrifty food plan," the cheapest of four USDA family food budgets. Thresholds were developed with adjustments for family size, farm/nonfarm status, by the number of family members who were children, gender of the head of household, and aged/nonaged status. Most experts believe that the poverty definition sharply underestimates—by as much as a factor of two—the incidence of poverty in this country today. Orshansky's method was adopted by the Office of Economic Opportunity,

Box 4.1 Students in Rural Schools
Do Better than Those in City Schools and
Less Well than Those in Suburban Schools

- A larger percentage of rural public school students in fourth and eighth grades in 2005 scored at or above the proficient level on the National Assessment of Educational Progress reading, mathematics, and science assessments than did public school students in cities at these grade levels. However, smaller percentages of rural public school students than suburban public school students scored at or above the proficient level in reading and mathematics.
- In 2004, the high school status dropout rate in rural areas (11 percent) was higher than in suburban areas (9 percent), but lower than in cities (13 percent).
- The average freshman graduation rate (those who enter as freshmen and graduate from that or another high school) for public high school students was higher during the 2002–2003 school year in rural areas (75 percent) than in cities (65 percent), but lower than in towns and suburban areas (76 and 79 percent, respectively).
- A larger percentage of teenagers in rural areas than in suburban areas were neither enrolled in school nor employed in 2004 (6 percent versus 4 percent).
- College enrollment rates for both eighteen- to twenty-four-year olds and twenty-five- to twenty-nine-year olds generally were lower in rural areas than in all other locales in 2004.
- A smaller percentage of rural adults than suburban adults in 2005 took work-related courses (24 percent versus 30 percent) or courses for personal interest (18 percent versus 23 percent), and a smaller percentage of rural adults (3 percent) than adults in cities and suburban areas (6 percent) participated in part-time college or university credential programs

Source

U.S. Department of Education, Institute of Education Sciences, National Center for Educational Statistics. 2007. *Status of Education in Rural America.* Online; available: http://nces.ed.gov/pubs2007/ruraled; accessed September 9, 2007.

Johnson's antipoverty agency, in 1965 and has merely been adjusted for changes in the Consumer Price Index (CPI) every year since, even though the cost of food in the family budget has gone down significantly and other things, such as transportation, housing, and health care, have risen in cost faster than the CPI as a whole. Child care, which for families with small children is even more expensive than housing, was not even a financial factor in 1965. One way of assessing the extent of underestimation of the official poverty rate is to calculate a self-sufficiency wage. A self-sufficiency wage is one that covers current expenditures for basic necessities for families of a specified composition (e.g., two parents and two children of varying ages). Jan L. Flora and others (2004) calculated self-sufficiency wages for Iowa that included no-frills expenditures for food, clothing, housing, health care, transportation (to work, for shopping, and to day care or school), day care (for preschool–age children), local telephone, and finally household expenses, personal care, and clothing. This bare-bones budget does not include money for savings, leisure activities, dining out, or the purchase of luxury or nongeneric goods. For 2002, Flora and colleagues estimated that between 19 percent and 28 percent of Iowa's children were in families with before-tax incomes that were insufficient to cover basic family expenditures, while according to the official poverty rate, approximately 13 percent of children were in poverty, suggesting that if we view poverty as the inability to afford basic necessities, the official poverty threshold should be increased by 50 percent to 100 percent.

Overall, rural poverty is higher than metropolitan poverty—in 2005 about 2 percentage points higher. However, if the metro population is divided into central city and suburban, rural poverty is intermediate: In 2005, 17 percent of all people living in central cities were (officially) in poverty, 9.3 percent of suburban residents were, and 14.5 percent of nonmetro people were officially poor. By 2006, a higher percentage of nonmetro than metro residents received food stamps (10.3 percent versus 7.3 percent).

If one breaks down poverty levels by race/ethnicity and family structure, then within each category, nonmetro poverty is higher than in central cities (see Table 4.1). (We chose to include only families with children under eighteen, since we wanted to focus on families that included the most vulnerable age group—children. The pattern within categories is similar for all families.) In the aggregate, rural poverty is intermediate between central city and suburb because European American families make

Table 4.1 Age-specific Poverty of Individuals in Households by Metro-Nonmetro Residence and Sex, 2005

Metro status/Age	Both sexes % below 100% of poverty	Male % below 100% of poverty	Female % below 100% of poverty
Inside Metro Statistical Area (MSA)			
Under 18 years of age	17.2	17.1	17.3
Under 6 years*	19.3		
6–17 years*	15.4		
18–24 years	17.9	14.5	21.3
25–34 years	12.3	9.5	15.1
35–74 years	7.6–9.2	5.9–7.5	8.4–10.9
75+ years	10.8	7.6	12.8
Outside MSA (Nonmetro)			
Under 18 years of age	20.0	19.1	21.0
Under 6 years*	24.3		
6–17 years*	17.0		
18–24 years	20.3	15.9	24.9
25–34 years	14.5	10.5	18.5
35–74 years	9.4–12.5	8.0–10.6	10.6–14.3
75+ years	14.7	8.4	18.8

* Not strictly comparable with other poverty indicators, because these childhood poverty rates are based on households rather than individuals in households, as are the other figures.
SOURCE: U.S. Bureau of the Census, Current Population Survey. 2006. "Pov 40: Age, Sex, Household Relationship, by Region and Residence—Ratio of Income to Poverty Level, 2005" (August 29). Annual Social and Economic Supplement. A joint project between the Bureau of Labor Statistics and the Bureau of the Census. Online; available: http://pubdb3.census.gov/macro/032006/pov/toc.htm; accessed July 28, 2007.

up a larger share of the total in rural (non-metro) areas than they do in central cities. Table 4.2 (p. 104) also shows that for married couples with children in rural areas, African Americans and Hispanics have poverty levels that are two and three times those for non-Hispanic whites. However, when one examines female-headed households, those geographic differences are substantially ameliorated—although the rates are much, much higher than for married couples of the respective race/ethnicity. The poverty rates for families headed by single dads (not shown, because they are small in number) are substantially lower than for those headed by single moms, indicating that when there is only one available breadwinner, gender trumps race as a predictor of poverty. Perhaps more importantly, rurality, minority status, presence of children, youth of parent(s), having only one adult in the family, and that adult being female, are cumulative in their prediction of family poverty.

In 2000, the poverty rate for persons in nonmetropolitan areas of the United States was as low as it had been in the mid–1970s: 13.4 percent. After a steady decline in the post–World War II era, poverty—both rural and urban—leveled off in the 1970s but grew noticeably in the 1980s. After 1979, the gap between rural and urban poverty, which into the early 1970s had steadily narrowed, began to widen once again. By 1985, the gap between nonmetro and metro areas exceeded 6 percentage points. By 2000, the difference was less than half that amount. However, there are regional differences. In 2005, rural (nonmetro) family poverty was greatest in the South (15.5 percent), followed by the West (12 percent), and least in the Midwest (8.8 percent) and Northeast (8.2 percent).

In 1974, children replaced persons over sixty-five as the poorest age group in the United States (see Figure 4.1). Nationwide 17 percent of children under eighteen years of age and 20 percent of children under six who are in families are officially poor (2005 data). However, the share of children in school who receive free or reduced-price lunches may be a better indicator of the childhood poverty rate. Thirty-one percent of rural schoolchildren receive free or reduced-price lunches, while the figure in metro schools is only 25 percent. The characteristics of poor households also have changed over the past three or more decades. Declines in family size and increased educational levels among young people have been offset by increased numbers of female-headed households and a decline in relatively well-paying jobs for those entering the job markets.

Poverty grew in rural areas in the 1980s for a variety of reasons. Most important was the fact that beginning in that decade, the quality of industrial jobs declined even faster in rural areas than in urban areas. In the 1970s, rural industrialization grew substantially, and urban industrial employment stagnated. Employment of educated and skilled persons grew, as did employment of unskilled workers in rural areas. In contrast, the 1980s were a period of unusually high out-migration of skilled and educated people from rural areas, reflecting the increasingly peripheral nature of the rural economy. The 1990s encompassed a long stretch of economic expansion, which accounts for a notable decline in rural poverty. There were record rates of job creation and the lowest rate of unemployment in more

Figure 4.1   Poverty Rates by Age, 1959–2005

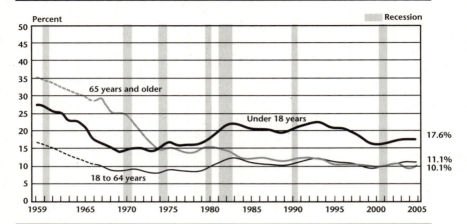

SOURCE: DeNavas-Walt, Carmen, Bernadette D. Proctor, and Cheryl Hill Lee. 2006. "Income, Poverty, and Health Insurance Coverage in the United States: 2005," 16. U.S. Census Bureau, Current Population Reports, P60–231. Washington, D.C.: U.S. Government Printing Office. Also online; available: www.census.gov/prod/2006pubs/p60–231.pdf; accessed July 27, 2007.

than thirty years. U.S. poverty increased beginning in 2001 and the metro/nonmetro gap again began to widen two years later (Jensen 2006).

Although the rural poor are more likely than the urban poor to be in the labor force, many of the employment opportunities in rural areas are with companies so small or in jobs so marginal that minimum-wage and benefits legislation does not cover them. The service sector, which tends to pay low wages, especially in rural areas, has replaced manufacturing as the rural growth sector. Furthermore, in rural areas there is a strong ideology against labor legislation and few labor unions to bargain collectively for higher wages.

Rural communities are noted for their ability to respond to extraordinary tragedies that lead to temporary poverty, such as a fire or, more recently, at least in some communities, the farm crisis. But rural communities are much less able to respond to conditions of chronic poverty. As discussed in Chapter 3, rural people tend to feel that proper attitudes lead to hard work, and hard work should lead to material success. As a result, lack of material success—such as an inadequate income or the lack of a decent home (preferably owned)—is viewed as a moral failing. The dominant view is that rewarding such moral failings by providing "handouts" to those out of work or with low incomes should be avoided.

The dominant cultural capital plays an important role in deciding whom people view as the worthy poor and the unworthy poor. The worthy poor usually are seen as being in poverty as a result of experiencing a catastrophe or as a result of inexorable forces, such as the aging process. The unworthy poor often are defined as able-bodied adults with no job or who work only part time.

According to dominant rural values, a higher proportion of the rural poor than urban poor should be "worthy." Rural families are more likely than urban (metropolitan) to be employed and still poor. In 1998, two-thirds of rural poor families had at least one member working at some time during the year; 29 percent of such families had one or more full-time, year-round worker, and 16 percent had two or more full-time year-round workers. The culprit is exceedingly low rural wages, particularly for workers with a high school education or less: In 1999, 27 percent of rural workers over age twenty-five received wages that if earned full-time, year-round, would not lift a family of four above the official poverty line (Fluharty 2002).

High poverty among young adults—who often are parents—means high poverty among children, who are part of the worthy poor. In rural areas, because young parents are able-bodied, neighbors may define them as the unworthy poor—even though they may work full time or at more than one job. As Table 4.2 shows, people ages eighteen to twenty-four are the most likely to be in poverty. Young women are considerably more likely to be in poverty than are young men, and their poverty rate remains quite high to an older age than that of young men. Young people also are likely to have small children. It is not surprising then that children are the age group most likely to be in poverty. If we use 150 percent of official poverty as a conservative indicator of family self-sufficiency, then nearly two-fifths (38.5 percent) of children under six in nonmetro areas are in families that earn less than is needed to meet basic needs. Thirty percent of children between six and seventeen are in such families. The high level of poverty among rural children—and not just in the South—is one of the best-kept secrets in this country.

The collective view that able-bodied people in poverty are undeserving affects the behavior of the rural poor. Because of the shame involved in

Table 4.2. Poverty Status for Families with Related Children under 18 by Family Structure, Race/Ethnicity, and Metro or Nonmetro, 2005

| Metro status/race | Family type (w/related children < 18 yrs old) | | |
	Total families % below poverty	Married couples % below poverty	Female householder % below poverty
Inside Metro Statistical Area (MSA)			
All races	14.0	6.3	35.0
Whites alone, non-Hispanic	7.8	3.1	26.4
Blacks alone	27.5	8.5	41.1
Hispanic, of any race	24.0	16.5	44.7
Inside MSA/Inside principal cities			
All races	20.1	9.4	40.7
Whites alone, non-Hispanic	9.8	3.6	29.2
Blacks alone	33.6	12.4	45.9
Hispanic, of any race	28.5	19.8	48.4
Inside MSA/Outside principal cities			
All races	10.3	4.7	29.5
Whites alone, non-Hispanic	7.0	2.9	25.0
Blacks alone	19.4	4.9	32.9
Hispanic, of any race	19.3	13.6	39.2
Outside MSA (Nonmetro)			
All races	17.4	7.9	43.1
Whites alone, non-Hispanic	13.9	5.8	40.0
Blacks alone	35.9	16.7	48.6
Hispanic, of any race	30.1	22.0	52.9

SOURCE: U.S. Bureau of the Census, Current Population Survey. 2006. "Pov 45: Region Division and Type of Residence—Poverty Status for Families with Related Children under 18 by Family Structure, 2005." *Annual Social and Economic Supplement.* A joint project between the Bureau of Labor Statistics and the Bureau of the Census. Online; available: http://pubdb3.census.gov/macro/032006/pov/toc.htm; accessed July 28, 2007.

admitting one needs help, many rural poor do not seek the help available to them. The rural poor are less likely than the urban poor to take advantage of the means-tested resources available to them.

Although composing a smaller proportion of families than in urban areas, single parents in rural areas face particularly severe problems. Poverty rates of rural families headed by single mothers are astronomical; 40 percent, 49 percent, and 53 percent of such Anglo (non-Hispanic white), African American, and Hispanic families, respectively, are below the poverty line (see Table 4.2). Furthermore, affordable day care generally is not available. Single parents who are in a family network often rely on female relatives to care for children, but those female relatives increasingly have had to join the labor force and no longer are available as babysitters. Thus, the single parent is faced with low wages and lack of daycare. Some communities, such as Harlan, Iowa, have instituted a community-supported day care system with a sliding fee scale that enables single parents and two-parent families in which both spouses work to find reasonably priced, reliable, high-quality child care. However, this kind of community action is the exception rather than the rule.

Another problem of poverty in rural areas is the fact that to gain better-paying jobs, workers need to travel great distances. The cost of transportation and the lack of public transportation often force families to depend on old and unreliable automobiles that get poor gas mileage. Not only is getting to work difficult, but it also is challenging and costly to get to places to purchase groceries and other necessities at a reasonable price. The declining availability of intercity public transportation as bus and train routes have vanished makes the rural poor even more vulnerable.

The one comparative advantage of living in rural areas for the poor is cheap housing. However, the high inflation in urban housing prices means that the rural poor who have housing are basically trapped. They are unlikely to be able to move to a place that pays better wages because they cannot afford the housing costs involved. To a degree, the cheaper housing reflects the fact that housing stock is older and more likely to be dilapidated. The rural poor are much more likely to live in mobile homes than are their urban counterparts. One of the strategies poor people have developed in rural areas is to send one member of the family to live temporarily in a higher-wage area, often with relatives, while the rest of the family remains at home, which often means having no vehicle and very little money. In turn, lack of transportation and of money limits the family members' ability to participate in community activities, which further isolates the rural poor.

Because of the moral connotations associated with poverty, integrating people who are poor into the rural community is often more difficult than integrating people who are elderly or who have developmental disabilities. Enabling the poor to participate involves providing basic necessities, such as health care, that often must be underwritten, at least partially, on a local basis. Local governments increasingly are challenged to provide health care and other welfare programs because of the sharp curtailment of federal funding for social programs.

In some communities, the farm crisis helped reduce the stigma of poverty and made the needs it represents more legitimate. Many communities responded to the consumption needs of the hardworking poor by such poverty-reducing mechanisms as winter coat trades, in which members of the community collected the clothing their children had outgrown, sorted it by size, and then made it available to everyone. Other mechanisms involve such seemingly trivial matters as exchanges of prom dresses; such solutions allow individuals to acquire some of the symbols of normal community participation at minimal investment and, therefore, to participate in mainstream community activities. These kinds of activities do not solve the economic problems of poverty, but they do reduce the social isolation of the rural poor and eventually can lead to the inclusion of similar efforts as part of community-level programs.

The central cause of poverty among the rural able-bodied poor is a lack of employment and low wages when employed. Rural areas should benefit significantly from the increase in the minimum wage that Congress passed in 2007 (to be gradually increased to $7.25 per hour by 2009), because of the large share of low-wage workers in nonmetro areas.

Economic development efforts that expand high-quality employment in both urban and rural areas will be the most effective long-term antipoverty program. Such efforts must be coupled with educational reform involving substantial investment in upgrading the capabilities of young and mid-career people, particularly in areas of persistent poverty. Unfortunately, the 1996 Welfare Reform Act allows for only two years of education during the time one receives Temporary Assistance to Needy Families. Realistically, that is not enough time even to get an associate of arts degree from a community college if one is a single parent. The welfare reform law was written more to get welfare recipients off welfare and into the job market than to encourage them to obtain the assets that would keep them permanently out of poverty.

Given the present antiwelfare mood, political support can be gained only for the worthy poor. Children are the most obvious target group. Expanding the Women, Infants, and Children program, State Child Health Insurance Program, and other programs benefiting children (and the families of which they are a part) is likely to be much more effective than the current spate of so-called workfare programs that followed passage of the welfare reform law. The Earned Income Tax Credit, by which low-income working families receive a tax benefit, is a form of bonus for performing low-wage work. Yet few rural low-income workers know of its existence or how to access it. Getting women off welfare (more than 80 percent of adults on welfare are women) is likely to be more effective if coalitions are made between advocacy organizations and urban and rural poor people. Only if the welfare of children becomes defined as a strategic interest of the United States is there a chance of making substantial inroads against poverty. The Child Care Tax Credit is another mechanism that supports working parents.

Health and Human Capital

Rural health care issues have both individual and social aspects. Many rural hospitals, clinics, and nursing homes are experiencing a fiscal crisis, and the changing structure of medical care is a factor. The fiscal crisis of rural health care is related to federal health policies. Because many rural communities have a very high proportion of elderly among their population, a higher percentage of patients in rural hospitals are on Medicare, whose reimbursements for particular procedures are lower than the rate hospitals charge patients with private insurance. Similar issues arise with Medicaid, which, unlike Medicare—a federally financed program—operates with shared financing between the states and the federal government. Among individuals under sixty-five, 15.3 percent of rural residents, compared with 11.2 percent of urban residents, had Medicaid as their primary source of insurance. With the current fiscal crisis, states are cutting back on Medicaid appropriations. In addition, nonmetropolitan hospitals are reimbursed at a lower rate for the same procedures than are hospitals in metropolitan areas. Members of Congress from more-rural states and districts are seeking to change that inequity, but urban representatives have dug in their heels on this issue, since it would involve either the shifting of large amounts of funds from urban to rural areas or the appropriation of substantial amounts of new money. And because rural people are more likely to be small-business owners or to be employed by small firms, they are less likely to have employer-provided insurance (although there is little difference in the proportion of workers who are totally uninsured in rural and urban areas). Those without employer-provided insurance will either pay higher premiums or have more-limited coverage, since they are less likely to get group rates. Nearly half of rural workers are without employer-provided health insurance.

Increased specialization of medicine, along with the accompanying expensive technology, means that rural people go more frequently to major medical centers for treatment of complex illnesses. Rural hospitals and clinics are left doing routine medicine, which has lower profit margins. Many rural hospitals host specialists from regional medical centers or metropolitan areas who come once a week or once a month to see patients with illnesses related to their specialty. In other cases, aggressive regional medical centers have purchased clinics, and the doctors who practice in those clinics become their employees. Telemedicine holds promise in linking rural patients to urban expertise. There is also a shortage of rural doctors. Only 10 percent of medical doctors practice in nonmetropolitan areas, although 20 percent of the population resides there (Moody 2002).

Poverty is highly related to *health status*. Poorer and less educated elderly women enrolled in Medicare+Choice plans reported poorer health, experienced more chronic illness, and reported that they felt depressed or sad more of the time in the preceding year than their more affluent and better educated counterparts, according to an analysis of data from the Medicare Health Outcomes Survey. Race and ethnicity also influenced elderly women's health status (Bierman, Haffer, and Hwang 2001).

Rural residents are more likely than people in urban areas to engage in behavior that can harm their health, because their level of self efficacy is often low. For example, smoking among people twelve to seventeen years of age was highest in the more remote rural areas and generally lower in central cities. Nationwide, in 1999, about 15 percent of adolescents reported having smoked in the preceding month. In the West and the South, they were much more likely to smoke if they were in rural areas, although those adolescents in the West in general were less likely to smoke than adolescents in the South and Midwest. Only in the Midwest did adolescents in the urban fringe smoke more than either central-city or rural adolescents. Except in the Midwest, cigarette smoking among those over eighteen years of age was higher in the rural areas than in metropolitan areas. People smoked less in the West than in other regions. Those most likely to smoke were rural residents in the South (Eberhardt et al. 2001). Smoking has obvious implications for health, as does obesity, which is higher in rural than in urban areas (see Chapter 10). However, if people see no point in improving their lifestyle, they are more likely to engage in harmful behaviors. Accidental death rates are also higher in rural areas.

What do these differences in health status mean for rural America? First, it is harder to work one's way out of poverty when one's health is poor, because the ability to show up for work on a regular basis is severely limited. Second, it is more difficult to get access to health care—preventative or curative—in rural America. Third, for children, poor health is associated with poor school performance, exacerbating the disadvantages that come from living in a home where the educational attainment of the adults is low. Increasing availability of health care would be an excellent investment for rural human capital and could translate into higher levels of financial and social capital.

CHAPTER SUMMARY

Gary Becker and other economists argue that education and training are the most important forms of human capital. Human capital also includes the personal attributes of individuals that contribute to their ability to earn a living, strengthen community, and otherwise contribute to community organizations, family, and self-improvement.

In the settlement period, attributes of human labor that were needed included physical strength, endurance, and, in some cases, innovativeness. Education often was denied to those who were expected to do only manual work all their lives. Where settlement was accompanied by relatively widespread access to property, education was more highly valued and more universally available, although rural schools were still segregated well into the 1970s in some places.

The employment opportunities in rural areas both determine the kind of education available and the degree to which students are motivated to take advantage of them. Workforce opportunities can be divided into two segments: the primary and secondary labor markets. The primary labor market recruits people based on educational and skill levels. Jobs in the primary labor market can be either managerial/professional or craft/skilled worker. Jobs in the secondary labor market generally have low status, low pay, poor benefits, and little or no chance for advancement.

In the past, miners and loggers, and often farmers as well, did not have high educational levels because they left school for work. However, this has changed. The interaction between educational level and type of jobs available has become a vicious cycle for many rural communities. Communities that invest heavily in education see the more educated young people leave because of the lack of opportunity—unless such communities work collectively to generate jobs they would like their children to take. Rural areas are losing their local schools to consolidation, which has hurt local economies without improving school effectiveness.

Rural poverty continues to be higher than urban poverty in the United States. People living in rural areas have fewer opportunities and may have less education, both of which contribute to rural poverty. Human capital thus suffers. Poverty is related to poor health status. People in rural areas are somewhat more likely than those in urban areas to engage in personal and occupational behaviors detrimental to their health. Rural areas are less likely to have the resources to invest in increasing human capital.

Key Terms

Achieved characteristics are those gained through education, training, experience, hard work, connections, or "native" intelligence.

Ascribed characteristics are social characteristics assigned by society to individuals and are based on physical (gender, race), cultural (race, ethnicity, religion), economic (social class), or demographic (young person, elderly) characteristics that were not chosen by those individuals. Ascription can readily lead to stereotyping or even scapegoating.

The *formal economy* includes economic activities that are regulated by laws and monitored through routine data collection.

Health status refers to physical and mental conditions that may be acute (temporary) or chronic (long term).

The *informal economy* includes economic activities that are not regulated by laws, such as noncontractual exchange of labor or goods. Such activity generally is not monitored through the use of invoices, paychecks, or formal accounting procedures.

The *labor force* includes all working-age persons within a community, local area, state, region, or nation who are able-bodied and who hold a paid job, are seeking one, or are self-employed in providing goods or services to the market. In most countries, including the United States, the decision was made early on not to count unpaid family members engaging in household or other economic activities as part of the labor force. The workforce is that part of the labor force that receives wages or salaries.

Labor market areas (LMAs) encompass both place of residence and place of work of a local population. It is a local region (often a cluster of counties), centered on a trade center or urban city, within which a pool of workers make their homes and can readily commute to work.

Opportunity structure describes the types of jobs and investment opportunities available in a community.

The *primary labor market* consists of jobs that provide good wages, safe working conditions, opportunities for advancement, reasonably stable employment, and due process in the enforcement of work rules.

The *secondary labor market* consists of jobs that do not require specific skills, are relatively low-paying, have few chances for advancement, and have high turnover.

REFERENCES

Becker, Gary S. 2002. "Human Capital." In *The Concise Encyclopedia of Economics.* Online; available: www.econlib.org/library/Enc/HumanCapital.html; accessed April 16, 2003.

Bierman, Samuel, C. Haffer, and Yi-Ting Hwang. 2001. "Health Disparities among Older Women Enrolled in Medicare Managed Care." *Health Care Financing Review* 22:187–198.

Castells, Manuel, and Alejandro Portes. 1989. "World Underneath: The Origins, Dynamics, and Effects of the Informal Economy." In *The Informal Economy: Studies in Advanced and Less Developed Countries,* ed. Alejandro Portes, Manuel Castells, and Lauren A. Benton, 11–37. Baltimore: Johns Hopkins University Press.

Eberhardt, Mark S., Deborah D. Ingram, Diane M. Makuc, Elsie R. Pamuk, Virginia M. Field, Sam B. Harper, Charlotte A. Schoenborn, and Henry Xia. 2001. *Urban and Rural Health Chartbook.* Hyattsville, Md.: National Center for Health Statistics.

Economic Research Service (ERS). 2007. "Rural Low-Wage Workers Face Multiple Economic Disadvantages." *Amber Waves* 5 (3):8.

Flora, Jan L., Martha M. Dettman, Stacy Bastian, Georgeanne Artz, and Margaret Hanson. 2004. "Iowa Self-sufficiency Wages." Office of Social and Economic Trend Analysis, Iowa State University. Online; available: www.iowapolicyproject.org/reports_press_releases/040216-wage-sum.pdf.

Fluharty, Chuck. 2002. "Toward a Community-Based National Rural Policy: The Importance of the Rural Health Care Sector." Presentation at the National Rural Health Association 25th Annual Conference in Kansas

City, Missouri, May 17. Online; available: www.rupri.org/presentations/; accessed May 13, 2003.

Gray, Jason. 2007. "The Pattern of United States Department of Agriculture Policy and Funding in Rural America's Low Wealth and Minority Communities." Southern Rural Development Initiative. Online; available: www.srdi.org.

Jensen, Leif. 2006. "At the Razor's Edge: Building Hope for America's Rural Poor," *Rural Realities.* Rural Sociological Society, 8 pp. Available at http://web1.ctaa.org/webmodules/webarticles/articlefiles/razor.pdf; accessed October 29, 2008.

Lyson, Thomas A. 2002. "What Does a School Mean to a Community? Assessing the Social and Economic Benefits of Schools to Rural Villages in New York." *Journal of Research in Rural Education* 17:131–137.

Moody, Robin. 2002. "Rural Health Care Faces Crisis." *The Business Journal* (Portland), December 30. Online; available: http://portland.bizjournals.com/portland/stories/2002/12/30/daily6.html; accessed April 16, 2003.

Parcel, Toby L., and Marie B. Sickmeier. 1988. "One Firm, Two Labor Markets: The Case of McDonald's in the Fast-Food Industry." *Sociological Quarterly* 29, no. 1:29–46.

Rural Policy Matters. 2006. "Anything but Research-based—State Initiatives to Consolidate Schools and Districts." Online; available: www.ruraledu.org/site/c.beJMIZOCIrH/b.1073911/apps/nl/content3.asp?content_id={16815E82–4187–4627–9C9E–62389AFE125B}&notoc=1; accessed September 8, 2007.

Schultz, Theodore. 1961. "Investment in Human Capital." *American Economic Review* 51:1–17.

U.S. Department of Education. 1998. *Violence and Discipline Problems in the U.S. Public Schools: 1996–97,* National Center for Education Statistics. Also online; available: http://nces.ed.gov/pubs98/98030.pdf; accessed September 8, 2003.

Whitener, Leslie A., and Tim Parker. 2007. "Policy Options for a Changing Rural America." Online; available: www.ers.usda.gov/AmberWaves/May07SpecialIssue/Features/Policy.htm; accessed September 9, 2007.

5

SOCIAL CAPITAL AND COMMUNITY

The farming community of Aurora, Nebraska, is located in the rich bottomland of the Platte River about five miles off Interstate 80. This town of 4,280 inhabitants (2005 figure, up from 3,700 in 1980) boasts a first-class library, an excellent community center, a hands-on science museum, two moderate-income housing corporations, and a farm museum. It has a lively industrial park and a farmers' cooperative that resulted from the merger of twenty-nine in central Nebraska and northern Kansas. In September 2006, groundbreaking occurred on the Aurora West Project, a joint venture between the Aurora Cooperative and private firms. The project eventually will include grain-handling facilities, an automated fueling station, an agronomy center, and a 220 million–gallon-per-year (mgy) ethanol plant, to be completed in 2009. (In a previous joint venture in the early 1990s, the cooperative was a partner in a 50-mgy ethanol plant, which still operates beside the site for the new larger plant; the Aurora Coop has sold its interest in the original plant.)

Citizens, out of habit or out of affection for the thriving locally owned telecommunications firm, still call it "the telephone company." This misnomer frustrates Phil Nelson, the CEO, because he has worked vigorously to make it much more than just a telephone company, and he corrects local residents to no avail. Hamilton Telecommunications provides sophisticated electronic communication for its customer base and has the state contract for a translation center for deaf and hearing-impaired telephone customers. The firm has trained and now employs forty-five skilled translators. The company also runs a telemarketing firm that employs nearly two hundred people.. In 1998, Hamilton Telecommunications was a key factor in attracting a software company that originally was based in Denver. The software company's president affirmed that the telecommunications company provided more options and better transmission power than was available in Denver. Aurora also recruited an Iams pet food plant in 1985. The plant uses as one of its ingredients corn from area farmers (as does the ethanol plant).

When researching Aurora in 1996, we (Jan Flora and Jeff Sharp) quickly became aware that Aurora was much more successful in building a collective life for its people and generating a sense of optimism about its future than was true of two other Midwestern communities that formed part of a comparative study of community development. What set Aurora apart?

Over the years, a number of people have played key roles in initiating ventures in Aurora, but their individual efforts paved the way for changes in community culture and organization with permanence unmatched in the other two communities. For instance, Aurora has twelve community-based foundations, the first of which was established in 1964. In the late 1960s, the culture of giving was solidified by a banker and his wife who died without progeny. They became benefactors of the foundation that funded construction and maintenance of the library. Other donors—large and small—followed suit, and it became the norm for financial advisers to suggest that people consider a bequest to one of the community's foundations, along with providing for their children and grandchildren. Currently the community's foundations have physical and cash assets greater than $44 million. These assets include a library, museum, educational center, leadership training center, senior center, community center, hospital expansion, and home-care and independent-living facilities. The original community foundation also funds university scholarships for local students.

As part of our study, we interviewed Ken Wortman (since deceased), a crusty, sometimes cantankerous, always decisive, and largely benevolent eighty-two-year-old who had established a car dealership in Aurora in 1948 with funds borrowed from his family after he was mustered out of the army following WWII. He was a founder of the Aurora Development Corporation (ADC), which brings together virtually all the movers and shakers in the community. Wortman cajoled and maneuvered to make sure that individuals representing all major local economic interests were at the table, and with others he devised a mechanism for bringing promising young men (few women have been groomed for leadership in the town) into an outer circle of leadership in the ADC. Once they were trained or schooled in how to operate in Aurora, they were invited into the inner circle.

But there are more subtle aspects to the Aurora story, including the following:

- The community demonstrated a willingness to generate money locally for a project, rather than first seeking a grant
- Similarly, Aurora showed a preference to spend money for a locally owned enterprise and reluctance to engage in "smokestack chasing" (subsidizing outside firms to locate in Aurora). A community-minded banker put it this way:

> You know when we . . . recruit industry here, we don't give them anything either. I mean, a lot of towns will give them a building, give them land, give them this. Our story is, everything's paid for here; you don't have to pay for it. All you got to do is come here and create jobs. We've paid for everything else. You don't have to pay for the schools and the libraries, and this city's infrastructure is all paid for and is in place. A lot of communities—they expect them to help pay for it all, you know, so that's been a big selling point—plus the quality of life.

- As the above quote shows, leaders in Aurora recognize the importance of both community development and economic development. The focus on making the community a good place to live—ensuring good health care, adequate housing, quality schools, and recreational and cultural opportunities, and, yes, a low tax ideology—is a better economic development tool than are tax abatements.
- In Aurora, city government is a facilitator, not an initiator. In fact, as is expressed in the 1989 strategic plan, one of the community's goals is "To continue to develop the new and enhanced facilities needed to provide a high quality of life for our citizens from private funds rather than tax dollars." The city could have proposed a bond issue to build a library, but these "conservative collectivists" prefer when possible to keep government out—even if it means using private funds for maintenance of the building, as in the case of the library.

• The city administrator summed up Aurora's key to success in the following way:

> But it's just—it's a unique town from the ones I've lived in. It's just got a great attitude. Hays [Kansas, where he worked prior to coming to Aurora] is factionalized, that if somebody got something and some other group perceived it to be at their expense. The debate and divisiveness is going on; we don't have that here. Not that we don't have disagreements. But they're left at the table; they're never personal.

—·—

Interactions among community residents transmit and transform community culture and legacy. It is people who must determine a community's development options, make decisions, and take action. Furthermore, this action often is most effective through groups. Ultimately it is the quality of community social capital that affects the extent to which people expand their scope of concern beyond self-interest and beyond their family to include the community as a whole.

Aurora clearly has a good deal of *social capital,* but how a community develops this social capital is a much more elusive consideration. Does it help to have financial and human capital? Can it be explained by the presence of one or of a small group of dedicated and visionary leaders? Does it help if the community is ethnically homogeneous (as is Aurora)? Or is the essence of social capital something much more intangible? In Aurora, community foundations to which all residents could contribute became important venues for building social capital. These efforts have created an ethic of generosity, rather than of scarcity. Having a comfortable but utilitarian community center (housing basketball courts, a weight room, and the like for organized youth and adult recreational sports) undoubtedly has contributed to greater civic-mindedness. Formal and informal luncheons are arranged regularly; it is around these meals that much of the community's business is completed. Private but collective decisions then are ratified and, where appropriate, implemented by city government.

Although the answer to all the questions asked in the preceding paragraph is "yes" (except perhaps the one regarding ethnic homogeneity), no factor by itself explains how community social capital is built. Precisely how social capital is constructed depends on the history and character of the individual community. In this chapter we will explore the elements of social capital to provide clues for building this particular form of capital so that it contributes to civic engagement and community betterment. We will also examine what Robert Putnam (2000) calls the "dark side" of social capital. For example, when does (or what configurations of) social capital have a negative effect on community well-being? Can social capital be used to exclude certain categories of community members? We will also introduce the concept of *entrepreneurial social infrastructure (ESI)* as a means of using social capital for community betterment. Finally, we will mention the interaction of social capital with other kinds of capital.

WHAT IS SOCIAL CAPITAL?

Human interaction is the foundation of all communities. People may inhabit the same place for extended periods of time and never see one another or socialize; conversely, people increasingly are interacting with others who live outside of their geographic community. Interactions in human communities are based not solely on proximity but also on history. Understanding the configuration of interactions, along with the inequalities, power differentials, and *social exclusion* that structure interactions, requires an understanding of the historical context as well as of current processes.

Social Capital Defined

Social capital is interactive. Although some scholars focus on the social capital of individuals, here we look at social capital as an attribute of communities, which is more than the summing up of individual social capital. It is a group-level phenomenon. Individuals do not by themselves build social capital. Sociologists often explain social capital in terms of norms of reciprocity and mutual trust (Coleman 1988). Norms can be reinforced through a variety of processes: forming groups, collaborating within and among groups, developing a united view of a shared future, forming or reinforcing collective identity, and engaging in collective action. All of these elements of social capital were developed in Aurora. For instance, telling Aurora's story, a pleasant task taken on by many of Aurora's leaders, both builds a united view of a shared future and reinforces collective identity. Putnam describes social capital as referring to "features of social organization, such as networks, norms, and trust, that facilitate coordination and cooperation for mutual benefit. Social capital enhances the benefits of investment in physical and human capital" (Putnam 1993b: 35–36).

Communities can build sustainable social capital by strengthening relationships and communication on a communitywide basis and encouraging community initiative, responsibility, and adaptability. Clearly it takes time for these processes to unfold and for social capital to develop. Stronger relationships and communications can result from fostering increased interactions among unlikely groups inside and outside of the community and increased availability of information and knowledge among community members. Community initiative, responsibility, and adaptability are enhanced by developing a shared vision, building on internal resources, looking for alternative ways to respond to constant changes, and discarding the victim mentality, which only causes the community to focus on past wrongs rather than future possibilities. To understand social capital, it is useful to look at the concept historically.

Is Social Capital New? From a Nation of Associations to Bowling Alone

Social capital is as old as human society. Emile Durkheim, a great nineteenth-century French sociologist/anthropologist, introduced the concept of *collective representations* or *social solidarity*. He drew his conclusions from the works of ethnologists who studied native North American and Australian aboriginal peoples, suggesting that all simple societies (that is, those with a noncomplex *social structure,* the order that shapes daily, weekly, and yearly interaction between and among people) engaged in sacred ritualistic behavior (Durkheim [1912] 2001). He concluded that such groups merged the mundane (day-to-day activities) and sacred realms: All activities were infused with religious meaning. He then applied the framework to modern people in terms of the development of a *civil religion,* that is, patriotic beliefs and related sacred rituals that unite a people. Examples of violation of sacred symbols include flying a Mexican flag in a U.S. parade or publicly imputing crass business or political motives to a leader during time of war. Neither act of protest is against the law, but those engaging in either act have, at different times in our history, been subjected to informal or extrajudicial punishment. Such in-group solidarity generally results in the drawing of sharp boundaries between insiders and outsiders and may even result in persecution of those who do not share (or who are perceived as not sharing) the values of the in-group.

These distinctions between those who do and do not share the in-group's values are strongest when the non-in-group values are perceived as outside threats. Examples of such persecution include the internment of Japanese Americans during World War II and the adamant refusal of the U.S. government to release the names of more than 1,200 suspects arrested after the September 11, 2001, terrorist acts in New York and Washington, D.C., or to indicate where they were incarcerated. Years after imprisonment, only a handful had been charged with terrorism, although it is believed that many have been deported, some to countries where human rights groups have evidence of their being tortured.

Pierre Bourdieu defined social capital as actual or potential resources that derive from "a durable network of more or less institutionalized relationships of mutual acquaintance and recognition—or in other words, to membership in a group—which provides each of its members with the backing of the collectivity-owned capital" (1986: 248–249). He said that to the individual member, social capital is a form of credit that allows him or her to claim certain elements of those resources when they are needed. Much as Durkheim did, Bourdieu argued that these networks—and one's place in them—must be constantly rebuilt through the giving of gifts (real or symbolic) that instill emotions of gratitude, friendship, and respect: "a continuous series of exchanges in which recognition is endlessly affirmed and reaffirmed" (1986: 250). From the individual's point of view, these exchanges are investment strategies, a claim on short- and long-term profit, symbolic or real. We might call these norms of reciprocity that foster commitment to the group and at the same time strengthen the group itself.

Bourdieu said there is a negative side of social capital, which is the obligation of each group member to be "a custodian" of group limits or boundaries. In other words, someone needs to keep out the "riffraff," that is, those who might change the essential nature of the group. This has important implications for geographic communities, since residents are—or should be—citizens of the community. But if they are excluded from community networks that provide credit or access to collective resources, how can they be full community citizens? Groups are excluded from key community networks for a variety of reasons: because of certain unconscious beliefs held by men regarding hierarchy of the sexes (men often perpetuate the myth "It's the women who really run this place—through their husbands" to maintain their own power), because a group is seen as being permanently "in training" for full community citizenship (young people: "We tried that before you were born; it didn't work"), because

Box 5.1   The Strange Disappearance of Civic America

For the last year or so, I have been wrestling with a difficult mystery. . . . The mystery concerns the strange disappearance of social capital and civic engagement in America. . . . I use the term "civic engagement" to refer to people's connections with the life of their communities, not only with politics. . . .

Evidence for the decline of social capital and civic engagement comes from a number of independent sources. Surveys of average Americans in 1965, 1975, and 1985, in which they recorded every single activity during a day—so-called time-budget studies—indicate that since 1965 time spent on informal socializing and visiting is down (perhaps by one-quarter) and time devoted to clubs and organizations is down even more sharply (by roughly half). Membership records of such diverse organizations as the PTA, the Elks club, the League of Women Voters, the Red Cross, labor unions, and even bowling leagues show that participation in many conventional voluntary associations has declined by roughly 25 percent to 50 percent over the last two to three decades. Surveys show sharp declines in many measures of collective political participation, including attending a rally or speech (off 36 percent between 1973 and 1993), attending a meeting on town or school affairs (off 39 percent), or working for a political party (off 56 percent).

Some of the most reliable evidence about trends comes from the General Social Survey (GSS), conducted nearly every year for more than two decades. The GSS demonstrates, at all levels of education and among both men and women, . . . a drop of roughly one-third in social trust since 1972. (Trust in political authorities, indeed in many social institutions, has also declined sharply since 1965, but that is conceptually a distinct trend.) Slumping membership has afflicted all sorts of groups, from sports clubs and professional associations to literary discussion groups and labor unions. Only nationality groups, hobby and garden clubs, and the catch-all category of "other" seem to have resisted the ebbing tide. Gallup polls report that church attendance fell by roughly 15 percent during the 1960s and has remained at that lower level ever since, while data from the National Opinion Research Center suggest that the decline continued during the 1970s and 1980s and by now amounts to roughly 30 percent. A more complete audit of American social capital would need to account for apparent countertrends.

continues

Some observers believe, for example, that support groups and neighborhood watch groups are proliferating, and few deny that the last several decades have witnessed explosive growth in interest groups represented in Washington. . . . With due regard to various kinds of counterevidence, I believe that the weight of available evidence confirms that Americans today are significantly less engaged with their communities than was true a generation ago. Of course, American civil society is not moribund. Many good people across the land work hard every day to keep their communities vital. Indeed, evidence suggests that America still outranks many other countries in the degree of our community involvement and social trust. But if we examine our lives, not our aspirations, and if we compare ourselves not with other countries but with our parents, the best available evidence suggests that we are less connected with one another.

Reversing this trend depends, at least in part, on understanding the causes of the strange malady afflicting American civic life. This is the mystery I seek to unravel here: Why, beginning in the 1960s and accelerating in the 1970s and 1980s, did the fabric of American community life begin to fray? Why are more Americans bowling alone?

SOURCES

Putnam, Robert. 1996. "The Strange Disappearance of Civic America." *The American Prospect* 7, no. 24 (December 1). An abbreviated version is online; available: www.prospect.org/print/V7/24/putnam-r.html; accessed April 2003.

_____. 2000. *Bowling Alone. The Collapse and Revival of American Community.* New York: Simon & Schuster.

they are undeserving (poor people: "They are too lazy to come to meetings; why else would they be poor?"), or because they are outsiders (newcomers and immigrants: "They don't know how we do things here").

A much earlier observer who viewed social capital (although he did not use the term) more positively was Alexis de Toqueville, an aristocratic Frenchman who traveled at length in the United States and who in 1835 and 1840 published the two volumes of *Democracy in America* ([1835 and 1840] 1956). He feared the "tyranny of the majority" and was generally suspicious of the motives and lack of formal education of the lower and working classes. However, upon observing the workings of communities of all sizes in the United States, he concluded that a fundamental bulwark against that tyranny was the degree to which Americans organized themselves into what we today would call *civil society.* The development of civic associations to accomplish different collective purposes involves building social capital: promoting interaction that strengthens members' commitment to particular values and goals and, in seeking to carry out those goals, forging a common identity. By and large, Toqueville's observations about the United States are still valid, although Putnam has documented that civic engagement has declined significantly in the past quarter century (at least in terms of historic indicators of civic engagement). Putnam uses the metaphor of bowling alone to represent the decline in civic engagement: Following World War II, bowling leagues regularly brought neighbors and colleagues together on weeknights in a relaxed atmosphere where they often discussed family and community topics. Now, although the number of lines bowled in the United States has remained more or less constant, most people are bowling alone rather than in leagues. Putnam does note, however, that although civic involvement of all kinds has declined, voluntary organization membership in the United States remains higher than in many other developed countries. (See Box 5.1 for a synopsis of Putnam's findings and interpretations.) He attributes the high levels of civic activity in the first two-thirds of the twentieth century first to the effects of the Progressive era and second to the mobilization of all U.S. citizens during World War II.

Toqueville rightly pointed out that in the first half of the nineteenth century, European societies were too stratified to be able to develop strong associations throughout the society: The wealthy did not often need them, for they had the resources to act alone. When they did need to work through an association, they were quite capable of forming one, accomplishing the objective, and then disbanding it. The working and lower classes, because they possessed so few cultural, financial, or human resources, effectively were barred from building associations; thus, great inequalities made it difficult for the lower classes to get organized. It is not surprising that in 1848, eight years after Toqueville published the second volume of *Democracy in America,* revolutions broke out in many parts of Europe as the subordinate classes perceived no alternative for redressing grievances.

What Toqueville did not capture—and it was more than half a century later that Durkheim provided the conceptual and empirical tools to do so—was the fact that strong associations did not necessarily add up to a collective will. Certainly what we now call a strong civil society made it more difficult for one leader or one group to capture political power and turn it to parochial and antidemocratic ends. The Civil War, which Toqueville foresaw because of the inequalities generated by slavery, was a case in point. Although the marketplace of ideas where American associations hawked their wares of values and desired futures was bustling, a large and important group—African Americans—was prohibited from entering that marketplace. Once slaves were emancipated and the secession of the Southern states from the Union was ended, the process of removing this greatest bottleneck to the achievement of democracy—the subjugation of black people—had begun, although it would take a century more for African Americans to fully gain their political and legal liberation.

But still the cacophony of voices that resulted from having many associations in U.S. communities did not ensure an improvement in well-being, happiness, or domestic or community tranquility. More than half a century after Durkheim completed his *Elementary Forms of Religious Life* (1912), Harold Kaufman and his student Ken Wilkinson, rural sociologists from Mississippi, examined this all-too-frequent contradiction between a flurry of activities by community-based organizations and a lack of improvement at the level of the community itself. Using an interactional approach, they proposed that it was important to distinguish the *social field* from the community field. According to Wilkinson, a social field is "a process of interaction through time, with direction toward some more or less distinctive outcome" (1972: 317). There are numerous social fields in a community, each of which consists of individuals and organizations working toward a particular goal. A good example in Aurora was the group of organizations and individuals that worked to establish a cooperative/joint venture for making grain ethanol as an additive to gasoline. The ethanol plant benefited the community secondarily, but its main beneficiaries were the farmer members from various communities in the central part of Nebraska, who had a guaranteed market for their irrigated corn at a modest premium, and the regional energy company, which provided additional capital in return for equity in the plant through a joint venture with the farmers' ethanol cooperative.

If a set of interrelated actions associated with a social field is focused on the whole community, we may talk of a *community field*. A set of actions within a community field serves a general community interest rather than specific private interests. A community field, then, is the pattern of interaction that focuses on the entire community. It can be a single organization

Figure 5.1 Interlocking Directorates, Civil Society Organizations, Aurora and Tryton (pseudonym), 1996.

Aurora Core Organizations and Direct Linkages

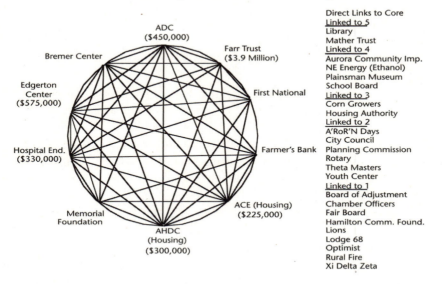

Direct Links to Core
<u>Linked to 5</u>
Library
Mather Trust
<u>Linked to 4</u>
Aurora Community Imp.
NE Energy (Ethanol)
Plainsman Museum
School Board
<u>Linked to 3</u>
Corn Growers
Housing Authority
<u>Linked to 2</u>
A'RoR'N Days
City Council
Planning Commission
Rotary
Theta Masters
Youth Center
<u>Linked to 1</u>
Board of Adjustment
Chamber Officers
Fair Board
Hamilton Comm. Found.
Lions
Lodge 68
Optimist
Rural Fire
Xi Delta Zeta

Tryton Core Organizations and Direct Linkages

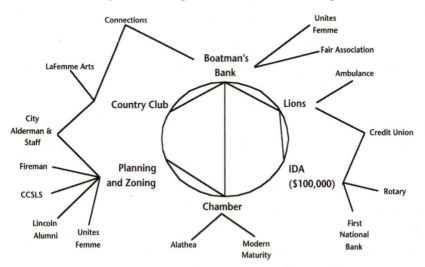

Adapted from Sharp 2001, 413.

that looks out for the interests of the community—the Aurora Development Corporation might qualify—or, more likely, it may be a web of associations, firms, and even governmental entities that collaborate for a common purpose. Figure 5.1 shows the interaction patterns of the core organizations in Aurora and in Tryton. Aurora's organizations and leadership are much more tightly linked with one another, particularly through ADC, than those of Tryton, which lacks a unifying organizational focus.

BONDING AND BRIDGING SOCIAL CAPITAL: HOMOGENEITY OR INCLUSION?

Social capital can be divided into two parts: *Bonding social capital* consists of connections among individuals and groups with similar backgrounds. These connections may be based principally on class, ethnicity, kinship, gender, or similar social characteristics. Members of a group with high bonding capital know one another in multiple settings or roles. *Bridging social capital* connects diverse groups within the community to each other and to groups outside the community. The ties that make up bridging social capital usually are single-purpose or instrumental, whereas bonding ties are affective or emotionally charged. Bridging social capital fosters diversity of ideas and brings together diverse people. This dichotomy is similar to the classical formulations by Ferdinand Töennies (*gemeinschaft* versus *gesellschaft*) and Durkheim (organic versus mechanical solidarity) and to Mark Granovetter's more recent strong versus weak ties (1973).

Deepa Narayan incorporates the notion of power into the bonding-bridging relationship. Regarding bonding social capital, she said,

> While primary groups and networks undoubtedly provide opportunities to those who belong, they also reinforce pre-existing social stratification, prevent mobility of excluded groups, minorities or poor people, and become the bases of corruption and co-optation of power by the dominant social groups. Cross-cutting ties which are dense and voluntary, though not necessarily strong . . . help connect people with access to different information, resources and opportunities. (Narayan 1999: 13)

Thus, Narayan suggested that the development of *weak* or *crosscutting ties* is important for breaking down inequalities of power and access. For instance, a contributing factor to racial inequality is the lack of information available to African American youth in central cities and in the rural

South about where they can find "good" jobs. A lack of parental connections to smooth the way for these youth to gain access to those jobs also contributes to inequality. These notions of exclusion are complementary to those presented by Bourdieu (1986), who proposed that elite French families and upwardly mobile middle-class families use family economic and cultural capital to gain strategic class-based ties (social capital) for their children, thereby excluding the children of parents who lack resources and the necessary strategic impulses for moving their children up the social ladder.

How do bridging and bonding social capital interact at the (geographic) community level in order to determine the extent of collective action that takes place in those communities? A simple fourfold table is used in an effort to predict levels of collective action (see Figure 5.2).

Bridging and bonding social capital can reinforce each other: When both are high, we get effective community action, or entrepreneurial social infrastructure (ESI), discussed later in this chapter. When both are low, extreme individualism dominates, which is reflected at the community level in social disorganization. Community action is low when residents mainly relate apathetically to their community. When bridging social capital is high but bonding social capital is low, there is *clientelism,* and the relationships formed within and outside the community are predominantly vertical. When bonding social capital is high but bridging social capital is low, conflict often occurs. The community may be organized against an outside entity or against itself. In the latter case, bonding social capital occurs

Figure 5.2 Social Capital Typology

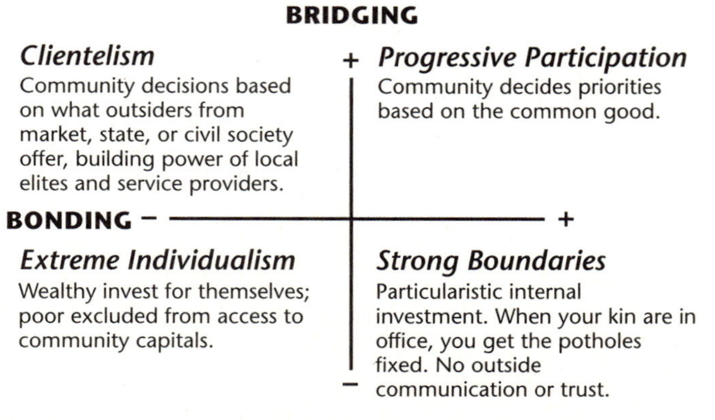

BRIDGING

Clientelism	**+** *Progressive Participation*
Community decisions based on what outsiders from market, state, or civil society offer, building power of local elites and service providers.	Community decides priorities based on the common good.

BONDING − ——————————————— **+**

Extreme Individualism	*Strong Boundaries*
Wealthy invest for themselves; poor excluded from access to community capitals.	Particularistic internal investment. When your kin are in office, you get the potholes fixed. No outside communication or trust.

−

within homogeneous groups within the community, and these groups oppose one another.

Four characteristics of networks build bridging social capital. First, networks include a *horizontal* dimension. Lateral learning is critical in networks; communities learn best from each other. Such social capital is built in the course of lateral learning, both between communities and within communities. Second, networks include a *vertical* dimension. It is critical that communities be linked to regional, state, and national resources and organizations; however, it is also critical that there not be just one gatekeeper who makes that linkage. Elected officials and members of organizations need to attend regional, state, and national meetings so that one person cannot say to other members of the community, "Well, the rules won't let us." Other points of view that are still within the rules can uncover alternatives. Third, networks are *flexible;* being part of a network should not be a lifetime commitment. Participation increases and burnout decreases when people are asked to participate in a network that has a finite life span or a regular rotation of leadership. People are willing to participate where they can make a difference and when they are asked to participate primarily in activities in which they have a genuine interest, although care must be taken that the larger vision is shared. Flexibility means that more people have the opportunity to become leaders. Fourth, networks have *permeable boundaries;* the community of interest is expanded and the community of place grows larger as new partnerships and collaborations form.

Exploring how the two dimensions of social capital relate to community change is a vital component in this discussion.

Absence of Social Capital (Bridging Low; Bonding Low)

Communities lacking bonding or bridging social capital also lack the capacity for change. Individuals in these types of communities view themselves as self-reliant—or as totally adrift. In the absence of social capital, some people can succeed by substituting financial capital for social capital. For communities without financial capital, the absence of social capital can be fatal, as health studies are increasingly showing and as was illustrated by the fate of the poor in New Orleans after Hurricane Katrina in 2005. People in communities that lack social capital are more likely to experience stress, hypertension, and mental health problems, among other difficulties. Crime rates are high where there is an absence of social capital; personal security is a major problem. The wealthy can protect themselves with expensive security systems. They install alarms and even hire their own police, but no protection is available in poor communities.

Conflict with the Outside/Internal Factionalism
(Bonding High; Bridging Low)

When bonding is high and bridging is low, communities resist change. This may occur in two ways. The community may organize in opposition to the outside in a kind of reactive solidarity; newcomers are viewed with suspicion in such communities. This reduces access to information and other resources from the outside. Alternatively, different homogeneous groups or factions within the community may have varying perspectives on the kinds of change that might benefit their community. The groups do not trust each other and therefore are unwilling to cooperate with one another. Conflict is internal and becomes the dominant community-level attribute. Although collective action may occur within groups in the geographic community, it is difficult to organize and carry out action at the community level if internal conflict persists. Social fields overcome the community field.

External Influence via Local Elites
(Bridging High; Bonding Low)

Where bridging social capital is high but bonding capital is low, some degree of control from outside the community is exercised through community elites, helping professionals or, in the most extreme form, local "bosses." This arrangement does not preclude collective action on the part of community residents, but that action is more apt to benefit outsiders or their local surrogates. Although this pattern of social capital is also built on norms of reciprocity and mutual trust (or at least mutual obligation), those relationships are vertical rather than horizontal. Power is clearly concentrated. Traditional patron-client relationships, typical of urban gangs or boss-run political machines, are created. Those at the bottom of the hierarchy—who are obviously beholden to the few at the top—are the majority of the population in such communities. As a result, recipients of favors owe substantial loyalty to their patron when it is time to vote for public office, to collect from a loser in the numbers racket, or to settle a score with a rival gang. As a result, horizontal networks are actively discouraged, particularly outside the sphere of influence of the patron, godfather, or elite clique. Such systems create dependency.

This type of social capital is prevalent in some persistently impoverished communities. For instance, the Appalachian coal-mining community of Blackwell (a pseudonym) studied by Cynthia Duncan (1999) involved control of most of the resources, businesses, and services by absentee-owned coal companies. When employment in the coal mines declined, jobs were in short supply. An elite group of families controlled many public-sector and private-sector jobs through their control of local government and the school system and through exclusive ties to state government. Gaining employment depended on whether one came from a "good" or a "bad" family. A more modern version of this hierarchical social capital is the power elite community model, in which social and economic inequalities are generally substantial. There is clearly a ruling clique that maintains its social distance from the rest of the community, but it preserves political influence either directly or through pliable middle- or working-class officeholders.

Entrepreneurial Social Infrastructure
(Bridging High; Bonding High)

Horizontal social capital implies egalitarian forms of reciprocity without necessarily implying equal wealth, education, or talents. Community resources or capital are broadly defined. Not only is each member of the community expected to give, earning status and pleasure from doing so, but each is expected to receive as well. Each person in the community is deemed capable of sharing something valuable with all members of the community, including contributions to collective projects, from parades to the volunteer fire department to Girl Scouts. Norms of reciprocity are reinforced, but payback to the donor is not required or even expected. Such communities also have diverse contacts with the outside, which provide needed information to the community, information that often can be used to generate outside resources without exercising control over the community. Aurora is a good example of a community with both high bridging and high bonding social capital.

With respect to bonding social capital, organizations within Aurora's community are closely linked to one another, with strong ties among civil society, market-oriented firms, and local government, although the latter is in a decidedly subordinate position. In Aurora, there is an organization that many leaders view as representing the community field, the ADC, and a common place for informal gathering, the community center. There is a tradition of making a conscious effort to recruit young males and new-comers into community leadership, particularly through the private development corporation. The community has a sense of identity and an ethos of progress or common purpose. Over the past few decades, the community has had impressive economic growth, resulting in substantial population expansion. Aurora is also an attractive place to live, with amenities such as attractive and affordable housing, an excellent library, and a science museum.

Regarding bridging social capital, Aurora's community has many contacts with the outside, and those contacts are not monopolized by a particular individual or clique. Because there are various centers of economic power, it is easy for a number of people to develop multiple ties with the outside. These ties tend to be ties between social, if not economic, equals. This has facilitated the development of joint ventures with outside firms and recruitment of firms that often stay for a long while, as in the case of the pet food plant. Another example of bridging social capital is the fact that the community has a very informative Web site, which aided greatly in updating the vignette above.

Clearly, Aurora has high bonding *and* bridging social capital. In one sense, Aurora had a limitation to expanding its community social capital that had not been overcome—or even substantially scrutinized at the time of our interviews: The community has not made a concerted effort to include people with different social characteristics in either the inner or outer circle of leadership. This most urgently can be seen in the subordinate leadership role played by women, although a few women had been incorporated into the outer circle of leadership when we conducted our study more than a decade ago. Professionals and businesspeople (including some farmers) dominate community leadership. With the expansion of industry, will the working class be welcomed and mentored in the same way that proprietors, entrepreneurs, and professionals currently are? The community is predominantly European American. One wonders, if a labor shortage developed and immigrant workers were recruited, would they be nurtured as professionals and entrepreneurs have been? Is there sufficient flexibility in cultural capital and in the leadership model being employed to resolve these issues of inclusion when they present themselves? In addition, the development model being pursued on the agricultural side consumes a great deal of natural capital, particularly fossil fuels and water. Will the social capital that has been built over the years allow for sufficient flexibility to adapt to the inexorable rise in the price of fossil fuels and to the major recombining of the different capitals that that will occur? The good news is that Aurora has more of both kinds of social capital with which to confront these changes than do most rural communities.

ENTREPRENEURIAL SOCIAL INFRASTRUCTURE

Communities that are high on both bridging and bonding social capital are poised for action, able to engage the community field. We use the term entrepreneurial social infrastructure (ESI) to indicate the structures and impacts that occur when both bridging and bonding social capital are high. The term social infrastructure was chosen because the name suggests that it operates in a parallel way to physical infrastructure (which we include under the term built capital) in community development. ESI is a measurable form of community action, conceptually distinct from social capital. We hypothesize that it is a consequence of high bridging and bonding social capital.

Two main characteristics distinguish ESI from social capital: First, ESI can readily be changed through an explicit collective effort; it links social capital to *agency*. A community with a well-developed social infrastructure tends to engage in collective action for community betterment, which is why we call this phenomenon *entrepreneurial social infrastructure*—ESI is a less abstract concept than the concept of social capital. For example, it is difficult to directly change levels of community trust, but it may be possible to encourage previously combative groups to cooperate through conflict management or by redefining issues.

Second, whereas *diversity*, the presence of different perspectives regarding means and ends, and social inclusion, ensuring that those groups usually without voice are empowered, are central to bridging social capital, ESI focuses on the outcomes of the inclusion of diversity—the willingness to consider and accept alternatives. In a community-planning process, diverse types of information are sought from individuals and groups with different values, backgrounds, and perspectives from both inside and outside the community. The flow of information is not channeled exclusively to or from a particular group but is dispersed widely throughout the community.

Furthermore, the inclusion of all citizens in the decision-making process itself ensures greater commitment to carrying out those decisions. Decisions, once made, are more generally accepted.

We have identified certain basic features within a community with high ESI, including legitimation of alternatives, inclusiveness and diversity of networks, and widespread resource mobilization.

Legitimation of Alternatives

Some communities seek a silver bullet to solve problems, whereas in others, various perspectives are discussed and combined. These latter communities recognize that there are alternative ways of reaching shared goals. As with continuous improvement in industry, definitive solutions are not sought. Instead, countermeasures are implemented as progress is monitored, and alternative ways of achieving goals are examined.

This leads to the acceptance of controversy, which contrasts with conflict. Acceptance of controversy means that people can disagree and still maintain mutual respect. In contrast, in a conflict situation, lines are drawn and labels are assigned according to one's stance on a particular issue. This is precisely the distinction that was voiced by the Aurora city manager in the quote at the end of the vignette that starts this chapter: Disagreements are fine as long as they do not become personal. Conflict-prone communities may tacitly agree to not deal with issues around which disagreement exists, thereby suppressing controversy. New issues are not brought forward, visions of the future are not shared, and alternative ways of achieving goals are not developed. In this situation, conflict often lies right beneath the surface.

In communities that accept controversy, politics are depersonalized. Ordinary citizens are willing to run for public office and feel able to implement measures to resolve community issues without having their character attacked by their constituents. There is awareness that the public sector is vital for supporting change at the local level; consequently, participation increases in both civic and governmental organizations. Furthermore, ESI is strengthened when market actors are involved. In the city of Marshalltown, Iowa, a community with a meatpacking plant and a growing immigrant population as the primary workforce in the plant, the addition of business leaders (market actors) and local government actors to a diversity group allowed it to succeed where it previously had failed in ameliorating the situation of immigrants.

In such communities, great attention is given to process. That meetings are conducted in a civil fashion and that all have the opportunity to present their viewpoints are given great importance. When controversy begins to spill over into conflict, specific conflict-management mechanisms are put in place, often with the assistance of an outsider trained in conflict management. On the positive side, individual and collective successes are celebrated. In communities where it is not legitimate to look at alternatives, the notion of a "limited good" is strong. One person's success is considered to have occurred at the expense of another. (The Aurora city administrator states that in the community in which he previously worked in local government, one person's gain was perceived as another person's loss; see vignette above.) These are communities where controversy does not occur because people are unwilling to risk expressing contrasting viewpoints.

The local newspaper can play an important role in conveying or failing to convey the information needed to make informed decisions. It can also set the tone of community dialogue on an issue. If it seeks to provide information and to suggest that controversy is legitimate, it will help prevent the conversion of disagreements into rancorous conflict with the potential to split the community. In a nationwide study of nonmetropolitan communities we conducted, one of the strongest predictors of whether a community had carried out a successful economic development project was the presence of a newspaper that not only reported community issues but also reported them fairly.

Unfortunately, in some small communities, the newspaper, often a weekly, tends to be long on ads and social announcements but short on news. The biggest zucchini of the season and the scores of the high school basketball games are highlighted, but there is seldom a reporter at school board or town council meetings. Often, no hint of any bad news is allowed to appear in print. In only a minority of communities is the editor willing to take on controversial issues or address emerging community problems and thereby risk offending people. At the same time, the editor must be perceived as fair by building a case on facts, rather than twisting those facts. Communities where controversy is openly aired and accessible factual information drives out rumors are best able to process information from a variety of sources and make choices that have the potential to enhance community well-being.

Focusing on process allows for the assessment of progress toward goals. When progress does not meet expectations, a discussion of countermeasures for advancement occurs. There is less concern about "Whose crummy idea was that?" or "Why didn't you listen to me? I had a better idea" and more consideration of "What did we learn from this last effort?" and "What will we try now?"

Inclusive and Diverse Networks

Several qualities of *social networks*—webs of relationships within a community—allow communities to gain control of their social and economic development effectively and to become entrepreneurial communities. They include depersonalization of politics, development of extracommunity linkages, diverse community leadership, and approaches to involving excluded groups. Each of these is discussed in turn.

Discussion of politics in many rural communities involves personalities, not issues. The quality of social networks is much higher in communities that accept and confront reasoned disagreement and do not turn a public stand on a controversy into a symbol of either moral rectitude or degeneracy. Those who disagree on one issue may be allies on another in a coalition that facilitates collective resolution of a problem. Furthermore, disagreements can surface early rather than being suppressed until they explode and divide the community. Political depersonalization requires the acceptance of controversy and debate as normal features of community life.

Through the development of linkages with the outside, a community gains access to information it needs to make choices about its future. Entrepreneurial communities foster extracommunity links and actively seek resources from other communities and from state and federal sources. They participate in regional planning groups, confer with the cooperative extension service, and apply for federal grants. They also engage in lateral learning from other communities. For instance, citizens of Decatur County, Kansas (its county seat, Oberlin, is another community with considerable entrepreneurial social infrastructure), decided to develop their own community carnival rather than relying on "sleazy" and "unreliable" itinerant carnivals to come to their 4-H fair. They inquired about communities that had built their own carnivals and dispatched a delegation to Hydro, Oklahoma, to learn from that town's successful effort. The delegation reported back to the community, adapted Hydro's experience to their situation, and built their own carnival, run entirely by volunteers. Civic groups from across the county are responsible for a particular ride or game each year. That gives every organization a concrete project and strengthens social capital among groups as they work together to plan the event each year. The proceeds from the carnival support new enterprises throughout the county.

By emphasizing flexible, dispersed community leadership, communities avoid becoming dependent on a single broker who has contacts or charisma. In entrepreneurial communities, members rotate through public offices and share informal leadership roles. Often newcomers to the community are active in leadership positions and bring with them a convert's appreciation of the community and an awareness of outside forces acting upon it. The Aurora Development Corporation does not leave to chance the integration of newcomers into the leadership structure. However, the incorporation of members of new ethnic groups, youth, and even women into leadership positions seems to present a challenge to many rural communities, including Aurora, that are perfectly willing to include white male newcomers.

Being inclusive does not simply mean having people at the table. Some youth programs intended to teach leadership skills, which the youth then can share with their community, have discovered this: A common response to the presence of these youths is, "Wonderful, here is someone to sell the donuts and do the cleanup." The youths may be willing to do these tasks, but they are also eagerly prepared to help plan the development activities. But when they try to participate in the planning, the response of the established leaders is, "Well, we don't do it that way here" or "We tried that twenty years ago and it didn't work." The mere presence of the youth does not equal inclusiveness.

The best approach to diversity is not to ask, "Are we being politically correct?" A more appropriate question is "Whose viewpoint is necessary as we move forward toward our goals?" For example, if a community development project's goal is to create more jobs, local people who take those jobs need to be part of the process so that there can be a better link between human capital and the built capital that offers employment opportunities.

Promoting diversity involves directly asking nonparticipants why they are not involved: Is it the time of day? Is the place too expensive for lunch? Is it the location? Meeting at lunch on workdays is impossible for people who work in factories or in hourly wage jobs. In addition, people who are poor or have mobility problems may find some meeting places difficult to access because of the lack of transportation.

Blanket invitations do not promote inclusiveness. Personal invitations are preferred over advertisements in newspapers. People who do not receive personal invitations and who are not part of the planning team generally attend meetings only if they are really incensed and want to protest. Personal invitations should explain how that person's or institution's special capabilities are critical to the effort.

When excluded groups are not organized, it is difficult to get effective participation from members of that group—or it is only the more educated or wealthy members of the group who participate. We have concluded in our work with rural immigrants that forming immigrant interest groups is an important prerequisite to their effective participation in communitywide organizations that represent the community field. Inclusiveness and diversity must go together, but inclusiveness sometimes means encouraging unorganized or excluded groups to form their own organizations to become more effective community participants.

Resource Mobilization

Resource mobilization is the last critical piece of structured community action, or ESI. First, resources in the community must be fully accessible. This applies to private resources, such as access to credit, as well as to public resources, such as high-quality schooling, recreational opportunities, and other opportunities. This does not mean there cannot be criteria for access, but the criteria should be publicized, and there should be opportunities for people to increase their chance for access.

When mobilizing private resources, financial institutions need to decide how to disperse appropriate loan amounts, with the appropriate terms, to all levels of entrepreneurs and citizens. In communities that successfully mobilize their resources, private citizens of all levels contribute financial aid when there is a need, and opportunities are available for individuals to contribute their time and goods to worthwhile causes. The ability to mobilize private resources is an important element of community action and gives everyone a chance to contribute. Aurora was excellent in mobilizing local resources. The leadership followed a simple rule: They are not afraid to use local resources if a potential economic enterprise or amenity looks like a good risk; local funds beget outside investments and industries in part because local investments send the message that the community is willing to partner with others.

Social capital–building for development, or ESI, includes communities of interest and place. We also find that ESI is enhanced by forming advocacy and action coalitions among institutional actors of the different sectors (market, state, and civil society) and at different levels (such as international,

national, regional, state, and local). Civil society is key to adding sustainability to the policy mix, and governments (the state) are uniquely able to provide rewards for market actors who conserve and protect natural and human resources and punishments for those who do not. Although market firms initially resist regulation of their treatment of employees or pollution, in the longer term many firms discover that pollution and not valuing workers are forms of waste; profits can be enhanced through environmental-cost accounting and by building employee commitment.

Conclusions

As suggested by Putnam's research in Italy (1993a), research done by the World Bank (2001), and other studies, development is enhanced when social capital exists. But when bonding social capital is not tempered by bridging social capital, it creates barriers to change. When bridging and bonding social capital reinforce each other, development can occur; local resources are innovatively combined with and augmented by outside resources. Situations must be established so that all community members have a chance to contribute to the collective endeavor—and have their contributions appreciated.

Although a balance of bridging and bonding social capital is needed at all levels of society, building bridging social capital of and to excluded groups is key. Unless a certain amount of social capital exists within excluded groups, it is difficult for a community to build its social infrastructure. And unless there is a certain degree of community bridging social capital—an inclusive orientation by the dominant community groups—increased social capital on the part of excluded groups may lead to reactive solidarity on the part of the dominant group within the community, further distancing a now well-organized excluded group. Attention to the components of entrepreneurial social infrastructure—legitimation of alternatives; building inclusive and diverse networks of those likely to be affected by the particular project, policy, or objective; and fostering widespread resource mobilization—can lead to community betterment.

Chapter Summary

Building social capital, which includes norms of reciprocity and mutual trust, is vitally important if small communities are to thrive. Communities can foster lasting social capital by improving communication within and outside the community. This phenomenon is not new; it is as old as human society and involves bonding and bridging social capital. Bonding social capital includes making multiple connections with individuals and groups from similar backgrounds. Bridging social capital ties different groups together within and outside a community. When both bridging social capital and bonding social capital are high, entrepreneurial social infrastructure (ESI) is enhanced. If bridging social capital and bonding social capital are low, individual solutions to collective problems are sought. There are several combinations of bridging and bonding social capital that can have positive and negative effects on community development.

Accepting controversy in communities can have positive results if people can disagree while maintaining mutual respect. If a community's local news media reflect only positive occurrences, then progress cannot be made because existing conditions are not being evaluated sufficiently. Social networks within and outside a community add economic vitality. These networks need to be inclusive and diverse. Diverse groups not only must be invited to sit at the table but also may have to be encouraged to organize among themselves before participating in communitywide coalitions.

Resources within a community must be accessible and mobilized effectively. Favoring only one form of capital can have negative results; each form of capital has the potential to enhance the productivity of others. Sustaining success in a community requires building synergy among forms of capital. All forms of capital can be utilized effectively if their relationships to one another are regularly considered.

KEY TERMS

Agency is the capacity to change social structure through the will of an individual or group to do so.

Bonding social capital involves multiple ties among people or organizations located similarly in the socioeconomic system.

Bridging social capital involves singular ties between individuals or organizations. Those ties are generally instrumental—that is, single purpose—and therefore do not involve an exchange of emotion or affect. Bridging social capital may be horizontal (between equals) or vertical/ hierarchical.

Civic engagement refers to people's involvement in their communities and in the civic life of their nation. It includes involvement in political life, but it generally relates to participation in civil society.

Civil religion is a set of cultural ideas, symbols, and practices oriented to the direct worship of society (or the nation-state) by its members. Generally, if certain members do not show sufficient deference or patriotism, they will be sanctioned negatively, either by state authorities or by other members of the society.

Civil society is the organized sector of a society that imparts or seeks to impart values to the society as a whole. Civil society consists of associations that are separate from government (state) and from market- or profit-oriented firms.

Clientelism is a system by which persons subordinate in the social structure are beholden to and do things for a patron. The patron, in exchange for loyalty from the client(s), provides certain largesse, but the patron is always in the more powerful position.

Collective representations or *social solidarity* are the common tightly held or sacred symbols deriving from shared practices (rituals) and strong networks. They are similar to bonding social capital and contribute to a strong sense of collective identity or bonding.

A *community field* is a social field that focuses on the whole community; that is, it consists of structured interactions among individuals, families, organizations, firms, and/or government agencies for the purpose of changing the community.

Diversity, as the term is used here, refers to the presence of different perspectives regarding means and ends and the recognition that individuals with different backgrounds and experiences will view an issue differently and therefore may contribute fresh ideas to the solution of a particular problem.

Entrepreneurial social infrastructure (ESI) is both the social capacity and the collective will of local communities to provide for their social, economic, and environmental well-being.

Flexible networks are those that expand, contract, or shift their composition in response to differing circumstances. Under such circumstances, people can readily move into and out of leadership in community organizations.

Horizontal networks are those that link people or organizations that are at the same or similar level in a system of authority.

Permeable boundaries are characteristic of communities or organizations that are not rigid in distinguishing members from outsiders and allow their boundaries to expand or contract according to the issue at hand. Such communities tend to be inclusive rather than exclusive.

Social capital includes norms of reciprocity and mutual trust. Norms can be reinforced through a variety of processes: forming groups, collaborating within and among groups, developing a united view of a shared future, building collective identity, and engaging in collective action.

Social exclusion is the shunning or leaving out of decision-making discussions and resource allocation of certain members of a community or group.

A *social field* is a process of interaction of individuals and organizations with specific interests through time, with direction toward some more or less distinctive outcome.

Social networks are webs of relationships that link individuals or organizations within a community or with the outside.

Social structure is the institutional framework that shapes order in daily, weekly, and yearly interaction between and among people.

Vertical networks involve ties between individuals, organizations, or communities that are in a hierarchical relationship with one another.

Weak ties are links with persons with values and experiences different from one's own. They are usually single-purpose links. Related terms include *crosscutting ties* and *bridging social capital.*

References

Aurora Cooperative News. "Aurora West Project Breaks Ground." September 7, 2006. Online; available: www.auroracoop.com/go.asp?id=001746016 #giltner; accessed July 30, 2007.

Bourdieu, Pierre. 1986. "The Forms of Capital." In *Handbook of Theory and Research for the Sociology of Education,* ed. John C. Richardson, 241–258. New York: Greenwood Press.

Coleman, James C. 1988. "Social Capital in the Creation of Human Capital." *American Journal of Sociology* 94 (Supplement S95–S120):95–119.

Duncan, Cynthia M. 1999. *Worlds Apart: Why Poverty Persists in Rural America.* New Haven: Yale University Press.

Durkheim, Emile. [1893] 1984. *The Division of Labor in Society.* New York: Free Press.

———. [1912] 2001. *Elementary Forms of Religious Life.* Trans. Carol Cosman. Abridged by Mark S. Cladis. Oxford: Oxford University Press.

Granovetter, Mark S. 1973. "The Strength of Weak Ties." *American Journal of Sociology* 78, no. 6:1360–1380.

Kaufman, Harold F. 1959. "Toward an Interactional Conception of Community." *Social Forces* 38 (October):9–17.

Narayan, Deepa. 1999. "Bonds and Bridges: Social Capital and Poverty" (August). Policy Research Working Paper 2167, Poverty Division, Poverty Reduction and Economic Management Network, The World Bank.

Putnam, Robert D. 1993a. *Making Democracy Work: Civic Traditions in Modern Italy.* Princeton, NJ: Princeton University Press.

———. 1993b. "The Prosperous Community: Social Capital and Public Life." *The American Prospect* 13:35–42.

———. 2000. *Bowling Alone. The Collapse and Revival of American Community.* New York: Simon and Schuster.

Sharp, Jeff S. 2001. "Locating the Community Field: A Study of Interorganizational Network Structure and Capacity for Community Action." *Rural Sociology* 66:403–424.

Töennies, Ferdinand. [1887] 1957. *Community and Society.* Trans. and ed. Charles P. Loomis. East Lansing: Michigan State University Press.

Toqueville, Alexis de. [1835 and 1840] 1956. *Democracy in America.* Specially ed. and abridged by Richard D. Heffner. New York: New American Library Mentor Books.

Wilkinson, Kenneth P. 1972. "A Field Theory Perspective for Community Development Research." *Rural Sociology* 37, no. 1:43–52.

———. 1991. *The Community in Rural America.* New York: Greenwood Press.

World Bank. 2001. *World Development Report, 2000–2001: Attacking Poverty.* New York: Oxford University Press. Also online; available: www.worldbank.org/poverty/wdrpoverty/; accessed September 2002.

6

POLITICAL CAPITAL

Joe and Ellen McDougal had grown up in Small Lake, in the boot heel of Missouri, a persistently poor area, and thought they knew the town well. As adults, they had decided to stay and raise a family in their hometown. Joe was employed in a small manufacturing plant. Ellen made crafts at home and worked part time as a waitress at the Down Home Cafe, the social hub in town.

As their children grew older, Joe and Ellen realized the area had few recreational facilities. What was available was in poor condition. In particular, they believed that lights should be installed at the city park's baseball diamond so that more games could be scheduled for the children's softball leagues.

For several years, they went to the city council with signed petitions, but there was no result. Their elected officials explained that funding was not available for "recreational luxuries" and that nothing could be done. Finally one of Ellen's regular customers at the cafe said, "Oh, if you want something done in this town, you really need to talk to Hank Jones." Ellen knew Hank, the owner of the local feed and farm supply store, because he drank coffee almost every day in the Down Home Cafe, but she was unaware that he was influential in town politics; he had never been elected to public office. Hank just seemed like "one of the boys."

Hank arrived at the cafe the following day, and Ellen poured his coffee and chatted with him about the need for lights at the city park and about how athletics played a vital role in keeping youngsters out of trouble.

Within a week, the item was brought before the city council again, passing easily and receiving funding through a small property assessment. Why had Ellen's casual conversation with Hank Jones been more productive than two years' work with the elected town officials?

———

In this chapter, we look at political capital in rural communities. We examine theories and ways of measuring community power, different sources of power or vested interests, and the importance of outside linkages to community power. Finally, we examine some of the implications that various power structures have for community development and change.

POLITICAL CAPITAL

Political capital consists of organization, connections, voice, and power. Political capital is the ability of a group to influence the distribution of resources within a social unit, including helping set the agenda of what resources are available. Political capital determines standards, the rules and regulations to ensure those standards are followed, and the degree to which they are enforced. Generally, political capital reflects the dominant cultural capital: There is a tendency to support the status quo. In many rural communities, high levels of bonding social capital reinforce the current situation and discourage groups with different ideas and agendas from coming forward to offer alternatives. Very often, those who control political capital are not in elected positions but are regularly consulted by elected officials. Sometimes they are not consulted, but elected officials, in giving reasons for not acting on new ideas, anticipate their response, as was the case in Small Lake when the McDougals were told funding was not available for "recreational luxuries." The city council, knowing that Hank was opposed to anything that might increase property taxes, automatically rejected any suggestion that might incur expenditures.

Our attention to political capital is to understand not only who runs things in rural communities but also how excluded groups whose issues are not on the agenda when resources are allocated can increase their voice and influence. Under what circumstances can excluded people organize and work together, know and feel comfortable around powerful people, and bring their issues forward for action?

Rural communities are greatly affected by outside forces; even the smallest places feel the repercussions of national and international events (see Chapter 9). Yet even very small communities have the power to generate and distribute resources (see Chapter 11).

Defining and Exercising Power

Power is the ability to create a situation that otherwise would not happen or to prevent from occurring an event that others wish to make happen. Hence, the ability to affect the distribution of both public and private resources within the community is called *community power*, or possession of political capital in the community realm. Often community power can be augmented by connections with the outside. Who possesses power and the degree to which it is widely available can greatly affect the quality of life for community residents and the future existence of the community itself.

An important dimension of power is the means by which it is exercised, including physical force, institutionalized force or authority, and influence. In totalitarian regimes, power is often based on the threat of exercising physical force. Institutional power—power that derives from occupying a position of authority in an institution—requires subordinates to follow orders or regulations if they want to remain part of that institution. Only when superiors go beyond institutional rules is it acceptable for subordinates to refuse to carry out an order. Even then, refusal can jeopardize one's longevity with the organization. Influence refers to power derived from more informal relationships, such as friendship or social status. Whistleblowers, such as Coleen Rowley in the FBI, Cynthia Cooper at WorldCom, and Sherron Watkins at Enron, are examples of individuals who withstand the cultural and political capital of their organization. Rowley, Cooper, and Watkins first went through the appropriate hierarchy to report discrepancies and, when corrective action was not taken by those with authority, then went outside the chain of command to try to correct the situation in the organizations in which they worked.

If excluded voices are to be heard, it is important to find out who really runs an organization or a community. Individuals who hold formal positions of authority may or may not actually set the agenda. People such as the McDougals can live in a place all their life without knowing who really makes things happen—or stops them from happening—in their community.

Patterns in the exercise of community power are called *community power structure*. In a community, we can map local power to determine the degree to which it is widely participatory or more concentrated. For instance, in Small Lake a hidden power structure has a great impact on town politics and decisions; the elected officials are not always the people running the town. In some communities, an influential network of individuals who never face public election or accountability greatly affect what does or does not happen.

Competing Theories

Social scientists disagree about the way power is exercised in North American communities and about how to determine the way community power is structured. In part the disagreements arise from the fact that not all communities have the same power structures. But researchers also bring diverse assumptions to their study of community power. This chapter describes four approaches to the study of community power: pluralism, elitism, class-based analysis, and "the growth machine," a variant of the class-based approach. Although most of the initial studies of community power were carried out in urban places, later elaboration and testing of the theories occurred in rural communities (Humphrey and Krannich 1980; Ramsey 1996; Sharp and Flora 1999). Consequently, we use these theories to explore power in rural communities.

Social scientists have devised several ways of determining who has power. Each of these measurement techniques is related to a supportable theory of power, and each tends to give a somewhat varied answer to the question "Who is running this town?" After each theory of power is discussed, the method of measuring community power most closely related to that theory is described.

Pluralism Versus Elitism

Early studies of community power were conducted from a pluralist perspective and focused mainly on who held formal positions in community government. After a more in-depth investigation into how communities worked, sociologists began to notice patterns of inequality in the exercise of power and distribution of resources. In many cases, small groups of individuals controlled the community by virtue of their economic and social position, leading to a competing view of power: elitism. This section explores these two models and the strategies each uses to measure power.

Pluralism and the Event Analysis Technique

The pluralist approach to power—whether in the community or on the regional, state, or national level—is based on fundamental assumptions about the way democracies work. Adherents of the *pluralism* theory of power assume that there is no dominant source of power. They assume that the capacity for acquiring power is widely distributed within the population unless analysis shows otherwise. Moreover, they hold, power is dispersed among competing interests. Although one particular group may prevail on one issue, it may not be influential on the next issue. Furthermore, without studying the situation, one cannot determine what is the interest of any particular group (Polsby 1960).

Community theorists who take a pluralist perspective see citizens in a democracy deciding on political issues in the same way they make decisions vis-à-vis the market: as unattached individuals with perfect access to information. Thus, the individual is the basic building block of politics. Individual citizens exercise their political influence principally through voting. The concept of "one person, one vote" is essential for pluralism to work. That vote may be exercised directly, as in the type of direct representation of a *New England town meeting*. Much more frequently, however, votes are cast for someone who represents a group of constituents. Under this system of representative democracy, citizens are not directly involved in making all public decisions. Instead, the chosen representatives periodically are subjected to electoral validation. It is assumed that this validation is a means by which representatives (be they school board members, town councilpersons, county supervisors, state officials, or presidents or prime ministers) generally reflect the desires of their constituents. Although individual voters may see their objectives deferred in the short term (particularly if they voted for the losing candidate), decisions should benefit the greatest number of people in the long term.

From the pluralist perspective, the U.S. democratic system is grounded in a legal system that prohibits power being used arbitrarily. One such mechanism introduced in the U.S. Constitution is a system of checks and balances among three branches of government: The legislative body makes the laws, the administration implements them, and the judiciary arbitrates when disputes arise. This is different from other forms of government, such as in England and in France, where the legislative arm of government also acts as the administrator of the policies it enacts. The Bill of Rights and other laws guarantee that those who do not share the majority opinion have freedom of expression and equality of opportunity. This equality includes the electoral system itself, in which those elected have only temporary power gained through periodic election and challengers have a reasonable opportunity of gaining office. All citizens share the civil right of participation in government through the election process, including the right to run for office themselves.

According to community theorists who take a pluralist perspective, representative democracy does not mean that everyone exercises equal influence in politics. Some may choose not to participate in voting, in party caucuses, or in contributing funds to a particular candidate. However, if they do participate and have the innate ability, their influence can roughly equal that of any other active citizen. Differences in influence among different classes or ethnic groups can be explained by the statistical tendency of certain groups or classes not to participate as actively in the political process as do others. It is an individual's decision to participate or not, and individuals who fail to participate have made the choice of noninvolvement.

The dispersion of economic, political, and social power that is assumed by community theorists who take a pluralist perspective also applies to the decision-making process. They believe that the best way to assess how and by whom decisions are made is to look at overt activity; in other words, decisions are made by those in positions of formal power. Community theorists who take a pluralist perspective are suspicious of analyses based on assumptions of behind-the-scenes influence. In fact, they reject the idea that certain groups have certain a priori interests. They do not subscribe to the notion that different classes have contradictory political interests. The degree to which class interests involve conflicting policies is a matter for investigation. Hence, lack of controversy on a particular issue is, for the community theorists who take a pluralist perspective, an indication that there is basic agreement among the citizenry on a publicly articulated position.

Those who study community power from a pluralist perspective use what is called the *event analysis technique*. This research methodology involves identifying and using controversial public issues to reveal the decision-making process. Newspaper coverage, observation, and interviews are used to determine which decisions were important and who made them. The information gathered through these sources generally shows a diversity of sources of inputs to public decisions; this diversity lends support to the pluralist perspective.

The classic pluralist study *Who Governs? Democracy and Power in an American City* (1961) was conducted by Robert Dahl in New Haven, Connecticut. Dahl examined three issues: political nominations, urban renewal, and public education. He found that no single group dominated the decision-making process in all three arenas; different groups and individuals were active in each. Only the appointed bureaucracy and the elected mayor were common to more than one issue area. Dahl concluded that his results supported the pluralist perspective.

G. William Domhoff (1983) reexamined the urban renewal issue, exploring what went on behind the scenes as well as during the decision-making process itself. He found that urban renewal in New Haven was predominantly the product of economic interests in New Haven that benefited handsomely from the program. The politicians were merely the implementers, not the decision makers. Dahl had looked at the decision-making process only after it became public, thus examining only the pluralist veneer. If one is using the event analysis technique to determine who has power in the community, it is important to study the period that preceded public airing of an issue to see whose agenda originally included the issue, the behind-the-scenes machinations that determined how the issue would be presented to the public, and which interests stood to gain when the decision was implemented.

Elitism and What Happens behind the Scenes

The elitist school of thought received its methodological orientation from Floyd Hunter (1953) in his study of Atlanta, Georgia. However, the perspective obtained its name from the work of sociologist C. Wright Mills, who wrote *The Power Elite* (1956). Mills argued that "a power elite"—a coalition of government officials, business executives, and military leaders—controlled the nation and that the political and economic interests individuals in the coalition shared were reinforced by their social similarities. Members of the elite had attended the same schools and universities, belonged to the same clubs, and relaxed at the same resorts. In addition, the branches of the elite interlocked professionally. Business executives became politicians, politicians had business interests, and retired military leaders sat on corporate boards; all of these connections further ensured and strengthened mutual interests. Domhoff's book *Who Rules America?* (1967) elaborated on and modified Mills's analysis at the national level, as did the work of Domhoff's followers.

Elitism is a perspective based on the assumption that power conforms to the stratification system. Community theorists who take a power elite perspective argue that power is distributed hierarchically. The premise is that sources of power (control over means of coercion, authoritative position, command of wealth or information, and prestige or other personal traits) can be accumulated. For instance, wealthy people often are viewed as having exceptional talents; otherwise, it is commonly believed, they would not be wealthy. Possession of wealth can then lead to prestige, control over information, and authoritative position. The pluralistic theory of power sees the community as having a series of factional coalitions: Group boundaries are fairly fluid, members disagree on specific issues over time, and no coalition dominates for any extended period. The community theorists who take a power elite perspective, on the other hand, see a pyramidal structure of power: A few individuals representing key economic institutions with like interests have the largest influence in what happens in towns, large and small.

Hunter, in one of the most significant works on community power, *Community Power Structure* (1953), developed the reputational technique for determining power in a community. Hunter collected lists of community leaders and activists from local newspapers and organizational membership rolls. He came up with a list of 175 names and then sought the aid of knowledgeable people in the community, who presumably knew about power and politics, to cull the original list, eliminating those who did not actually exercise much power. The forty people who remained on the list were then personally interviewed. Each individual was asked a number of questions, including "If a project went before the community that required decisions by a group of leaders, leaders that nearly everyone would accept, which ten on this list of forty would you choose?" The responses gave him a list of top reputational leaders.

As a result of using this reputational technique, which has been modified by multiple researchers studying different cities, Hunter found an elitist power structure in the form of a pyramid. At the top was a small group of business leaders, an elite upper class that dominated the city's economy through a web of interlocking directorships. Those leaders lived in the same exclusive neighborhoods, belonged to the same expensive clubs, and entertained one another in their homes. The elites rarely held office and were not visible to the general public. In fact, only four of the forty top elites were public officials. The rest were bankers, manufacturers, and other business leaders. Their power was informal. Elected officials were subordinate to them, doing their bidding but not seeing them socially.

Hunter found this small policy-making group, largely from the business class, to be in overall agreement on most major issues. He noted that "controversy is avoided, partly by the policy-making group not allowing a proposal to get too far along if it meets stiff criticism at any point in decision making" (1953, 111). Hunter did not conclude that this small group had absolute control over major issues, but he did propose that it played a major role in setting the public agenda.

Community theorists who take a power elite perspective criticize the event analysis approach on the grounds that it often focuses on controversial issues, defining power in terms of who makes decisions politically. They argue that most decisions are not controversial and are never debated publicly. Many of these decisions systematically support one set of interests in the community over another. Viewed from this perspective, power is held by those who control the public agenda but who may not be visible players in the political process. It becomes important, then, to look at what issues in the community are never publicly decided: the nondecisions that happen abruptly. Matthew Crenson, in a study conducted when pollution became an issue in urban communities, concluded that the problem of dirty air became a "key political issue" in those communities where "industry's reputation for power was relatively puny," suggesting that the critical stage is not at the point of public decision but when "a community sifts out subjects that will not be given political attention and so will never become key political issues" (1971, 131 and 90).

POWER AND ECONOMIC INTERESTS

Class-based theories of community power focus attention on the economic roots of power. This theory and its variations assume that those who control the corporate economic system control the wider society. It is often in their economic interest to influence or to control political decision making. This section explores the class-based theory of community power and one of its more recent variations, the growth machine.

Class-Based Theory of Power

According to the *class-based analysis* of power, it makes little difference to the economic elites which person or group actually makes decisions as long as those policy and allocation decisions facilitate profit making. Those in official decision-making positions may not be the economic elites themselves, but the decision makers tend to represent the interests of the economic elites. This appeared to be the case in Small Lake, where Hank Jones, a local businessman, had a good deal of informal control over the city council.

The influential study undertaken in the 1930s by Helen and Robert Lynd (1937) found that economic institutions were key to understanding power and the distribution of resources in "Middletown," the name they gave to Muncie, Indiana. Now a metropolitan city, in the 1930s Muncie was a fast-growing nonmetropolitan community, increasing from fewer than thirty-nine thousand inhabitants in 1925 to more than forty-seven thousand ten years later.

The locally based Ball family owned and operated the Ball Jar Company, the largest producer of home-canning equipment in the world. The Lynds found that after the "bank holiday" in 1933, the family controlled or had a major interest in all surviving local financial institutions. The Balls were also heavily involved in local real estate and shaped the city's growth. Through philanthropy they influenced the growth of the local college (now Ball State University), the hospital, the community fund, and the YMCA and YWCA. Although family members only occasionally held local public office, they controlled the Republican Party and had influence in the Democratic Party and thus were able to bring about or prevent change in many arenas. In short, the Ball family exercised political power in Muncie.

The Lynds found abundant evidence that questioned the independence of those holding political office. According to the Lynds, elected officials were of meager caliber: people the Ball family and the rest of the inner business group ignored economically and socially yet used politically. Those who controlled the economic institutions (the Balls were among these elites) did not want to bother with direct political involvement, but they did need to limit government interference in their concerns. Elected officials thus were considered a necessary evil. Using that insight, Vidich and Bensman (1968) found similar results in Candor, New York, in the 1960s.

A case study of business-class control and citizen mobilization in a small Kansas town by Eugene Hynes and Verna Mauney (1990) offers insight into the reasons that the elites, particularly specific business interests, are concerned about city government and want to control decisions.

Many rural communities own their own utilities; this was the case in the town Hynes and Mauney studied. Utility pricing policies and rate structures in this Kansas town were such that domestic households paid higher rates than did commercial and industrial enterprises. The business group that almost invariably owned these enterprises was from the same town as the officials. By charging high domestic utility rates, officials made it possible to keep property taxes low. This was to the advantage of those who owned a lot of property. Zoning decisions also were systematically made in favor of those with direct influence on the city council. Special-interest groups also influenced the public financing of business projects that might otherwise have been funded through private sources. People with these vested interests had tangible reasons for controlling both the community government and the nongovernmental institutions involved in distributing resources. Generally, they were very accomplished at doing so.

Working-class people in rural communities have a set of interests different from the interest groups just described. Of primary importance to them are wage levels, benefits, and actions that would increase the prevailing wage. Local governments influence wage levels by how much they pay their own employees, by whether they consciously recruit high- or low-wage firms, and by other such actions. Yet a number of structures in small communities prevent working-class citizens from influencing these decisions: They rarely sit on the public boards, and even when elected to office, they often find it difficult to attend the informal and sometimes the formal meetings called during daytime working hours. Hynes and Mauney document well the case of the working-class mayor in the town they studied. He was publicly ridiculed in the press because of his irregular attendance at city council meetings. His job kept him from the impromptu meetings called by the city council, which was composed of small-business operators who had flexible schedules.

Hynes and Mauney also clearly demonstrated the chilling nature of a local elite's tight control that was preventing people from running for office or publicly addressing issues they knew were negatively affecting them. People often were reluctant to act because of their perceived vulnerability. For example, Hynes and Mauney reported that one prominent member of the town's concerned citizens group became inactive when she came to fear that her cousin, a schoolteacher, would lose his job if her activities continued. When individual members of a power elite occupy economic, political, and civic roles almost interchangeably, one can expect little participation in decision making. The more widely dispersed economic, political, and civic roles are within the community, the more likely it is that various citizen voices will be heard.

The Growth Machine

With the publication of "The City as a Growth Machine" in 1976, Harvey Molotch introduced a variation of the class-based theory of community power. Studies in a number of urban areas had identified the importance of a group, which later came to be called the "growth machine." The *growth machine* is a coalition of groups that perceive economic gain in community growth. Led by certain groups within the business class, the growth machine works to encourage growth and to capture its benefits. These groups tend to include a combination of interests of developers, construction companies, providers of home insurance, real estate agents, and owners of commercial buildings, rental units, banks, and other businesses dependent on an increase of aggregate rent levels through the intensification of land use (Logan, Whaley, and Crowder 1997). The ability to increase aggregate rent levels (income from land or other real property) depends heavily on increases in the community's population. These growth machines compete with growth machines in other communities to attract capital that, in turn, will attract residents to increase return on land, buildings, merchandise, and services.

The most active elites in the local power structure are generally members of the *rentier class,* those who receive their income from property. Members of this class promote population growth (and thus constant construction and city expansion to office and house the new population), usually in the name of increasing jobs. These modern rentiers have financial interests in the use of local land and buildings and include developers, commercial and residential landlords, and those who speculate in real property. The rentier class does not produce goods or services but, rather, makes money by preparing the foundation for manufacturing, service, or retail firms by providing them with desirable sites. Profits for the rentier class depend primarily on population growth but secondarily on their degree of political capital with local governments. Local government in the United States has unique powers to regulate land use (see Chapter 11), and it is land use that provides potential profit to this class of people. As a result, the rentier class works very hard to make sure that the people with formal decision-making power have the rentier class's interests at heart. They are big political contributors at the national level, ensuring tax deductions for interest paid on mortgages and federal government disaster funding to help them continue to profit when building on flood plains. On the local level, this class is generally well organized to explain why its members need an exception to zoning, the extension of a sewer or expansion of a sewage treatment plant, the paving of a road, or tax relief.

The growth machine and the rentier class are eager to attract industry because it generates commercial and residential construction and results in increased land values. That may explain why, despite the large number of studies that universally show that the incentives given to attract industry do not repay the local area, such incentives continue to be offered, jeopardizing the quality of life that other uses of that money would bring, such as schools, parks, and libraries. Therefore, there is minimal discussion about what is produced, the wage levels paid by new employers, or the impact of new industrial or service firms on the quality of life. Industry is often put in the low-income part of town, even in rural communities. Thus, people in the wealthy part of town gain the profits, and costs of development are borne by the poor, often in terms of decreased quality of life because of polluted air, overcrowded schools, and traffic congestion. Or, in some rural areas, the residents get the pollution, and the investors, who definitely do not live there, get the profits. When this occurs in predominantly African American, Native American, or Hispanic communities, it is referred to as environmental racism. Those who are poor and further excluded because of race or ethnicity have little political capital with which to counter that of industrial investors seeking profit. Those communities often are chosen because they have few environmental laws and little means to enforce those that exist.

As a result, the central conflict in many communities is between the growth machine and neighborhoods. This conflict can be understood in terms of a conflict between use value and exchange value—two terms that are almost self-explanatory. Something that has *use value* is valued because of its use, instead of its monetary value. *Exchange value* is realized only when the commodity is sold.

For example, an apartment building has little use value to the owner. It has exchange value in terms of the income generated either from its rental units or from its sale. On the other hand, one's ancestral home has only use value because there is no intention of selling it. It may be sold when the individual dies, giving it exchange value, but the owner, now deceased, did not realize any exchange value from it—only use value. Properties have values that lie between these two extremes. For example, the home of a professional who expects to move several times has use value while the person lives in it, but maintaining its market value is of concern because of the expectation of selling it at some time in the not-too-distant future. Any improvement the owner makes must be made with dual concerns: First, does it increase the owner's enjoyment of the house (use value)? Second, does it increase the salability of the house (exchange value)?

Attempts to develop and gentrify older neighborhoods often expose the conflict between use value and exchange value. Those who live in the targeted neighborhood embrace use values. They first seek to preserve their homes (the longer they live in them, the greater their use value compared with their exchange value). Neighborhood associations work to improve that use value through enhancing natural and built capital in ways that do not convert immediately into financial capital through publicly or collectively owned amenities such as parks, playgrounds and sports fields, and natural areas. Second, neighborhood people have an interest in keeping the value of land low because it means lower property taxes. Those who are part of the growth machine thrive on profit derived from increasing land values and support efforts at urban renewal. Yet neighborhood associations often are willing to tax themselves to create the kind of amenities that increase the use value of the neighborhood.

In rural communities, the growth machine has a similar composition to that in the cities. David McGranahan points out that "locally owned banks, utilities, law firms, and other firms operating largely within local trade areas," for which "income and wealth depend on the volume of business, especially to the extent that there are economies of scale," are likely to be part of the growth machine (1990, 160). Because growth is in itself supposed to be good, everything should be done to promote it. The dominant cultural capital provides the values that undergird the activities, justify public and private investment, and support the regulatory setting that makes growth profitable for at least some of the community. Although outside interests, such as multinational firms seeking to locate a branch plant, may mobilize the political capital of the local growth machine to get special tax benefits or environmental exceptions, the core of the growth machine is made of local firms and individuals.

Smart Growth

Smart-growth coalitions first sprang up in urban areas in the 1970s to combat urban sprawl and excessive suburbanization. These principles increasingly are being applied in rural areas as well.

Smart-growth rural communities often have lively art groups, as well as active outdoor recreation, and they often sponsor regular farmers' markets and community gardens.

The principles of smart growth below (from www.smartgrowth.org/about/principles/default.asp) address all the capitals and attempt to use the power of zoning and planning to maintain and increase quality of life while fostering a vital economy.

- Create range of housing opportunities and choices
  Providing quality housing for people of all income levels is an integral component in any smart-growth strategy. (built capital and financial capital)
- Create walkable neighborhoods
  Walkable communities are desirable places to live, work, learn, worship, and play, and therefore are a key component of smart growth. (human capital and social capital)
- Encourage community and stakeholder collaboration
  Growth can create great places to live, work, and play—if it responds to a community's own sense of how and where it wants to grow. (social capital and cultural capital)
- Foster distinctive, attractive communities with a strong sense of place
  Smart growth encourages communities to craft a vision and set standards for development and construction that respond to community values of architectural beauty and distinctiveness, as well as of expanded choices in housing and transportation. (cultural capital, natural capital, built capital)
- Make development decisions predictable, fair, and cost-effective
  For a community to be successful in implementing smart growth, it must be embraced by the private sector. (financial capital)
- Mix land uses
  Smart growth supports the integration of mixed land uses into communities as a critical component of achieving better places to live. (natural capital)

- Preserve open space, farmland, natural beauty, and critical environmental areas
  Open-space preservation supports smart-growth goals by bolstering local economies, preserving critical environmental areas, improving our communities' quality of life, and guiding new growth into existing communities. (natural capital)
- Provide a variety of transportation choices
  Providing people with more choices in housing, shopping, communities, and transportation is a key aim of smart growth. (built capital)
- Strengthen and direct development toward existing communities
  Smart growth directs development toward existing communities already served by infrastructure, seeking to utilize the resources that existing neighborhoods offer and to conserve open space and irreplaceable natural resources on the urban fringe. (social capital, cultural capital, built capital)
- Take advantage of compact building design
  Smart growth provides a means for communities to incorporate more compact building design as an alternative to conventional, land-consumptive development. (built capital)

Decorah, Iowa, is part of the rural smart-growth movement. Taking advantage of its natural capital in terms of a natural riverbank setting, the town has over the years sought to control strip malls and unplanned growth. Through a coalition of civic and business leaders, including the local college, the town maintains a growing economy within established boundaries. Determined to become even more sustainable, it is part of the recently launched Northeast Iowa Food and Fitness Initiative.

Other groups in rural communities might be characterized as no-growth coalitions, though that coalition differs somewhat from its urban counterpart. Unlike in cities, a rural no-growth coalition tends to dominate, especially in the smaller, non–trade center communities, though its precise nature depends on the principal source of the community's wealth.

The no-growth coalition in small communities includes manufacturers, processors, commercial farmers, and others who produce for an export market (for products sold outside the community). Their interest is in having low-cost labor, not in generating a larger local market. Bringing in new employers, particularly branch plants that have paid higher wages in metropolitan areas, is not in this group's interest. For instance, the peanut processors who dominated politics in Early County, Georgia, until the 1980s not only opposed higher wages but also were against spending on public schools because they feared that educating the largely black population would result in higher wages. In the 1970s, affluent whites there often attended a white private academy, keeping down public school expenditures. Lower school funding was doubly in the interest of the powerful group because (1) it helped keep wages down by keeping the bulk of the labor force unskilled and (2) it resulted in low taxes.

Another example is in Midwestern farm communities, where farmers (often retired) usually dominate the board of county commissioners or supervisors. They favor a limited government, no-growth approach because they do not depend on the local population to buy their products and because they have an interest in low real estate taxes. Their interest in improved roads and bridges to get their products to market more efficiently is an exception to their low-expenditure perspective.

Retired people, whose concern lies more with the use value of their homes than with their exchange value, also are part of the no-growth coalition. This group makes up a substantial part of the population of rural communities that are experiencing out-migration. Although retirees may not participate actively in community affairs, they tend to vote in large numbers and sometimes can defeat industrial revenue bonds, as well as school and other infrastructure bonds.

The small village of "Springdale" in upstate New York studied by Arthur Vidich and Joseph Bensman is an example of a community where the no-growth mentality dominated. After a long period of decline, Springdale became a low-rent bedroom community for industrial workers from nearby Binghamton, New York. The business elite controlled local politics through an "invisible government" that consisted of the three members of the village Republican committee: a feed and seed dealer, the editor of the weekly newspaper, and a lawyer who was the clerk (counsel) to the village board. This group determined the nominees for village offices and manipulated voting behavior so that their candidates always won. (Because the Democrats who voted were a distinct minority in the village, nomination on the Republican ticket was tantamount to election.) The hours that the polls were open were not convenient for the industrial workers, and "safe" voters could be recruited as soon as it appeared that too many of the "wrong" kinds of people were voting during a local election.

Vidich and Bensman found the following informal requirements for being on the village board: (1) being a resident of the community for at least ten years, though lifelong residency was preferable; (2) either being economically vulnerable, and hence amenable to being manipulated by those holding real power, or having a kinship connection with one of the dominant figures of machine politics; (3) having little knowledge about the way government works; and (4) subscribing to a low-tax, low-expenditure ideology. The authors summed it up accordingly: "It thus happens that the incompetent, the economically vulnerable, and the appropriately kinship-connected individuals are elected with regularized consistency . . . to a village board on which they find they have nothing to do because, in their own perspective, the routine affairs of government are automatic" (1968, 116).

Vidich and Bensman indicated that another characteristic united the members of the village board as well as the invisible government: They all owned rental property. As owners of real estate, they logically should have been part of the growth machine. However, decline was so deeply imprinted in their experience that they had developed a low-tax approach to making money in real estate: keeping their expenses low and seeking to make money on rentals rather than on sale of real estate. The modest influx of commuter residents allowed them to reap some benefits of growth without having to spend their own or others' money to bring it about. Making sure that the "right" kind of people were elected to the village board was imperative. Restricting the vote and ensuring that individuals believing in limited—very limited—government were elected to the village council made this happen.

In somewhat larger rural communities, influence over city government is more commonly exercised through such semigovernmental units as the chamber of commerce. (Chambers of commerce often channel government funds, but without much public accountability, to promote tourism and economic development.) Both no-growth and growth-machine business interests choose to be active in the local chamber of commerce or similar civic organizations in order to seek to impose their view of local development.

Unlike urban communities, where the growth machine typically dominates, rural communities vary substantially in projecting a no-growth, smart-growth, or pro-growth orientation. Smart-growth groups have the most influence in creative communities, where there is a high probability of locally initiated entrepreneurial manufacturing plants and the adoption of advanced technologies and management practices (Wojan and McGranahan

2007). The ability of the no-growth group, as in Springdale, to make automatic the routine affairs of government is sufficient in some communities to defeat the growth machine and to keep new economic activity out. Pro-growth groups dominate other nonmetropolitan communities, which often are regional trade centers. In other instances, such as during times of crisis and population decline, the rentier class and those who benefit individually from low taxes may join together to save their rural community by seeking to attract or generate capital to increase employment in the community. Rural communities that elect to do nothing when faced with decline are much more numerous.

Local Versus Absentee Ownership

In a modern capitalist system, ownership is separated from management. Those who provide the capital or have inherited it are not assumed to possess the managerial knowledge and talents necessary to enhance capital accumulation (profits and corporate growth). Furthermore, modern businesses require huge amounts of capital, often more than a single individual or family can readily save or borrow. A limited liability corporation allows for the sale of stock to raise capital, in exchange for a vote on who will sit on the board of directors, which sets policy for the company. When a business or corporation sells shares of itself in public offerings on a stock exchange, it is known as a "publicly held corporation." When a family or only a few people hold those stocks, it is known as a "privately held corporation." Does who owns community businesses matter in terms of what happens to the people and the place? Does it matter if the parent corporation is based in the community, the same state, the United States, or overseas? If a parent corporation is not locally based, does the company have the same kind of local political capital and does it utilize what local political capital it does have in the same way a locally based company does? Is it more likely to threaten to leave if a community does something it does not like? Or is it more likely to let other voices be heard?

Both the San Jose study discussed later (Trounstine and Christensen 1982) and the growth-machine literature suggest that the increasing international ownership of firms will result in less involvement in day-to-day community issues by industry and business and more involvement by an increasingly diverse group of players. In addition, the awareness citizens have of nonlocal ownership encourages them to mobilize collectively as insiders against outsiders to address serious issues such as environmental pollution. At the other extreme, an outside firm may threaten to leave a community if it does not win concessions on issues that directly affect its profitability (see the discussion in Chapter 8, Built Capital).

Increased nonlocal ownership could lead to a bias favoring the growth machine. Nonlocal firms tend to have managers who are geographically mobile and as a result exert less long-term influence in the community. Managers of absentee companies generally do not invest their human, social, financial, or political capital in community affairs or charitable activities. In contrast, local industrialists often take part in all civic realms, may be linked to the rentier group through co-ownership of speculative property, and frequently are local philanthropists providing a trickle-down of local wealth through community-based foundations with a local range of giving.

Nonlocal firms usually are linked to national or international supply networks; local entrepreneurs do not benefit from such commercial links. There are smaller multiplier effects from absentee-owned firms than from those locally owned. When local businesses are aligned with the growth machine, these benefits, both tangible and symbolic, can be exploited to foster the growth mentality and to generate support for policies that benefit local firms.

The concentration that is occurring in manufacturing firms is also occurring in the media. Daily newspapers are less likely to be locally owned than they used to be. Chain newspapers, with limited links to individual communities, are less likely than locally owned newspapers to actively promote the local growth machine and therefore are more likely to take an independent editorial stand. Domhoff (1983) points out that local newspaper publishers are committed not to a particular faction of the growth machine but to the growth machine in general: The newspaper's interest is in selling more newspapers and, in particular, more advertising. It follows that the local publisher often serves as an arbiter among groups within the growth machine, acting as a spokesperson for the growth machine as a whole. When the newspaper is no longer locally owned, the growth machine loses an important integrative element.

Similarly, banking is becoming more concentrated in fewer interstate firms that have less interest in controlling the uniquely local resources of tax rates and land use. Unlike its locally owned predecessor, the consolidated bank usually is not allied with the local growth machine. It may also be less interested in investing in the local community.

Absentee-owned enterprises have a contradictory impact on the community by creating space for greater community pluralism through their lack of interest in local politics. That lack of interest will mean less commitment to the interests of the dominant community elites, and the lack of political coordination among economic elites provides a greater opportunity for nonelites to organize in their own interest. Alternatively, when an issue arises that affects the absentee-owned firm directly, the company may threaten to leave the community if the issue is not resolved in a way favorable to it. That threat may carry considerable weight if the firm makes a large contribution to the community's economy.

POWER STRUCTURE AND COMMUNITY CHANGE

With the decline of branch manufacturing plants in rural areas as they move to areas with even cheaper labor and no environmental controls (see Chapter 9, The Global Economy) and with the expanded growth of service-sector activities, the growth machine—whether local or national—has found it more difficult to manage community symbols to its own benefit. Because industrialization generally was seen as the solution to all communities' problems, the local growth machine could convince local governments to offer tax breaks to new industries. Such offers were made, even though people on fixed incomes found that they lost more than they gained from the presence of such plants, and unemployed people often did not benefit because more-educated commuters took the new jobs. Now the service sector has replaced manufacturing as the growth sector, creating new problems for nonelites and for some elites in rural communities. Even in small cities, downtown malls built through urban renewal have uprooted people from poorer neighborhoods, and suburban malls have replaced locally owned stores with chains and franchises within the mall. Merchants in small communities have been "Wal-Marted" by the general-merchandise chain store in the nearby larger community (see Chapter 10, Consumption in Rural America).

Environmental awareness has increased as people have become more concerned about urban garbage filling rural landfills or about nuclear-waste dumps and missile sites replacing farmland and ranchland. In some cases, the interests of the entire community coalesce if such facilities do little to generate wealth for local elites. Just as frequently, such issues split communities that are desperate for jobs and income.

In rapid-growth communities, the new in-migrants often are professionals with a strong commitment to the residential value of the community, organizational skills, and a willingness to participate in community affairs. Their commitment includes concern for the environment, often coupled with an unwillingness to pay the fiscal and social costs of development. They have political capital outside the local community that allows them to counteract the power of the growth machine.

National economic elites are mobilizing anew to have an effect at the local level. Management-level personnel in branch firms are required to become active in local organizations, form their own associations to lobby local governments, support political candidates, and publicize their views on zoning, land use, and the free enterprise system. As the interests of national and local elites diverge, the national elites and national power structure seek to convince local elites that the ideology of the national growth machine should also be their ideology. To this end, local chambers of commerce may come up with programs that seem antithetical to local development needs but that match the U.S. Chamber of Commerce's political and ideological agenda—which is that of the national growth machine.

Communities vary enormously in the degree to which power is concentrated and in the degree to which it is wielded by local or absentee individuals, firms, and institutions. It is important to assess the structure of local power in analyzing how change takes place within a community and what kinds of tactics are needed to institute grassroots change. Challenging the power elite is an empowering experience because disenfranchised groups can learn to be successful through their mobilization. However, it is also risky because of the ability power elites often have to control information and symbols (cultural capital), enabling them to totally discredit people who oppose them, not by systematically attacking their position on issues but by casting doubt on their personality and character.

Understanding Power Structure and Increasing the Political Capital of Excluded Groups

Selecting one technique for use in a community study would bias the results in favor of that perspective. More recent studies have introduced new analytic techniques (such as network analysis) and combined research methodologies to create a more complete picture of community power structures. For excluded groups, understanding the power structure is key to gaining political capital.

Jeff Sharp and Jan Flora (1999) uncovered vital information about power structure in communities by asking four key questions: "Who can best represent this town to the outside?" "Whose support do you need to get things done?" "Whom do you need to implement a project?" "Who can stop a project in the community?" From the answers, it was evident that "old guard," middle-aged males were more likely to be project stoppers.

Drew Hyman, Francis Higdon, and Kenneth Martin (2001) combined positional, reputational, and event analysis to see what differences in power structure identification emerged in a town that contained a major university. They found that who had influence depended on the specific issue area under consideration; no one group influenced everything that went on in the community, suggesting that people felt the power structure may be different for various issues or aspects of community affairs. In their findings, the positional method and the reputational method did not identify the same individuals, although there was overlap. The researchers concluded that both methodologies were necessary to achieve an understanding of who exercises political capital and that if they had used only these methodologies, they would have determined that the community had an elitist power structure. But when they looked at the public record and key informant interviews using event analysis of issues important for growth machine interests (zoning of public lands, whether to build a new school building, and local government consolidation), they found a different set of individuals influential in each event. But almost all of the individuals found influential in each event were on the positional list, the reputational lists, or both. The researchers saw that on each issue, the local growth machine was a player, and each time it was defeated by organized citizen interests. Political capital was relatively dispersed and had countervailing influences.

They concluded that although growth-machine proponents have an advantage over local citizens in that they have careers that depend on pursuing growth (and are paid to make sure that growth happens through developing political capital with key decision makers), "if citizens are willing to maintain some continuity and even 'infiltrate' local government, boards, and commissions, there can be very pluralistic outcomes" (2001, 218). The key to building and maintaining political capital for disadvantaged groups is persistence and permanence. It is critical to organize, stay active, and form coalitions, and to know about other groups organizing with opposing views. Often a group may organize to stop a project (such as a large shopping center) and then disband, only to have something equally disadvantageous to the area's social and natural capital put in its place.

Both community theorists who take a power elite perspective and the class-based theorists of community power use network analysis of the key positions in major institutions in a community. Class theorists use the method to determine the corporate structure and to identify the top corporate leaders.

Network analysis involves obtaining the names of the members of the boards of directors or officers of all the important firms or organizations in town, determining linkages between organizations or individuals, and assessing patterns of linkages. Network analysis in various circumstances shows a single power elite or different power factions. The people then are ranked according to their number of connections and their centrality in the networks. Networks of interlocking firms can be examined to determine the kind of resources they bring together and whether they represent a growth machine or other type of resource network.

Balanced studies of power structure often combine a number of these mechanisms to limit the theoretical bias of the studies. An example of a study that combines methods is *Movers and Shakers,* a study of community power in San Jose, California, by Philip J. Trounstine and Terry Christensen (1982). They did a reputational study, conducted a network analysis, and, finally, looked at actual decisions using a historicojournalistic approach. (Trounstine, now director of the Survey and Policy Research Institute at San Jose State University, was a journalist. A political scientist, Christensen has published widely on California politics.) The historical analysis helped identify the most important issues, including annexation and land-use policies, urban renewal, and district versus at-large elections. Research on how decisions were made went beyond examining the formal decision making to include examination of agenda setting and manipulation of symbols. The authors found that there was indeed a pro-growth power structure. However, the power structure changed over time. Mechanisms evolved to increase democratic participation and flow of information and hence the degree of pluralism. These included changes in ownership of the newspaper from local to absentee and the change from at-large to district election of public officials. As pluralism increased, the strength of the pro-growth faction declined.

Trounstine and Christensen also found that as ownership of major firms in the area shifted from local to multinational companies, pluralism increased. The multinational firms were very interested in specific decisions directly affecting their operations but less interested in other decisions within the community, so their strategy was to decrease the range of their power but to keep it relatively strong in areas directly affecting their immediate financial interests.

There are a number of ways to identify which groups and individuals have power. Important vested interests in local communities need to be identified and linked to the exercise of community power. Participating groups will mainly define specific arenas in which power is sought and exercised.

WHO GAINS?

Joe and Ellen McDougal were able to enlist Hank Jones's influence in getting lights for the city park's baseball diamond. Had the issue been more sensitive, however, they might not have been so successful. Issues that directly affected Hank's feed and farm supply store, for example, might have had a different outcome. Sociology has long been concerned about power in modern society. A major sociological problem has been to determine which segments of the population gain from what kind of activities.

Studies of community power structures have shown that in different circumstances, different power actors are important. For example, upper-middle-class environmentalists have been able to confront the growth machine in certain U.S. cities (Molotch 1976). Other sociological studies show different winners. For example, a study by Clarence Lo (1990) suggests that the tax revolt in California began in working-class communities because these citizens were hard-pressed financially and felt that taxes were the reason they had little discretionary income (money to spend once basic expenses were paid) and that government was inefficient and uncaring. However, business interests joined that group to have an impact. Ultimately the tax revolt favored real estate developers.

From early studies that concentrated on a power elite that exercised monolithic control (Mills 1956), the focus has shifted to particular issues to reveal a range of who controls what and profits from it. Even rural communities such as Small Lake can have complex power structures. Political capital is key in determining not only how issues get resolved but also which situations become issues.

CHAPTER SUMMARY

Political capital can be transformed into built capital, social capital, cultural capital, and financial capital. That transformation is the exercise of power. Community power is the ability to affect the distribution of both public and private resources within the community. Power can be exercised by physical force, economic force, institutionalized force, and influence. The patterns in the exercise of community power are the community power structure. That structure affects communities and how they function.

Social scientists do not agree about how power is exercised, nor do they agree about how to measure it. Pluralism assumes that the capacity for acquiring power is widely distributed within the population. This model relies on the event analysis technique to detect and measure power. Researchers identify controversial public issues and then use the decision-making process employed to resolve those issues as a device to measure power. The elitist perspective of power assumes that power conforms to the way a community is stratified. Power is not widely dispersed; instead, it is held by just a few. Researchers who use an elitist model of power rely on the reputational technique to measure power, asking knowledgeable people in the community to identify those who have the greatest reputation for power.

The class-based theory of community power assumes that those who control the economic system control the community. A more recent variation of this model is the growth-machine model. The growth machine is a coalition of groups that perceive economic gain in community growth. This coalition exercises power to promote economic growth. The model has been applied successfully to urban areas. Rural communities differ more in terms of whether they project a pro-growth, smart-growth, or no-growth orientation.

To make power structures more pluralistic, broad participation in setting the community agenda is important. Once issues are made public, they need to be discussed and debated adequately. However, without the first two steps of community empowerment and broad participation in agenda setting, the final decision-making process of discussion, debate, and compromise is relatively meaningless.

KEY TERMS

Class-based analysis as a theory of power assumes that those who control the economic system control the community.

Community power is the ability to affect the distribution of both public and private resources within the community.

Community power structure consists of the patterns identified in the exercise of community power.

Elitism as a perspective of power assumes that power generally conforms to the social stratification system; wealth, prestige, and power tend to be associated with one another.

Event analysis is a research methodology that involves identifying and using controversial public issues to reveal the decision-making process.

Event analysis technique is the preferred strategy for measuring power from a pluralist perspective. Researchers identify controversial public issues and then look at the decision-making process used to resolve those issues. Those who make the decisions are deemed to have power in that issue area. Frequently, different issues are examined to determine if the same or different people exercise power across issues.

The *exchange value* of an object, such as a house, is its value to the owner insofar as it can be exchanged for money.

The *growth machine* is a coalition of groups that set about to use power to encourage growth and capture its benefits.

Network analysis is a way to measure power by looking at the patterns of linkages between organizations and individuals considered to be important in the community.

A *New England town meeting* is a form of direct representation where all residents in a geographic jurisdiction come together to make decisions on local policies, rules, regulations, and budgets.

Pluralism as a theory of power assumes power is an attribute of individuals and that the capacity for acquiring power is widely distributed within the population.

Power is the ability to make something happen that otherwise would not happen or to prevent something from happening that others wish to make happen.

The *rentier class* is made up of those whose principal income derives from rent or an increase in the value of property. It includes landlords of residential, commercial, and industrial establishments and of agricultural land as well as speculators in land and buildings.

Reputational technique measures power by asking knowledgeable members of a community who they think has power.

The *use value* of an object, such as a house, is its value to the owner for her own uses. Factors taken into consideration include comfort, sentimental value, prestige imparted by the object to the owner, pleasure in possessing or using the object, and so on.

REFERENCES

Crenson, Matthew A. 1971. *The Un-Politics of Air Pollution: A Study of Non-Decisionmaking in the Cities.* Baltimore: Johns Hopkins University Press.

Dahl, Robert. 1961. *Who Governs? Democracy and Power in an American City.* New Haven: Yale University Press.

Domhoff, G. William. 1967. *Who Rules America?* Englewood Cliffs, N.J.: Prentice-Hall.

———. 1983. *Who Rules America Now? A View for the '80s.* Englewood Cliffs, N.J.: Prentice-Hall.

Humphrey, Craig R., and Richard S. Krannich. 1980. "The Promotion of Growth in Small Urban Places and Its Impact on Population Change, 1975–78." *Social Science Quarterly* 61, no. 314:581–594.

Hunter, Floyd. 1953. *Community Power Structure.* Chapel Hill: University of North Carolina Press.

Hyman, Drew, Francis X. Higdon, and Kenneth E. Martin. 2001. "Reevaluating Community Power Structures in Modern Communities." *Journal of the Community Development Society* 32:251–270.

Hynes, Eugene, and Verna Mauney. 1990. "Elite Control and Citizen Mobilization in a Small Midwestern Town." *Critical Sociology* 17:81–98.

Lo, Clarence. 1990. *Small Property versus Big Government: Social Origins of the Property Tax Revolt.* Berkeley and Los Angeles: University of California Press.

Logan, John R., Rachel Bridges Whaley, and Kyle Crowder. 1997. "The Character and Consequences of Growth Regimes: An Assessment of 20 Years of Research." *Urban Affairs Review* 32:603–630.

Lynd, Robert S., and Helen Merrell Lynd. 1937. *Middletown in Transition: A Study in Cultural Conflicts.* New York: Harcourt, Brace, and World.

McGranahan, David A. 1990. "Entrepreneurial Climate in Small Towns." *Regional Science Review* 17:53–64.

Mills, C. Wright. 1956. *The Power Elite.* New York: Oxford University Press.

Molotch, Harvey. 1976. "The City as a Growth Machine." *American Journal of Sociology* 82, no. 2:309–330.

Polsby, Nelson W. 1960. "How to Study Community Power: The Pluralist Alternative." *Journal of Politics* 22 (August):474–484.

Ramsey, Meredith. 1996. *Community, Culture, and Economic Development: The Social Roots of Local Action.* New York: State University of New York Press.

Sharp, Jeff S., and Jan L. Flora. 1999. "Entrepreneurial Social Infrastructure and Growth Machine Characteristics Associated with Industrial-Recruitment and Self-Development Strategies in Nonmetropolitan Communities." *Journal of the Community Development Society* 30, no. 2:131–153.

Trounstine, Philip J., and Terry Christensen. 1982. *Movers and Shakers: The Study of Community Power.* New York: St. Martin's Press.

Vidich, Arthur, and Joseph Bensman. 1968. *Small Town in Mass Society.* Princeton, N.J.: Princeton University Press.

Wojan, Timothy R., and David A. McGranahan. 2007. "Ambient Returns: Creative Capital's Contribution to Local Manufacturing Competitiveness." *Agricultural and Resource Economics Review* 36:133–148.

7

FINANCIAL CAPITAL

Tina Fernandez wanted to be the first person in her family to go to college. A daughter of immigrant farm workers in the Rio Grande valley, a persistently poor region in Texas, she had started working in the fields when she was six years old. She was accustomed to hard work. Her parents could not afford to send her to college, so she decided to forgo her dream and marry her high school sweetheart. Unfortunately, the marriage lasted only three years, and Tina was left alone to raise a son. They moved back to the *colonia* to her parents' home, where she had someone she trusted to help care for her son and someone she loved to help put food on the table.

The economic downturn of the early 1990s made it difficult for her to find work, even with a high school diploma. She finally found a part-time job waiting tables at a locally owned restaurant in McAllen, a fifty-minute drive in her unreliable car, for less than minimum wage. Fortunately, her mother provided child care and her father was a skilled mechanic who kept many of the *colonia*'s cars running by swapping parts on the junkers he kept in his yard.

Her excellent service and friendly manner resulted in good tips, and the owner liked Tina's work ethic. She showed up regularly on time, followed directions—and even anticipated what the owner might ask next—and got along well with the cook and the other waitresses, for whom she served as peacemaker when tension arose in the restaurant. The owner began to depend on Tina to do some of the administrative tasks for the

restaurant and recognized her knack for business; soon Tina was pro-
moted to assistant manager, a full-time position with benefits. Encouraged by her parents, Tina took a night course in bookkeeping at the local
community college. Tina felt that she was earning the degree she had always wanted as she began to learn the inner workings of the restaurant
business. The owner acquired another restaurant in McAllen and made
Tina the manager.

Tina was making good money, but she knew that she wanted to be a
restaurant owner, an entrepreneur. However, she had only $7,000 in start-
up capital of her own to use, even after her parents and cousins loaned her
what they could. She decided to look at low-cost resources to help her start
a restaurant business of her own. She turned to a small-business development center for women to help her research and develop a successful business plan. The center informed her about alternative credit resources that
she could tap into for her start-up costs. Tina soon found out about a few
restaurant-supply companies that provided equipment for start-up businesses; the interest rates were favorable, and the equipment itself would become collateral. She would need many commercial appliances for her new
restaurant, and the expenses would be well above $7,000. She joined the
Latino chapter of the chamber of commerce in McAllen, despite the time
driving took away from her business and family. There she began network-
ing with local businesspeople who offered their expertise, including a few
investment bankers who offered more advice about alternative forms of
credit, including private placement deals where investment banks are offered *minority ownership* in exchange for capital to begin the business.
Within a few months, the plans were drawn up, and she had built up
enough social and financial capital to begin her entrepreneurial career.
Finding sources of alternative capital had been a key factor in her success.

Her restaurant, with its Latino flair, was a local hit. She hired dependable
waitstaff and trained them well. Her chef was new, but extremely creative
and talented. Within three years, Tina had opened two more restaurants in
the valley, and she had a great start on her son's college fund. She now lives
across the street from her parents and has added rooms and indoor plumbing to both dwellings, working with the barrio organization.

Financial capital is important because it can be transformed into more
productive labor as it is invested to increase human capital and built capital. Tina Fernandez needed financial and bridging social capital to convert
her idea into a profitable business. Yet for rural communities and busi-

nesses alike, there is a crisis of capital availability. As savers and investors are lured by higher profits outside the local area and are facilitated by new laws making it easier to move from one place to another, financial capital is becoming more and more mobile.

As capital becomes more mobile, rural communities lose control. Tina Fernandez had to go outside the *colonia* to build social capital that helped her learn how to access and invest financial capital. Her restaurant is one of the few in the *colonia,* and it is doing very well, attracting people from as far away as McAllen.

This chapter examines financial capital in its various forms. The extent to which communities depend on financial capital is explored, as are the various institutions created to provide loans to businesses. Traditional sources of financial capital are contrasted with the new sources rural communities must develop to adapt to the changing rules of the financial playing field.

THE CONCEPT OF FINANCIAL CAPITAL

The term financial capital often translates to money: the money needed to start a new business or the money used to *speculate* in the currency market. But money is not always financial capital, nor is financial capital simply money. This section explores the definition of financial capital, the various forms financial capital can take, and both the public and private character of financial capital.

Defining Financial Capital

Capital is any resource capable of producing other resources (see Chapter 1). Financial capital represents resources that are translated into monetary instruments that make them highly liquid, that is, able to be converted into other assets. This definition forces us to distinguish between consumption and investment. If you buy a car for personal enjoyment, the car is not considered a form of capital. But if you buy a car to run a shuttle service, the car becomes a means for generating income. A resource (the car) is capable of producing other resources (your income).

Although financial capital is more than just money, examples based on money are helpful in building a definition of financial capital. Money can be used for a variety of purposes. We use it to buy things, such as a new stereo or food for dinner (both goods), or a ticket to a movie or trash-collection services (both services). These uses of money are part of consumption (see Chapter 10). Money also can be used to make more money. Money invested in a savings bond, for example, generates more money in the form of interest. People invest money in a business because they expect to receive part of the profits in addition to the money they originally invested. Money is a form of financial capital when it is used to make more money.

Keeping Track of Financial Capital

Sociologists have been intrigued with the interaction between social organization and economic organization. Some theorists (Weber 1978) have suggested that the way money was accounted for can be linked to the emergence of capitalism. In earlier days, the most common form of accounting was cash accounting, keeping track of the money coming in and going out in a business. There was no way to keep track of exchanges in which money was converted to capital goods, as happens when a business invests in a new plant or accumulates an inventory. When accountants began keeping track of assets rather than simply of cash, capitalism as a form of economic organization began to emerge.

The scandals of the early twenty-first century around accounting practices—what was counted where for what—demonstrated the importance of having clear, standard rules and of a transparent presentation of financial assets. Energy companies falsified their profits, and at the same time they created artificial power shortages.

CEOs of publicly traded companies are generally assessed, and therefore given larger or smaller bonuses, on two things: the net worth of the company and its quarterly earnings. Lax accounting practices and lack of oversight allowed executives to inflate both during the 1990s. However, the story told to stockholders (who lost a great deal of money because of padded bottom lines) was not the same as was told to the U.S. government (which also lost a great deal of money because of tax avoidance by the companies and the CEOs). For example, publicly available data from 1996 to 1999 shows that Sprint (a single company) reported $5.8 billion more in earnings to its stockholders than to the Internal Revenue Service.

The cultural capital of major corporations and the accounting industry legitimated tax avoidance, overstated earnings, and maximized personal profit. The former commissioner of the U.S. Securities and Exchange Commission (SEC), Arthur Levitt, made this point clearly in the *Wall Street Journal* of June 17, 2002 (Pacelle 2002, 7):

Enron is not an aberration. What troubles me is that what is fueling these corporate implosions are not strategic misjudgments, the rise of new competitors, the sudden appearance of rival technologies, or even basic managerial mistakes. Instead, it is the uncovering of accounting irregularities, inflated balance sheets, and outright corporate deceit and malfeasance.

The SEC tried for ten years to reform the accounting industry, in the face of huge opposition mustered in Congress to block any changes, even passing retaliatory budget cuts for the agency. Political capital was mobilized to allow those who controlled financial capital to obscure what they were doing as they sought short-term personal and corporate economic gain. That cultural capital again was shown as the CEOs of money-losing corporations received huge salary increases and bonuses at the same time that stockholders lost money, workers were laid off, and pension funds were decimated.

Self-regulation seemed like a good idea. The thinking was that if one firm let another firm get away with something, its own reputation would be tarnished. Yet the opposite happened: If one firm let another get by with something, that firm would repay the favor. In performing "peer reviews" of each other, Big Five accounting firms repeatedly unearthed what the SEC staff considered major flaws in the way audits were conducted. Nevertheless, they gave each other clean bills of health in public reports of the reviews (Weil and Paltrow 2002).

Clearly, a number of institutions have to be in place for a modern economy to emerge and prosper. The people in those organizations and the conventions they have for keeping track of assets and evaluating loans play an important role in influencing who has access to financial capital. Do we need new conventions, new ways of keeping track of financial capital to support rural economies? The deregulation of banks and the increased mobility of financial capital in a global economy suggest that we need something new.

Forms of Financial Capital

The tangible forms of financial capital are relatively easy to identify. *Capital goods* (built capital) include the physical objects (cars, machines, buildings) that individuals or businesses invest in to generate new resources. A sawmill in Oakridge, Oregon, invests in the equipment needed to saw timber. The meatpacking plants in Garden City, Kansas, invest in the buildings, feedlots, and transportation equipment needed to move cattle in and processed meat out. *Land* becomes an investment because of the resources it has or the development space it offers. Timber companies purchase land, in part for existing stands of timber but also for the land's capacity to sustain new growths of timber. Real estate agents buy land, hoping to realize a profit if the land increases in value. Finally, *financial capital* includes financial instruments—stocks, bonds, derivatives, market futures, and letters of credit—as well as money.

Public Versus Private Capital

Capital can be further classified in terms of who invests it. When individuals or groups invest their own resources, they have used *private capital*. Land, buildings, equipment, and the inventory associated with a small business are part of its private-capital stock. Land owned by farm families, timber companies, or oil companies is private capital. The investment you make in your education is also an example of private capital.

Public capital refers to the resources invested by the community. Tax dollars are used to build roads, install sewer lines, maintain public parks, and finance schools. Governments raise the needed funds and then authorize their investment on behalf of the public good. Capital goods are then owned by the public, typically at the level of government involved in the original purchase. Communities own their street system or industrial park. Counties often own courthouses, county road systems, or landfills. The state owns its state road system and state universities. The federal government owns national parks and federal lands.

Public capital and private capital are often linked through partnerships. For example, some logging companies in the Northwest harvest trees on land owned by the U.S. Forest Service. The logging companies gain access to federal lands in exchange for fees paid to the government. Postsecondary education is funded by both public and private capital. When individuals pay tuition to attend colleges and universities, they are investing private capital in their own development. However, tuition covers only a fraction of the costs of maintaining public institutions. State tax dollars support public colleges and universities; city or county taxes support community colleges.

Mobility of Capital

These various forms of capital differ in how easily they can move. Land and many forms of capital goods, such as buildings and roads, are not mobile, so individuals and communities have to figure out how to make these forms of capital productive. By contrast, financial and human capitals are very mobile. Money can move to wherever it can earn the highest return. People can move to wherever they can earn the best salaries. The mobility of both causes problems for rural communities.

Financial capital has become increasingly mobile. Electronic transfers of capital can take place in seconds not only between communities on either coast but from a rural community to an urban center halfway around the world. Wealth created in New Hampshire can end up as an investment in California or Malaysia as savings deposits in the local bank become financial capital attracted to wherever the money can earn the highest rate of interest.

For example, a farmer in Iowa may sell a truckload of hogs when prices are high and costs of production are low. The profit made becomes savings that the farmer can now invest. That farmer phones a broker in Des Moines who buys shares in a New York–based mutual fund by computer. The mutual fund then invests in a garment factory in Malaysia, where the funds receive a higher return than they would have had they been invested in a garment factory in rural Iowa. Capital created in Iowa then turns into wages paid in Malaysia.

FINANCIAL CAPITAL AND COMMUNITY NEEDS

Nearly all rural communities have depended on financial capital from their very founding. Financial capital not only helps individuals set up homes and businesses but also enables local governments to provide roads, schools, sewers, and other services needed by community residents and businesses. This section examines the public and private needs for financial capital and describes the role played by rural financial institutions.

Public and Private Need for Capital

Seeking to expand and protect its boundaries, the federal government encouraged settlement of the frontier by making capital available in the form of land. During the settlement period, the government had few liquid assets, for the cost of wars kept the federal treasury in debt. Although many families homesteaded, much of the public lands went to large companies, such as railroads. The government encouraged the privatization of land by removing it from the public domain and selling it to private holders at reduced prices. This policy encouraged the development in rural communities of private capital held by businesses as well as individuals.

From its inception, the U.S. government recognized the role public financial capital played in community development and growth. First through the Northwest Ordinance of 1787, the federal government gave newly established communities land on which to build public goods (schools and roads) considered necessary for a community to exist and the nation to prosper. The United States and Canada are among the few nations of the world that grant local governments the power to raise public capital through local means, such as property taxes. This ability to tax gave communities a powerful tool by which to become self-reliant, unlike rural communities in other countries that have had to depend on the central government to finance roads, schools, or a water system.

The increasing cost of public services, combined with a decreasing population and tax base, has made most rural communities more dependent on state and federal sources of financial capital. In turn, this dependence has made communities less able to control their capital investments. For example, a school district that needs to introduce instruction in Spanish because of an influx of new migrants might instead find itself creating a gifted program because federal funds are available for the gifted program but not for the Spanish-language program. Despite the need to improve a local water system, a county board of supervisors might decide to lengthen a local airport runway, again because of the availability of federal funds. As communities find it increasingly difficult to raise financial capital locally, the locus of control for capital investment shifts to the state or federal level. Communities find themselves acting on state or federal priorities rather than on local ones.

To develop, communities require private capital other than land. Many rural communities originally depended in one way or another on farming. Agricultural production, unlike industrial production, is consecutive. Farmers must plow before they plant and plant before they harvest. There are long periods between the major production activities, particularly in crop production. Consequently, selling is done well after initial production decisions are made. That means that many farming communities have erratic income flows; a lot of money comes into the community when the harvest is sold, but little is generated at other times.

During the settlement period, women often sold eggs and cream throughout the year in an effort to even out income flow. When crops failed or a buyer could not be found, however, local residents created other mechanisms for generating financial capital. Individuals and groups formed banks or cooperative financial institutions to provide credit for both consumption and production loans. These institutions were especially important in communities dependent on agriculture, timber, and mining, because fluctuations in production—and therefore in income—often were typical.

Rural Financial Institutions

The names of many small-town banks, such as Miners and Merchants Bank (Grundy, Virginia), Farmers and Drovers Bank (Council Grove, Kansas), and Farmers and Miners Bank (Lucas, Iowa), reflect the character of the needs that led to their creation. Capital was also needed for small businesses (Merchants Bank) and for workers seeking credit between paydays (Union Bank). Rural banks generally had local roots and were structured much the same as other local businesses, being either privately held or organized as cooperatively held credit unions. What do the names of the banks in your community tell you about the history of financial capital there?

Because of the amount of capital and risk involved, banks generally formed corporations that separated the owners' assets from those of the bank. Incorporation is a legal strategy often used to limit personal liability. Banks that were incorporated were required to be chartered by the state or federal government. "State" in a bank's name means it is chartered under state law. The terms "national" or "federal" in a bank's name mean it is chartered with the federal government.

Banks make loans to individuals on the basis of risk. The lower the risk, the more inclined the banker is to advance the capital. Common factors used to assess risk include (1) net worth, (2) cash flow, and (3) personal knowledge of the borrower. As banks consolidate, the third factor to assess risk is used less and less. Instead, banks turn to individual credit ratings, which are privately controlled central databases (credit bureaus) of an individual's financial history, current assets, and liabilities.

Although some rural residents are wealthy in terms of land, that wealth has low *liquidity;* that is, it cannot easily be converted into cash. (This feature of land gave rise to the saying that one could be land-rich and money-poor.) When these individuals need money to invest in their businesses, they use their capital assets (land, livestock, or machinery) as collateral to guarantee the repayment of a loan.

For a financial institution, money that is deposited is carried as a debit, or liability, on its books. A *liability* is an obligation to pay back on demand to depositors the amount credited to their accounts. A loan, on the other hand, is an asset, because the bank is owed that money by a third person. A financial *asset* is money or property that can be used to meet liabilities.

Loans made on the basis of net worth compare collateral with indebtedness. Collateral is important to the lender, because if the loan is not repaid, the property can be claimed and sold to repay the loan. Loans based on net worth (the value of collateral minus outstanding indebtedness) are relatively safe loans to make, despite the fact that the lender assumes the assets will retain their value. Consequently, net worth is a traditional criterion for making a loan, introducing a bias into the flow of financial capital. Those who already have wealth are best able to acquire additional capital.

More adventurous bankers make loans based on a borrower's ability to repay. Determining ability to repay involves a detailed comparison of the costs of expanding production weighed against the increased sales that would result from expansion. Cash flow, not net worth, is the criterion for such loans. Determining cash flow involves gathering more data about a business operation than is necessary when the criterion for loaning money is net worth. It is also somewhat more inexact. Bankers have to estimate not only the future value of assets but also the future costs of needed inputs, future demand for the product, and future prices that will be paid for what is produced.

Basing loans on a borrower's ability to repay avoids the bias created when the net-worth method is used. Because the loan is based on an individual's future prospects for repaying the loan rather than on present assets, those with few assets can obtain a loan. However, loans based on the ability to repay introduce yet another bias. Those who can keep good accounts and work through cash-flow projections are more likely to receive loans. These loans favor the more educated individual.

Bankers in rural communities traditionally have had a third criterion for making loans: knowledge of the character of the borrower. In a sense, this is a shorthand way of calculating ability to pay. A young person known to be thrifty and hardworking could get a loan based on a handshake, indicative of the faith a banker put in the individual. In small-town settings, such loans were often biased against women and minorities, who were traditionally excluded from those considered worthy of credit. Bankers who know the community well are not likely to make bad loans—but they may fail to make some good loans.

This criterion was especially important in allowing those with little property an opportunity to become small-business owners. For the most part, however, this informal way of assessing risk is disappearing. Although state laws on branch banking and multibank holding companies vary, personal knowledge of the potential borrower by the individual with authority to make the loan is declining. As control of rural banks shifts to metropolitan areas, personal knowledge of the borrower is no longer valued as a method by which to assess risk.

In most cases a poor credit rating comes from two major events: divorce or medical emergencies. Poor credit ratings, in turn, increase financial vulnerability. Predatory lending—cash-on-demand and very high interest rates—is increasing in rural areas, further decreasing the money available to families.

SOURCES OF CAPITAL

To create more productive capacity or to get the inputs needed for production, individuals and businesses need capital. One way to get capital is to sell an asset. Another is to spend less money than taken in and thus accumulate savings. But many people, companies, and communities need a large amount of capital at one time to purchase a farm, a business, or a major piece of machinery. They do not have enough assets to sell to finance the purchase, and even if they did, selling those assets would mean selling their productive capacity. They also do not save enough to purchase the capital asset in a timely fashion. Therefore, they must borrow the money, which banks can provide in a number of ways.

Savings

For most people in the world, income seems insufficient to provide for the necessary expenses of family maintenance and reproduction. Others are able to take in more money than they spend in a given period of time, so they save it. Some savings are voluntary; others are involuntary, such as the contribution to Social Security or other government-mandated pension funds. Regardless of whether they are voluntary or involuntary, savings represent a major source of capital.

In most communities, savers with moderate incomes tend to deposit their money in their local financial institutions. This money is then reinvested by the bank, savings and loan, or credit union to earn interest. Despite the fact that rural financial institutions often offer somewhat lower interest rates than other institutions for savings and investment, rural banks remain a preferred investment for many citizens. Deposits in most rural banks steadily increased during the 1980s, but in the 1990s, deposits in these banks dropped due to the growing popularity of money-market and mutual funds. These investment alternatives offer services much like those of banks, including automatic teller machines (ATMs) and debit cards. In 1999, Congress passed the Gramm-Leach-Bliley Act, which increased small banks' access to Federal Home Loan Bank funds to finance agricultural, rural, small-business, and low-income community development investments (Dolan 2000). This membership offers many benefits for rural banks, including a steady source of long-term funds. It can provide rural credit markets with another source of liquidity, which may improve a bank's profits, since such funds are less costly than *core deposits*. This has compensated for the drop in deposits for some rural banks.

Interest

In lending money for a business, the lender generally secures the loan through the collateral of the capital goods acquired with the loan funds or through a lien on the product produced. In short, banks have the right to collect the capital goods purchased or the products produced by the business if it fails to repay the loan. There is also a charge to the borrower for use of the money, called *interest*. A portion of that money goes to the individuals whose savings are used to provide capital. This encourages them to put the excess capital they have into the bank instead of under their mattress or into the purchase of additional consumer goods. A portion of the interest remains with the bank, credit union, or savings and loan. These funds are used to cover the costs associated with managing the loan and to provide the bank with a profit.

The *nominal interest rate* (the interest rate charged to the borrower) varies according to the supply of money available for lending and the demand for money among competing borrowers. However, interest rates are not influenced by local supply and demand for capital. Even in isolated rural communities, interest rates are set daily responding to monetary and fiscal policies adopted by U.S. and foreign governments. This control decreases the ability of local institutions to redeploy capital to local investments.

To compete in the global financial market, projects must have high rates of return and low risk. Investments in rural communities traditionally are the reverse: low return and high risk. As interest rates become bound to global markets, capital leaves rural areas. This phenomenon, known as *capital flight,* describes the extent to which capital originally invested in rural areas eventually is moved elsewhere in search of a higher return.

Interest rates indicate the costs of capital. When interest rates are high, fewer people are able to borrow. When rates are low, more people may be inclined to borrow because it appears easier and cheaper to pay back the loan and interest on it. However, it is important to calculate the *real interest rate,* which is the nominal interest rate minus the rate of inflation. This is the real cost of capital.

In periods of high inflation, nominal interest rates are high, but they are often exceeded by the rate of inflation. In this case, it pays to borrow. The interest charged for the loan is less than the increased value of whatever was purchased. Savers, on the other hand, often lose money on bank deposits, bonds, and other ordinary financial investments. Consequently, they often look for investments whose market price will rise at a rate likely to equal or exceed the inflation rate. Commodities or real estate are frequent choices for such investments. During the 1970s, for example, farmland and urban real estate prices escalated at an extremely rapid rate as investors sought inflation-proof investment opportunities. During the 1990s, farmland prices increased, but at a more gradual rate than during the 1970s. By 2002, prices for farmland had doubled from what they were in the mid–1980s; however, even with the increase, prices when adjusted for inflation were still 15 percent below what they had been in the 1970s. Urban real estate prices declined in the 1990s, whereas prices for real estate in rural areas increased. In many regions, rural areas grew more rapidly because of new housing developments that were built on the metropolitan fringe.

Local banks cannot provide the required financial capital for larger or more risky investments. The risk may be too great, the amount needed may be too large, or the banker may simply lack the expertise to judge the appropriate loan period and rate of return. Rural banks accustomed to making agricultural loans may be unsure when asked to finance a cabinet factory, for example. Agricultural loans are equally difficult for urban banks to evaluate. Several other sources of private financial capital are available for such undertakings, such as bonds and equity capital.

Bonds

When a large amount of financial capital is needed for a long-term capital investment, loans can be made in more formal contractual agreements, such as bonds. Bonds pay interest and constitute a promise of repayment of a designated amount of money (often more than the amount received as a loan) at the end of an established period of time, usually twenty or thirty years. Businesses can pledge securities or future income to repay the money raised through bonds.

In the 1980s, deregulation of U.S. financial markets allowed the marketing of *junk bonds,* high-risk, high-interest securities that often are sold at a deep *discount,* an amount well below their face value. The money raised by these bonds was converted into equity capital in new or established businesses. Because the businesses were risky, the bonds paid high rates of interest. Most of these ventures were in urban areas, drawing financial capital out of rural areas. When the businesses failed, many savings and loan institutions, which had invested in venture capital firms and in urban real estate, went under. Rural people contributed to the bailout of urban savings and loans through their taxes.

Governments, including rural towns and counties, can issue municipal bonds to raise public financial capital. Usually state law disallows the use of bonds to pay the operating expenses of local governments, schools, and hospitals but permits their use to support buildings or structural improvements. These bonds are guaranteed by the good faith and taxing power of the issuing government. The U.S. government feels so strongly that these local financing mechanisms should be in place that interest earned from personal and corporate investment in these bonds is usually tax-free; this feature provides additional incentive to make financial capital available to local communities.

Bonds are an important mechanism by which rural communities raise financial capital but retain local control. Industrial revenue bonds, for example, can provide investment capital for a local firm. Too often, however, the money raised by such bonds goes to attract a business from another area rather than to create a local firm. Communities run the risk that the business will eventually move, despite local efforts to make it financially attractive for the firm to stay. Privately issued, publicly regulated bonds can provide an important source of seed financial capital for new firms or investment capital for local firms wishing to expand.

Equity Financial Capital

Sometimes a business has neither enough capital assets to provide collateral for a loan nor the proven excess of income over expenses to ensure a steady repayment of further indebtedness. In this case, other sources of financial capital must be found.

One mechanism is to "go public," selling shares in the company to the general public through the stock market. Individuals with savings (or other access to financial capital) invest in shares of the company. In exchange for their financial capital investment, these individuals receive a portion of the company's profits in the form of dividends paid on their shares. Stockholders can also make (or lose) money on their investments by selling their shares on a stock exchange.

Once a business has decided to sell stock, the company no longer belongs solely to the original business owner. However, the company's assets have increased as a result of the capital investment of the new shareholders. The business's equity is still defined as the total assets less the total liabilities, but the partners or stockholders now hold that equity. In exchange for the financial capital invested in the company, the partners or stockholders share in determining who will manage the company and how it is managed.

Employees can become owners as a way to raise capital through wages invested in the company or through stock earned through bonuses. Such stock options were given by many start-up companies in the 1990s as a way to attract talented, highly skilled workers. Partial ownership in a business can be a way to attract reliable labor in areas where there are relatively few available workers (see Box 7.1).

The market price of stock is largely dependent on the company's earnings. Stocks are of two types. Preferred stock guarantees a dividend of a specified rate and a specified portion of the assets if the corporation is liquidated. Common stock has a rate of return that fluctuates depending on the corporation's profits. Stockholders have voting rights in choosing the company's management. Their votes are weighted according to the amount of stock owned. These votes are used to select the board of directors, which then sets policy and names the CEO of the corporation. In seeking financial capital by selling equity, a business owner gives up management control.

Once companies have started up, they often need a high level of initial capital investment to upgrade technology and develop markets. Furthermore, they require financial capital that comes from investors who are

BOX 7.1 WORKERS AS PART OWNERS

Jose Hernandez is going to be able to retire well someday. At forty-one years old, he has accumulated more than $80,000, and he works only from April to November, for $20,000 a year. As a migrant worker, he has worked hard all his life, but fortunately he has worked for a company that takes care of its workers.

Migrant workers at McKay Nursery in Waterloo, Wisconsin, are reaping the benefits of their difficult work. The nursery has always been known for its generous employee benefits, such as paying migrants overtime, which is very unusual. In 1984, McKay took an extremely bold step and began offering its workers shares in the company through employee stock ownership plans. In 1998, the company employed sixty full-time workers and nearly a hundred migrant workers at the height of growing season. Migrants are eligible for the plan once they have worked 1,000 hours in a season, which goes from late March through the end of November. Workers are promised that at least 10 percent of their gross wages for the year will be set aside for retirement; the amount depends on how much the company earns for the year and how many employees it has. Typically, workers have had 20 percent to 25 percent of their wages set aside, and they can then invest the cash portion in a variety of mutual funds. Money in the workers' retirement plans cannot be withdrawn until they have been with the company for five years. At that time, they can take money out to pay for college bills or to purchase a home. Workers who decide to leave after five years take the cash with them after they sell their shares back to the company.

The nursery's president, Griff Mason, admits that hiring on a seasonal basis is difficult, and it was challenging to find dependable workers—until he started this plan. Since migrant workers are a critical component to the company's success, he wanted to ensure that many would return every year. As word spread to friends and family members of the migrant workers employed at McKay, the nursery saw a return rate of 90 percent. McKay has found that building human capital and social capital within the migrant worker community has enhanced the financial capital not only of the workers but also of his business.

SOURCE

Jonathan Kaufman. 1998. "Sharing the Wealth." *Wall Street Journal,* April 9. www.mckaynursery.com/employment.asp; accessed August 5, 2007.

willing to take risks and be patient as they wait for a return. This kind of equity capital is referred to as *venture capital.* Some have argued that a shortage of venture capital stifles would-be entrepreneurs and as a result retards growth and development.

The availability of venture capital boomed in the 1990s due to the rise of technology companies. In 2000, venture capital investment in the United States reached $35.6 billion, a high never seen before. In 2006, venture capital investment was down from its previous high, to $26.1 billion for the year (Money Tree Report 2007), but still was far higher than during the 1980s. Venture capital brings with it a say in the management of the company. For start-up businesses, this access to human and social capital often is as helpful as the access to financial capital.

Although selling stock is a useful strategy for raising business financial capital, it is not always viable in rural areas. To sell stock on a stock exchange, a business must meet several requirements related to financial disclosure. For small companies in rural areas, putting these statements of financial disclosure together can be expensive relative to the amount of financial capital being raised.

THE CHANGING RULES OF FINANCIAL CAPITAL

One of the reasons banks were chartered by states or the federal government was to ensure that financial capital would be available locally for local investments. But the control exercised by government and thus the risk involved for the rural community have varied over time. Entering banking was easier when the National Bank of the United States (a forerunner of the Federal Reserve banking system) did not exercise disciplinary and restraining influences; control was loose during the periods 1781–1791, 1811–1816, and 1837–1863. State charters were the exclusive method for creating banking corporations during these periods. During the era of unregulated banking between the 1830s and the 1920s, any entrepreneur who could meet minimal capitalization standards to set up a bank could obtain a state charter. Banks proliferated, particularly in rural communities, peaking at thirty thousand banks in the United States in 1921.

The Age of Regulation

More than ten thousand banks, a large proportion of which were in rural communities, failed during the Great Depression of 1929–1933. The

Banking Act of 1933 established more demanding criteria for charters, including tougher requirements for capitalization and management based on the convenience and needs of the community along with competitive circumstances.

Other limitations were placed on banks in 1933, setting lending limits, limiting insider lending, and restricting bank investments. Interest-rate ceilings were established, and interest was prohibited on *demand deposits*—that is, deposits, such as checking accounts, whose account holders could demand their money at any time. In 1933, the *Federal Deposit Insurance Corporation (FDIC)* became a supervisory agency for all national banks and state banks seeking protection for their depositors. *Federal deposit insurance* offers borrowers insurance on deposits up to $100,000 in banks that agree to be supervised by the FDIC. Few rural banks were established once the regulations were enacted, but few banks failed. In regulating banking activities, the government played a major role in reducing the financial risk to society.

These regulations, which were in effect between the mid–1930s and the early 1980s, specified that different organizations should specialize in different financial functions. For example, banks could not engage in real estate brokerage. Thrift institutions (savings and loans) were forbidden to offer demand-deposit accounts. These prohibitions had two major purposes: (1) to further certain social goals, such as home ownership, and (2) to prevent conflicts of interest within individual firms. As Anthony Downs, an economist concerned about the real estate capital markets and real estate finance, points out,

> Congress apparently believed that the average patron of each financial institution should not have to pass prior judgment on the quality of that institution's management in order to have confidence that the institution's assets would be prudently handled. Such judgments would require knowledge and expertise far beyond the capabilities of the average citizen. (1985, 41–42)

Federal regulatory agencies therefore were established to provide collective supervision of financial institutions, to oversee the safety and socially responsible use of financial capital.

Bank regulation provided a governmental mechanism whereby public trust could be maintained in the major institution that linked financial capital to producers and consumers. In return for the security provided to savers through state and federal deposit insurance, financial capital was made available to borrowers. Public trust in banks and thrifts was gained not only through the insurance of savings but through the oversight provided by the federal and state regulatory agencies.

Deregulation

With the shift in the world economy, which involved devaluation of the dollar in 1971 and the rise in oil prices in 1973, there was a substantial decrease in the real cost of money as a result of inflation. Savers found they could get higher yields from uncontrolled financial institutions by putting their money into newly developed financial instruments, such as *money market funds*. Banks found that they did not have the financial capital to lend at the rates they were legally able to offer; in other words, they were no longer competitive.

In the 1970s, rural areas found their locally owned and controlled financial institutions competing with nonfinancial institutions not restricted by banking regulations, such as Sears and Merrill Lynch. These institutions, which are multinational in character, channeled financial capital out of rural areas by offering investment opportunities such as money-market funds. A financial capital exodus from traditional banks, including rural community banks, occurred as savers increasingly sought higher interest rates elsewhere.

In addition, the savings and loan institutions, which traditionally had lent money for long-term real estate purchases, found that the short-term interest rates they had to pay to attract depositors far exceeded the long-term rates they were charging borrowers. In the early 1980s, savings and loan institutions were given the right to engage in activities formerly reserved for other institutions in an attempt to shore up their profitability. These changes offered short-term help for savings and loans, but rural banks lost their competitive edge.

Banking deregulation involves a decrease in the degree to which the government limits and oversees (1) the costs of credit and services, (2) the geographic location of financial institutions, and (3) the variety of services offered by financial institutions. The goal has been to increase the *efficiency* of distribution of financial capital. What the lawmakers mean by efficiency is the ability of funds to move to where they offer the investor the greatest possible return consistent with the risk involved in their use. With deregulation, return on investment is assessed over an increasingly shorter time frame.

Deregulation has made it relatively easy for financial institutions to capture savings from rural areas and add these funds to a national pool of financial capital that can be directed wherever the highest short-term profit can be made. From the rural perspective, it has become increasingly difficult to keep local financial capital invested locally. Facilitated by a variety of national policies, financial capital now flows easily from one city to another or from one country to another. This international financial capital market has increased the outflow of financial capital from rural areas.

Bankers and other lenders see investments in rural communities as having high risk and low payoffs compared to other options. Deregulation has increased the relative cost of credit for rural areas as compared with urban areas and decreased the availability of credit for rural borrowers. It has further decreased the availability of financial services for the rural poor. The balanced exchange of public trust through regulation and deposit insurance has been moved off center. Gary Green, a rural sociologist who has studied rural banking extensively, advocates reregulation of a type that permits greater flexibility in the form and content of banking practices and organizational structure in return for social responsibility on the part of banks, including reinvestment in rural communities.

BUSINESS FINANCIAL CAPITAL AND COMMUNITY

For the most part, financial capital has always been less available in rural areas than in urban areas. Changes in the U.S. financial market recently have made it increasingly difficult for rural areas to attract and retain financial capital. This section explores some of the strategies by which financial capital can be attracted to and retained in rural communities.

Keeping Financial Capital Local

In many ways, banks and other lending institutions are like other businesses in rural communities. They also require investment capital, not just savings, to get started. Individuals wanting to start a bank or purchase an existing one take out an individual or business loan from another financial institution.

Starting or acquiring a bank often requires more financial capital than can be obtained through the usual loan procedure. Increasingly, banks require equity capital gained from stockholders. As more and more of those stockholders and owners come from outside the community, concern mounts that decisions on the use of savings deposited in the bank will be used in ways that benefit the shareholders but not necessarily the community. Under the previous ownership pattern, local owners were more likely to perceive benefits that were more consistent with benefiting the community.

Because banks and thrifts enjoy special privileges from the public sector in terms of deposit insurance and oversight, many think that banks should be required to serve the public good as well as stockholders' short-term interests. For banks, however, it is difficult to argue that the interests of the stockholders, who may now live anywhere in the world, are identical with those of the community. Stockholders tend to encourage financial capital use that favors short-term gain, which pays them higher dividends and makes their stocks worth more. This conflicts with the needs of communities, which often need "patient" capital that can be invested locally. This use of financial capital emphasizes long-term gain in recognition of the multiplier effect such financial capital can have in the community. The *multiplier* is the extent to which money is recirculated in the local economy. In the example shown in Figure 7.1, each dollar turns over six times before leaving the locality and has a cumulative impact on the local currency of $1.66.

The extent to which financial capital leaves a community can be seen in the declining loan-to-deposit ratios among rural banks. A decreasing ratio means that less of the money deposited by community residents is being reinvested in the community through loans. Instead, the money deposited is exiting the community through urban municipal bonds, certificates of deposits at larger banks, and government securities. The farm crisis significantly reduced traditional loan opportunities in rural communities, and bankers have not found it easy to identify nontraditional loan options.

The Community Reinvestment Act of 1977 encouraged banks to invest their financial capital within the local community. The legislation was aimed primarily at poor urban areas, and few rural banks were forced to reinvest in rural communities under the terms of the act. Until the farm crisis of 1982, lack of rural reinvestment did not appear to be a major problem. Rural banks were eager and able to make agricultural loans

Figure 7.1   Income Multiplier

Capital and Community

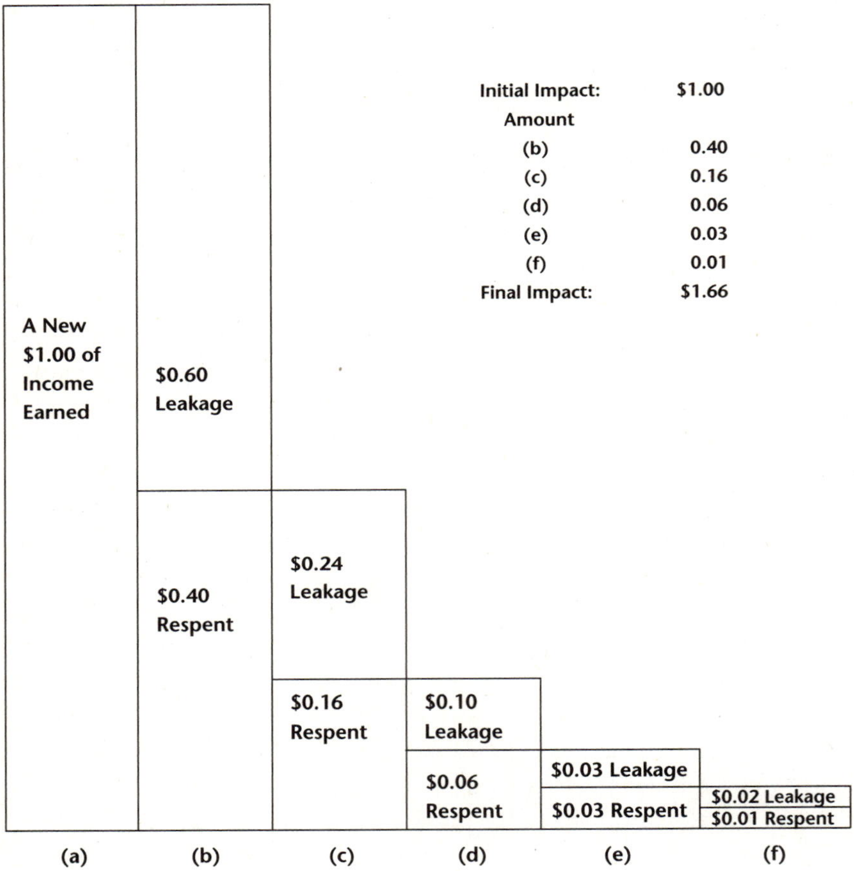

	Amount
Initial Impact:	$1.00
Amount	
(b)	0.40
(c)	0.16
(d)	0.06
(e)	0.03
(f)	0.01
Final Impact:	$1.66

A New $1.00 of Income Earned

$0.60 Leakage

$0.40 Respent

$0.24 Leakage

$0.16 Respent

$0.10 Leakage

$0.06 Respent

$0.03 Leakage

$0.03 Respent

$0.02 Leakage

$0.01 Respent

(a)   (b)   (c)   (d)   (e)   (f)

locally and they often diversified with energy-related loans. The Community Reinvestment Act was revised in 1995, and regulations were put into place to reduce paperwork for evaluation. This new revision, named the Brownfields Act, worked in conjunction with the Environmental Protection Agency to help clean up and restore industrial sites in low-to-moderate-income communities. This action eased fears of financial regulations, liability, and burdens.

Government securities are used to finance the federal debt. They are either short-term or long-term securities sold by the federal government. Rural banks have a much greater percentage of their assets in government securities than do urban banks.

New Sources of Financial Capital

Traditional ways of generating financial capital for rural communities now appear to be inadequate. Indeed, the flow of financial capital from rural areas seems to have exceeded the out-migration of people. Governments as well as private entities and new public-private ventures are attempting to generate investment financial capital in new ways. By 2001, thirty-seven states had implemented targeted investment programs for rural areas. These states subsidize loans or offer loan guarantee programs, grants, tax abatements, or other financial incentives to businesses that process agricultural products (Kilkenny and Schluter 2001).

Rural communities and regions can create community foundations to capture some of the intergenerational transfer of wealth that is expected to take place between 2000 and 2020 as elders who acquired wealth in the 1980s and 1990s die. These foundations provide a number of ways for individual citizens to contribute to a fund that, through the interest it earns, then is invested in their communities in both public and private ventures. The Montana Community Foundation has worked hard to build these funds by utilizing political capital to maintain state tax deductions for charitable contributions. Nebraska and other states have enacted similar legislation.

Rural-based venture capital funds are also in place, such as Northeast Ventures in Minnesota. In response to economic restructuring in Minnesota's Iron Range as the mines closed, in 1989 Northeast Ventures was developed to intervene strategically to reduce dependence on a single industry that was in turn dependent on the fickle steel market. Northeast Ventures has the Northeast Entrepreneur Fund, which provides loans and guidance to firms, and the Northeast Ventures Corporation, which makes equity investments in home-grown companies.

Congress created the Community Development Financial Institution Fund in 1994 to expand the availability of credit, investment capital, and financial services in distressed urban and rural communities. By stimulating the creation and expansion of diverse locally based community development financial institutions (CDFIs) and by providing incentives to traditional banks and thrifts, the fund's investments strengthen private markets, creating healthy local tax revenues, and empowering residents. CDFIs are specialized financial institutions that work in local market niches that have not been adequately served by traditional financial institutions. CDFIs provide a wide range of financial products and services, including mortgage financing for first-time home buyers, financing for needed community facilities, commercial loans and investments to start or expand small businesses, loans to rehabilitate rental housing, and financial services needed by low-income households and local businesses.

The Lakota Fund was established in 1986 by members of the Oglala Lakota tribe to develop a private sector in the Pine Ridge Reservation in South Dakota. The fund was certified as a CDFI in 1999, giving it access to additional sources of financial capital. The goal was to help tribal entrepreneurs establish jobs, products, and services close to home. New businesses were started by Lakota people on the reservation, and the Lakota Fund diversified to meet other needs for financial capital, including a fund for housing.

Many of these nontraditional lenders and investors are successful because they offer far more than financial capital. They also increase the human and social capital of the entrepreneurs with whom they work. Michelle Sweedman has cared for children in her own home in Bigfork, Minnesota, ever since her first child was born. More and more families came to her seeking high-quality child care, but she could take care of only four children at a time, given her space. She saw the need in the community for affordable, high-quality child care and felt that she could hire a few more child care workers and set up a real business that would increase her income and serve the community. But she had no business experience, and only about $150 in savings. The Northeast Entrepreneur Fund showed her how to plan her business and manage income and expenses, and it then lent her the down payment on a suitable house. She now has two employees who, like Michelle, are working on a child care credential on the weekends at Itasca Community College.

Financial Capital Retention through Risk Reduction

Risk to commercial banks on any given loan can be reduced through the use of secondary markets for rural business loans. Secondary markets allow rural banks to package together a number of business loans, which they initiate and service; investors who purchase those securities bear the risk. Such secondary markets have been in place for many years for home mortgages and were initiated for farm loans in 1989. This approach to sharing risk could help rural banks recirculate local financial capital within the community.

Another way to make loans less risky is to provide technical assistance in such areas as personnel management, marketing, accounting, and planning. Both the Small Business Administration of the federal government and the Cooperative Extension Service at the state and local levels have programs that aid small businesses and that can be tied to financial capital investment. Microfinance organizations have been successful because of the social capital and human capital investment that accompany loans.

Loan guarantees by the state and federal governments spread the risk of financial capital investment in rural areas between the public and private sectors. Such guarantees function much as does the student loan program, in which private banks make the loan. The individual who borrows the money is obligated to repay the financial capital plus interest, usually at below-market rates. The federal government guarantees that the lender will be repaid at least a certain percentage of the initial loan if the borrower defaults. This strategy is cheaper than if the government makes capital investment directly, and it allows financial capital to be invested in a far greater number of enterprises.

Government's Indirect Role

Another way that governments direct financial capital is through tax concessions. Tax abatements reduce taxes for investments that are made in certain business ventures deemed socially desirable. Alone among developed countries, the United States has viewed home ownership as so socially desirable that its tax code allows a federal tax deduction of all interest paid on home mortgages and local taxes on homes.

Other laws reduce the tax burden of those who invest in specific geographic areas by starting new businesses or expanding existing firms. Governments offer tax abatements in an effort to attract industry. The problem with this strategy is that although it benefits private financial capital investment in a specific area, it may not increase total financial capital investment in the nation. Furthermore, the tax breaks given often increase the need for public financial capital investment in the form of schools, prisons, fire stations, sewers, and roads. The reduced taxation offered to new businesses erodes the tax base needed to support public financial capital investments.

More and more communities are trying to retain financial capital locally by stopping financial capital leakage and forming local corporations and cooperatives to generate financial capital and invest it locally. When successful, these enterprises build on the strengths of an area and the solidarity of its citizens. Such mechanisms of financial capital generation increase local control. They also tend to have a longer-term time frame than do firms brought in from the outside that have stockholders who provided financial capital in the hopes of reaping short-term gains.

Firms recruited from the outside are often branch plants of large multinational firms that are seeking some advantage such as cheap land or lower wage scales. Transplants often create real difficulties for local financial capital formation in rural communities. Among the problems are low-wage employment, few purchases of local inputs for production, and cutbacks and shutdowns that are more frequent and more likely because of the absentee nature of ownership and management. Still, such an option has great allure for a desperate rural community.

Recent studies have pointed to the weakness such short-term approaches have inserted into community development efforts. Rural communities are being forced to address the problems created by rapid financial capital movement to capture short-term gain. As rural areas organize to create options in providing public and private financial capital needed for their communities to function, they may generate alternative investment models that strengthen the economic base of the country. The Earned Income Tax Credit (EITC) is a federal tax benefit for low- and moderate-income workers—the working poor—who are eligible for and claim the credit. The credit reduces the impact of payroll and income taxes paid by these workers, supplements the earnings of very low-wage workers, and may be returned in the form of an IRS refund check.

Many families with children who qualify for the EITC may also be eligible for the Child Tax Credit (CTC), which reduces federal income tax liability. Some low-wage families who don't earn enough to owe income tax may still qualify for a CTC refund (Center for Budget and Policy Priorities 2007). It is often more difficult for low-income rural workers to file the appropriate papers than for urban workers because they lack the assistance network to help them do so.

Alternative Sources of Financial Capital for Rural Communities

Federal programs have long recognized the need to make capital available for investment in rural America. Rural utilities receive low-interest government loans. Although those rural electric cooperatives had nearly $11 billion of outside investments in 1997, only $61 million (0.5 percent) went into local business ventures or rural infrastructure. Rural utilities could be an important source of capital for rural America if they were to actually invest locally or in other rural places (to spread their risk).

Most banks are making it more and more expensive to be an account holder, requiring higher minimum balances and charging higher fees for services. Yet poor people need to cash checks, wire money to relatives, pay bills, and borrow money in a pinch. The number of check-cashing outlets doubled between 1996 and 2001, and they charge 3 percent of a check's face value when they cash it. Many individuals who wire money to their relatives do not realize that a substantial proportion of what they send does not actually reach the recipient, even though they have paid a sending fee, because each financial institution through which the transaction passes takes its cut. These same outlets also offer loans, charging annual rates of 300 percent to 400 percent per year. And when people conduct financial transactions through these outlets, they do not build a credit history and are not offered a way to save some of the money so they will not need a payday lender the next time the car breaks down.

Most federal funds to rural areas are in the form of a variety of commodity payments. These are highest in some of the poorest rural counties in the United States. *The Mississippi Analysis* by the Southern Rural Development Initiative found that for every dollar spent on rural development in the 364 poorest counties in America, $15.65 went to agricultural commodity direct payments—most of it to a small number of very large farm operations.

CHAPTER SUMMARY

Capital is any resource capable of producing other resources. Financial capital consists of instruments that express exchange value and that have a high degree of liquidity compared to other forms of capital. When individuals or groups invest their own resources, they have used private capital. Public capital comprises the resources invested by the community.

The forms of capital differ in how easily they can move. Natural capital, social capital, and some forms of built capital are relatively immobile. Human capital is somewhat mobile, and financial capital is highly mobile. The mobility of political and cultural capital varies; for excluded peoples, it is relatively immobile.

Nearly all communities depend on financial capital, either for private investment in local businesses or for public investment in community services. Communities often have relied on federal and state governments in gaining access to financial capital for local improvements. Individual businesses have turned to local banks. Traditionally, rural banks have made business loans based on an individual's net worth or cash flow, or a banker's knowledge of that individual. As control of rural banks shifts to metropolitan areas, this last criterion becomes less important.

Financial capital is available from a number of sources. Businesses take out loans for which interest is charged. Businesses can also choose to sell stock to raise the financial capital needed. In exchange for making financial capital available to the business, stockholders participate in selecting the management of the company and share any profits. Municipal bonds typically are used as a device by which communities borrow the larger amounts of money needed for financial capital improvements.

Deregulation of the banking industry in the early 1980s changed the economic environment in which rural banks functioned. In limiting the interest rates that could be charged for loans or paid out on deposits, banking regulations had been more favorable to rural banks. When the regulations were dropped, financial capital began moving to where it could earn the highest short-term return. Financial capital began to flow out of rural areas. Rural communities are working to retain local financial capital, reduce the risk associated with local investments, identify innovative sources of venture capital, and enlist governmental help in making financial capital available to rural businesses.

KEY TERMS

A financial *asset* is money or properties that can be used to meet liabilities (debts owed). Assets minus liabilities equals net worth.

Capital is defined as resources capable of producing other resources.

Capital flight occurs when funds originally invested or generated in a particular area are moved in order to take advantage of increased earnings elsewhere.

Capital goods consist of objects used to produce other goods or resources.

Collateral, or assets of a borrower that can be sold for cash, is required by many lenders to secure a loan. If the loan is not repaid by the borrower, the lender takes possession of the assets, which it then sells to repay the loan.

Consumption is the use of goods and services for personal enjoyment, which removes them from the stock of goods and services available.

Core deposits are acquired in a bank's natural market area, counted as a stable source of funds for lending. These deposits have a predictable cost, imply a degree of customer loyalty, and are less interest-rate sensitive than short-term certificates of deposit and money market deposit accounts. Included are small-denomination time deposits and checking accounts.

Demand deposits are deposits in commercial banks and savings institutions that may be withdrawn upon demand of the lender.

Discount refers to the sale of a security at a price lower than its face value or to a loan on which the lender withholds interest from the principal amount, lending only the net amount (a "discounted" loan).

Efficiency describes the goal of allocating capital in different places to maximize the return on the investment, given the level of risk.

Equity is the net worth of a firm or corporation (total assets less total liabilities) belonging to the partners or stockholders.

Federal deposit insurance is a federal program that insures each deposit account to a level of $100,000 and that will provide up to $100,000 to depositors of failed banks and thrift institutions that are insured by the FDIC, the Federal Savings and Loan Insurance Corporation (FSLIC), or other federally sponsored insurance agencies.

Federal Deposit Insurance Corporation (FDIC) is an agency created in 1933 to provide insurance for bank depositors and supervision of insured banks.

Federal Reserve Act of 1913 is the legislation that created the Federal Reserve system to stop recurring money panics through pooling and lending bank reserves.

Financial capital includes stocks, bonds, market futures, and letters of credit as well as money.

Government securities are either short-term or long-term promises to pay sold by the federal government, such as U.S. savings bonds.

Interest is the charge made for borrowed money.

Junk bonds are high-interest, high-risk securities that are sold at a deep discount, that is, at an amount well below their face value.

Land is a form of natural capital when it is used to produce other resources.

Liability is the claims of creditors.

Liquidity is the difficulty and cost of converting assets into money. The greater the degree of liquidity, the faster and cheaper the conversion process.

Minority ownership is the status of an investor who owns less than 50 percent of a business. Minority ownership entitles an investor to a voice and part of the profits, but not control of the business.

Money market funds are a type of mutual fund that invests in short-term (less than a year) debt securities of U.S. government agencies, banks and corporations, and U.S. treasury bills.

A *multiplier* is the degree to which change in aggregate demand causes a further change in aggregate economic output.

Municipal bonds are debt obligations of a state, locality, or municipal corporation. Interest on these bonds is exempt from U.S. income taxes.

National Banking Act of 1863 was the first legislative step in the United States toward establishing a stable and uniform currency. It required that all nationally chartered banks meet uniform regulations, back their note issues with government bonds, limit the amount issued to their paid-in capital, and maintain a fund of lawful money in the U.S. Treasury for bond redemption.

Nominal interest rate is the stated or published percentage cost or return on capital, not corrected for inflation.

Private capital is capital owned and controlled by individuals or groups of individuals.

Public capital is capital owned and controlled by governments or communities, such as public schools or bridges.

Real interest rate is the nominal interest rate minus the rate of inflation.

Investors *speculate* when they invest in an asset in the hope it will greatly increase in value. The profit (or loss) is made from the difference in the buying price from the selling price, not from what the asset produces.

Stock options are opportunities given to employees to buy stock at pre-determined prices in the company that employs them. Start-up companies that cannot pay competitive salaries often use stock options to attract highly skilled workers and executives.

Venture capital is the capital provided by investors willing to take a higher than average risk for an anticipated higher than average profit in an expanding but capital-short enterprise.

References

Center for Budget and Policy Priorities. 2007. "The Earned Income Tax Credit." Online; available: www.cbpp.org/pubs/eitc.htm; accessed September 9, 2007.

Dolan, Julie. 2000. "Rural Banks and the Federal Home Loan Bank System." *Rural America* 15, no. 3:44–49.

Downs, Anthony. 1985. *The Revolution in Real Estate Finance.* Washington, D.C.: Brookings Institution.

Green, Gary. 1991. "Rural Banking." In *Rural Policies for the 1990s,* ed. C. B. Flora and J. A. Christenson, 36–46. Boulder, Colo.: Westview.

Kilkenny, Maureen, and Gerald Schluter. 2001. "Value-Added Agriculture Policies across the 50 States." *Rural America* 16, no. 1: 12–18. Also online; available: www.ers.usda.gov/publications/ruralamerica/ra161/ra161c.pdf; accessed September 9, 2007.

Money Tree Report. 2007. Online; available: www.pwcmoneytree.com/MTPublic/ns/index.jsp; accessed September 9, 2007.

Pacelle, Mitchell. 2002. "Former SEC Chairman Levitt Decries Business Ethics in U.S." *Wall Street Journal,* June 17, C7.

Weber, Max. 1978. *Economy and Society.* Vols. 1 and 2. Berkeley and Los Angeles: University of California Press.

Weil, Jonathan, and Scot J. Paltrow. 2002. "Peer Pressure: SEC Saw Accounting Flaws." *Wall Street Journal,* January 29, C1.

8

BUILT CAPITAL

In Knott County, Kentucky, a persistently poor rural area, Sara Johnson turns on the faucet. A mucky, grayish solution trickles from the spout. The water system isn't working again. She'll have to go out and buy water for drinking, washing dishes, and even bathing. Sara will have to take the family's laundry to the Laundromat, a round trip of at least twenty miles. She hasn't the money for gasoline, let alone the time to spare for such a trip. Installed by the coal company, taken over by a private water company, and now owned by someone in another state, the local water system doesn't work half the time.

In Hebron, Nebraska, located in a rural county adjacent to a metropolitan area, Carl Jones no longer takes the most direct route to Center City. To deliver his fresh vegetables to the farmers' market, Carl now drives an extra forty miles in his old pickup truck because the bridge over the creek collapsed when an overloaded grain truck exceeded the old bridge's weight limit. Carl wonders when or if the county plans to replace it. The cost of the extra gasoline and its increase in price sure take away from what he can make selling vegetables at the market.

Emily Bailey and her husband, Jim Smothers, moved to Scottsburg, Indiana, in the fall of 2002, eager to bring their business from Chicago. They loved the small-town atmosphere and the way their children could participate in after-school activities and walk to play with their new friends. Their customers were already using the Internet to place most orders, which assured them a quick turnaround. But Emily and Jim quickly found that dial-up Internet access did not allow them to give their customers the service they had grown to expect. The large telecoms that served urban Indiana did not calculate enough profit from expanding to rural areas, so Emily and Jim were unable to get the services they needed.

Both Sara and Carl have limited incomes. The extra costs they bear in buying water or traveling an extra forty miles can mean the difference between remaining economically independent or having to turn to others for financial help. Emily and Jim enjoy living in a small town, but if they cannot use standard business equipment, they have little choice; they will have to move elsewhere.

These problems are equally serious to the communities. Knott County finds it hard to attract businesses to take advantage of its mountain setting. Basic services, such as clean water, are often unavailable. Hebron continues to decline as more and more of the small vegetable farmers realize that they cannot market their produce. Scottsburg was unable to take advantage of the new opportunities created by technology. Many businesses no longer need to be located in large cities, but Scottsburg needed to find a way to upgrade its technology to be able to keep people like Emily and Jim.

Water services, bridges, and broadband access are all part of what social scientists call the built capital of a community. How we function in everyday life depends on the type, quality, and condition of the infrastructure available to us. How rural communities function in the new economy will depend on the infrastructure available to their residents. This chapter defines the term built capital and discusses how it is provided and how rural communities can organize to maintain it.

DEFINING BUILT CAPITAL

Built capital provides a supporting foundation that facilitates human activity. Rural development policies are often geared toward enhancing built capital, on the assumption that people's lives will improve, particularly people who are disadvantaged, once new physical structures are in place. Yet concentration on built capital while ignoring social capital has led to the installation of rural water systems that have led to rural sprawl or gentrification of rural areas to the point that the original residents can no longer afford to live there. Communities are far more than built capital.

Built capital can support the life of the community, but it can also exclude certain people (those on "the wrong side of the tracks") and divert financial capital from other investments.

In the late 1990s, upstate New York communities along the historic Erie Canal made significant investments in tourism facilities and services, with the aid of federal funding from the Department of Housing and Urban Development (HUD). A study by Susan Christopherson of Cornell University and her city and regional planning colleagues (1999) found that investment in built capital by public and private entities to build tourism facilities can have a positive impact on the local and regional economy. However, community capacity (social and human capital) to construct a broad strategy that can take advantage of new and sometimes unexpected opportunities (strategic readiness) is key to long-term, successful economic development that includes investment in built capital.

Small towns (along with state and federal governments) for decades have invested in built capital. Currently, many rural communities give huge tax incentives to locate grain ethanol plants in their communities, supported by federal and state subsidies to that industry. Prison construction has been framed as a community economic development strategy.

The theory is that prisons and ethanol plants will bring jobs, the jobs will bring wages, and those wages will multiply through the local economy. Prisons are certainly a growth industry. The number of people incarcerated has grown extremely rapidly with mandatory sentencing and heightened concern for national security. But many towns have found that prisons do not buy their supplies from local vendors, nor do they employ local people. Rush City, Minnesota, about sixty miles north of Minneapolis, found that the presence of a prison did not fill empty Main Street shops or employ many Rush City people. The town's future growth depends on it becoming a bedroom community for the Twin Cities rather than a bedroom community for convicts. Built capital has limitations in what it can do for rural communities. Although the state of Iowa experienced a large increase in the number of ethanol plants and in ethanol production in 2006, the economy of rural communities with a plant was positively impacted by the construction phase as workers came to the communities to construct the multimillion-dollar plants. The price of corn increased, but that was immediately translated into the cost of land, making it even more difficult for new farmers to access land. Built capital can create problems or solve them.

This section defines what we mean by built capital and explores current issues that rural communities face in transforming financial, natural, and social capital into built capital.

Built Capital

Built capital is the permanent physical installations and facilities supporting productive activities in a community. It includes roads, streets and bridges, airports and railroads, electric and natural gas utility systems, water supply systems, police and fire-protection facilities, wastewater treatment and waste-disposal facilities, telephone and fiber-optic networks and other communications facilities, schools, hospitals, and other public and commercial buildings, as well as playgrounds and soccer fields. As is obvious from the list, the built capital of a community refers to the physical infrastructure that enables network communication and access to services and markets.

Built capital can facilitate production in and of itself. Buildings enable a factory to make products that can then be sold. Roads are used to take goods to market or to bring raw materials to a production facility. Power plants provide electricity that is converted into light and energy for a variety of business and domestic functions. These and other elements of a community's built capital enable individuals and businesses to be more productive within the community. Although the built capital of a community is necessary, it cannot ensure the economic health and well-being of that community. People must be able to use the infrastructure in productive ways.

Access and Consumption

Two issues, access and consumption, are involved in people's use of the community's built capital. This section explores each of these dimensions. The following section looks at the types of built capital that emerge from the interaction of these two issues.

Goods and services are considered to be *exclusive access* built capital when particular groups or individuals can be denied access to them. Elements of built capital are *inclusive access* built capital when they are available to all users. Access to many utilities, such as water, electricity, or telephones, is exclusive because people must be hooked up to the utility in order to use it. Most streets and roads are available to anyone who wants to use them and are thus inclusive. Access to public parks or recreational areas is often inclusive, whereas access to Disneyland is exclusive.

The decision as to whether a good or service is inclusive or exclusive depends on a number of factors. One factor is the extent to which access can be controlled. Radio stations, for example, might have a hard time making radio signals exclusive. Television signals are scrambled on pay-per-view channels, which makes the signals exclusive, dependent on possession of the right equipment with the right code. A second factor is the decisions made about how a service is organized. Water, for example, can be treated as an inclusive or exclusive service; the category is determined by the way the community chooses to organize delivery of the water.

A second feature of a good or service is the notion of joint consumption versus rival consumption. *Joint consumption* means that even if one person uses a good or service, others are nevertheless able to use it as well. By contrast, *rival consumption* means that if one person uses a good or service, another cannot use it. Roads, television and radio signals, and zoos are all capable of supporting joint consumption. Electricity is subject to rival consumption; clean water is rapidly becoming so also.

The distinction between joint and rival consumption is obviously not clear-cut. Goods or services can appear to support joint consumption in some circumstances and rival consumption in others. To some extent, the match between the resources and needs affects how we characterize different forms of built capital. Furthermore, cultural capital determines how built capital is viewed. In some Hopi cultures, a washing machine in a private home is considered open access, whereas most Americans of European descent would be deeply offended—or would call the police—if a distant relative put seven loads of laundry through the washing machine in their back entryway while they were gone.

Types of Built Capital

The two dimensions of access and consumption can be used to define different types of built capital. As shown in Table 8.1, crossing the two forms of access with the two types of consumption leads to four categories of built capital. The extent to which control by the private or public sector seems better suited for each category is explored briefly in this section.

In the lower right corner of the table are goods or services characterized by exclusive access and rival consumption; these are defined to be *private goods*. A landfill for which individuals must pay a fee to dispose of garbage

Table 8.1 Types of Goods and Services

	Consumption	
Access	Joint	Rival
Inclusive	Collective	Common-pool
Exclusive	Toll	Private

is an example of a private form of infrastructure, regardless of whether it is publicly or privately owned.

Until recently, people did not think of waste disposal in terms of rival consumption. When people were free to dispose of garbage wherever they wanted, waste disposal was not even a form of built capital. Once it became clear that dumping garbage in ditches by the road, in ravines, or down old wells contaminated water supplies, bred pests, and was unsightly, disposal of garbage was characterized as rival consumption. Now most people are aware that the amount of garbage one household puts in the landfill limits the amount another household will be able to put in. For example, if rural communities agree to take in out-of-state garbage, that community's capacity to dispose of its own garbage may be limited.

Toll goods or services are those subject to exclusive access and joint consumption. Access is limited, usually by the requirement that a fee be paid, but anyone who can afford the fee can use the facility. Toll roads, long-distance telephone lines, and fiber-optic communication systems are examples of built capital that are toll services. These are goods or services that can be jointly consumed by different people simultaneously. If one person uses a toll service, another person can use the same service without having to replenish it.

Goods or services for which inclusive access is matched with rival consumption are referred to as *common-pool goods*. Public school buildings normally are an example of this type of infrastructure. School buildings are available for use without a fee, but they can accommodate only a limited number of people. Use made of the school by one child might limit the opportunity for another child to use that same facility. Demands for use by a larger number of people require additional buildings or expansion of existing ones.

Finally, goods or services that link inclusive access with joint consumption are referred to as *collective goods*. Streets, roads, and public sidewalks are the most obvious examples. Schools can be considered collective goods if the community decides to have the school run two shifts of children each day or increase class size rather than turn children away.

Cultural capital has a great deal to do with the meaning of property to different groups, and thus, different cultures classify built capital in diverse ways. Some argue that the more goods can be classified as private, the higher the level of innovation. Others argue that the more goods are common-pool goods, the greater the chances for all members of a society to achieve their potential. How does your community view consumption of and access to different kinds of built capital? Has it changed over time?

Issues Facing Rural Communities

A large question for rural communities is who will own and maintain built capital? Many utilities in communities across the nation are privately held. Others are local government enterprises. A number of communities, from the City of Los Angeles to Harlan, Iowa, generate their own electricity and collect the revenues from it. The decision to function as a utility is based on assumptions about equity, efficiency, and the proper role of government in providing built capital.

What is appropriate for the state to own, versus what should be owned by private investors, is not set in stone. Construction of the aqueduct by the City of Los Angeles led to the development of other built capital by Los Angeles. For example, a great deal of cement was required to construct the aqueduct. Rather than buy the cement from private contractors, Los Angeles constructed its own cement plant at Monolith, California. The city invested public funds in an element of built capital that is private in most parts of the United States.

Failure of the built capital of rural areas has become a pressing problem. Much of the existing *infrastructure* was built in the 1930s, in conjunction with efforts to rebuild the country economically after the Great Depression. Community planners realized that rural people would prosper only if their communities had a well-developed foundation of streets, roads, public buildings, and utilities. Thus, a variety of public programs and private initiatives were established to assist rural communities in developing stronger infrastructures.

That infrastructure is now deteriorating. In the 1980s, one out of every five rural communities reported that two-thirds of its water pipeline had been in use for more than fifty years. At the end of the 1990s, an estimated forty-five thousand of the nation's fifty-five thousand community water systems served fewer than 3,300 people; that infrastructure needs extensive upgrading, and the cost of doing so is high. Improving water systems in these areas would take $31.2 billion dollars over the next twenty years. Many rural communities in the twenty-first century are still waiting for pipeline replacements to have fresh, clean water. In rural and remote McKenzie County in North Dakota, the McKenzie Rural Water Association was formed in 1996 to work toward improving the water quality. Many people who had well water were not able to drink it because of contamination; some of the people in town would not wash their clothes with it because it left stains. Farm animals were becoming sick from drinking the water because of the high levels of sulfates. It took a lot of organization within the district to build its technical, managerial, and financial capacity. In 2003 its plans and specifications were approved by the North Dakota Department of Health. The county actively worked with the State Water Commission and other local coalitions to gain access to state-operated revolving loan funds for pipeline replacement throughout the rural areas of McKenzie County.

The August 2007 collapse of the Interstate 35 West bridge in Minneapolis was a fatal reminder of the fragile state of the nation's bridges and other infrastructure. In 2005, there were 307,000 "on system" bridges (owned and maintained by the federal government or state departments of transportation) across the United States, 23 percent of which were deemed structurally deficient or functionally obsolete. Of the 286,000 "off system" bridges (typically owned and maintained by local agencies, or by state agencies on rural and other low-volume roads), 30 percent were deficient. The gap between the cost of replacement and the dollars available to rural governments is huge. Thus, rural areas are faced with difficult choices: to prioritize built capital investments, realizing some built capital will be abandoned; to share what built capital they can; or to change the specifications to have affordable built capital. An example of the last possibility would be for rural bridges to be used as one-way-at-a-time bridges, which would decrease the weight load they would have to be built to hold.

Responsibility for maintaining and replacing water and sewer systems, roads and bridges, and public buildings increasingly has shifted from federal and state to local governments. Locally, infrastructure improvements often are financed through tax-exempt municipal bonds. These bonds can be either general-obligation bonds or revenue bonds. General-obligation bonds commit the community as a whole to repayment of the bonds. Consequently, funds are raised through increased taxes or a reallocation of existing tax revenue. The revenue collected through rate increases and increased numbers of users as a result of the improvement repays revenue bonds.

Rural communities face a number of problems in financing infrastructure improvements. Rural communities often lack an economic base sufficient to support the large financial outlays required to solve their infrastructure problems. For the many communities that now have a declining tax base, general-obligation bonds are of limited use. *Revenue bonds* depend on a population large enough to make the increased costs manageable. In most cases, the per capita costs of improving or even maintaining built capital in rural communities tend to be rather high. Thus there is substantial motivation to form collaborations, as they have in the Northwest Missouri Water Partnership, so that the eighty-three water districts in twelve counties could maintain their independence but share water sources and water treatment through new collaborations.

High per capita costs in rural communities are a function of several factors. Because of the lower population densities there, rural areas often must function under unfavorable economies of scale (low number of users per investment). Serving greater distances makes both the installation and maintenance of many forms of built capital more expensive. That is often the reason given for lack of broadband access in rural and remote and persistently poor areas. In some cases, the higher costs may be offset by simpler technology or individual solutions. Septic tanks and private wells, for example, may substitute for expensive sewage treatment facilities and water distribution systems needed by more densely populated areas. Fewer streets are needed in rural areas, and they do not need to accommodate the heavy traffic common in urban areas. In general, however, built capital costs considerably more per citizen to build and maintain in rural areas.

Some rural communities are turning to other alternatives, such as special districts or impact extractions. Kentucky, for example, went to a system of creating special districts to fund infrastructure improvements. Special districts allow the costs of improving the infrastructure to be paid only by those who will benefit directly. Impact extractions involve shifting the costs of development from the public to the developer. Bethel, Maine, a growing amenity-based community, gives developers two alternatives in connecting into the municipal sewer system: The developer can either construct a replacement for existing lines or pay a sewer-system-development charge.

Both options provide the funds needed to upgrade and maintain the community's sewer system.

In recent years, the new term rural sprawl has appeared. In Missouri, people who are looking to "get away from it all" are causing small towns to grow faster than the big cities surrounding them. In the 1990s, more than 3,500 new housing permits were issued for outlying areas. One of the issues involved in rural sprawl is the handling of municipal waste. In 2002, Oronogo, Missouri (population 976), a rural community outside of Joplin, Missouri, put a stop to new development because of infrastructure constraints. Its wastewater treatment plant reached full capacity, and the town faced a $2.6 million bill to expand its water system. Water bills would nearly double if expansion were to begin. Developers in the area argued that they were not promoting sprawl but rather trying to meet the needs of people who wanted to live outside of the city. The developers overcame the ban, and the town grew 104 percent in four years. Rates indeed increased. Alternatives, such as those found in Maine, are necessary in areas like Oronogo.

PUBLIC VERSUS PRIVATE
PROVISION OF BUILT CAPITAL

Built capital can be provided for and supported in a number of different ways. Public schools and roads, for example, are provided for totally through public investment and control. Private schools and private roads, in contrast, have at least some private financial capital invested. Other forms of built capital, such as telephone systems, are developed through the private sector. Public versus private control is not a simple dichotomy, however. It is a continuum, such that elements of public and private support can be combined in varying degrees. This section examines the four types of infrastructure in terms of how they are provided for and proposes a framework from which to examine the choices a community makes.

Private and Toll Forms

Private and toll goods or services can be supplied by either the private or the public sector. The choice of control, public or private, is typically a function of historical development, economic entrepreneurship, or fiscal prudence. Bridges, housing, water supplies, recreation facilities, and fire protection can all be offered directly to users by private suppliers for a fee that includes cost plus profit. On the other hand, some local governments provide (for a fee) goods usually classified as private, such as electricity or telephone service. Some built capital originally constructed at public expense may be converted to private and toll goods controlled by the private sector. Land in industrial parks or speculative buildings placed on that land are sometimes turned over to private firms as an incentive for them to come to the community. Thus, the three most common alternatives seem to be private development and maintenance, public development and maintenance, and public development but private maintenance.

In many rural communities, natural monopolies maintain segments of the built capital. *Monopolies* are single companies that control the delivery of goods or services without competition, and they can be either public or private. They typically form in cases when, even though different providers could offer competitive services, the services are best handled by a single provider in the interest of efficiency. Water services, electricity, and fire protection tend to be offered by single providers through regulation. The company accepts government intervention, usually in the form of price controls and requirements that service be provided to all, in exchange for exclusive rights to do that kind of business in a given area. The 1990s saw increasing deregulation of many of these monopolies, which led to differential impacts for rural and urban areas. Although the deregulation of telephone service resulted in increasing price competition, in many areas where electricity was deregulated, the companies supposedly in competition instead colluded, creating artificial scarcity, brownouts, and high prices. Although monopolies seem natural when only one delivery system exists, it is possible to provide service on a competitive basis. The restructuring of long-distance telephone service is an example. The infrastructure (telephone lines, cables, and switches) is owned and leased to competitors.

Some of the goods and services that now come from monopolies were once provided on a competitive basis. In colonial Maryland, for example, fire protection initially was provided through insurance companies. Private companies sold insurance policies that included firefighting services from any number of competing companies. If a fire did break out, only the firefighting service identified by the insurance policy responded. One person might purchase such a policy; a neighbor might not carry any insurance at all. Such erratic access to fire protection was inefficient, as well as a danger to the public welfare.

Many communities moved to provide more uniform fire protection through firehouses and firefighting equipment purchased and controlled by the community. In some communities, salaried firefighters were hired. Other rural communities organized volunteer fire departments. No longer competitive, firefighting has become a monopolized part of the built capital in communities.

As local resources become scarcer, some communities use their built capital to generate income. Bethel provides fire protection to several surrounding towns. It charges each town an availability fee—a flat rate for making its fire department available—that is reminiscent of the old insurance policies sold in Maryland. When actually called to a fire, the Bethel Fire Department charges a rental fee for the trucks that show up at the fire scene, labor costs for the firefighters involved, and a fee to cover the overhead for providing the service. The fees have increased nontraditional sources of revenue available to Bethel and, presumably, have made a higher level of fire protection available to the smaller communities.

In Scottsburg, the town was unwilling to wait for a private provider of high-speed Internet access. The city established its own wireless network, which then not only enabled businesses to be more efficient but also gave residents better access to medical care, government services, and education. However, Scottsburg was lucky. Nineteen states regulate or ban government-operated Internet services. Emily and Jim worked hard with State Senator David Ford to defeat such a ban in Indiana. Meanwhile, Scottsburg extended its service to nine counties where private telecoms chose not to invest.

Rural communities still face many issues pertaining to funding these services. Decisions must be made as to whether fire protection should be supported through public or private means and whether it should be operated as a profit-generating or not-for-profit activity. Are volunteer firefighters sufficient to meet the needs of the local area, or must there be full-time, paid staff? Should states intervene to mandate a certain level of training or commitment to firefighting, or should communities be allowed to organize the service in response to local resources? If the community opts for public support, what proportion of funds should be derived from public moneys such as assessments of property taxes?

Common-Pool and Collective Goods and Services

Generally, collective goods or services can be provided only by the public sector. Common-pool goods or services are often also provided by the public sector. Because these include types of infrastructures that are accessible without a fee, the private sector has little incentive to provide them.

When collective goods and services are provided to an entire community, they are referred to as *public goods and services.* No one can claim an exclusive share; public goods and services are free to everyone. It is assumed that access to any particular good or service is a right of citizenship or residency.

Semipublic goods and services are those for which only part of the infrastructure cost comes from fees (a variant of private goods) or for which the full cost for a restricted facility comes from public funds (a variant of toll goods). Many municipal swimming pools, libraries, and landfills fall into this category. Generally, the public provides the costs of construction and maintenance, and fees cover the continued operating expenses of the facility.

In contrast to collective goods and services, common-pool goods and services can be made exclusive. Charging an access fee limits who can purchase the good or use the service. If the fee is relatively low, the common-pool good or service begins to resemble a collective good or service. Setting the fee relatively high, however, effectively limits access.

Other methods of exclusion involve limiting access to people of specific ages, ethnic groups, or races, or of a certain gender. At the beginning of the 1990s, two public institutions of higher education in the United States continued to prohibit the entrance of women: the Virginia Military Institute (VMI) and the Citadel in South Carolina. By the end of the decade, both had begun admitting women to their institutions. In Georgia, the Augusta National Golf Club, home of the Masters Tournament, allows only men to belong to the club. Until recently, only white men could play on the course. Women still are not allowed to buy a membership, and they can play at the course only if they are accompanied by a male club member. This exclusive golf club maintains that it has the right to deny access to certain individuals because it is "tradition." Well into the 1960s, blacks were denied access to community services such as schools, swimming pools, motels, restrooms, and drinking fountains. This exclusion ended when blacks staged large-scale protests and initiated legal challenges, making clear that their rights of citizenship included access to built capital constructed at public expense. Furthermore, citizenship rights also meant that certain goods previously defined as private, such as restaurants and bowling alleys, actually had a semipublic status.

Community Choices

Deciding whether the public or private sector should be involved in organizing for a community's built capital ultimately relates back to the values of the community and its decision makers. Max Weber, a nineteenth-century German sociologist, argued that there were really two forms of logic involved in these types of decisions. The first, called *formal rationality*, is used when the provision of needs can be calculated in quantitative terms of profit and loss. *Substantive rationality* applies to situations in which goods or services are provided to people based on values rather than profit. Whether the enterprise is profitable is not important or is of secondary concern. Therefore, profit or loss often is not even calculated. The values sought might involve a concern for maintaining status distinctions, being fair, or gaining and maintaining power.

Through their local governments, communities make decisions about what infrastructure to develop. These decisions are based on the perceived needs of the local people, often as voiced by organized groups, as well as on the resources available. A community can decide to invest in a new landfill rather than a public swimming pool or in a new school rather than an industrial park. In many cases, investments in built capital generate insufficient profit or are too risky for the private sector to undertake. Thus, local communities must assume construction and maintenance costs if there is a belief that access to the service is a right of citizenship or residence in that community (substantive rationality). If that value is not held so strongly, then the community may choose to do without that particular service.

In the past, the federal government helped local areas with investments viewed as a right of citizenship—for a clean water supply and sewage treatment, for example. These forms of a community's infrastructure were considered valid, regardless of whether a profit could be made. Substantive rationality based on concern for equity placed this form of infrastructure in the public sector. Federal involvement declined in the 1980s and 1990s, however. Access to a clean water supply and sewage treatment is now being approached through mandates. This strategy is less effective, but it is also less costly to the federal government. As we discuss in Chapter 11, the costs are shifted to either the state or local level.

All of these decisions involve choices on the part of the community as well as for other levels of government. The examples that follow enable us to explore the choices states and communities face in providing for various types of infrastructure and the problems created by these choices.

PUBLIC CHOICES: WATER SYSTEMS

When we think about water as part of a community's infrastructure, we normally focus on the system established to deliver water to homes and businesses. Water, like air, is assumed to be available to all.

In parts of the rural West, however, this assumption is no longer valid. Urban growth increases the demand for water, threatening its availability for rural communities. Various governing bodies affect whether water is viewed as inclusive or exclusive and whether its consumption is joint or rival. Water services may be viewed as a source of profit, so that access is determined by formal rationality, or a right of every citizen, and thus a matter of substantive rationality. This section explores the larger political context that influences the availability of water as well as the local decisions communities face in providing and maintaining water systems.

Water Services

Assuming that water is available (see Chapter 2), communities can offer access in a number of ways. People can haul their own water or dig wells, assuming individual responsibility for getting water. Communities can organize a shared water system that then can be publicly or privately owned.

Theoretically, water as part of a community's infrastructure can be subject to both exclusive access and rival consumption. Water, especially clean water, typically is distributed throughout the community through pipes. Consequently, potential users can be excluded. Moreover, water resources are finite. Use by one member diminishes the use by another. Until recently, the characteristic of rival consumption of water seemed less noticeable on the local level. The "watering patrols" now used to control the use of public water on lawns or the rationing procedures used during periods of drought illustrate the extent to which water now is seen to involve rival consumption. Wastewater and its storage and treatment also have become a significant problem throughout the rural United States because of outdated or insufficient infrastructure. It is vitally important that the consequences of toxic wastewater are understood (see Box 8.1).

Because of these characteristics—exclusion and rivalry—the distribution of water at the local level potentially is suitable for private control. Rural areas are more likely to have private water supplies: wells sunk by individual homes. In urban areas, water is typically managed by the public sector. In general, the belief that all citizens have a right to clean water at a

---

Box 8.1   What Exactly Is Wastewater? Why Treat It?

Have you ever considered the journey your drinking water made before it came out of your tap? Wastewater is generated by everyone, and each person in the United States uses 75 to 100 gallons of water per day. Seventy-three percent of the population is connected to a centralized (municipal) wastewater collection and treatment system, and the remaining 27 percent uses on-site septic systems. Water does not magically disappear into the earth when it is used on a daily basis; it becomes wastewater, or sewage that is filtered before it can be returned to the environment for reuse. Wastewater contains disease organisms and hazardous substances such as cleaning fluids and disinfectants. It is easy to ignore wastewater treatment, until that sort of bacteria appears in the water that comes from your tap at home. If these organisms are in the water, people can become seriously ill. In rural areas, the infrastructure is often outdated and has deteriorated, making it easier for bacteria to form and get into drinking-water supplies. Keeping up with the maintenance of wastewater treatment is difficult, and paying for it is sometimes impossible.

Source

Olson, Ken, Bridget Chard, Doug Malchow, and Don Hickman. 2002. "Small Community Wastewater Solutions: A Guide to Making Treatment, Management and Financing Decisions." University of Minnesota Extension Service.

---

reasonable price has led to public control or regulation. In other words, substantive rationality has dominated over formal rationality.

Water Quality

For people like Sara Johnson, the problem is the quality of water, not its availability. The water that reaches residents of Knott County is unusable. For years, rivers have been dumping grounds for industry. Sewer systems owned by cities often discharge into rivers or bays that later are used as sources of drinking water. Toxic chemicals from dumps, industry, and agriculture seep through soil to taint groundwater. Runoff of the chemicals used in fertilizers and pesticides contaminates the water of lakes, streams, and reservoirs.

For the most part, rural communities are not prepared to deal with increased concerns about water quality. Coliform bacteria are a source of gastrointestinal diseases and are one of the most common problems found in rural water supplies. If each household provides its own well, it is even more difficult to assure periodic testing and water quality.

The susceptibility of water to physical, cyber, biological, chemical, and radiological threats was realized after the terrorist attacks on September 11, 2001. For example, a computer hacker can disrupt a distribution system. Water-related agencies and organizations made security a high priority on their agendas, and even smaller water systems needed emergency plans. Close scrutiny pinpointed needed improvements in security and emergency preparedness, and correcting these deficiencies required additional funding. The Environmental Protection Agency set aside approximately $23 million to support small and medium drinking-water facilities; most federal funding is for large systems in the United States. Outreach to small communities is necessary to implement security-related measures. The Rural Community Assistance Program Inc. and its affiliates around the country work with small communities to help them plan and implement solutions for built capital that fit their situation and their goals.

Part of the solution is to treat wastewater and to maintain sewage and water lines. Citizens in the small communities throughout Knott County are insisting that the small, privately owned water companies make the investments needed to maintain water quality. These citizens rely on local and state governments to ensure that these investments in infrastructure are made.

Another part of the solution is to stop contamination of local water supplies. In some communities, citizen groups work together to see that clean-water laws are enforced. These groups trace contamination back to its source and then take public action to block the release of the contaminants. Citizen groups serve as watchdogs to ensure that private individuals and companies do not dispose of their waste at public expense. Private companies are encouraged to increase their investment in built capital for reasons of substantive rationality.

PRIVATE CHOICES: SOLID WASTE

Built capital includes a means to provide for the collection and disposal of solid waste generated by households and industries. Urban areas are finding that they no longer have room for the volume of waste they produce and have arranged to transport it to rural areas for disposal. In many rural communities, waste disposal has become a source of revenue. Like water, waste disposal can be placed under either public or private control. As increased demand for disposal sites has been countered with environmental concerns, waste disposal has become an intriguing issue.

Waste as an Economic Venture

Waste disposal involves exclusionary access and rival consumption. It is exclusionary in that most dumps and landfills restrict access, regardless of whether they are publicly or privately owned. Users must pay a fee to dump solid waste. Waste disposal involves rival consumption in the sense that land used to store solid waste is land unavailable for other purposes. Urban areas are well aware of these rival uses; indeed, some have run out of land on which to dispose of their waste. In rural areas, people sometimes simply leave waste where it is or toss it into the river. Even such casual disposal is ultimately a rival use of land or rivers because these areas fill up and no one else can use them.

In 2005, U.S. residents, businesses, and institutions produced nearly 245 million tons of municipal and solid waste, which is approximately 4.6 pounds of waste per person, per day (Figure 8.1). This statistic does not include the hazardous waste and toxic waste that also are produced in large quantities and that are even more difficult to dispose of. Because waste disposal is both exclusionary and rival as well as potentially very profitable, private interests have been drawn into providing this type of built capital. Rural communities themselves are looking toward waste disposal as an economic venture.

Jerry Wharton, an independent strip miner, started the Kim-Stan Landfill Company in Virginia. His previous company had specialized in quick profit: clearing ground, mining coal, and leaving the land exposed. Once the coal ran out, Wharton decided that waste disposal was one way to use the holes he had made in the earth. With little investment on the part of Wharton and his Chicago-based partners, the Kim-Stan Landfill Company was launched in a persistently poor area of Virginia. The landfill did a booming out-of-state garbage business as cities and industries desperate for a place to dump their garbage took advantage of the Virginia mountains. This proved extremely profitable, and a great deal of waste was moved into the landfill site.

Figure 8.1 Trends in Municipal Solid Waste Generation, 1960–2005

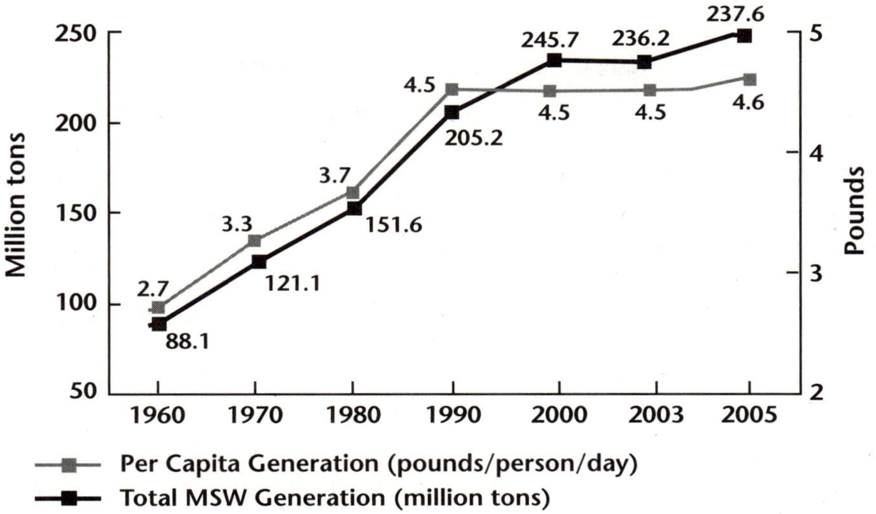

— ■ — Per Capita Generation (pounds/person/day)
— ■ — Total MSW Generation (million tons)

SOURCE: www.epa.gov/epaoswer/non-hw/muncpl/facts.htm

People paid little, if any, attention to what happened to the waste products once they reached the site. When an unusually high concentration of dangerous contaminants was noticed in the nearby Jackson River, however, an investigation was launched. In May 1990, the Commonwealth of Virginia closed the landfill. After first paying $250,000 to Wharton, the Kim-Stan Landfill Company declared bankruptcy. The public—the Commonwealth of Virginia—was left with the cleanup costs and remaining company debts. The waste at the landfill included five thousand gallons of waste oils contaminated with mercury, asbestos, and medical waste, which reached depths of eighty feet (Environmental Protection Agency 2002). Soon after the site was closed, the EPA put the landfill on its Superfund list, meaning that U.S. taxpayers pay 90 percent of the cleanup costs; Virginia taxpayers have to pay the remaining 10 percent. The public is paying for cleaning up toxic substances generated by a now-bankrupt private firm.

Private landfills and waste disposal operations are now common. Certainly, the notion of accepting solid waste from other areas is not especially new. In most rural areas, landfills have been developed regionally, or larger communities have simply charged neighboring towns for the use of their facilities. What is new is the profit that can be made from accepting out-of-state garbage. Strip mines in northern Kentucky have been adapted for use as private landfills. A private firm has proposed a six thousand–acre landfill three miles from Welch, West Virginia, a persistently poor rural community. In return for permits to open the landfill, the developer promised to build the city a sewer system that would clean up the Tug Fork River (Kilborn 1991). There was much discussion in town both in favor of and against the landfill. Those in favor saw it as providing good jobs (increasing financial capital). Those who opposed it were concerned about pollution and health risks (natural and human capital). The plan was stopped, but as the area's economy continues to decline into the twenty-first century, some still regret the lost jobs. The idea of out-of-state garbage entering the county landfill did not sit well with some Welch residents; others saw it as an opportunity for job growth in the area. There also were concerns about past mining activities that had occurred beneath the proposed landfill site. Protest groups formed to stop the landfill from being built, and by the late 1990s, Capels Resources Ltd., the company that had applied for a permit to build the waste facility, decided not to construct it. The county put into place several restrictions, including a limit on the size of the disposal area, which ultimately was decreased to thirty-five acres from five hundred acres. Capels withdrew its application for a permit, making protesters happy; however, many residents are still upset by what they see as the loss of new jobs with decent wages and benefits in the area. Such conflicts over which capital should be favored often leave long-term divisions in rural communities. Focusing on waste as impacting only natural capital ignores its negative impacts on other capitals (see Box 8.2).

Virginia's experience with the Kim-Stan Landfill illustrates the complex issues involved. Solid waste disposal has implications for the environment shared with others as well as for the profits generated within a private enterprise. Even when the public would profit, as in Welch, decisions made today could compromise the use of land for other purposes in the future.

Governmental Responses

Because of inadequate government oversight, disposal of solid waste, particularly toxic waste, has been more profitable to private waste management firms than valuable to society as a whole. The social costs often become apparent only years after the waste has been improperly disposed

Box 8.2 The Hidden Costs of the Landfill on Dunlap Road

On the weekend of Cinco de Mayo, when several northeast Georgia counties were walking to raise money for a well-known cancer organization, residents of Dunlap Road were walking to raise awareness at the second annual Making the Link Environmental Health Awareness Walk. Over fifty people turned out to highlight the associations between chronic diseases that come from repeated exposures to toxic chemicals, like those that lurk in our local landfill.

Hidden cost #1: **Natural capital:** the price of safe air, soil, and water for the residents on Dunlap Road. What is the dollar value of their loss?

Human capital: Cancer is not a stranger in this community, which has suffered tremendous environmental damage from the Athens Clarke County Municipal Solid Waste Landfill for the past thirty years. Groundwater contamination prompted the ACC government to make city water available to residents, but not everyone has chosen that option.

Hidden cost #2: **Financial capital:** decreased value in property of Dunlap Road. Who wants to purchase land that could kill you?

When the state Environmental Protection Division came to Athens in 2006 to discuss renewing the air permit for the landfill, residents were shocked to discover that no ambient (outdoor) air monitoring is done to determine which gases/particles migrate from the landfill to the air they breathe. There is also some concern that vapors could potentially intrude into homes from the contaminated groundwater. Residents will not know the extent of their exposure until reliable testing is done. What residents do know is that the smell can be unbearable enough to make them stay inside on given days.

Hidden cost #3: **Cultural capital:** How much do residents pay for odor trespassing that results in decreased quality of life, liberty, and the pursuit of happiness?

Along with the Dunlap Road Community, the event was sponsored by Billups Grove Baptist Church, the Northeast Georgia Children's Environmental Health Coalition, and MICAH's Mission. Members of all four groups came together before the walk with Athens Clarke County Commissioners Kelly Girtz and Doug Lowry to discuss their concerns over the possible expansion of the landfill. Dr. Richard Field, ACC environmental coordinator, was also in attendance and listened to the requests of citizens.

continues

Box 8.2   *continued*

Hidden cost #4: **Political capital:** How much have residents spent in time, emotions, and discouragement in the past thirty years asking to be treated like decent human beings only to be constantly ignored until now?

Dunlap Road community leader and organizer Charles Nash led the walk, which journeyed to the Oglethorpe County line and looped back. ACC landfill shares a cooperative agreement with Oglethorpe County: ACC uses Oglethorpe's C&D (construction & demolition) landfill while privileges to Oglethorpe County are given at the ACC municipal solid waste landfill.

Dunlap Road lies in both Athens-Clarke and Oglethorpe counties. Is there contamination migration into Oglethorpe County? Will both county governments adopt better recycling and reduction ordinances, which will promote a shift from the burden of taxpayers to continue burying waste to a more excellent and greener way? When will producer responsibility be taken for the disposal of toxic materials such that product life cycles never require shoveling them into the ground at all?

Hidden cost #5: **Financial capital:** How much money has been paid and will be paid out in legal fees and settlements to compensate for the ecological damage done to Dunlap Road from ultimate product liability?

Commissioner Carl Jordan brought along his two canine daughters, who also completed the walk. He noticed how poorly maintained Dunlap Road is, which was another indicator that the community is constantly bothered with high traffic of large diesel-emitting, waste-hauling trucks.

Hidden cost #6: **Human capital:** What price tag shall we put on the perpetual health effects from these polluting commercial trucks and the poor planning of the built environment, which placed an unwanted dump in the middle of a residential community in 1976?

Social capital: While many in northeast Georgia were remembering their loved ones stricken with cancer this past weekend, Dunlap Road residents also wondered how many of their children never made it because of the landfill. How much premature death has been caused on Dunlap Road from the holes in the ground to which our throwaway society transports its trash?

continues

Hidden cost #7: **Human capital:** What is the price tag on a lost human being? **Political capital:** If one adds up all these irretrievable losses on Dunlap Road, it is plain to see the negative bottom line for them: *a travesty of justice for three decades*. And yet, there is hope for residents to be heard, for we live in a country where democracy gives all a place at the table. Pull up a seat, Dunlap Road. Come, let us reason together.

SOURCE

McElheney, Jill. 2007. "The Hidden Costs of the Landfill on Dunlap Road." *The Networker* 4, no. 12 (July). Science & Environmental Health Network.

of. Consequently, waste management firms have found it easy to pass part of the true cost of waste disposal on to the government. Ultimately, taxpayers pay for the cleanup. Consequently, the public must assume a more active role in solid waste disposal. Governmental involvement may be of two types: regulation of private companies or direct public control of solid waste disposal.

If the first option is chosen, governments must find a way to retrieve the costs of cleanup or insist that those costs be integrated into the operation of the private landfills. As is illustrated by the actions taken by Kim-Stan Landfill Company, retrieving the costs of cleanup can be difficult. Alternatively, governments can develop regulations designed to protect the environment. Firms would be required to take certain precautions designed to protect the groundwater, the air, and the appearance of the landscape. The cost of those precautions would then be integrated into the cost of the business and passed along to the customer through higher disposal fees. These costs would be closer to the true cost to society and certainly would be cheaper for society as a whole than toxic-waste cleanup after the fact.

If the second option is chosen, both governments and the general public must acknowledge the need to deal with the social costs as well as the physical costs of disposal. This means greater use of recycling, careful selection of landfills, segregation of toxic from nontoxic waste, and the selection of appropriate means for disposing of toxic waste. If the local governments do not have the technical capacity to deal with these issues, state or federal governments may need to assume responsibility for developing appropriate procedures and regulations.

Community Responses

Solid waste is now recognized as a collective problem that communities can solve through organization. Solutions are not always arrived at easily, however. As occurs on most issues, opposing forces organize to protect their respective interests. NIMBY ("not in my backyard") groups organized early as wealthy suburban communities sought to protect themselves from private landfills. Other community groups formed coalitions to support recycling or to promote or oppose the choice of a location for new landfills. In Greenup, Kentucky, an organization called Greenup Residents Opposing Waste Landfill (GROWL) was created to block the approval of a private landfill, based on fears that groundwater would be contaminated. Groups may protest the acceptance of waste from out of state or the proposed construction of toxic-waste incinerators. They may also propose delaying a decision until the community can educate itself on both the benefits and risks; the people of Harlan, Iowa, sought a delay when faced with the possibility of a medical-waste incinerator being built.

Recycling is a common response to the growing volume of trash. Participation in recycling programs is voluntary in some locales, mandatory in others. Community-organized programs have been successful in reducing the volume of solid waste needing disposal. Although some recycling enterprises can be profitable or at least break even, most incur costs for the community. Communities offer recycling programs to decrease the amount of solid waste to be processed rather than as a means to generate municipal revenue.

Because recycling programs cost money, the decision to recycle involves substantive rationality. Communities recycle because they are concerned about the environment, not because recycling generates a profit. As the costs of waste disposal increase and as regulations require that the true costs of solid waste disposal be passed on to the consumer, recycling may become more formally rational. Individuals may find it personally profitable to recycle much of their solid waste rather than pay the true costs of having it collected. Communities themselves may find it more profitable to recycle than to open new landfills. As that occurs, private firms may find it possible to earn a profit, and recycling programs may shift to the private sector. Ultimately, recycling works only when the demand for recycled materials offsets the costs of recycling. Governments can increase the demand for recycled products by purchasing them for the military, prisons, and other government institutions. Recycling in the United States grew rapidly until 2000, then slightly slowed beginning with less EPA support in 2001 (see Figure 8.2a). Although some dangerous materials, such as car batteries, are almost all recycled, the growing number of plastic soft-drink and water containers are not (see Figure 8.2b).

Figure 8.2a Municipal Solid Waste Recycling Rates, 1960–2005

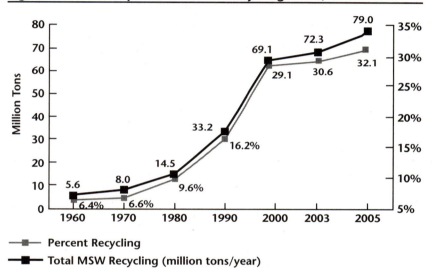

Figure 8.2b Recycling Rates of Selected Materials, 2005

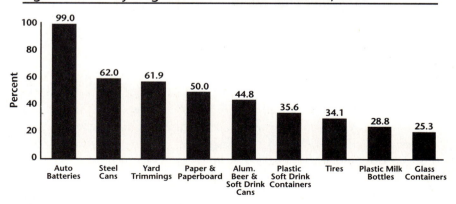

SOURCE: www.epa.gov/epaoswer/non-hw/muncpl/facts.htm

The Climate and Waste Connection

Every stage of a product's life cycle—extraction, manufacturing, distribution, use, and disposal—indirectly or directly contributes to the concentration of greenhouse gases (GHGs) in the atmosphere and affects the global climate. For instance, product manufacturing releases GHGs directly from the manufacturing process and indirectly from the energy produced to run the plant. Extraction and distribution require gasoline-powered vehicles that release CO_2. Discarded products typically end up in a landfill, which releases methane as products decompose.

Waste prevention and recycling—jointly referred to as waste reduction—offer significant potential for decreasing GHG emissions. The EPA estimates that simply increasing our national recycling rate from its current level of 30 percent to 35 percent would reduce GHG emissions by 10 million metric tons of carbon equivalent. That amount is equal to the average annual emissions from the electricity consumed by roughly 4.6 million households.

FEDERAL ROLE: MAKING LINKAGES

By definition, rural residents are more isolated from markets and information than are urban residents. Two forms of built capital, transportation and communication technologies, reduce that isolation. These span larger distances and involve public-private partnerships to ensure rural access, however. Rural communities must provide the local infrastructure, but they then hope to be linked with other networks and hope that private companies will provide the needed services. In the past, the federal government has played an important role in maintaining these forms of built capital.

Transportation

Transportation continues to be crucial to rural areas. At the local level, rural transportation systems suffer from four major problems: inadequate new construction, deferred or otherwise inadequate maintenance of existing structures, inadequate fiscal infrastructure to serve economic needs, and financing problems.

Inadequate maintenance of roads and bridges is particularly acute. Seventy percent of the bridges in the north-central United States, not atypical of other parts of the country, were constructed before 1935 and were designed for a fifty-year life (Chicoine 1986). As this infrastructure deteriorates, people such as Carl Jones in Hebron are unable to transport goods to market.

Although some bridges were repaired or rebuilt, many still have outdated constructions, and with increased traffic in rural areas due to farm equipment and heavy trucks, bridges need attention. The costs of maintaining rural roads and bridges are escalating, in part because of inflation but also because of deterioration of the system.

The 1998 Transportation Equity Act for the Twenty-First Century (known as TEA–21) authorized $171 billion to improve the transportation system in the United States. Although this amount of money is significant, rural funding was not sufficient, in part because of the classification system that was implemented. Local roads and minor collectors, which are defined as low-traffic roads, make up 77 percent of rural roads but received only 15 percent of rural federal highway funds, which equates to $7.7 billion (Brown 1999). Rural areas, under the Surface Transportation Program, are defined as those having populations of less than five thousand, which leaves out many rural communities. There are rural areas that have unmet needs because of this classification, and the condition of roads and bridges in those areas continues to deteriorate because they lack funding.

Public Transportation

The viability of a transportation network is a function not only of well-sited and safe bridges and roads but also of what means of transport are available. The federal government's decision to deregulate transportation has significantly decreased access in rural areas. Railroads abandoned a number of lines, isolating rural communities that produced low-value but high-volume products, such as wheat or timber. Communities such as Garden City, Kansas, invested in their own railroad spur to maintain regional linkages to their local infrastructure. Other towns were less able to step in where the private sector had withdrawn. The loss of those linkages meant the loss of a part of the community's economic base.

Public transportation, always deficient in rural areas, has become virtually nonexistent in many communities. Railroads abandoned most passenger service entirely. The interstate bus network has substantially reduced its service.

Bus service illustrates the character of the public-private partnership involved in transportation. The public provides the roads, but private companies provide the means of transport. Prior to 1982, decisions made to regulate bus service were based on substantive rationality. The goal was equity: ensuring that rural residents had access to public transportation. Regulations linked profit with service. In exchange for the right to serve profitable routes, bus lines were required to serve unprofitable ones. The expectation was that the profit generated along the better routes would exceed the loss generated along the more rural routes.

The Bus Regulatory Reform Act of 1982 reflected a shift from substantive to formal rationality. It was justified in terms of increasing competition and thus lowering the price of bus tickets. But reduced service to small communities compensated for those lower ticket prices. Communities no longer had the right to bus service. Routes are now selected strictly in terms of their profitability. The routes abandoned were those to rural communities with neither air nor rail service.

Rural communities also have been affected by deregulation in the airline industry. Regulation of bus service was designed to ensure access. Regulation of the airline industry was designed to ensure equity in fares. When the airlines were deregulated in 1978, commuter airfares increased sharply. It now costs as much or more to fly the 225 miles from Roanoke, Virginia, to Washington, D.C., as it does to fly five times that distance, from Kansas City, Missouri, to Washington, D.C. Although these charges reflect a difference in cost resulting from the lower passenger travel between Roanoke and Washington, they also reflect the lack of competition that exists along such routes. Deregulation initially reduced airfares, but the number of carriers has decreased gradually through economic failure. Fares and services have been left in the hands of fewer companies. Service to some rural communities has been abandoned altogether. Other service continues with the help of funds designated for Essential Air Service, a federal program meant to bridge the transition from regulation to deregulation.

Telecommunications

As the world economy becomes more integrated, information becomes more central to business operations. Information-age technologies can improve both the economic efficiency and the competitiveness of today's rural commercial enterprises. Rapid information flow is facilitated through modern electronics and telecommunications. These require not only investment by the individual (in computers, modems, and facsimile machines) but also investment by the public (in switching systems, underground cables, and satellite links). E-commerce in small, rural towns, necessary if rural businesses are to compete effectively, has been on the rise.

Many rural and remote areas still either do not have Internet service or cannot acquire it at a reasonable cost. Rural areas are now distanced from global business not only by miles of land and water but also by miles of phone lines, or lack thereof.

At almost every income level, rural households are less likely to have broadband Internet access. In 2006, 48 percent of urban and suburban residents had broadband at home, compared to only 29 percent of rural residents. Sharon Strover's work at the Telecommunications and Information Policy Institute at the University of Texas (1999) vividly illustrates the continued struggle that rural areas have with accessing Internet technology. Internet service providers, or ISPs, may choose not to enter a rural market because they think it is too costly. Even when rural infrastructure exists, ISPs are leery of entering the market because the price at which they can offer the service limits the number of customers. In Scottsburg, Indiana, the local people had to figure out how to band together to establish their own ISP—and had to fight policies pushed by telecoms to limit the ability of community self-development through local public-private partnerships.

Many rural linkages to the world economy are being made through Internet connections. The Telecommunications Act of 1996 was put into place to eradicate the monopoly of large telephone companies; it was intended to give smaller telephone companies a chance to compete. The hope was that phone service would become more economical and that more rural customers would have access to more telecommunications services. A Universal Service Fund, money generated by a surcharge on every phone bill, was established to ensure investments were made to incorporate hard-to-reach customers. As a result, between 2003 and 2007 there was a tenfold increase in government subsidies paid to a handful of so-called "completive" providers—wireless phone companies paid by the Universal Service Fund to offer services in rural areas where an existing carrier also receives a subsidy.

Government involvement is crucial to the development of telecommunications infrastructure in rural areas. Yet often the incentives become entitlements for firms who take advantage of them. Rural communities often are not attractive to private companies, which prefer to lay cables in more densely populated areas. Although wireless technology and publicly subsidized satellites have greatly lowered the costs, the subsidies for wireless companies are the same as for wired service. Because information infrastructure links communities to one another and therefore crosses local government boundaries, both state and federal levels of government are involved. Such participation could involve direct public ownership, independent quasi-public or private collectively owned entities (such as the rural electric cooperatives organized to bring electricity to the nation's farmers), or subsidies to private firms. Regardless of the form of ownership chosen, the decision to subsidize telecommunications infrastructure in rural areas is a public choice that should be constantly reexamined in the light of changing technologies.

Motivation to Act

To what degree and under what conditions do communities and governments provide the needed infrastructure? When will the communities in Knott County insist on adequate water and sewer facilities? Can Hebron convince the county to repair its bridge? What will motivate private telecoms to ensure that remote areas receive affordable Internet service?

Assuming that a community has the capacity to mobilize investments in support of different forms of built capital, whose needs prevail? Are community choices a reflection of the community as a whole, or do they respond to the elites?

Chapter Summary

Built capital includes the permanent physical installations and facilities supporting productive activities in a community. Examples include roads, bridges, telephone and Internet services, and water and sewage treatment and distribution facilities.

Access to various types of infrastructure can be exclusive (limited to some) or inclusive (available to all). Consumption of goods or services provided through the infrastructure can be either joint (simultaneous use) or rival (use by one diminishes the use by another). If we cross the two forms of access with the two forms of consumption, we can identify four types of built capital: private, toll, common-pool, and collective.

The form of built capital is a factor in whether it is provided and supported through private or public organizations. Either the public or the private sector can supply private and toll goods or services. Collective and common-pool forms of infrastructure typically are provided by the public sector. Selection of the provider, public or private, is ultimately a choice made by the community.

Two forms of logic govern such decisions. Formal rationality relies on a quantitative assessment of the choice: The choice must result in profit. Substantive rationality relies upon values other than profit. Federal or state support of local infrastructure often is based on substantive rationality.

Four categories of built capital—facilities for water distribution, solid waste disposal, transportation, and telecommunications—illustrate some of the issues now faced by rural communities. Two issues, water availability and water quality, affect decisions related to the provision of water services. State and federal governments have become involved in issues related to water rights. Communities focus on the distribution and quality of water. For the most part, water access is placed under public control.

Because solid waste disposal involves exclusionary access and rival consumption, private control is a possibility. Local, state, and federal governments have found it necessary to intervene, however, to protect the environment. Current interest is focused on strategies that ensure consideration of the social as well as the physical costs of disposal.

Finally, transportation and communication technologies all depend on some state and federal involvement. E-commerce has become increasingly important for all businesses; however, rural communities continue to have difficulty getting affordable Internet access. In an unregulated environment, access to services at a reasonable price ceases to exist for many rural communities.

KEY TERMS

Built capital in a community includes the permanent physical facilities and services needed to support business and community life. Examples are roads, bridges, telephone service, and schools.

Collective goods are forms of infrastructure that involve inclusive access and joint consumption. Roads and public sidewalks are the most common examples.

Common-pool goods are forms of infrastructure that involve inclusive access and rival consumption. An example is a public building with a defined capacity.

Exclusive access is a characteristic of built capital such that individuals can be denied access to the good or service. Utility companies typically are exclusive.

Formal rationality applies to decisions made on the basis of economic calculation of profit or loss.

Inclusive access is a characteristic of built capital such that there is unrestricted access to all who would use it. Public roads are an example of inclusive infrastructure.

Infrastructure is the foundation or supporting framework needed for a structure or organization.

Joint consumption is a characteristic of built capital such that the use of a good or service by one person does not diminish its availability to another.

Monopolies are single enterprises that have sole control over the sale and distribution of a particular class of goods or services in a particular geographic area.

Private goods are forms of infrastructure that involve exclusive access and rival consumption. In most communities, waste disposal in local landfills has become private.

Public goods and services involve forms of built capital that are provided to the entire community at no cost.

Revenue bonds are a type of municipal bond where principal and interest are secured by revenues such as charges or rents paid by users of the facility built with the proceeds of the bond issue. Projects financed by revenue bonds include highways, airports, and not-for-profit health care and other facilities.

Rival consumption is a characteristic of built capital such that the use of a good or service by one person diminishes or even eliminates its availability to another.

Semipublic goods and services include forms of built capital that are supported in part by fees collected from the user.

Substantive rationality applies to decisions made on the basis of values rather than on economic calculation.

Toll goods or services are forms of infrastructure that involve exclusive access and joint consumption. Toll roads are the most common example.

REFERENCES

Brown, Dennis. 1999. "Will Increased Funding Help Rural Areas?" Economic Research Service, U.S. Department of Agriculture. Agriculture

Information Bulletin no. 753. Online; available: www.ers.usda.gov/publications/aib753/aib753.pdf; accessed April 14, 2003.

Chicoine, David L. 1986. "Infrastructure and Agriculture: Interdependence with a Focus on Local Roads in the North Central States." In *Interdependence of Agriculture and Rural Communities in the Twenty-First Century,* ed. Peter F. Korsching and Judith Gildner, 141–163. The North Central Regional Center for Rural Development.

Christopherson, Susan, Todd Alexander, Pierre Clavel, Jeffrey Lawhead, Kenneth Reardon, Karen Westmont, and Eric Wilson. 1999. *Reclaiming a Regional Resource: A Progress Report on the U.S. Department of Housing and Urban Development's Canal Corridor Initiative.* Ithaca, N.Y.: Department of City and Regional Planning, Cornell University. Also online; available: www.hud.gov/library/bookshelf18/pressrel/canalrpt.pdf; accessed April 16, 2003.

Environmental Protection Agency (EPA). 2000. "The Drinking Water State Revolving Fund: Financing America's Drinking Water." Online; available: www.epa.gov/safewater/dwsrf.html; accessed January 21, 2003.

———. 2002. "Region 3: Mid-Atlantic Region Hazardous Site Cleanup Division: Kim-Stan Landfill." Online; available: http://epa.gov/reg3hwmd/super/VA/kim-stan/pad.htm; accessed January 22, 2003.

Kilborn, Peter T. 1991. "In Despair, W.Va. County Looks to Trash." *New York Times,* October 16: A1–A2.

Strover, Sharon. 1999. "Rural Internet Connectivity." Rural Policy Research Institute (RUPRI) report. Online; available: www.rupri.org/pubs/archive/reports/1999/P99–13/index.html; accessed December 5, 2002.

Weber, Max. 1968. *Economy and Society: An Outline of Interpretive Sociology.* Eds. Guenther Roth and Claus Wittich. Vol. 1. Berkeley and Los Angeles: University of California Press.

PART TWO

THE TRANSFORMATION OF COMMUNITY CAPITALS IN A CHANGING WORLD

9

THE GLOBAL ECONOMY

When John Brooks, at age fifty-five, acquired the old shoe factory in Nelsonville, Ohio, in 1975, he never realized the long journey that his new company and its footwear would take. John felt compelled to buy the company because his uncle had once owned it, but John could not afford to purchase it by himself. He gave the sellers, who had no other buyers, only $500 as a down payment, but he needed to come up with the rest, nearly $600,000. John's son Mike contacted a high school friend, who later became the company's chief financial officer, for help. They contacted a congressman in Ohio who did not want the local shoe factory to close. Soon after, they attained assistance from the Farmers Home Administration, which guaranteed 90 percent of the loan. Five local banks lent them the money, which secured their ownership; however, John sensed that the road ahead would be challenging. If the company failed, John knew he would lose everything.

Mike Brooks, who was selling leather for a Milwaukee tannery, decided to help his father, even though John vehemently opposed his son's joining this risky venture. Mike had prepared for such an opportunity when, just out of high school, he had attended a shoe-design school in Milan, Italy. It had appeared that he had lost his chance to make his mark in the shoe business when his great-uncle sold the company out from under the family in 1959. He now had a second chance, and he was not going to pass it up.

The people of Nelsonville were thrilled because the shoe company would have closed otherwise; there were no other buyers. It would be locally owned again. However, the business needed more money for operating costs. Soon Brooks Shoes bypassed the local banks for most of its working capital; only banks in Cincinnati and Columbus had the financial capacity to service this growing shoe-manufacturing company. The company first marketed to big retail merchandising firms such as Sears and J.C. Penney, who slapped their own brand names on the shoes. These mail-order giants continued to place orders with Brooks Shoes because it provided high-quality shoes at low prices. John Brooks was selling a commodity, not a product. Mike concluded that if they wanted to make a decent profit and generate capital for expansion, they needed a brand name for their footwear. The company began targeting working people who did a lot of walking, including postal workers and law enforcement officials. Soon the company became Rocky Shoes and Boots. The Rocky label received a boost in 1977 when Mike won an award for a square-toed work boot he designed for the company.

Mike believed that they needed to increase the prices of their shoes, but John disagreed, staunchly maintaining "I did not buy the company to get rich." After many arguments, Mike was able to convince his father that they should sever ties with buyers who would not pay them more for their shoes. Mike had success at a trade show, where people lined up and demanded his new footwear for hunting. They had found their market niche: consumers of rugged, outdoor footwear.

John did not agree with some of Mike's ideas about how to run the family business, and he became upset when Mike decided to pursue overseas labor. John believed in using local labor to benefit the community. Mike thought the company would have a difficult time sustaining itself without employing cheaper labor. By 1987, Mike, along with their sales manager, the factory manager, their financial adviser, and John (a silent partner), purchased a Dominican Republic plant where the leather uppers were made. The uppers were shipped to Nelsonville, where local workers stitched them into the rest of the boot. A few years later, they opened a Puerto Rican plant.

In 1991, John decided to work only part time, and he handed his business and its debts equally to his five children. Mike remained president of the company, a position he had occupied since the mid–1980s. Mike was concerned that the heavy debt load stood in the way of obtaining capital for expansion. Mike decided to seek outside investors in Rocky Shoes and Boots through the stock market. In February 1993, Rocky Shoes was listed on the NASDAQ. Good economic times helped double the value of the stock from the initial offering—from $10 to $20—in a few short months. This sudden infusion of capital reduced the debt by $10 million. John Brooks was impressed with his son's achievement. Mike handed him a $1 million check for his share of the Dominican plant—his last remaining investment in the company. Mike began planning for a major expansion: "We have a chance to become a Timberland or a Wolverine," he told the *Columbus Dispatch* in 1997.

Mike's decision to expand at the beginning of 1999 was not matched by an increase in demand for Rocky shoes. The company was overloaded with unwanted boots and shoes and had to sell them at cheap prices to elated customers. This meant a net loss of $5 million; Mike had to make some difficult decisions. He did not want to move the factory jobs overseas, but he knew it would be a possibility if profits continued to decrease. Furthermore, he had to share profits with other owners who had bought the company's stock on the NASDAQ. Unlike John, they were in the business for the profit; in fact, that was their only interest in the company. Labor in other countries was much cheaper, and Mike knew that it might be a way to recover profits.

Mike would have to make this critical decision on his own; he could not debate the situation with his father, who had passed away in 1996. What Mike and his fellow executives had ignored was that the competitors they had identified (Wolverine and Timberlake) focused on fashion to grow their firms; the rural and blue-collar workers, such as postal workers, who bought Rocky hunting boots and hiking shoes were not that interested in fashion. The market was dependable but not prone to expand rapidly. He decided to strengthen that market by selling his shoes at Wal-Mart, a company that sells one-third of America's hunting licenses each year. Although the value of Rocky's stock rose again after this marketing move, difficult times were still in sight.

By November 2000, 110 people had been laid off in Nelsonville, as Mike moved these manufacturing positions to the Dominican Republic. The company's stock had plummeted to a fifty-two-week low of $3.69 per share after the layoffs, and many people were angry with Mike because of the way he was handling the business. They scoffed at his new car and even jeered at him at the factory in Nelsonville. The workers felt that he had failed them and the community, and he recognized their pain.

In November 2001, Mike Brooks moved the remaining sixty-seven manufacturing jobs to a factory in Moca, Puerto Rico. An overall mood of sadness was apparent as the last pair of boots produced in Nelsonville came down the assembly line. Manufacturing shoes in Nelsonville meant paying a worker $11 an hour, versus $6 in Puerto Rico, $1.25 in the Dominican Republic, and 40 cents in China. Mike felt that the only way the company could thrive enough to pay dividends to stockholders and revalue its stock was to take full advantage of cheaper overseas labor.

Rocky Shoes also took advantage of overseas tax breaks. Five Star Enterprises Ltd., a Cayman Islands corporation and subsidiary of Rocky Shoes, operates the manufacturing facility in La Vega, Dominican Republic. The Cayman Islands is a Caribbean tax haven. Earnings repatriated from the company's subsidiary in the Dominican Republic are subject to U.S. federal income tax but are exempt from state and local taxation. In 1999, the company elected not to repatriate all 1999 and future earnings of its subsidiary in the Dominican Republic. It pays no property, income, or sales taxes in the Dominican Republic; the factory is located in a free trade zone. In 1988, Rocky Shoes established a subsidiary, Lifestyle Footwear Inc., in Delaware to operate the manufacturing facility in Puerto Rico. The company thus paid minimal income taxes on income earned by its subsidiary in Puerto Rico due to tax credits it received under Section 936 of the Internal Revenue Code (enacted to assist in industrializing Puerto Rico), local tax abatements, and the fact that Delaware charges no income tax on corporations operating within the state. However, when Section 936 was repealed, future tax credits available to the company were capped beginning in 2002 and terminated in 2006. In addition, the company's local tax abatements in Puerto Rico expired in 2004. Rocky Shoes also sources products manufactured to its specifications from independent manufacturers in the Far East, primarily China, to be able to further cut prices. In 2000, this represented 36 percent of the company's sales.

Although many of the factory workers in Nelsonville were unionized, none were offered replacement jobs with the company. Judith Collins, age sixty-one, said, "I've been here thirty-six years. I wanted four more, and then to retire. This is the only job I've ever had." The number of white-collar workers in the corporate headquarters in Nelsonville exceeds 260—more than the number of factory workers employed during most of the firm's existence—but working-class jobs for those with a high school education or less are much more scarce in this Appalachian town of five thousand than at any time since before coal was mined locally. In 2006, Mike Brooks received $662,390 in current and deferred compensation plus $91,000 in stock options—a quite modest package, compared to most CEOs of publicly traded companies.

Rocky Shoes was the last shoe company to close its factory doors in Ohio. The U.S. Department of Labor has reported that fewer than 15,000 shoe jobs (USDOL/BLS 2006) remained in the United States by 2004, down from 235,000 in 1972.

Not only are rural and urban areas alike being drawn into a world economy, but the character of the economy has also changed. Financial capital, the money businesses need to finance their operations, now can be moved easily from one country to another. New financial instruments constantly evolve that further separate both debt and investment capital from management—and responsibility. The Internet has made this even more effortless. Businesses across the globe can be accessed from a consumer's home. Businesses, through online advertising and stores, can target another business's customers; businesses can also sell supplies to one another via the Internet. Thus, the price of money, not the price of raw materials, is driving many business decisions. This chapter explores (1) traditional linkages between rural areas and international markets; (2) changes that have altered the character of the world economy, including e-commerce; (3) the impact these changes are having on rural communities; and (4) the opportunities and problems this new economic environment creates.

RURAL LINKAGES TO A WORLD ECONOMY

Newspaper accounts and after-dinner speeches often characterize the world economy as though it were something new, as though the U.S. economy previously had been insulated from world events. Although the character of the U.S. economy has changed, the United States has always been linked to other countries through trade. In the past, rural communities were tied with the world economy through the primary products (e.g., lumber, food and fiber, seafood, energy, precious metals).

Exporting Natural Capital

International trade motivated and financed European immigration to and settlement in the New World. Trading companies, eager to profit from the natural resources the new land offered, financed early European settlements in the New World. New England communities found furs, fish, and lumber to be their most profitable exports. The South depended on rice, cotton, and tobacco. For the colonies, these international linkages were so important that the tariff England imposed on American tobacco was among the causes of the Revolutionary War.

Nearly all natural-resource-based economies move through cycles, influenced by nature and by trends in world markets. Mining towns have gone through boom-and-bust cycles as mineral prices fluctuated on the international market. In the 1870s, the silver streaming out of Nevada nearly ruined Germany, which had a currency based on silver. During World War I, cotton prices soared in response to the demand for uniforms. Once Europe recovered in the 1920s, however, prices dropped to historic lows. Increased grain production in Europe sent American wheat prices plummeting following both World Wars. Until railroads opened up markets in the Midwest and the East, Oregon lumber interests depended more on foreign than domestic markets. Today, raw logs are exported to Japan from the United States; Japan is the greatest volume buyer of logs, purchasing virtually all sizes and species. The United States generally sends more wood fiber, whole logs, and wood chips overseas than any other country.

Oil towns from Texas to Montana prospered when the members of the Organization of Petroleum Exporting Countries (OPEC) limited their oil production in 1973. The OPEC cartel represents the interests of major oil-producing countries, most of which are located in the Middle East. Decreased oil production in the Middle East meant increased prices worldwide, high enough to encourage the development of domestic oil reserves, triggering an economic boom in states such as Texas and Oklahoma unequaled since the days of the gold and silver rushes of the past century. Less than a decade later, however, the same towns that had boomed were struggling. Increased oil production from the OPEC nations had sharply reduced the price of oil worldwide, making U.S. domestic oil no longer competitive.

In 2000, OPEC decided to limit production to five million barrels of oil per day, increasing the demand for domestic oil, which caused higher prices. OPEC's decision, along with concern over the war in Iraq, caused oil prices to rise. International events, such as the September 11, 2001, terrorist attacks and the military conflict in Iraq, create uncertainty about supplies, which leads to price fluctuations. With increasing conflict in the Middle East, members of OPEC have had difficulty reaching a consensus over production targets and exporting strategies. Despite OPEC's lack of coordination, the growing demand for fossil fuels by emerging countries, China and India in particular, and increased petroleum imports by the

United States that dwarf those of any other country, has increased demand and raised prices. Luft and Morse (2006) of the Washington Office on Near East Policy state, "[b]etween 1990 and 2005, U.S. oil imports increased by six million barrels per day, higher than the total oil consumption of all other countries except China, and equal to total Chinese demand."

Importing Human Capital

Early linkages with the world economy also included movement of workers, the people needed to harvest the vast natural resources available in the New World. European immigrants seeking to escape religious persecution or simply to get a new start on life harvested New England's furs, fish, and lumber. Slaves were brought involuntarily from Africa to harvest rice, cotton, and tobacco in the South. The need for low-cost labor to perform domestic work along railroad lines or in mining camps led to heavy conscription of Chinese laborers. Mine owners in West Virginia recruited experienced miners from eastern Europe. Europeans who were eager to own land settled farms throughout the Midwest.

The need for labor, especially in rural areas, was so great that the United States maintained open borders for nearly a hundred years after independence, until the Chinese Exclusion Act of 1882. Immigration hit an all-time high in the first decade of the twentieth century, leading some to propose that limits be imposed. In 1921, Congress passed the first quota act, limiting the annual number of immigrants from each country to 3 percent of the number of people born in that country and residing in the United States as reported in the 1910 census. The Immigration Act of 1924 was even more restrictive: It used the national origin of each individual in the United States in 1890 as the basis for allocating admission to the flow of immigrants. It was not the numbers of immigrants but their racial and cultural backgrounds that inspired these exclusionary efforts, which were clearly aimed at reducing immigration from Asia and southern and eastern Europe. National-origin limitations were lifted in 1965, but numerical limits still remain in place, although the limit is referred to as a "flexible worldwide cap." There are country quotas on immigrants who are family members of U.S. citizens, and there is a major backlog in processing applications.

To complicate the contradictions of migration policy and labor demand, the U.S. and Canada populations are aging, particularly in rural areas. As a result, economic survival requires that new sources of labor be found from outside current national borders. Yet the small number of immigrants allowed to enter legally forces choices between economic stability or population homogeneity.

In an effort to safeguard the United States from future terrorist attacks, recent changes in immigration regulations have been imposed, making it more difficult for immigrants to enter the country. Some of these changes include a program that makes getting and keeping student visas more difficult and an extended waiting period on nonimmigrant visa applications, especially for men from Middle Eastern and Muslim populations. These changes make it far more difficult for well-intentioned immigrants to enter the country, and racial and ethnic discrimination can be a by-product. In fact, many Mexican immigrants have been searched and questioned exhaustively when they cross the U.S. border. Julio Sandoval is one such immigrant. Julio is not seeking U.S. citizenship; he emigrated from Mexico in 1989 and is already a naturalized citizen. However, when he and three male friends returned to the United States from a recent visit to Mexico, they went through hours of investigation, including a check of police and citizenship records (Adame 2002). Even though Julio understands that strict surveillance of U.S. immigrants is necessary and important, it is clear from this example that men of varied ethnic descent are being targeted at the border because of the events of September 11. More recently, widespread raids by the Department of Homeland Security's Immigration and Customs Enforcement have detained large numbers of workers with full documentation of their legal residence, including many native-born Hispanics and African Americans.

Although U.S. immigration restrictions have increased, it is important to remember the extent to which economic activity in rural areas depended on labor imported from other countries. For example, much of the labor in food processing, the hospitality industry, and construction is provided by migrants.

ALTERING GLOBALIZATION:
THE GROWING IMPORTANCE OF FINANCIAL CAPITAL

Linkages to world markets are not new, but the character of those linkages has changed dramatically. *Commodities,* bulk natural resources or standardized manufactured products bought and sold on markets, once drove the international economy. The country that could mine copper or weave high-quality cloth at the lowest cost exported the most. Consequently, national industries sought to make their operations more efficient to remain competitive.

Today, it is the flow of capital from one currency to another, even more than trade in goods or services, that drives the international economy. Corporations have become multinational, moving their operations to wherever the financial conditions enhance profitability. Tax havens in small countries of the Caribbean are used by firms the size of Rocky Shoes and larger to reduce their tax burden, thus loosening their ties to the particular country where they were founded. High-speed electronic communication allows different operations in the value chain to be carried out in different countries to enhance the bottom line. As a result, local areas have less control over what happens to them economically. To understand how this came about, we need to examine (1) changes in international monetary policy, (2) the impact of trade relations and domestic fiscal policies, and (3) and the true internationalization of corporations.

International Monetary Policy

As World War II drew to a close, world leaders met in Bretton Woods, New Hampshire, to grapple with the problem of how to reestablish trade. Most felt that the economic chaos of the 1930s had contributed to the Nazi takeover in Europe; thus, they were anxious to develop mechanisms that would ensure stability in the world economy. The Bretton Woods Agreement (1944) created a system of fixed exchange rates among national currencies. *Exchange rates* set the value of countries' currencies relative to one another; consequently, they are important in facilitating trade among nations. Under the agreement, the United States fixed the value of the U.S. dollar to gold at $35 per ounce. The exchange rates of other countries were then fixed relative to the U.S. dollar. This system of *fixed exchange rates* did not allow the value of the dollar to fluctuate on world markets.

During the 1950s and 1960s, the United States enjoyed economic predominance throughout the capitals of the world. Its economy grew steadily, filling gaps in trade as the nations of Europe and Japan turned their attention to rebuilding what had been destroyed during World War II. The United States generally favored open trade of its products and enjoyed a trade surplus, exporting more than it imported. The dollar occupied a unique position in the world economy as the standard against which the values of all other currencies were fixed.

As the world economy recovered from World War II and as other nations strengthened their industrial base, U.S. exports faced increased competition. By the early 1970s, the United States was importing more than it was exporting, in part because the dollar was valued much higher than other currencies. There was a net flow of dollars out of the United States and into countries from which it was importing goods.

When the dollars held by other countries exceeded the gold reserves the United States had with which to buy back those dollars, financiers assumed that the United States would increase the price of gold. In other words, increasing the exchange rate for gold from $35 to $40 per ounce in effect decreases the value of each dollar relative to gold and is an example of currency devaluation against a standard, gold. Financiers began trying to unload their dollars on world currency markets, hoping to sell the U.S. dollars before they were devalued. The flood of dollars on currency markets forced the United States to do just what the financiers feared: devalue the dollar. In August 1971, the United States also suspended the conversion of dollars into gold.

Efforts to establish a new fixed exchange rate failed. In May 1973, President Richard Nixon negotiated the Smithsonian Agreement, which established a *floating exchange rate,* allowing currency values to fluctuate and find their market values. Central banks, including that of the United States, could no longer fix exchange rates except in cases when a nation's currency began fluctuating widely. In general, national controls on currency were reduced and country-to-country banking restrictions were eased.

Financial capital, the money available for investment, now moves more easily from one country to another. This allows private speculators to buy and sell currencies in an effort to make a profit as exchange rates fluctuate, which can have devastating effects on the countries whose exchange rates are in disfavor. Capital markets established through this exchange of currency generate a flow of money that is thirty times as great as the money exchanged through countries importing and exporting products. Whether a nation's corn is competitive on the world market, for example, depends as much on the current exchange rate of that country's currency as on the costs of growing that corn. A strong dollar discourages foreign tourists from visiting the United States, but U.S. tourists travel enthusiastically to other countries. When the dollar is weak relative to other currencies, visitors flock to the United States, and Americans are more likely to visit Yellowstone or New York City, rather than Europe or Asia. However, recently imposed difficulties in getting tourist visas has reduced the number of foreign tourists in the United States, even when the dollar is low on world markets.

The movement of people across borders, whether for pleasure or work, decreased sharply after September 11, 2001, temporarily slowing the flow of money across international borders. The concurrent *recession,* defined by the National Bureau of Economic Research as "a period [two consecutive quarters] of declining output and employment," caused some instability in the value of the dollar, and since travel to and from the United States decreased, the economy did not bounce back quickly. Scandals involving large corporations such as Enron and WorldCom created skepticism among international investors. The euro's introduction in an additional twelve countries of the European Union on January 1, 2002, added competition for the dollar. The dollar's value decreased, reaching a one-to-one parity with the euro in July 2002 and declining more than 25 percent since then.

A decline in the dollar reduces the value of U.S.-based assets, thereby reducing the wealth of foreign investors. A plunging dollar could negatively impact the global economy by deflating consumption and causing international investors to withdraw their investments from the United States in favor of countries with stronger currency. If the dollar weakens substantially more, domestic interest rates could increase to encourage investment to finance the U.S. debt. After the low interest rates of the early years of the twenty-first century, rising interest rates in the United States had serious negative impacts on the housing market and other investments that drive the U.S. economy. On the other hand, moderate and gradual weakening of the dollar might encourage exports and reduce the massive trade deficits the United States has experienced over the past decade and a half. In the absence of a worldwide recession, such a change should strengthen U.S. agricultural and manufactured exports, benefiting rural areas.

Trade Relations and Domestic Fiscal Policies

However, the continued weakening of the dollar since 2002 has not led to an improvement of the U.S. trade deficit—in fact it has deepened. The main reason is that China has kept its currency artificially undervalued (by linking it to the U.S. dollar) to ensure a continued flow of exports to the United States. In turn, this has dampened inflation in the United States by having doubly cheap consumer goods available to American consumers— doubly cheap because of the low wages in China and because of China's artificially weak yuan. Hence the sharp increase in petroleum prices—and gasoline in particular—in the United States since 2005 has contributed to only moderate inflation—particularly in conjunction with a series of hikes in the Fed's prime interest rate. The price of gasoline has increased because of uncertainties in the Middle East, but also because of limited refining capacity in the United States. (There is evidence that over the years certain major oil companies have deliberately limited their refining capacity to boost the price of gasoline.) The federal budget surplus during the later years of the Bill Clinton administration turned into a growing deficit due to the wars in Iraq and Afghanistan and to the tax cuts passed by the Republican Congress in the first six years of the George W. Bush administration. That could lead to a crowding out of private investment funds by the government as it attempts to finance an increasing national debt. However, cheap consumer goods from China and elsewhere, and the self-interest China has in continuing to invest in U.S. public and private offerings, dampens interest rates. Thus, the U.S. government pushes China to revalue its currency—but not very hard.

The New Corporation

What is the impact of these changes? Companies have become multinational in a new sense. Computerization, the free flow of capital, and tariff reductions around the world allow networks of firms to source raw materials and components from different parts of the world. No longer confined to one country, many of today's corporations have developed branches and relations with supplier companies in countries throughout the world. These diversified locations ensure that the company has access to local markets and the flexibility to move resources quickly in response to changes in capital and labor markets (and to reduce tax liability, as we saw in the case of Rocky Shoes). The organizational structure of these companies reflects the multinational character of their operations. Stockholders reside all over the world, as do the board members who make decisions on behalf of the company. Individual countries can do little to control the activities of these new corporations.

Trade Agreements and International Labor Markets (Human Capital)

Beginning in the 1980s, a debt crisis, quite similar in its origins to the farm crisis that occurred within the United States, befell debtor countries (mostly developing countries without large quantities of exportable oil). To discipline those debtor countries to pay back their staggering debts, the International Monetary Fund and the World Bank implemented neo-liberal policies to help them streamline their state apparatus and to open their economies to international competition in hopes that enterprises in those countries would become "lean and mean." If they did not survive this competition, foreign firms would take their place. To pay back the debt, countries had to generate more foreign exchange and by definition had to be export oriented. By bringing about lower tariffs, the General Agreement on Trade and Tariffs and its successor, the World Trade Organization (WTO), were an important part of this neoliberal international economic model. Each nation was to specialize in those productive enterprises in which it had a comparative advantage, and the world system as a whole would become more productive.

The WTO is the only global organization dealing with the rules of trade between nations. The goal of the WTO is to help producers of goods and services, exporters, and importers conduct their business with the least friction or nonmarket barriers. The organization, created by the Uruguay Round of trade negotiations, which lasted from 1986 to 1994, was formally established January 1, 1995. Based in Geneva, Switzerland, the WTO administers trade agreements, serves as a forum for trade negotiations, handles trade disputes, monitors national trade policies, and provides technical assistance and training for developing countries. Many groups take issue with the WTO's authority to set and enforce universal rules of trade, although there are special exceptions from the most stringent rules barring state support for exports for developing countries. The rules are set on the basis of financial capital goals; many criticize the rules of trade because they do not include standards regarding human capital (prohibitions against slave or child labor, workers' rights to collective bargaining, etc.) and do not allow individual countries to set standards regarding natural capital (for instance, a member state's setting of green standards would be prohibited as a "restraint of trade"). The WTO says that its goal is to facilitate world trade, and that is what most alarms critics, who feel that world trade harms excluded people by further disadvantaging them through increased competition and lower prices for what they produce.

Backers of the WTO saw regional trade agreements as complementary to the organization, and indeed spelled out the relation between the WTO and such agreements. The North American Free Trade Agreement

(NAFTA) was one such regional agreement. Implemented on January 1, 1994, it provided for a reduction of tariffs among the three partners—Canada, Mexico, and the United States. NAFTA illustrates what is perhaps the greatest shortcoming of free trade—that in practice there is no free trade: political advantage generally trumps comparative advantage. NAFTA included reduction and eventual elimination of agricultural tariffs, but it could not resolve the larger agricultural conundrum that the WTO was wrestling with—how to deal with protection afforded farmers from the economically most powerful countries, namely the United States, Japan, and those in Europe. Prior to NAFTA, Mexico had eliminated subsidies on corn as part of structural adjustment. Under NAFTA, they experienced an additional shock as tariffs on subsidized U.S. corn were eliminated in just thirty months. U.S. corn was cheapened further in Mexico by the weak dollar, which had a devastating effect on the countryside in traditionally corn-growing areas. As industrial jobs fled to cheaper Asian venues, migration to Mexican cities was not a solution for those from the depressed countryside. In 1997, with a worldwide dip in commodity prices, migration of rural Mexicans to the United States began to grow, becoming a flood by the turn of the new century. It is not a great exaggeration to say that under NAFTA the United States traded corn for immigrants. Rural parts of the Midwest and the rural South were particularly attractive to the new migrants as confinement livestock and poultry operations, located in depopulating rural areas, were in need of workers. The neoliberal model of development requires rapid flow of financial capital, quick construction of built capital, and highly mobile human capital. The model also rests on cheapening labor. The main bottleneck to the system working smoothly is that human capital is subject to serious limitations on mobility across national boundaries imposed by the national state.

Impact on Rural Areas

Any discussion of capital flows, fluctuating commodities prices, floating currency exchanges, and foreign investment seems abstract until their collective impact on rural areas is examined. Two examples, one drawn from agriculture and the second from rural manufacturing, illustrate how rural areas have been affected by the changed global economy. We also discuss the changing character of the rural labor force.

The Farm Crisis of the 1980s

The 1970s brought another milestone in the transition to a global economy. As mentioned earlier, OPEC decided to limit oil production. In making oil scarcer, OPEC effectively increased the price of oil. Urban people in the United States remember long lines at gasoline pumps and occasional fistfights as motorists jockeyed for position to buy the scarce gasoline at unbelievably high prices. Rural people remember $5-per-bushel wheat and $12-per-bushel soybeans—prices two to three times higher than usual.

The sudden increase in oil prices meant that the oil-producing countries developed a trade surplus. The money they received from the oil they exported exceeded the money they spent on imports. Oil-producing nations had "petrodollars" to spare and were suddenly able to import more goods. The Soviet Union, for example, was a major exporter of oil. It also needed food and feed grains with which to support its people. The trade surplus created by higher oil prices enabled the Soviets to purchase larger quantities of basic commodities such as wheat and soybeans. Oil-producing countries, particularly those with small populations but lots of oil, were eager to lend poorer, non-oil-exporting countries money to purchase oil, wheat, and other commodities.

The increased price for commodities that followed set off a period of worldwide inflation. *Inflation* occurs when the currency in circulation or the availability of credit increases faster than production grows, leading to a sharp rise in prices. The devaluation of the dollar made U.S. exports extremely competitive in world markets. Percentages and volume of crops exported were higher than they had been during the previous fifty years.

Economic conditions during the 1970s encouraged farmers to borrow money. Land was rapidly increasing in value, giving farmers more equity in the land they already held. The shift to floating exchange rates and the devaluation of the dollar made U.S. products very competitive in world markets. Business was booming, and capital was readily available. Moreover, inflation was outstripping interest rates. If inflation averages 10 percent and interest rates are only 8 percent, it makes sense to buy land or equipment rather than to put money into a savings account. Farmers and other borrowers were being paid to borrow money—as long as real interest rates remained negative. Land itself became an excellent investment and a hedge against inflation. The real value of land, when controlled for inflation, nearly doubled during the 1970s. When the effects of inflation are added in, the price per acre nearly tripled during this same period (U.S. Department of Commerce 1986).

By the end of the 1970s, U.S. economic growth depended heavily on the rest of the world, particularly as a market for agricultural products. As worldwide demand for imported agricultural and manufactured products became saturated, the United States moved into a period of "stagflation": high inflation with no real economic growth.

Efforts to curb inflation in the United States focused on internal fiscal and monetary policy. In 1979, the Federal Reserve Board, the governing body that sets monetary policy for the U.S. central bank, effectively withdrew dollars from circulation in the economy by increasing the rate that banks charge their best customers, other banks. This strategy reduces inflation. Investment slows or declines because money is more costly, workers are laid off, and people have less money to buy products, all of which reduces demand and stabilizes prices.

To counteract the recessionary impact of the Federal Reserve Board's action, the Reagan administration decreased the federal income tax and, despite making spending cuts in many areas, increased spending for defense, farm programs, and the interest paid on the increasing national debt. Massive tax cuts were made in 1981, with the high-income and corporate sectors of the economy being the primary beneficiaries. The rationale was that tax cuts would free up money for investment in the domestic economy and stimulate economic growth. Increased economic growth did not occur at the projected rate, however. As a result, the federal deficit grew rapidly. The United States became the largest debtor nation in the world, borrowing money from foreign countries at the new higher rates rather than raising taxes or cutting spending.

The United States took these actions in an effort to deal with its internal economic problems. As it turned out, however, these actions had an enormous negative impact on the world economy. Economic theory predicts that if the money supply is reduced, the economy will slow down. The trade-off is reduced inflation. A gradual tightening of the money supply could result only in a decrease in economic growth. This was not the case in the early 1980s. The abrupt actions taken by the Federal Reserve Board under presidents Jimmy Carter and Ronald Reagan slowed inflation but also triggered a worldwide recession.

Why should action taken in the United States to cure its own economic ills affect the world economy? The answer lies, in part, with how easily capital flows from one country to another. Dollars withdrawn from the national economy were also dollars withdrawn from the world economy. In fact, that was an objective of the Fed—to regain control over U.S. currency. The growth of the federal deficit meant that the federal government itself was competing for scarce dollars, which also boosted real interest rates.

High real interest rates made U.S. government securities a good investment. Foreign capital flowed into the United States because the U.S. government needed to borrow so much money to service its debt. The U.S. deficit became something of an international black hole, pulling in any and all liquid capital. This made capital scarce for others and deepened the worldwide recession. The spiral of increasing demand and higher prices for commodities came to an abrupt end. Prices of commodities on the world market dropped precipitously.

As real interest rates climbed and as the value of the dollar rose, those who had borrowed money—whether American farmers or Third World countries—found themselves paying more interest with increasingly scarce dollars. When commodities prices fell dramatically, both crops and land on which they were produced lost much of their former value. Agricultural land prices in the United States dropped by more than 50 percent, reaching the point where farmers no longer had the equity to repay loans that were still outstanding. In short, a great many farmers faced financial ruin. By 1985, the number of farm foreclosures, forfeitures, or loan defaults reached levels not seen since the Great Depression.

Farmers were not bad managers, nor were banks unusually greedy. Both applied tried-and-true investment principles to the economic environment created by the floating exchange rate and increased oil prices. Monetary and fiscal policies initiated by the federal government (decreasing taxes) and the Federal Reserve Board (cutting the money supply) simply changed that environment and changed the rules of the game.

Although recovery from the recession was evident in urban America by the middle of the 1980s, rural communities that were natural-resource-dependent did not experience substantial economic growth until after the rather mild 1991 recession—and then only from a notably smaller population and institutional base than had existed in the 1970s. During the 1990s, rural areas shared to a degree in the prosperity of the nation as a whole. Many communities diversified away from such heavy dependence on natural resource–based activities into services and routine manufacturing, availing themselves of a gradually shrinking niche in the world system, one that combined willingness to work for low wages (relative to metropolitan U.S. wages but still very high when compared with wage scales in developing countries) with an educated and dedicated workforce (human capital) and adequate built capital along with strong social infrastructure. Persistent-poverty areas in the South, Southwest, and Great Plains did not fare so well. The rural routine manufacturing sector, as we saw in the case of Rocky Shoes, is very vulnerable to the shifting of production jobs to Latin America initially and later to China and other low-wage parts of Asia.

In mid–2007 (as we write this chapter), conditions in the United States are very different from those of the 1970s, 1980s, and indeed the 1990s. The burst of productivity led by the electronic and telecommunications sectors in the 1990s kept inflation well under control. In 2002, the economy pulled out of a brief recession. Since inflation was not a problem, interest rates dropped to the lowest point in thirty years. However, people continued to be cautious about spending their money because of the military conflict in Iraq, distrust of large corporations, the instability of the economy, and increasing economic inequality. (Real wages had not increased since the 1970s.) Americans and foreigners were not investing in the stock market as readily, causing the market in the second half of 2002 to have its worst performance since 1991. The uncontrolled secondary market of *subprime lending* led to an increase in ownership of homes beyond the investors' real ability to pay, as well as high speculation in the housing market. As the favorable introductory terms of those loans ended, borrowers were unable to make their higher monthly payments, driving down the price of homes, with repercussions across the economy.

When a recession looms (and there is fear of reentering the recession), consumers, concerned that they may lose their jobs, spend less money on frivolous goods, which ultimately hurts retailers. Locally owned retail stores often feel the effects of the economic downturn the most, since they often do not have the flexibility of large corporate firms to shed unprofitable activities, slash their workforce, or sell off built capital. The slow recovery of the economy and stagnation of wages caused frustration for many; however, the low interest rates on real estate gave many people the chance to buy a home or to refinance the one they already owned—investments that are viewed as much more solid than the alternatives. Further, lenders offered extremely low adjustable interest rates (ARMs, or adjustable-rate mortgages) for the first several years of the loan, and borrowers often bought a more expensive house than they had intended or consolidated their debts in home equity loans. Because of the increasing value of their asset, borrowers assumed they could simply refinance if their mortgage rate adjusted upward. Housing prices soared nationwide as the upper middle class moved up the ladder and homeownership increased among the lower middle class. By 2006, interests rates and ARMs had increased, and housing prices, particularly in urban areas, became much higher than was merited by the ability of all but the wealthy to repay their mortgages, and demand began to decline. Much as occurred in the farm crisis, as housing values declined, people who had hoped to refinance when the initial favorable terms of their loan ended simply were unable to make the new higher payments.

Like the Reagan administration, the second Bush administration attempted to stimulate the economy by cutting taxes and (whether intended for that purpose or not) greatly increasing military spending. Farm program expenditures, too, have reached all-time highs. Low interest rates decreased the cost of the national debt, but the deficit increased at record rates. Beginning in 2005, the upward adjustment in interest rates (although still moderate by historical standards) further increased interest payments on the national debt.

U.S. farmers now function in a changed economy. The increased worldwide production stimulated by the high commodities prices of the 1970s and farmers' positive responses to overproduction stimuli has flooded the market. With the so-called Freedom to Farm Act, the United States began subsidizing major commodities without supply-limiting mechanisms after 1997; Europe—until recently—and Japan continued to protect domestic production through high import tariffs and export subsidies. The increase in world inequalities, in part a result of the structural adjustment policies instituted by the World Bank and the IMF, has meant that the number of poor people in developing countries who were poor clients for the increased amount of traded food has actually grown, although commodity prices continued on a downward trajectory. Finally, the worth of a farmer's produce has become as much a function of currency and futures markets as it is of the inherent productivity of the farm operation.

That was the situation until October 2006, when the demand for corn for ethanol increased sharply in the United States due to the increase in petroleum and gasoline prices, which enabled lobbyists for the grain industry to gain further federal and state ethanol and biodiesel subsidies. Those subsidies increased the prices of crops that compete with corn for land in the Midwestern and Southern United States. As the strong demand for agricultural commodities works its way through the international system, it may stimulate production of basic commodities in developing countries, but in the meantime, urban consumers in Mexico City protest the soaring price of tortillas.

In agriculturally dependent counties of the United States, the effects of this boom in agricultural commodity prices would appear to be good for farmers and for rural communities, but there are some problems. Not all farmers benefit from high commodity prices, since landowners tend to capitalize the increase into land prices. Thus land owners benefit. Because of the skipping of a generation of farmers due to foreclosures and low prices during the 1980s farm crisis, management companies now farm a significant portion of Midwestern land on behalf of urban inheritors of family farms. Owner-operators farm a decreasing share of farmland; absentee owners will benefit from higher land prices, but not renters. Since farm program payments tend to go out of county and often out of state, the communities where the farmland is located benefit less from farm subsidies than they used to. Large management companies bypass the local community in buying machinery. Farming-dependent counties of the Midwest and South are the least likely of rural counties to retain population and to generate economic development.

Rural Manufacturing

Economic conditions that encouraged U.S. farmers to expand also stimulated the growth of rural manufacturing. In about 1960, relatively mature industries began looking to rural areas for cheaper land, an ample labor supply, and lower wage levels. This trend was bolstered by decisions to devalue the dollar and shift to a floating currency. The cheaper dollar made U.S. exports more competitive in world markets. The country's products also became more competitive within domestic markets, because it was less costly to manufacture some products at home than to import them from Germany or Japan. The rapid increases in commodity prices that followed OPEC's decision to limit oil production put money in the hands of many developing nations, and their greater purchasing power further increased demand for U.S. products.

Growth in U.S. rural manufacturing employment continued during the 1970s, increasing at an annual rate of about 1.4 percent until 1976. By contrast, manufacturing employment in urban areas was declining at a rate of 1.1 percent per year. The availability of low-wage, hardworking, nonunionized rural labor forces attracted many light-manufacturing plants. Rural communities invested heavily in industrial parks and infrastructure developments designed to attract industry. Tax abatements, new-job tax credits, training programs, low-interest loans, and a host of local, state, and federal subsidies added more incentives for industry to move to rural areas. High demand, low wages, and inexpensive capital made it profitable for industries to relocate their more routine production activities to rural counties. By 1979, manufacturing had become the largest employer of the rural workforce.

Actions taken to control inflation and stimulate the domestic economy brought this expansion to a halt. Between 1979 and 1982, employment in rural manufacturing dropped 5.6 percent as nearly every state in the nation lost manufacturing jobs; recession hit the U.S. economy. As the 1980s progressed, the value of the dollar increased, and U.S. goods and services became more expensive on the world market. By the mid–1980s, rural areas found themselves in an entirely different economic environment. The strong U.S. dollar made it more difficult for the United States to compete on world markets. To maintain their profits, some companies felt it necessary to move their plants to the developing nations of Mexico, Thailand, and Bangladesh, where labor could be acquired more cheaply. The sustained economic growth of the 1990s resulted in a renewal of nonmetropolitan manufacturing growth, but the comparative advantage that rural areas had over metropolitan ones remained cheap labor. Since the raw materials usually were not locally produced and low-wage labor was employed, the local multipliers for these plants were not very high. Agriculturally related manufacturing plants, such as meatpacking, had a greater impact on the rural communities and were less likely to move to developing countries.

The recession of 2002 shrank the number of rural manufacturing jobs further, as occurred in Nelsonville, Ohio, when Rocky Shoes closed out its manufacturing activities and moved overseas. In the past, rural areas have led the country out of recessions, but recently they have followed metropolitan areas (Henderson 2002). Rural communities will need to find innovative ways to enhance the productivity of local manufacturing companies and to develop flexible, high-end manufacturing firms and service businesses. Perhaps e-commerce will help in this effort.

An International Labor Market (Human Capital)

As discussed earlier, rural areas historically have depended on immigrant labor. In the two decades after World War II, only a little more than 60 percent of the legal quota of immigrants entered the country. Labor was needed, however, as the economy expanded.

Permitting temporary immigration offered one solution to the problem, and this was provided through the Bracero Program (1942–1964), a series of bilateral agreements that temporarily admitted agricultural workers to the United States from Mexico, Barbados, Jamaica, and British Honduras. Migrant workers harvested fruits and vegetables, providing low-wage labor at crucial times in the production cycle. Undocumented immigrants, those without any formal documentation, also began moving into both urban and rural areas.

As international capital flow increased, so did international immigration to the United States. Foreign-born residents accounted for only 4.7 percent of the U.S. population in 1970, the lowest proportion in the twentieth century. That percentage had more than doubled by 2000, to 10.4 percent, reaching 12.4 percent by 2005 (Migration Policy Institute 2007). Compare that number with the high mark of 13.6 percent recorded in the 1900 census. Despite a temporary decline in illegal immigrants after the amnesty law of 1986, undocumented migration to this country is again high, estimated by the Pew Hispanic Center at twelve million undocumented immigrants in the United States as of 2006 (Passel 2006). By 2006, immigrants, documented and undocumented, represented more than 15 percent of the U.S. labor force, nearly three times the proportion of the 1960s; more than one in four new workers was an immigrant. For the first time, in 2000, half of all nonmetropolitan Hispanics lived outside the Southwest. While almost all nonmetro counties experienced Hispanic population growth, roughly a third of this growth occurred in just 150 counties dominated by low-skill industries. Between 1990 and 2000, the nonmetro Hispanic population more than doubled in twenty (mostly Southern and Midwestern) states. The number of nonmetro counties in which Hispanics constitute at least 10 percent grew from 211 to 287. All else being equal, more than 100 nonmetro counties, largely in Midwestern and Great Plains states, would have lost population between 1990 and 2000 if not for growth in the Hispanic population (Jones et al. 2007).

Even with the clampdown after September 11, 2001, and the wave of Immigration and Customs Enforcement raids targeting undocumented workers that began in 2006, immigrant workers continue to enter the United States. Many immigrants—particularly those from Mexico and Central America—work in jobs that do not demand a lot of recognized skills, jobs that native-born Americans scorn: as meatpackers, hotel maids, fast-food attendants, fruit and vegetable pickers, nursery and landscape workers, and construction workers. Many rural places in the United States could not survive without immigrant workers.

Agriculture in many parts of the United States has depended on migrant labor at planting, harvesting, and weeding time, but both service and manufacturing communities now increasingly employ immigrants also. Packing plants in the Midwest, such as the two in Garden City, Kansas, hire mostly Latinos and Southeast Asians, many of them women. In the small town of DePue, Illinois, manual farm work is done mostly by Hispanic and Laotian immigrants. Non-native-born workers can be found in mushroom farming, which includes picking mature mushrooms out of manure. These immigrant laborers show an immense work ethic, and they recognize that native-born Americans generally will not do the manual work, only the mechanized labor (Lydersen 2002). Many employers are hoping for more liberal migration laws. However, post–9/11, with more stringent immigration policies and enforcement, these migrant workers will not have an opportunity to regularize their status until at least after the 2008 elections.

Imported labor will continue to be a feature of rural community life. Rural areas have benefited from the immigration of medical doctors and nurses from developing countries by gaining access to professional skills that have been lacking. The majority of the new arrivals to nonmetropolitan areas, however, have limited education. As in DePue, they are viewed as hardworking employees and thus are often favored over U.S.-born workers of equal skill levels; this keeps wages low among unskilled workers, although there is little evidence that immigrants contribute to lower wages for occupations in which a high school diploma or more is the norm (Congressional Budget Office 2005). In good times, immigrant labor helps rural areas deal with a labor deficit. In bad times, immigrants are seen as competing with native workers for jobs, and they present communities with a complex set of social issues.

OPPORTUNITIES AND RISKS: RURAL AREAS IN THE GLOBAL ECONOMY

Most experts now agree that the world economy has changed and that the U.S. economy is restructuring in response to these changes. Rural communities have become part of this transformation, and although they exert limited control over the nation's fiscal policies and even less control over what are now worldwide capital markets, they can make intelligent choices. Those choices need to be based on a firm understanding of what drives the global economy. This section examines features of the new global economy and their implications for rural communities.

Features of the Changed Global Economy

The shift to floating exchange rates for currencies and the economic response to OPEC's actions in the early 1970s led to a series of features that now characterize the global economy. According to Peter Drucker (1986), these features are that (1) the industrial economy has become uncoupled from the primary-goods economy; (2) production has become uncoupled from employment; and (3) the movement of capital has replaced trade as the driving force of the economy. An added feature that Drucker could not have yet realized is the effect of online purchases and e-commerce shipments on manufacturing businesses.

The first feature refers to the fact that manufacturing and other sectors of the economy no longer seem to change in response to prices for natural resources. In the past, the economic health of the industrial sector was linked to the economic health of the raw materials or natural-resources industries. Now U.S. industrial firms get fewer of their raw materials from U.S. sources and sell fewer of their products back to the producers of primary goods. In addition, the materials component of products has diminished as a proportion of the value of those products. This is obvious in the case of the miniaturization of computing that has occurred over the past two decades or so, but it is also true of automobiles, appliances, and other goods not generally considered high-tech. Our industrial economy appears to be functioning independently of our raw-materials economy.

The second feature of the changed world economy is that manufacturing production has become uncoupled from employment. Again, traditional models of the economy predicted that as manufacturing production increased, so would manufacturing employment and wages. For example, when Henry Ford increased wages at the Ford plant, workers were able to buy more cars, thus increasing production. Expanding the industrial base of the economy created more manufacturing jobs.

The worker-to-market-to-manufacturer linkage has changed. Manufacturing production in the United States increased by nearly 40 percent from 1973 to 1985, but manufacturing employment decreased over that same period. From 1970 to 2000, manufacturing employment dropped by 5 percent, and after the terrorist attacks, more layoffs occurred. Rural manufacturing jobs in 2001 were 5.5 percent below the previous year (Hendersen 2002). Paralleling the economic uncoupling of raw materials from industry, this uncoupling between production and employment results from both a decreased dependence on labor and a shift in the types of manufacturing producers. As an alternative to moving operations overseas to wherever labor costs are lower, industries are looking for ways to mechanize their operations and reduce labor needs. In addition, newer industries are more dependent on knowledge and information and consequently use less labor. The challenge for rural communities is to show that they can become knowledge centers and can provide amenities that will attract knowledgeable workers.

Production itself is growing more international. Capital-intensive parts can be made where capital is cheap and abundant, and parts can be assembled in countries having low labor costs. Workers also move to areas of potential labor demand, whether the work is in an assembly plant along the border at El Paso, Texas, or a meatpacking plant in rural Kansas, often in spite of the fact that their movement is restricted by national governments. The free movement of financial capital and national restrictions on movement of human capital are a major contradiction of the global economy as presently constituted.

Third, the movement of capital rather than the movement of goods and services drives the global economy. Traditional economics teaches that the relative value of goods and services is what determines exchange rates. Financial transactions once occurred as a function of trade. The growth of capital markets now means that most financial transactions occur independently of trade. These transactions are what determine exchange rates and hence the extent to which a nation's products are competitive on the world market.

Finally, *e-commerce*—business transactions made over the Internet—is affecting trade and manufacturing businesses. More and more businesses have decided that e-commerce is a successful way to buy and sell goods; in fact, the Internet has become a basic business component for most companies, in terms of selling and purchasing goods and services. Internet businesses that sell goods online employ 17 percent of manufacturing workers, but revenue grows significantly faster than employment. Businesses online either sell to the consumer directly or to other businesses, and both types of transactions are considered to be more efficient. Measuring e-commerce is difficult because of the rapidity of sales and business expansion that can occur on the Internet. For example, Amazon.com used to sell only books, but now it has an expansive range of products, including DVDs, CDs, toys, and other products. Increasingly, businesses have both online and "brick-and-mortar" stores, such as Wal-Mart or Target. These stores actually compete against themselves for sales and product availability. E-commerce is a way to market to an immense audience of consumers.

In a physical, brick-and-mortar business, there are several layers of employees; likewise, there are layers of Web-related jobs within e-commerce. Internet businesses for large companies need Web consultants and designers as well as marketing managers for an online audience. Instead of depending on transportation and raw materials, e-commerce depends on high-speed networks and effective software that is easy for the consumer to navigate. Business-to-business e-commerce relationships have the most influence on the economy because intermediaries are eliminated, cutting costs for consumers. The world economy has become dependent upon these relationships, which will have a large effect on business practices in the long term. E-commerce has and will continue to have an enormous presence in the global economy.

Rural Communities in the Global Economy

The changed global economy has a number of implications for rural communities, some of which have already become obvious. Tariff reductions and present trade agreements make the effects of globalization on rural communities more immediate, contributing to greater volatility in prices for agricultural products and less certainty about the length of tenure of industries in rural areas. The collapse of commodities markets and the flight of manufacturing industries during the 1980s suggest that no single economic activity offers stability to rural communities. Urban areas were affected by these same changes; Pittsburgh, Pennsylvania, had a steel slump, and Detroit, Michigan, lost automobile manufacturing jobs. But because they typically have more diversified economies, cities and surrounding suburban areas often are better able to adapt to changes. Clearly, rural communities need to broaden their economic base as protection against the increased uncertainties created by the changing global economy.

Low-wage labor and natural resources, the traditional strengths of rural economies, today offer little advantage, unless the natural resources are sustained and enhanced to offer amenities. Most natural-resource-based industries, especially agricultural production, are experiencing increased competition internationally at a time when markets are already flooded. The flight of manufacturing jobs to developing nations and the importation of low-wage workers are phenomena that demonstrate that rural labor has been drawn into competition with labor in other countries. In Puerto Rico, the Economic Revitalization Act of 2001 has been embraced with bipartisan support. This act would work to eliminate any potential exploitation by large corporations and loss of jobs to other countries. In the previous five years, twenty-seven thousand jobs were lost to other countries, such as China, Singapore, and Malaysia. And in any case, the overall decline in blue-collar jobs underscores the futility of capturing low-skill manufacturing industries. Although natural resources and light manufacturing probably will continue to be important contributors to rural economies, the character of these enterprises must change in response to the changed global economy.

The rate at which many natural resources are being depleted has become alarming. Communities relying on natural resources for their economic well-being are beginning to emphasize constructive measures for replenishing those resources. In 1991, the Chesapeake Bay oyster industry in Maryland and Virginia, for example, called for a three-year ban on oyster harvesting. The oyster beds, for centuries a source of food and income for Maryland communities around the bay, had been reduced to less than 1 percent of their estimated original stock. Without a complete ban on harvesting to allow the oyster population to reproduce, the entire economic role of the bay would have been altered permanently. The preservation of oysters in the Chesapeake Bay area continues as aquatic reefs are being restored and created. This is a long-term project that planners hope will enhance oyster reproduction tenfold by 2010. People are beginning to acknowledge the need for economic practices that maintain rather than deplete finite resources. Choices, both private and public, are being made accordingly.

Natural-resource industries, including food producers, are beginning to expand into value-added activities or to look for market niches. Logging communities, for example, are adding small wood-manufacturing operations to existing milling facilities. This enables the community to capture the economic benefit of value-added activities as well as that realized from the extraction of natural resources. It also diversifies the local economy.

Other communities are beginning to make imaginative use of the resources at hand. After decades of trying to rid their fields of milkweed, some farmers in Ogallala, Nebraska, are now harvesting it. The pods are separated from the stalks, and the fibers within are extracted. This "Ogallala down," as it is called, is then used as filler for pillows, quilts, and other household products. These products are being marketed and sold online by various bath and linen businesses as high-priced items. Because Ogallala down is considered hypoallergenic, standard Ogallala down pillows sell for almost $140 each online; comforters are sold for as much as $500. These items have a large target audience because of the many consumers who suffer from allergies.

Local economic planning now takes place within a new context: constant change in a global economy. The world is becoming smaller; people are now global citizens. Cyclical trends in national and global economies affect the stability and growth of even the smallest, remotest rural community. At the same time, improved transportation and communication linkages have increased rural-urban connections, fostering regional and national economic integration. If local planning is to be successful, it must strengthen the international competitive position of local businesses and take advantage of the new opportunities for employment, marketing, tourism, and local cooperation.

Beat 'Em or Join 'Em?

The future of rural America may depend on the three A's: agriculture and energy, amenities, and amistades (friendships). The first two focus on natural and social capital, while the third relates particularly to human and cultural capital. How they are dealt with depends heavily on political capital and which social groups are most successful in mobilizing it.

Agriculture and Energy Policy (Natural and Political Capitals)

How rural areas respond to the threat of global warming and the need for renewable fuels as well as how the food system is configured are central to the future of rural areas. Although agriculture and natural resource extraction employ only somewhat over 1 percent of the U.S. labor force and perhaps 5 percent of the nonmetro labor force, these activities involve the majority of the land area and set limits and offer opportunities for other human activities in this vast region that people call rural America. Unfortunately, for the short term, the choices being made are not very encouraging. The recent spike in commodity prices as a result of the ethanol boom brings more factors in line with the situation of the late 1970s that led to the farm crisis of the 1980s: high commodity prices that could collapse with a shift in the volatile energy economy, land prices that are being bid up by the high commodity prices to approach levels of the late 1970s, increasing federal indebtedness as a result of massive tax cuts and an unexpectedly long-lasting foreign military venture, and sharp increases in energy costs and agricultural commodity prices (USDA/NASS 2007).

However, a number of factors are different: only modest inflationary pressures in the United States and abroad, and much lower U.S. farmer indebtedness. Also, there is arguably a greater dispersion of international economic power. The consolidation of Europe as an expanded economic and political bloc and counterweight to the United States is noteworthy, as are emerging countries such as Brazil, India, and China.

Two elements of future U.S. national policy will have important worldwide repercussions: farm policy and energy policy. Diversification of policy is important in both areas. Farm policy should be crafted so that not only is there a safety net for producers of the five basic commodities (rice, cotton, corn, wheat, and soybeans), but also fruits and vegetables and local, organic, and sustainable agriculture are encouraged. Greater diversity of production, consumption of more foods that are raised locally, and more ecological food production result in greater resiliency at the farm and community level, less production of greenhouse gases (GHG), less pollution of lakes and streams, and improved soil quality. Similarly, energy policy should give much greater emphasis first to conservation, then to renewable energy (wind, solar), rather than to growing more corn for energy. Corn ethanol, by the most optimistic calculations, uses 75 percent as much fossil fuel in its production as does gasoline and could replace at best 6 percent of the gasoline currently used in the United States—if all corn currently produced were converted to ethanol. We are already seeing the environmental effects of expanding corn production at the expense of soybeans and other crops and encroachment on Conservation Reserve lands, in the projected expansion of the hypoxic zone in the Gulf of Mexico (Brasher 2007). (Corn requires considerably more nitrogen fertilizer than do soybeans, which fix nitrogen; many Midwestern and Southern farmers are shifting to a corn-after-corn rotation rather than alternating corn and soybeans.) Concerns are being expressed about reduced wildlife habitat, pollution of lakes and streams, and the amount of land that will be taken out of the Conservation Research Program to be put into continuous corn production for ethanol.

Thus, instead of exporting corn down the Mississippi River, the United States will import nitrogen fertilizer, a petroleum derivative from the Middle East, up the Mississippi River to grow more corn. Of course, a great deal of the nitrogen will flow back down the river into the Gulf of Mexico.

Amenities and Services (Natural and Social Capital)

The coexistence of industrial agriculture and rural amenities is possible, but not readily accomplished. Confinement livestock production has perhaps the most notable incompatibility with amenity-focused rural development. Conflicts between farmers and "city people" (those who live in the small towns) are reported by extension field specialists in Iowa as the rural-urban question highest on their agenda and that of their constituents, and many of those conflicts revolve around livestock confinement operations. The research of Monchuk and colleagues on counties of Iowa and the surrounding states indicates that although growth in livestock sales has a modest positive effect on county income growth, the contribution of outdoor recreation amenities is more than five times as great (2005, 17–18). Because of the odor of concentrated hog manure, recreational amenities and concentrated animal feeding operations (CAFOs) cannot exist cheek to jowl. Presence of CAFOs also is negatively associated with surface water quality (Flora et al. 2007).

Rural communities must enter the digital economy if they want to interact in the global economy. E-commerce, telecommuting, telemedicine, distance education, cell phone access, and other digital technologies yet to be invented or commercialized are a necessary progression if rural areas are to hold their own in the global economy. For many remote areas, the physical barriers for phone lines and telecommunications services are palpable. However, farmers and agribusinesses are already marketing agricultural products on the Internet. Fertilizer, chemicals, seeds, produce, equipment, and livestock are all advertised and sold online (Staihr 2000). Online transactions allow consumers to arrange for shipping and the transfer of funds without personal contact, which is a growing business practice across the country. Rural businesses that do not participate in e-commerce run the risk of being thought outdated by consumers and other businesses. Experts see a need for rural businesses to catch up with the global economy if they do not participate in e-commerce now. However, personal communication and building social capital are still necessary components of business practices. Personal contact and e-commerce can work hand in glove.

Under the present policy regime, e-commerce is a double-edged sword for rural communities, in that it has been protected from taxation since 1998 by the Internet Tax Freedom Act. The Internet Tax Nondiscrimination Act of 2001 extended this moratorium on taxation, and the more goods are sold over the Internet, the more local communities are adversely affected. Small brick-and-mortar business owners do not think e-tailers are reinvesting in the community as frequently, even though they use community infrastructure to "reap the benefits of doing business in local communities" (Glick and Grossfield 2001). Most experts agree that the Internet is becoming a basic component of all businesses. The digital divide must be closed if rural companies are to compete in a global economy.

The larger issue that concerns many social scientists is the relationship between development and equality. Can the shift to a global economy lead to greater equality among people? Increasingly, sociologists are looking at the impact that investment and trade dependence have on indicators of quality of life: nutrition, health services, mortality, and education. Closing the gap in education and health care with digital capabilities is a way to alleviate the negative effects of remoteness, distance, and shifting demographics. Distance learning, which bridges educational gaps for adult learners, is available in rural communities. Telemedicine is an advance that allows rural physicians to teleconference with specialists. These advances in technology suggest that development, if defined as increased linkages to the world system, need not always increase inequality, particularly if that development is embedded in a policy framework that focuses on equal access.

Amistades (Cultural and Financial Capital)

Should the increasing cultural diversity of rural communities be viewed as an asset or a liability?

Table 9.1 contrasts characteristics of native-born and immigrant residents in nonmetro areas of the United States. Two overall differences stand out. First, immigrants are considerably younger, a higher percentage is of working age, and, largely because of the age difference, they have an average of one more child in the household than do native-born families. The other obvious difference is in levels of education. Rural communities

**Table 9.1   Selected Nonmetro Demographic Indicators, 2000
and 2003**

Characteristic	Hispanic	Non-Hispanic White
Demographic		
Percent foreign born (2003)	34	2
Median age (2003)	27.7	37.8
Percent of population under 18 (2000)	37	23
Percent of population 65 and older (2000)	6	18
Male/female ratio (2000)	1.09	0.96
Average persons in household (2003)	4.1	3.1
Average children in household (2003)	1.8	1.0
Socioeconomic incorporation and assimilation		
Percent speaking English "very well" (2003)	73	99
Percent citizens (2003)	75	99
Education (persons age 25+)		
Percent with a high school diploma (2003)	53	86
Percent with a college degree (2003)	6	17

SOURCE: Compiled by Economic Research Service using the 2002, 2003, and 2004 Current Population Survey, March Supplement. U.S. Department of Agriculture, Economic Research Service. 2005. "Rural Hispanics at a Glance." *Economic Information Bulletin* 8 (December):4. Online; available: www.ers.usda.gov/publications/EIB8/eib8.pdf; accessed August 2, 2007.

and the states will have to invest considerable resources toward educating immigrant children and adults to ensure that they become as productive as the native-born population.

Immigration from Mexico and Central America in particular poses a dilemma for the country as a whole, but the contradiction is even greater in rural areas: On the one hand, immigrants are repopulating certain rural communities and filling jobs that would otherwise go unfilled because of the scarcity of native persons in the early productive age groups. They also are reinvigorating schools with declining enrollments, fixing up old houses, becoming new homeowners, starting new businesses, and filling local tax coffers. At the same time, they pose a challenge to the schools because of the expense of accommodating limited-English students, to the hospitals because of their heavy use of emergency rooms because they lack health insurance, and to soup kitchens and food pantries, because of the low wages many of them receive and the seasonal nature of their work.. If immigrants became legal residents, they perhaps would make a substantial claim on social welfare resources (those who are not documented or are but have been in the country fewer than five years are not eligible for many public social services). In addition, undocumented workers often pay social security and withholding tax that they will never be able to claim, take low-paying jobs, and fail to claim Earned Income Tax Credits because they don't know about them or because they do not file tax returns, and thus their tax payments remain in the federal and state treasuries.

Finally, for a society that knows little about people of other cultures because of the size and wealth of our own country, the parochialism of our mass media, and the chauvinism of many of our leaders, having the opportunity to get to know people of another culture is an incredible opportunity.

How rural communities view the newcomers will determine whether those communities prosper through a vibrant labor force and new economic ventures or spend a lot of their social and political capital in conflict in deporting millions of people to their countries of origin.

CHAPTER SUMMARY

Rural communities are being affected by worldwide economic restructuring. Historically, rural areas were linked to international markets by the natural resources they exported and the labor they imported. The character of these linkages has changed dramatically in recent decades. E-commerce has had a huge impact on global links.

Since the close of World War II, national economies have been moving toward integration into a global economy. The shift from a fixed exchange rate (the Bretton Woods Agreement) to a floating exchange rate (the Smithsonian Agreement) reduced controls on international currency. Capital now moves easily from one country to another. OPEC's decision to limit oil production in the early 1970s eventually led to increased production of commodities, drawing more competitors into international markets. Finally, steps taken to control inflation and stimulate the U.S. economy ultimately led to an economic recession worldwide. National economies are now linked to one another, digitally and physically. The events of September 11, 2001, have since limited and negatively affected international tourism, which has interrupted some cash and cultural flows between countries.

The events that signaled the transition to a global economy have had an impact on rural communities. The farm crisis of the 1980s was triggered in part by the same series of events. The expansion in commodities production created by OPEC's decision to limit oil production encouraged farm lending. Steps taken to control inflation and stimulate the local economy later made it impossible for those who had expanded their farm operations to service their debt load. Similar conditions encouraged manufacturing companies to move their operations to rural areas and then, more recently, to foreign countries. Imported labor has become a feature of rural community life.

Most experts now agree that the world economy has changed and that the U.S. economy is restructuring in response to these changes. Features of the new global economy are that (1) the industrial economy is less dependent on the natural-resource economy, (2) manufacturing production is less dependent on labor, (3) the movement of capital is the driving force in the world economy, and (4) the development of instantaneous communication among knowledge centers around the world and the development of e-commerce have allowed for the physical separation of production and marketing components, a separation that was impossible even as recently as the early 1990s. In this changed economic environment, rural communities need to diversify their economies, must be creative in locating market niches or finding new uses for existing resources, and need to develop regional, national, and international linkages that help local businesses remain competitive. Researching e-commerce and finding an online target audience are an important step in this process.

KEY TERMS

Commodities are natural resources or manufactured products bought or sold on markets.

Devaluation of a currency is a decrease in the value of that currency in relation to other countries' currencies. Devaluation used to occur when the exchange rate changed in such a way that more gold was required to equal the same unit of currency; now it occurs when more of a particular currency must be used to buy other currencies.

E-commerce (electronic commerce) is business transactions made over the Internet.

The *exchange rate* is the amount of one currency needed to purchase another currency. Exchange rates vary from source to source for commercial reasons. Banks, credit card companies, and other providers of exchange-rate information will likely differ from the rates provided by the Federal Reserve Bank. When an exchange rate is high, imports are cheap, and a country's exports are less competitive on the world market. When an exchange rate is low, imports become expensive, and it is easier to sell products on the world market. Exchange rates are increasingly determined by market mechanisms—supply and demand—although governments often intervene by either buying or selling their own currency when they see their currency changing in value.

Fixed exchange rates establish a fixed standard against which one currency can be exchanged with another. The Bretton Woods Agreement of 1944 fixed the price of the U.S. dollar relative to gold.

Floating exchange rates allow the value of one currency to change relative to another in response to the demand for and the availability of currencies.

Inflation occurs when the currency in circulation or the availability of credit increases, leading to a sharp rise in prices.

Neoliberal policies liberate private enterprise from government rules, including favoring international trade and investment through free movement of capital, goods, and services; weakening the power of organized labor; cutting public expenditure for social services such as education, health care, and welfare for the poor; deregulating banks and industry; privatizing services previously provided by the government, such as prisons, Social Security, and the welfare system; and focusing on individual responsibility rather than the public good. Powerful financial institutions, such as the International Monetary Fund, the World Bank, and the Inter-American Development Bank, as well as the U.S. government, demand the implementation of these policies as a condition for receiving international financial assistance.

A *recession* typically is defined as an overall slowing of economic activity. Since there are many measures of economic activity as well as what constitutes a "slowing," there can be many definitions of what exactly constitutes a recession. The National Bureau of Economic Research, a nonprofit organization that assigns dates to the beginning and end of downturns, defines a recession as "a period of declining output and employment."

Subprime lending refers to making loans to borrowers who do not qualify for the best market interest rates because of problems in their credit history. Because the loans are risky for lenders, interest rates are higher, making it more difficult for borrowers to repay.

References

Adame, Vicki. 2002. "Immigration Anxieties: Changes in Immigration Law Meet with Concern as Well as Understanding" (September 11) Tri-City Herald: Columbia, Washington.

Associated Press. 2002. "Cheaper Labor Moves Rocky Shoes Production to Puerto Rico." *Cincinnati Enquirer,* April 29. Also online; available: http://enquirer.com/editions/2002/04/29/fin_cheaper_labor_moves .html; accessed September 1, 2007.

Brasher, Philip. 2007. "Report Says Ethanol May Fuel Dead Zone." *Des Moines Register,* July 1.

Congressional Budget Office. 2005. *The Role of Immigrants in the U.S. Labor Market.* Online; available: www.cbo.gov/ftpdocs/68xx/doc6853/11-10-Immigration.pdf; accessed September 1, 2007.

Drucker, Peter. 1986. "The Changed World Economy." *Foreign Affairs* 64:768–791.

Flora, J., Q. Chen, S. Bastian, and R. Hartmann. 2007. *Hog CAFOs and Sustainability: Local Development and Water Quality in Iowa.* Iowa Policy Project: Mount Vernon, Iowa.

Glick, Gary, and Scott Grossfield. 2001. "Who's Plugging the E-Sales Tax Leak?" Online; available: www.ccnlaw.com/Articles/sales_tax.html; accessed December 5, 2002.

Henderson, Jason R. 2002. "Will the Rural Economy Rebound with the Rest of the Nation?" *The Main Street Economist.* Kansas City, Mo.: Center for the Study of Rural America.

Jones, Carol A., William Kandel, and Timothy Parker. 2007. "Population Dynamics Are Changing the Profile of Rural Areas." *Amber Waves* 5:30–35.

Kowalczyk, Nick. 2001. Part 1: "Rocky Shoes and Boots: A Historical Profile"; part 2: "Shoemaker Fulfills Dream, Revitalizes Company"; part 3: "Rocky Boots Historical Profile"; and part 4: "Rocky Boots Historical Profile." *Post,* Ohio University, Athens, Ohio, January 30, 31, and February 1, 2. Also online; available: http://thepost.baker.ohiou.edu/archives3/jan01/013101/today.html; accessed September 1, 2007.

Luft, Gal, and Edward Morse. 2006. "Is Oil Independence Attainable and Desirable?" *PolicyWatch* no. 1085: Special Forum Report, March 16. Also online; available: www.washingtoninstitute.org/templateC05 .php?CID=2450; accessed Aug. 4, 2007.

Lydersen, Kari. 2002. "On the Farm, an Immigrant's Work Is Never Done." Alternet.org, October 7. Online; available: www.alternet.org/story .html?StoryID=14240 ; accessed September 1, 2007.

Migration Policy Institute. 2007. "Percent Foreign Born by State, 1900, 2000, and 2005." Online; available: www.migrationinformation.org/DataTools/ MigrationInformationSource-ACS-2005-PercentForeignBorn.xls; accessed September 1, 2007.

Monchuk, Daniel C., John A. Miranowski, Dermot J. Hayes, and Bruce Babcock. 2005. "An Analysis of Regional Economic Growth in the U.S. Midwest." Working paper 05-WP392, April. Online; available: www .card.iastate.edu/publications/synopsis.aspx?id=586; accessed August 4, 2007.

Ohio University Telecommunications Center. 2002. *Rural Communities Legacy and Change: Think Globally.* Part six of a twelve-part video series, directed by Keith Newman and Gary Mills. Annenberg/CPB Collection, fifty-eight minutes (includes an approximately twenty-minute segment on the William Brooks Shoe Company).

Passel, Jeffrey S. 2006. "Size and Characteristics of the Unauthorized Migrant Population in the U.S.: Estimates Based on the March 2005 Current Population Survey." *Research Report,* Washington, D.C.: Pew Hispanic Center, March. Online; available: http://pewhispanic.org/files/reports/ 61.pdf; accessed August 3, 2007.

Staihr, Brian. 2000. "Rural America's Stake in the Digital Economy." *The Main Street Economist.* Kansas City, Mo.: Center for the Study of Rural America.

U.S. Department of Agriculture, National Agricultural Statistical Service. "Agricultural Prices." Online; available: www.usda.gov/nass/PUBS/ TODAYRPT/agpr0807.pdf, 2007.

U.S. Department of Commerce. 1986. *Statistical Abstract of the United States.* Washington, D.C.: Bureau of the Census.

U.S. Department of Labor. 2006. "Textile, Apparel, and Furnishings Occupations." *Occupational Outlook Handbook.* Washington, D.C.: Bureau of Labor Statistics. Also online; available: www.bls.gov/oco/ocos233 .htm#emply; accessed August 4, 2007.

World Trade Organization (WTO). Official Ministerial Web site, www.wto .org/english/thewto_e/thewto_e.htm; accessed September 2, 2007.

10

Consumption in Rural America

It is almost 6:00 PM as the Archer family settles into the Tuesday evening meal. They live in a rural community about sixty miles from a metropolitan area. Susan Archer produces small metal parts for automobile air conditioners at the local manufacturing plant. Her shift began at 7:00 AM and ended at 4:30 PM. Her husband, Dan, just came in from his job as an auto mechanic at a local car dealership. They and their three children crowd around the Formica table where Jill, age six, says grace. Susan sets on the table a large bowl of salad greens taken out of a bag that says "triple washed" and tops it with the package of dressing and croutons that came inside. The evening meal and the conversation begin in earnest.

Eric, thirteen years old, opens the conversation with a plea for some new athletic shoes. He is trying out for the middle-school basketball team and asserts that he needs a particular pair, a brand-name shoe endorsed by a professional basketball star. Dan grouses at this request: "Jeez, Eric, those shoes cost a bundle, and they aren't any better than a pair that's half that price. Besides, you'll grow out of them by spring." Eric is visibly upset and begins listing the shoe's features, adding, "And the other guys have already bought theirs!"

Susan finally intervenes on Dan's behalf. She points out that the pair Eric wants is equivalent to about twenty hours of her take-home pay. She then suggests that the family will pay for part of the expensive department-store shoes if Eric pays the rest with his wages from his part-time job with a neighbor, who has a dog-grooming business at home. Eric

279

quickly calculates the difference and estimates that the shoes will cost him about eight weeks' work. A deal is struck.

Dan is curious about where Eric is going to go to buy these sneakers, because none of the local merchants carry the expensive brand. Eric smiles and says he can get them on the Internet, which he can access at the public library, if his parents will let him use their credit card. He knows they have it only for emergencies, but he figures this may qualify as one. His parents disagree, saying that they will not use their credit card to buy shoes for growing feet. Eric mentions that they are sold at the Central City Mall, about an hour's drive away. Susan asks him how he will get there and who will take him. After a brief silence, Eric says he'll buy them on the next trip the family makes there. He can wait; they usually go to Central City about every fourth weekend. Susan nods quietly as she glances at Dan.

There is an insistent ding from the microwave oven. The main course is ready. Susan gets up and pulls out a large frozen-food package consisting of turkey and gravy. The peas, also from the freezer, are already on the table. Then she scrapes the instant rice out of a pot on the stove into a bowl that she also sets on the table. She puts the pot in the sink to wash after dinner, which she will do with water from their well.

Eric's plea for new shoes seems to have reached a compromise, so Jake, ten years old, makes his pitch to get a new video game system, the Wii, when they make their trip to the mall. He says it's the "coolest new interactive video game on the market!" Dan's head jerks up. "We just bought you an Xbox for Christmas!" Jake sighs, rolling his eyes. His parents clearly do not understand how quickly the new games come out. "But I know I would use it all the time, and it's really fun, because I tried it out at Sam's house!" Dan asks how much it costs, and Jake tells him that it's more than $200. Jake's mother ends the conversation by saying, "We are not talking about that right now." Dan shakes his head in disbelief over the price. Susan is concerned because Jake is heavy for his age, and more time with the screen on a new video game means less time being active outdoors.

After cleaning up the dishes, Jake takes the day's trash out to the garbage can and then takes the can to the road for the Wednesday-morning pickup. The two bags join others full of discarded aluminum foil, newspapers, jars, and plastic containers. None of the garbage is sorted for recycling, for the town of two thousand has no recycling program. The garbage will end up in a landfill about five miles away.

What a difference from a hundred years ago! The majority of rural North American and western European consumers in the early 1900s either grew their own food or purchased it raw and unprocessed. The homemaker cooked over a wood-burning stove in a house with no indoor plumbing, no mechanical refrigeration or freezing, and no electricity. Centuries-old procedures for food preservation commonly were used: drying, salting, smoking, or storage in root cellars. Up to 50 percent of a household's disposable income and an equal proportion of a household's labor were needed simply to eat. Moreover, the common diet was extremely unhealthy, with an excess of salt and fat and a lack of fresh fruits and vegetables (Cotterill 2001).

What we buy and consume has changed as dramatically as the way in which goods and services are produced. Most people are disconnected from the production of what they consume; even most farmers do not directly consume what they produce. Most Americans are capable of sustaining healthier diets for a smaller proportion of our disposable income. More items that once were produced at home are now available for purchase: bread, clothing, suntans, and fingernails. We often work in buildings with windows that do not open, process enormous amounts of information on personal computers, and access weather information on our computer that is based on satellite pictures only minutes old. Most people drive automobiles and rely on in-home, high-tech sound equipment, video recorders, television, compact disc players and recorders, and Web-available music for entertainment. Rural grandparents in the Midwest receive photo images or videos of their grandchildren in Dallas, Texas. Our current consumption habits were not even imaginable just a few years ago.

Consumption has many faces: inputs used for production, needs for day-to-day living, preferences for leisure time, and confirmation of personal identity. As the Archer family illustrates, consumption starts with inputs and ends with landfills, both of which are important to rural communities. This chapter explores various facets of rural residents' consumption patterns and how and why those patterns have changed in rural areas.

WHY IS CONSUMPTION IMPORTANT?

In 1899, sociologist Thorstein Veblen coined the term *conspicuous consumption*. Veblen used this term to characterize the habits of middle- and upper-class individuals who achieved their identity and prestige by what they consumed rather than by what they produced or by the nature of their character. At the time of his writing, such consumption was relatively new. Rich people have always consumed more than poor people, but they tended to limit the visibility of their greater wealth to their own circles. This was partially out of fear of mass uprisings in the face of large inequalities. In some rural areas in the twenty-first century, particularly in the Northeast and the Midwest, wealthy people conceal their affluence, driving modest cars and wearing ordinary clothes and jewelry.

Sixty years ago, it was fairly easy to distinguish rural residents from urban ones. Rural residents, particularly those who lived on farms, tended to wear homemade clothes and eat food they produced and processed themselves. Urban residents bought their food and clothing at the store. Urban residents were consumers; rural residents were producers. But by the turn of the twenty-first century, consumption patterns no longer easily distinguished urban from rural residents, although rural residents dressed more conservatively and were more cautious in trying new things.

The seeds for the transformation of country people into consumers were planted in the late 1800s with the development of mail-order catalog companies, such as Sears, Roebuck, and Co. and Montgomery Ward. Congress greatly aided these firms by authorizing rural free delivery (RFD) in 1896. Before then, country people had to travel to the nearest post office to pick up their mail, rather than having it delivered to individual mail boxes near their residences. Lobbied hard by the National Grange and other farm organizations, Congress passed RFD over the objection of general-store operators in small towns. It became an official service in 1902 and was expanded in 1913 with the introduction of rural parcel post service. A similar shift occurred nearly a century later when Wal-Mart threatened merchants in small towns with its computerized and centralized inventory system, just-in-time delivery, and dictation of prices to its merchandise suppliers.

Where we consume, what we consume, and why we consume certain types of commodities and services shape the quality of our lives. Our consumption affects the natural environment as well as our relationships with others.

Societal Trends Related to Increased Consumption

In the United States and Canada, as in other developed nations, most people consume more things than ever before. Economic expansion and the rise in real wages after World War II meant that more and more Americans could afford to buy a wider variety of goods. Increased demand meant increased production, and more companies entered the market, seeking to differentiate themselves from other producers by more than price. Henry Ford's dictum about the Model A—that the consuming public could have any color car they wanted as long as it was black—became a thing of the past. By the year 2001, car buyers could choose between internal combustion engines and hybrid cars that linked those engines with electric batteries charged by the cars' wheels to power electric motors. Color, style, and source of energy became ways of differentiating products and their consumers. The development of commercial television in the 1950s allowed manufacturers to shape but not dictate consumer tastes. Cable television added to this by targeting specific populations and increasing product differentiation, thereby furthering the tendency to base personal or collective identities on what is consumed. The Internet has extended this targeting and segmentation of consumer groups even further.

Our consumption patterns have also changed with the transformation of the labor force. As women entered the labor force in greater numbers after World War II, precooked frozen food became more readily available. By the end of the twentieth century, prepackaged salads, precut vegetables and meats for stir fry, and a variety of precooked roasts and ribs were on the shelves of many rural supermarkets. Deli sandwiches, pizza, and hot dogs are available at every convenience store, even in rural areas. Time once spent preparing food has been given over to other work around the house and to leisure. Even in rural areas, carryout meals and fast-food restaurants are growing more popular as working men and women grab a double cheeseburger with large fries rather than pack a lunch. But increasing income inequality means that many in rural areas must choose carefully what they consume, making hard choices between fixing the car to get to work and paying the electricity bill. It may be easier to buy fast food instead of preparing a home-cooked meal, but it is not always the most economical. Money spent on cheeseburgers over the course of a month can add up, which decreases money needed for paying the household bills.

Janice, age forty-five, lives in a small rural, remote town in Kentucky with her husband and sixteen-year-old daughter. Janice cares for neighbors' children and receives $1 an hour per child—when the neighbors can pay. Her husband works for the sanitation department, only making $6.10 an hour, although he does get benefits. They are not eligible for welfare, and their struggle to survive is immense. Each month, paying the bills causes Janice to have anxiety attacks. She often has to choose between paying part of the electric bill or buying groceries. Consumption in Janice's household is minimal, for basic needs are barely being met.

In the last quarter of the twentieth century, new methods of production and distribution increased the variety of products we could consume. Flexible production, made possible because of the use of computers in operating machine tools, managing inventories, and scheduling transportation, has replaced mass production. The global economy makes it possible to produce clothing in Malaysia that will be available across the United States at the same time as U.S.-made clothing and for a cheaper price.

These and other changes have had a direct impact on consumption patterns in both rural and urban areas. We can buy more consumer goods for less money, while prices of the investments that enhance the accumulation of household assets, such as homeownership and college educations, increase dramatically in terms of total household income. Although a number of economic and social forces have contributed to this change, four phenomena have had significant impacts on rural consumption patterns. All are nationwide trends, but they affect rural communities differently from urban areas:

- consolidation of retail and service enterprises
- changes in the structure of the labor force
- targeted marketing to segmented markets
- increased income inequality

CONSOLIDATION

Why do businesses consolidate? Why do services become regional rather than remain local? One explanation given for centralization is provided by *central-place theory*, which proposes that population centers, whether small crossroads communities or large cities, are organized geographically into hierarchical retail and public-service markets. Moreover, according to the theory, any particular hierarchy of places reflects a division of labor such that the larger places possess greater economic diversity of products and services for consumption than do smaller places. Correspondingly, the smallest places offer the fewest commodities and services. Thus, there is a system of nested markets. But central-place theory does not predict the steady loss of services by smaller, more remote communities as increasingly larger firms provide those services in central towns and cities. Part of this consolidation and centralization occurs as a result of larger and more expensive technology used to provide improved services, as in the case of health care. It is also due in part to economies of scale as fewer firms handle ever greater volumes of goods at less cost per unit, or competitive advantage deriving from providing a uniform product nationwide coupled with national advertising strategies, as in the case of fast-food chains. Technological change, such as computerized inventory control systems, also can favor larger firms. Finally, there is the raw power that derives from size that gives ready access by large companies with fat pocketbooks to the state and federal executive and legislative branches, and resulting policies that favor larger firms.

Perhaps no other aspect of changing consumption patterns is more symbolic of rural social change over the past four decades than the loss of Main Street businesses. The Archer family's trips to Central City Mall are typical of the changing consumption pattern of rural families. This section explores the consolidation of rural businesses, factors that explain why consolidation occurs, and the impact that consolidation is having on rural social services.

Business and Social-service Consolidation

When the railroads pushed across the country, they facilitated mail-order buying, which led consumers to bypass local merchants who could neither provide the wide variety of products nor take advantage of the quantity wholesale discounts available to the mail-order firms. What was true then continues to be true today. Across most retail trade, rural businesses find it difficult to offer the variety available in large central markets, such as urban malls or on the Internet. This has meant a loss in business for local merchants and a decline of revenue for many local governments.

Consolidation has occurred across both the business and social-service communities. Many locally owned stores have disappeared or been purchased by larger retail chains; department stores have either closed or moved into suburban malls, leaving empty buildings on Main Street. Locally owned banks are now members of regional consortiums or have been taken over by large regional banks. Local businesses and services have consolidated at different times and in different ways.

Some small businesses have been replaced by nationally based chain stores. Mom-and-pop stores became franchises that later became national chains, especially in the hardware and automotive businesses. Family-owned and -operated firms first were replaced by franchises such as Western

Auto, Gambles, and the like. The franchises are now fighting a losing battle with Wal-Mart and Target, national firms that have incorporated hardware and automotive sections into their diversified merchandising stores. In the grocery business, local groceries and markets were replaced by regional chains, which were then bought out by chains that are national and international in scope. For example, Dillons stores, a regional chain based in Wichita, Kansas, purchased small supermarkets. Kroger, a national chain, eventually purchased Dillons stores. Now Kroger and other supermarket chains are struggling against Wal-Mart, which, once it entered the grocery business, used the same inventory control and consignment sales strategies used in its soft goods to advance a meteoric rise in its share of national retail grocery sales.

In contrast, franchise convenience stores/gas stations occupy an important niche. Their comparative advantage is convenience, not price. Consequently, their location is more important than the prices they charge. Because economies of scale are not a driving force in their marketing, the parent firm has no advantage in directly managing individual outlets.

This transformation in retail trade is characterized both by a decline in the number of retail merchandising and service enterprises in rural communities and by the introduction of firms that are national in scope, often in regional trade centers. This pattern is illustrated by comparing Iowa communities influenced by Wal-Mart to similar-sized communities not affected by Wal-Mart. Kenneth Stone (1995) found that the introduction of a Wal-Mart store in ten small trade centers with populations of at least three thousand resulted in a slightly greater increase in retail trade in those communities compared to the state as a whole. However, rural towns within a twenty-mile radius of trade centers that had acquired a Wal-Mart within the previous three years showed a greater decline in retail sales than did comparable-sized communities within twenty miles of trade centers without Wal-Marts. Wal-Marts draw business into the regional center, decreasing retail sales in surrounding small towns. (See Box 10.1 for a summary of research on the impact of Wal-Mart on rural communities.)

The public sector has also responded to the need to maximize scarce revenue resources. Increasingly, private firms are buying previously public services, such as rural hospitals. Firefighters, police, public education, and other community services continue to undergo consolidation as rural areas address the demand for increasing quality of service and their accompanying expenses. As in the retail sector, central trade centers siphon off businesses that once supported local hospitals and clinics.

Box 10.1 The Wal-Marting of Rural America: Who Wins and Who Loses?

Wal-Mart has affected many small towns since the first store opened in 1962, and the opening of each new Wal-Mart store has been met with mixed reactions: resistance because of the loss of businesses and excitement for job opportunities. Many groups have retaliated against the opening of a Wal-Mart near their small towns by petitioning and using town zoning rules to make it impossible for Wal-Mart to enter the surrounding area. However, there are definitely numerous sides to the issue of Wal-Mart's force. Because it offers a variety of goods for low prices, many small-town businesses have had to close their doors, but Wal-Mart also provides jobs for people who need them. For example, in Donaldsonville, Louisiana, a small town on the Mississippi River, arguments over Wal-Mart arose when it proposed moving into town. People who owned small businesses in town felt that a Wal-Mart would wipe out their business, and when they heard that one might be opening outside of town, they panicked. Shop owners closed their businesses without even waiting to see if they would be affected; their theory was that they should "get out while the getting's good" (Ortega 1998). Several other small businesses ended up closing their doors as well. However, the other side of this debate was led by a large population of poorer black residents, who saw Wal-Mart as an opportunity for jobs and cheaper goods. They argued that the rich white business owners feared honest competition. After several debates that ended before the state board commission, Wal-Mart opened a 45,000-square-foot store (Ortega 1998).

What Wal-Mart does has import for us all. Wal-Mart is the largest corporation in the world. It had total revenues of $285 billion in 2005. The company generates more than 2 percent of U.S. GDP. It employs over 1.2 million workers in the United States in over 3,600 stores and is aggressively expanding overseas. Wal-Mart stirs passions because it is variously accused of offering low wages, encouraging its employees to go on welfare, contributing to the decline of manufacturing in the United States, squeezing suppliers until they cry "uncle," etc. *Business Week* reports that the average wage for an "associate" (employee) in 2001 was $8.23 per hour, generating $13,861 on a full-time year-round basis, which at that time was below the poverty level for a family of

continues

Box 10.1   *continued*

three (cited in Goetz and Swaminathan 2004: 4). But what do we *really* know about the impact of this giant firm, which began in rural Benton County, Arkansas, and used a decidedly rural strategy to become almost ubiquitous in both urban and rural America?

How does the coming of Wal-Mart to a particular county affect employment and how does it affect incomes? (Later we will address the question of how it affects community social capital.) These straightforward questions have answers that are more complicated to reach, in part because one has to separate out employment and income growth that would have occurred without Wal-Mart from that which resulted from a Wal-Mart store opening. Since Wal-Mart stores opened in Benton County in 1962, Neumark and colleagues (2007) determined the Wal-Mart employment effect essentially by calculating the expected growth rate in county retail employment independent of the Wal-Mart opening. The authors based the expected growth primarily on retail employment growth during the four years prior to the advent of a Wal-Mart store. That figure subtracted that from the retail employment growth following the coming of a Wal-Mart store to that county. If one failed to take into account this "endogenous" effect of Wal-Mart's siting its stores in growing counties, there was a positive relationship between Wal-Mart's coming and retail employment growth of some forty-five jobs. However, when the expected retail employment growth in these counties was subtracted, aggregate retail job change *due directly to the advent of one Wal-Mart store* was negative by some 147 jobs. This is not surprising, since part of the reason that Wal-Mart is able to outcompete its mom-and-pop rivals (and to a lesser extent other big-box stores) is its greater productivity per worker; Neumark et al. (2007) estimate that each Wal-Mart employee replaces 1.4 employees in the rest of the retail sector. This is due to automation and centralization of inventory, just-in-time delivery, careful selection of store locations so as to minimize distance between stores and distribution centers (hence the concentric-ring expansion of Wal-Mart stores), combined with high sales volume per square foot of store space and low cost of land due to the rural strategy employed.

Regarding payroll, although the retail payroll grew by some $282 million in counties in which a Wal-Mart store opened, the annual retail sales figure was $1.22 million less than it otherwise would have been

continues

had Wal-Mart not entered. In other words, retail payroll would have grown more than $1.5 million in such counties had there been no Wal-Mart store. This of course was due in part to the slower growth of employment but may also be due to the dampening effect of Wal-Mart on wages. An additional effect, as Goetz and Swaminathan (2004) point out, is the transfer of wealth to Wal-Mart stockholders and to the Walton family in particular, who rarely live in communities where Wal-Marts are located, unlike the family-run stores they often replace.

Neumark et al. (2007) are not able to say anything about Wal-Mart's effects on wages, because the source they used—*County Business Patterns*—does not distinguish between full- and part-time jobs. They do indicate that the average yearly payroll per worker is $13,700 in the retail sector, while the annual payroll per job of general merchandise retail stores—which include Wal-Mart, other big-box stores, and department stores—is $600 lower than for the retail sector as a whole. This suggests that Wal-Mart and other big-box stores have fine-tuned the art of using part-time workers to lower wages and to avoid paying benefits where possible.

Goetz and Swaminathan (2004) use a different methodology to determine whether existing and new Wal-Marts acquired by counties over the decade of the 1990s contributed to higher or lower poverty than would have occurred without their presence. Both led to modest increases in poverty rates. They estimate that each new Wal-Mart store slowed the decline of the poverty rate by greater than 0.2 percent and the presence of a Wal-Mart at the beginning of the period slowed it nearly 0.1 percent (the expansive economy of the late 1990s contributed to substantial overall declines in poverty rates), after controlling for location factors, pull factors, education levels, self-employment levels, social capital, and other variables. The authors conclude that the positive relation of Wal-Mart presence and expansion to the poverty rate results from former employees of small independent retail firms not having opportunities for work comparable to their old jobs, even in these growing local economies. Since Wal-Mart purchases virtually nothing locally, the economic multipliers may be lower than the retail firms they replaced, and because Wal-Mart pays its employees less, the employees have less to spend locally. The authors also suggest that the weakening of the local business community contributes to lower social capital and the weakening of entrepreneurialism, which then results in slower growth

continues

Box 10.1   *continued*

in employment than would have occurred without Wal-Mart. However, this is more a hypothesis to be tested than a finding.

A third way of looking at the impact of Wal-Mart expansion in rural areas is to assess the distributional impacts between growing trade centers and hinterland counties (Stone, Artz, and Myles 2002; Artz and McConnon Jr. 2001; Stone 1998, 1997, 1995). These studies, rather than being national in scope, generally focus on a single state, and rather than looking at employment and earnings, focus on business closures and retail sales. In general, counties that are adjacent to counties where a Wal-Mart store is sited tend to lose retail sales faster than those counties that are more distant from a Wal-Mart. In the host county or trade center, total retail sales rise and eating and drinking places and home-furnishings sales tend to increase because they are not in competition with Wal-Mart, which draws in shoppers from adjacent towns and counties. On the other hand, sales of grocery items and building materials, and in apparel stores and pharmacies decline because they are in direct competition with Wal-Mart.

The final question is whether and how much consumers benefit from the lower prices charged by Wal-Mart, and if that offsets the negative effects Wal-Mart stores have on retail employment and payroll. Basker (2005) compared prices of ten items before and after entry of Wal-Mart into 165 cities over a twenty-year period and concluded that for items normally sold in drugstores, such as toothpaste, laundry detergent, shampoo, and aspirin, the effect of Wal-Mart's entry was a price reduction of between 1.5 percent and 3 percent in the short run and between 6 percent and 12 percent in the long run. Items such as cigarettes, soft drinks, and apparel showed little decline. Other factors that make Wal-Mart's low prices possible include the company's strong shift in the early 1990s to purchasing goods made in developing countries, particularly China, where wages are extremely low when compared to those in the United States. There is consensus that this movement of industry to such low-wage countries has dampened inflation in the United States but at the same time has continued to erode industrial jobs in the United States—jobs that paid considerably more than do retail jobs.

continues

How then does one assess the overall benefits and costs of the Wal-Mart effect? Is a family that lives near the poverty level better off having a member who works at Wal-Mart than at the independently owned grocery store, pharmacy, or local department store that Wal-Mart replaced—if they can also buy the cheaper goods offered by Wal-Mart? What is the impact on local leadership and civic engagement when a Wal-Mart comes in?

Sources

Artz, Georgeanne M., and James C. McConnon Jr. 2001. "The Impact of Wal-Mart on Host Towns and Surrounding Communities in Maine." Working paper, Office of Social and Economic Trend Analysis, Iowa State University. Online; available: www.seta.iastate.edu/retail/publications/artz_narea_paper.pdf; accessed September 7, 2005.

Basker, Emek. 2005. "Selling a Cheaper Mousetrap: Wal-Mart's Effect on Retail Prices." *Journal of Urban Economics* 58, no. 2:203–229. Online; available: http://ssrn.com/abstract=484903; accessed July 19, 2007.

Goetz, Stephan J., and Hema Swaminathan. 2004. "Wal-Mart and County-Wide Poverty." AERS Staff Paper No. 371, Department of Agricultural Economics and Rural Sociology, Pennsylvania State University. Online; available: http://cecd.aers.psu.edu/pubs/PovertyResearchWM.pdf; accessed September 7, 2005.

Neumark, David, Junfu Zhang, and Stephen M. Ciccarella, Jr., "The Effects of Wal-Mart on Local Labor Markets," *Working Paper No. 2545, IZA, Bonn, Germany,* January 2007. Available: http://ftp.iza.org/dp2545.pdf; accessed October 28, 2007.

Ortega, Bob. 1998. *In Sam We Trust: The Untold Story of Sam Walton and How Wal-Mart Is Devouring America.* New York: Times Business/Random House.

Stone, Kenneth E. 1995. "Impact of Wal-Mart Stores on Iowa Communities: 1983–93." *Economic Development Review* 13, no. 2:60–69.

———. 1997. "Impact of the Wal-Mart Phenomenon on Rural Communities." In *Increasing Understanding of Public Problems and Policies,* ed. David P. Ernstes and Dawne M. Hicks, 189–200. Chicago: Farm Foundation.

———. 1998. "The Effect of Wal-Mart Stores on Businesses in Host Towns and Surrounding Towns in Iowa." Working paper, Department of Economics, Iowa State University. Online; available: www.econ.iastate.edu/faculty/stone/Effect%20of%20Walmart%20%201988%20paper%20scanned.pdf; accessed July 23, 2007.

Stone, Kenneth E., Georgeanne Artz, and Albert Myles. 2002. "The Economic Impact of Wal-Mart Supercenters on Existing Businesses in Mississippi." Mississippi State University Extension Service, fall. Online; available: http://msucares.com/pubs/misc/m1283.pdf; accessed September 7, 2005.

Urban clinics now expand into nearby rural areas, often buying out local clinics and absorbing their doctors. Rural hospitals and clinics may provide space for urban specialists who come weekly or monthly to perform tests and treat people with a particular disease or condition. The more lucrative procedures are referred to urban hospitals, while the rural clinics and hospitals provide the routine and less remunerative follow-up care. Rural hospitals have closed for a number of reasons. Medicare reimbursement policies pay rural hospitals less than urban hospitals to treat the same medical conditions; the result is lower revenues. Additionally, rural hospitals are unable to purchase expensive medical technologies or attract trained health care specialists. In response, some rural communities are joining together to develop collaborative health care systems that are locally coordinated and driven.

The notion that larger, consolidated schools increase the quality of education in the information age, when advanced courses can be delivered via distance education, has been challenged by research showing that small schools had higher levels of achievement and that more students finished school in smaller schools, although this varies by region. Better student attitudes about themselves and others and higher extracurricular involvement are two aspects of small schools that continue to differentiate rural schools from urban ones. Retaining small schools has a positive impact on rural communities (Lawrence et al. 2002).

The food industry also is increasingly concentrated. Not only do a few transnational firms dominate retail grocery stores, but concentration in the fast-food industry also is increasing at the same rate as fast-food outlets. In 1992, the four largest firms in the industry (McDonald's; Yum!Brands Inc., which owns the Taco Bell, KFC, and Pizza Hut brand names; Burger King; and Wendy's) controlled only about 11.9 percent of total fast-food sales. By 2000, they accounted for 39.5 percent of the fast-food sales category.

Another factor favoring consolidation is *economies of scale*. Such economies occur when a greater volume of business can occur at one particular site, since volume is a way to spread fixed costs (of transportation, land and buildings, equipment, labor) over a larger number of units manufactured, distributed, or sold. Distance and low population in the market area make it difficult for rural businesses to take advantage of economies of scale. Central-place theory suggests that there is constant pressure to centralize economic activities in larger places.

The theory does not explain when and why consolidation occurs in a particular sector. Other factors, such as the opportunity to generate profit based on favorable macroeconomic trends, tax policies, capital availability, and organizational innovation, help explain why centralization occurs at a specific time in a specific industry. In retail trade, enterprises tend to spill over into rural areas when several elements are in place. New, more efficient forms of economic organization that are already fine-tuned in urban areas are introduced in rural areas when they appear to have promise for profit there. Centralization also occurs when capital is abundant and the marginal advantage offered by increased urban investment is no greater than what rural areas provide or when the cost of labor becomes critical and the cheap labor available in rural areas is central to profitability or the accumulation of wealth.

Retail grocery chains moved into rural areas in the 1960s, after they had already organized the grocery business in urban areas. These chains developed a transportation system that was sufficiently well organized to enable them to move perishables from warm-climate areas to regions lacking year-round growing seasons. When rural consumers acquired incomes large enough to demand vegetables and fruits year-round, that organization could be matched to new markets, and chains began appearing in rural communities. However, by 2000, grocery stores were leaving small towns as it became more and more expensive to be supplied by national distributors, who prefer more densely populated distribution routes. Driving sixty miles for one small store does not fit into their profit plan. This has resulted in the development of so-called food deserts, much as has occurred in inner-city neighborhoods (see Box 10.2). The transaction costs of distribution have become critical for retailers, and the integrated chains that most reduce them are poised to make the greatest profit.

Wal-Mart was a pioneer in bringing retail discount general-merchandising stores to rural areas because it organized itself economically to support volume sales by attracting rural customers over a wide geographic area through excellent record keeping and stock management. As the corporation's volume grew, it negotiated with suppliers to wait longer periods between delivery and payment, something that disadvantaged small suppliers with limited credit. Wal-Mart was able to offer lower prices and more diverse stock than the mom-and-pop stores, which paid in cash for their stock. Increased numbers of cars and trucks per household and relatively cheap fuel costs facilitated consumers traveling long distances to purchase the perceived bargains and the variety of goods offered. Strategic site selection

Box 10.2 Food Deserts

William Laste of Pittsburgh, New Hampshire, thinks nothing of driving more than four hundred miles round trip to buy groceries, or of supplementing his shopping with fiddlehead ferns and dandelion greens gathered in fields near his home.

In this mountainous outpost of 870 people along the Canadian border, good food at fair prices is hard to find. There are no supermarkets, and the community's two convenience stores offer little fresh produce and plenty of high prices.

"Up here, you're so far out they've got you over a barrel," the sixty-nine-year-old retired plumber said recently. "I couldn't afford to shop up here."

Such is life in "food deserts," increasingly common rural—and inner-city neighborhood—areas where supermarkets with healthful and affordable food are many miles away.

For people like Laste, who have the vehicles, time, and patience to go the distance, it's an inconvenience. For the poor and elderly, it can mean stocking the refrigerator with the pricey, fatty fare of gas station convenience stores.

The term food desert was coined more than a decade ago in Great Britain, where it was used to describe the phenomenon of supermarkets withdrawing from cities to build larger stores on the outskirts.

Rural sociologists Lois Wright Morton and Troy C. Blanchard identified counties in which at least one-half of the population lives more than ten miles from a large food store, which they defined as "low-access" places. The largest concentrations of low-access counties are in the Great Plains and Rocky Mountain regions of the country. Low access is also prevalent in select areas of the Deep South and in the Appalachian region of Kentucky and West Virginia. The researchers found 803 counties with low-access areas in the United States.

Those who live in these low-access areas did not consume adequate amounts of fresh fruits and vegetables and dairy, and many did not consume adequate amounts of protein, with serious health repercussions.

Sources

Associated Press. 2004. "Residents Do Without in America's Food Deserts." MSNBC.com. Online; available: www.msnbc.msn.com/id/5353901/; accessed August 5, 2007.

Morton, Louis Wright, and Troy Blanchard. 2007. "Starved for Access: Life in Rural America's Food Deserts." *Rural Realities*. Rural Sociological Society.

coupled with careful inventory control and control of labor costs enabled them to be profitable. In general, Wal-Mart stores maintain less inventory and use more part-time workers than do traditional retailers. They also do not allow labor unions, do not pay suppliers until an item is sold, and use part-time employees, who receive fewer benefits. (See the discussion of the impact of Wal-Mart in Box 10.1.)

This progression from mom-and-pop stores to franchises to the "Wal-Marting" of rural America has multiple impacts. Small, family-owned stores had a limited variety of goods and generally used family labor. When they did hire, these businesses paid low wages to employees who often worked only part time, particularly women and youth, who provided an important labor supply for these stores. In general, their inventory and sales were not organized as efficiently as in the chain stores. Mom-and-pop stores generally had higher prices than either the franchises or the nationally based discount stores that replaced them, as their low volume required substantial markups, and they could not take advantage of volume buying. These locally owned businesses provided a more personal atmosphere for customers, especially those who came from a similar social class as the proprietors and the workers. The locally owned and operated stores often provided better service, such as providing information about the features of competing products, offering repair services, and greeting customers as they came into the store and immediately helping them find what they sought.

Retail franchises had features of both a family firm and a national chain. They offered variety in their inventory and some of the same friendly helpfulness that characterizes small towns, although they often hired clerks who knew little about the products. They were able to use national advertising and had frequent sales. Their regular prices, however, were not discount prices.

National merchandising firms offer "everyday low prices" but provide little in the way of customer service. For those who define shopping as recreation, and for poor people and minorities, who risked unfriendly treatment by the proprietors of family firms, these changes have been acceptable. Others view the reduction in the number of clerks, the use of part-time labor, and the resulting lack of personal service as problematic.

CHANGES IN THE LABOR FORCE

Changes in the rural labor force have followed national trends since the end of World War II. Among these, two have had important consequences for consumption patterns of rural people: the entry of women into the nonfarm labor force and the growth of the service sector.

Entry of Women into Nonfarm Labor

It now takes more than one income earner in a household to make what one alone could earn in the 1960s. Reduced earning power has led to the entry of more women into the labor force. The increased proportion of women working outside the home has meant that less time is available for household production, such as gardens, food preparation and preservation, the making and maintenance of clothing, housecleaning, and child supervision. Outsourcing these goods and services previously provided by unpaid household labor has contributed to an expansion of consumer goods and the service sector and increased the amount of money a household needs to have.

The Archer family is a typical American family for the current time. Both parents work. This puts a strain on both spouses in fulfilling traditional role expectations, but it is particularly stressful for women. Women may have entered the workplace, but there is little evidence that they have transferred any of their traditional caretaker roles to other members of the family. Women are still the primary caregivers; they continue to prepare meals, take care of the laundry, and look after the children. For women who are single heads of households, especially women in or near poverty, the burden of being both wage earner and caregiver can be a tremendous source of stress. To cope with their increased time in the workplace while continuing to shoulder their traditional caregiving roles, women have changed their consumption patterns. Evidence of this is the growth of convenience foods and the popularity of microwave ovens, to which Susan Archer can attest.

In rural areas, lack of child care has put a special burden on female-headed families, who are an increasing proportion of the rural population and are much more likely to be living in poverty.

Growth of the Service Sector

The service sector has grown because activities previously performed within firms, farms, and households now are acquired in the market. Consolidation has supported the growth of the service sector because as farms and rural businesses consolidate into large enterprises, the workload is no longer manageable within the family unit. These enterprises purchase goods and services that they once produced themselves because of their growing specialization. Outsourcing by firms decreases their costs in infrastructure, labor, and benefits and pushes the risk onto the suppliers of both goods and services.

In earlier times, farm women would prepare and take lunch to the field. Now it is much more likely that one spouse or the other will have an off-farm job and that prepared meals will be purchased for whoever operates the farm machinery. In addition, if the family has small children, child care will become a commodity part of the time; in earlier times, it was handled entirely within the family. Also, since today's farmer is unlikely to obtain the training legally required to apply lethal chemicals, the application of pesticides to crops may be contracted out to a firm that is licensed to apply them but may not have the links to neighbors to be sure that pesticide drift does not occur.

At one time, the wife kept the books of the family farm or business, whereas now bills and receipts may be sent to an accounting firm and returned in the form of a computerized monthly balance sheet. If the family business has grown large enough, a full-time bookkeeper is hired. In either case, a price has been placed on the cost of keeping accounts, making this activity a commodity.

Typically, both adult members of a family hold multiple jobs in rural areas. Teenagers, too, often have jobs, thereby modifying family consumption patterns. Ironically, leisure time, an objective of these efforts to maintain or increase family income, becomes scarcer. When young people work more hours, there is a resulting reduction in their effective consumption of education and extracurricular activities.

In summary, the increases in the number of jobholders per family and the growth of the service sector and volume of consumption goods to ease household production and service demands influenced household consumption patterns. Families have substituted prepared foods and fast-cooking technologies, particularly microwave ovens, for the time once spent preserving and preparing food from scratch. Constantly expanding offerings of highly processed food give the illusion that time can be saved in meal preparation over that required by using raw ingredients. However, research has found that the actual time spent in meal preparation by either method is approximately the same. The difference lies in the complexity of meal presented, particularly since the availability of prepared foods and the decline of family meals often means preparing a different meal for each member of the family The Archers' family evening meal is much less common than a generation before, even in rural communities.

TARGETED ADVERTISING
AND SEGMENTED MARKETS

Radio has long targeted its advertising to its desired listener. Rural radio stations in farm country followed daily commodity price information with advertisements for agricultural inputs.

Television and now the Internet have become powerful tools for marketing products. During the early days, advertising was directed at as broad an audience as possible. Advertising became a powerful influence on the consumption patterns of people, rural and urban alike. The introduction of cable television and the rapid proliferation of highly specialized channels now enable advertisers to use this tool to reach very specific audiences. For example, MTV and VH1 television networks can be considered continuous advertising that is targeted to very specific groups. The Web pages entered by a computer are tracked through "cookies," and this tracking allows advertising related to one's past behavior to jump onto the screen. When entering the pages of an Internet bookseller, a customer is immediately informed of purchases made by consumers whose tastes are similar to his or her own. In this sense, markets have become segmented. Consumption patterns now reflect both mass advertising and the introduction of segmented markets. These two trends have affected those least prepared to deal with increased consumption, the poor.

Targeted Advertising

The Archer family conversation over shoes and video game systems is one repeated among both rural and urban families. Decisions on what is consumed have moved beyond mere functional necessity. Eric Archer's willingness to spend allowance money on a pair of sports shoes that he probably will outgrow in a short time is not driven by a rational comparison of the characteristics of competing brands and their relative prices. Rather, his decision is based on the social acceptance he gains by consuming the more expensive pair. The disparity in the quality of the merchandise probably is not great enough to account for the significant difference in price. However, the status he acquires from consuming a particular style of shoe has implications at school or with his peers and suggests the importance of cultural capital over financial capital. Mass media advertising and product placement in movies and television shows aimed specifically at young males help reinforce the cultural meaning of the particular item consumed.

Since World War II, the use of multiple media to advertise and differentiate commodities has expanded. Some observers suggest that the introduction of mass advertising was a calculated response to lagging consumption and the futility of competing just by price. Instead of responding to consumer demand, manufacturers now create a demand for a particular product or elaboration of a product. The effort has been so successful that the resultant spending patterns are one reason the United States has one of the lowest savings rates in the industrialized world.

Mass advertising often uses values that are deeply seated in popular culture to create demand. Advertisers employ the rural myth to create positive images of their products. Soft-drink commercials that celebrate the honesty of farm work, family, and the land seek to connect these values to consumption of the manufacturer's product. Other advertisements rely on status attainment. Advertisements for designer athletic shoes and jeans propose that the consumption of a certain piece of clothing or footwear will bestow a particular status on the consumer.

Segmented Markets

Network television and general-interest magazines first enabled advertising to be aimed at as broad an audience as possible. The expansion of cable and satellite dishes has led to the proliferation of channels, many of which are highly specialized in terms of intended audience. Now advertising can be targeted to the specialized audiences those channels attract. MTV and many other targeted channels include product placement in their noncommercial air time, as well as specific commercials aimed at teenage and preteen consumers.

Similar targeting has occurred in the print media with the proliferation of professional, sports, hobby, and other types of magazines. Rural areas early on were targets of segmented market publication. *Wallaces' Farmer* was founded in 1895, during the golden ages of farming and journalism, the last era of parity prices for farm commodities and the era when Americans relied on newspapers for all of their news and information. At the time, more people lived on farms than in towns. Farmwork was done with oxen, horses, mules, and manual labor. Farm families often had many children to help with the work. Families seldom went to town and had limited opportunities to socialize with other families. Newspapers and magazines provided the primary source of information as well as a means of communication with other farm families (Goldman and Dickens 1983).

Farming was a family affair, and *Wallaces' Farmer,* written during this era, was aimed at farm families, not just at farmers. There were sections for every member of the family: plenty of information and advertising about agriculture, "Hearts and Homes" for women, "The Boys' Page," "The 4-H Girls' Club Page," and "Little Recipes for Little Cooks."

More recently, the growth of desktop publishing, made possible by the continued miniaturization of computer technology, has strengthened segmentation, with advertising and news often combined almost seamlessly. One example of such targeting is a beef-industry magazine called *Beef Today,* produced by *Farm Journal.* The magazine is free but is provided only to cattle growers. It is virtually impossible for even a public library to obtain a subscription.

The digital revolution is representative of the current revolution in the quantity and availability of all kinds of information. Although we may or may not be consuming any more information now than our parents did, we are consuming far more specialized information.

Changes in the character and price of communications technologies have made it easier for wealthier rural residents to participate in telecommunications consumption. Indeed, some observers have argued that telecommunications technology represents the greatest leveling force for rural and urban residents. However, digital divides between rural and urban and rich and poor still exist. There is less demand in rural areas for broadband access partially because it is difficult for rural businesses to know how they would use the new technology. The Cooperative Extension System, which includes national, state, and local extension staff, was authorized in the 2002 Farm Bill to help rural firms link their business plans to e-business options, much as the extension system previously gave away free hybrid seed and conducted artificial insemination on cows and sows. In those cases, once the usefulness of the innovation was established and legitimized, private-sector firms took over the distribution.

Income Inequality

Mass advertising and the mass media in general have become powerful influences on the consumption patterns of rural people. Mass media can inspire universal demand for certain consumer products. However, economic differences within rural areas make these purchases extremely difficult for some families. Class replaces rural residence as the feature that distinguishes people's consumption patterns.

Income inequality has been growing in the United States since the early 1970s. The incomes of the working class have stagnated or declined. The purchasing power of the average hourly wage in 2007 is no higher than it was in 1965. The new national minimum wage legislation will be implemented gradually in July 2008 and July 2009.

The pressure to spend discretionary income is felt by all, though different groups are encouraged to buy different things. Discretionary income is very unequally distributed. Among teenagers, this inequality becomes obvious as many take on part-time work to consume such products as the latest in athletic shoes or, in rural areas, to invest in a four-wheel-drive pickup truck. Often they work many hours a week, which has a negative impact on their studies.

What we consume ultimately is limited by income more than by point of sale. Outlet malls, for example, are a current growth area in retail trade. Initially these stores were located near factories to market flawed goods, called "seconds." Because factories often were located in rural areas, outlet malls offered inexpensive merchandise to rural consumers. By the 1990s, major manufacturers had found that outlet malls enabled them to keep up production and sales in the face of economic downturns in the U.S. economy. The discount malls have continued to expand in rural areas, in part because of the availability of cheap land in rural areas and in part because upscale department stores that carry the same designer products dislike direct competition located nearby. However, shoppers frequenting these malls often are not rural residents; they are predominantly upper-income suburban residents seeking name brands at bargain prices.

Rural people in the immediate area shop the local Dollar Store or Wal-Mart. As in inner-city neighborhoods, rural low-income residents shop at used-clothing stores set up by churches and other volunteer groups. Families can indeed get high-quality clothes at these local shops selling previously owned attire. Teenagers, however, cannot buy faddish items in the year they are fashionable. Level of income continues to affect consumption patterns.

Are Consumers Really Poor?

The Archer family illustrates the dilemmas encountered in defining inequality. Compared with their parents at the same stage of their life cycle,

Susan and Dan consume many more products. To do so, they both must work. The trend toward two incomes is well documented and frequently cited as evidence of growing economic inequality. Ultimately, sociologists wonder to what extent these social patterns actually reflect inequality. Sociological research shows a dramatic increase in inequality in the U.S. economic structure since the 1970s. Sociologists differ, however, in their interpretation of how this inequality actually affects individuals. There is growing evidence that inequality, coupled with racial discrimination, contributes to reduced health and life expectancy of African American males. Whether the hidden injuries of class and social inequality by themselves contribute to stress and stress-related illnesses is less clear. Recent studies have shown similar impacts of inequality on health and social outcomes for rural whites, Native Americans, and Latinos.

Children who are raised in rural, single-mother households are the poorest demographic group in the country (Duncan and Chase-Lansdale 2002). Poor, single mothers in rural areas would need to double their income to escape poverty, which means that many single mothers have to double up and live with other families. Rural child poverty is widespread, from Appalachia to the Deep South to California's Central Valley. These children are unable to consume large amounts of material goods; they often are denied such basic needs as adequate health care or safe drinking water.

To summarize, it is clear that changing consumption patterns are having a significant impact on rural life. The service industry and the variety of products sold have expanded to meet the increased demand for services the family once performed. Increased consumption has placed added stress on the environment. Young people define themselves according to the products and services they consume, which ultimately affects the community's culture. Finally, wealth rather than place of residence now determines what and how much families consume. And as the world becomes more connected, the status implications of consumption are clear. No longer can rural residents proclaim, "We didn't know we were poor."

IMPACTS OF INCREASED CONSUMPTION

Human Capital

Health. Recent changes in consumption patterns have had a significant impact on human capital in terms of health and education in the United

States. The dense calories in fast foods and their constant presence—from school lunchrooms to shopping malls—have increased serious health problems such as obesity, diabetes, and high blood pressure. Due to the ease of eating provided by fast food and microwavable meals, even rural residents spend less time cooking and more time eating than they did thirty years ago. Overproduction of food has been translated into overconsumption. Agribusiness now produces 3,800 calories of food a day for every American, 500 calories more than it produced thirty years ago, and at least 1,000 calories a day more than most people need. Our taboo against gluttony is tempered by the "bargains" we get in supersized everything and all-you-can-eat buffets. According to Michael Pollan (2006), a man named David Wallerstein is credited with having invented supersizing of popcorn and soft drinks in the 1960s as a way to make a chain of movie theaters in Texas more profitable. He later went to work for McDonald's and after a time convinced Ray Kroc, the founder of McDonald's, to use the supersizing strategy, which of course depends on cheap raw materials (potatoes for french fries, high fructose corn syrup for soft drinks, and even the beef in hamburgers, subsidized by cheap corn that farmers overproduced because of government commodity programs) so that fast-food chains can increase profits by convincing us to eat more than we would if we had to think about whether we should order a second standard-sized helping.

The National Health and Nutrition Examination Surveys found that 32 percent of adults in 2003–2004 were obese by the technical medical definition (having a body mass index greater than or equal to 30). That percentage is up from 22 percent in 1988–1994 and 14 percent in 1976–1980. Obesity has negative health consequences that rival smoking—higher levels of diabetes, high blood pressure, and greater risk of stroke. In the United States, obesity is a main focus for research because it is so prevalent in both adults and children. A Healthier U.S. Initiative was launched in June 2002 with a focus on overall health through exercise, proper nutrition, and screenings for disease prevention. The U.S. Department of Agriculture food pyramid was modified in 2005 to be more individualized. The new pyramid more strongly recommended exercise, reduced total calorie recommendations, suggested more daily helpings of fruits and vegetables, advised whole-grain and more complex carbohydrates, and somewhat strengthened wording about limiting fats and sugar.

Table 10.1 Obesity among Persons 18 Years of Age and Over, United States, 1997–1998 (by sex, region, and urbanization level)

Region and Urbanization level	Total (%)	Men (%)	Women (%)
All regions	19.6	19.3	19.7
Metropolitan counties			
Large central	19.1	17.9	20.2
Large fringe	17.7	19.0	16.3
Small	19.8	19.6	19.9
Nonmetropolitan counties	21.6	21.0	22.1
With a city ≥ 10,000 population	20.5	20.1	21.0
Without a city ≥ 10,000 population	22.7	22.0	23.3
Northeast			
Metropolitan counties			
Large central	19.1	18.9	19.2
Large fringe	17.7	19.0	16.3
Small	19.5	19.4	19.3
Nonmetropolitan counties	21.3	19.9	22.6
Midwest			
Metropolitan counties			
Large central	21.9	18.7	24.8
Large fringe	18.5	18.3	18.5
Small	19.8	19.0	20.4
Nonmetropolitan counties	22.8	23.1	22.4
South			
Metropolitan counties			
Large central	19.9	18.9	20.8
Large fringe	18.5	20.5	16.5
Small	20.4	20.3	20.4
Nonmetropolitan counties	21.9	20.4	23.2
West			
Metropolitan counties			
Large central	16.7	15.8	17.5
Large fringe	15.5	17.8	12.7
Small	18.4	18.8	18.0
Nonmetropolitan counties	17.3	17.8	16.9

NOTE: Percents are age-adjusted.

Rural people in the United States are more likely to be obese than are urban people, partly because at one time rural life required enormous physical effort by both men and women. Large meals with lots of meat and potatoes were regularly consumed. The quality of a restaurant in most rural areas is still judged by the size of its portions. The problem is particularly grave among low-income populations, because healthy diets are more costly and require preparation skill and planning time. Furthermore, socioeconomic status is closely linked to a number of health-related behaviors other than diet, including smoking, the use of seat belts, and physical exercise. On all these measures, rural people's patterns of consumption have a negative impact on their health. (See Table 10.1 on comparative obesity by region and by distance from urban centers.) Rural people also are more likely to smoke than are urban people, although everyone in the West is less likely to smoke than people in other areas of the country. Smoking by youth also is higher in rural areas. (See more on this discussion in Chapter 6, Human Capital, and Box 10.3.)

Education. The second impact of increased consumption is on male educational levels. In the early twentieth century, Eric would have turned his earnings from his part-time job over to his mother to help run the house; now he uses them for his own consumption goals. Normative consumption for young males often includes a car, high-end entertainment equipment, and other expensive items (although these goods are relatively much cheaper than they were even in 1950). Because young men can earn good money in jobs such as construction, they tend to spend more time at work, to devote less time to their studies, and to be less likely to graduate from high school and go to college. Although this ultimately will affect their lifetime earnings, desires for immediate consumption—and the need to make payments on the debt they run up to acquire things—make the workforce seem a more attractive option. Whereas young women in rural and urban areas are more likely to finish high school and go on to college than they were in 1990, young men are less likely to do so.

Female students now outnumber males on college campuses, making up 57 percent of the college population in 2007. There are several explanations for the shift in the proportion of men and women enrolled in colleges, including the feminist movement, but many young males are entering the workforce directly after high school. Many seek jobs in construction or technology where they can have a steady income without needing a college degree. The gap between Hispanic, Native American, and African American males and females is even larger, with more females attending college than males (Mather and Adams 2007). One could conclude that male identity, even more than female identity, is based on consumption during the teens and early twenties. By comparison, as late as the 1980s in many rural communities, it was assumed that if anyone went on to higher education after high school, it would be the males. By 2000, more rural females than males were going on to college.

Box 10.3 Obesity and Physical Inactivity among Rural Children Aged 10–17

Although other studies suggest that patterns of obesity are not significantly different between urban and rural areas, analysis of the 2003 National Survey of Children's Health by the South Carolina Rural Health Research Center indicates otherwise. The report used the U.S. Department of Agriculture urban influence codes, with a focus on differences between metro and nonmetro areas. The authors based definitions of overweight and obese on height-weight ratios. Since parent-reported height and weight are not reliable for children under ten, analysis was limited to children aged ten to seventeen. Here are some of the more provocative findings from the report:

Overweight and obesity

- In 2003, 30.6 percent of children ages ten to seventeen were overweight, 14.8 percent of whom were obese. Rural children (16.5 percent) were more likely to be obese than urban children (14.4 percent). At least 10 percent of children were obese in forty-eight of the states.
- Children living in rural areas adjacent to metropolitan areas (16.7 percent) and micropolitan rural areas (17.1 percent) were more likely to be obese than those living in small remote rural areas (14.3 percent).
- Minority children were more likely to be overweight than either urban or rural white children:
- African American children (41.2 percent) were more likely to be overweight (including obese) than Hispanic (38.0 percent) and non-Hispanic white children (26.7 percent).
- Nearly one in four African American children was obese (23.6 percent) versus 19.0 percent for Hispanic children and 12.0 percent for non-Hispanic white children.
- Rural African Americans had the highest level of overweight (44.1 percent) and obesity (26.3 percent) of any race/ethnicity group.
- As family income increased, the proportion of children who were overweight decreased significantly among both rural and urban residents.
- Children living in the South were most likely to be overweight or obese (33.1 percent), followed by the Midwest (30.2 percent), the

continues

Northeast (29.5 percent), and the West (28.1 percent). Children living in the rural South had the highest likelihood in the country of being overweight.

Physical Activity

- Nationwide, more than one in four children (28.6 percent) ages ten to seventeen failed to meet recommended physical activity levels; that is, not participating in moderate to vigorous exercises for at least twenty minutes three or more days per week. (Note: Under new guidelines, the recommendation has increased to 1 hour for those seeking to lose weight.)
- Fewer rural children (25.4 percent) failed to meet physical activity recommendations than urban children (29.3 percent).
- Older children (ages fifteen to seventeen), girls, Hispanics, African Americans, and children from low-income families were less likely to meet physical activity recommendations.
- Rural children living in the Midwest were more likely to be physically inactive (26.1 percent), followed by the South (26.0 percent), the Northeast (23.7 percent), and the West (23.5 percent).
- More than two out of five children, whether urban or rural, did not participate in any after-school sports teams or lessons in 2003.
- Rural African American children (50.1 percent) and rural Hispanic children (48.6 percent) were more likely not to participate in after-school sports teams or lessons than rural white children (38.9 percent) and urban white children (35.6 percent).
- About half of the children spent at least two hours a day with electronic entertainment media, including television.
- Among rural children, high electronic media use was more common among blacks (63.7 percent), overweight children (54.0 percent), and obese children (54.8 percent).
- Rural children (20.1 percent) were less likely to live in an environment perceived to be unsafe than urban children (25.7 percent).
- Among rural children, black children (38.3 percent), Hispanic children (32.6 percent), and children from low-income families (36.1 percent) were more likely to perceive unsafe environments.
- Overweight children were more likely to feel unsafe, in both urban (28.9 percent) and rural environments (23.2 percent).

continues

Box 10.3   *continued*

- The proportion of children living in perceived unsafe environments ranged from 11.6 percent in Vermont to 50.0 percent in
  Washington, D.C.

SOURCE

Liu, Jihong, Kevin J. Bennett, Nusrat Harun, Xia Zheng, Janice C. Probst, and
  Russell R. Pate. 2007. "Overweight and Physical Inactivity among Rural
  Children Aged 10–17: A National and State Portrait—Executive Sum-
  mary." Columbia, S.C.: South Carolina Rural Health Research Center.
  Also online; available: http://rhr.sph.sc.edu/report/SCRHRC_Obesity-
  Chartbook_Exec_Sum.pdf; accessed July 24, 2007.

Social Capital

Changed consumption patterns have affected the way people interact. As
people work more hours, their interaction with other people decreases.
As more goods and services undergo commodification (being moved from
use value to exchange value), more activities previously done in groups are
now done individually. Putnam discusses the problems of "bowling alone,"
as bowling leagues declined at the same time that the number of lines
bowled increased. Prior to the 1950s, entertainment required getting together with friends for community events or going to the local picture
show. When television first was introduced in the 1950s, the person in the
neighborhood with a high antenna and a television set had all the neighbors in to watch the favorite network shows. As more homes purchased televisions, viewing became a family activity. But by the 1990s, many homes
boasted multiple televisions, and children and adults watched separately.
Videos in rural areas substituted for the few rural theaters that remained,
and there were fewer opportunities to run into friends in a public gathering
to discuss the movie and community issues. In both urban and rural areas,
reading among young people, which is strongly associated with later civic
engagement, has given way to television and video games, which are negatively associated with social capital and community involvement.

The burgeoning service industry now responds to needs that previously
were met within the household or the firm. Goods and services once pro-

duced at home have become commodities, items to be bought and sold. Leisure once involved reading or visiting neighbors, but now even entertainment is purchased rather than being created at home. A growing sector of the economy now generates new alternatives for the use of leisure time, from extreme sports to reality television shows.

Natural Capital

There is an intimate relationship between consumption and rural areas. Rural areas represent 97 percent of the country's land area. It is primarily this part of the country in which food and energy for the future—including wind energy, solar power, and biofuels—will be produced; waste from human consumption is disposed of; and if we are to be successful in combating global warming, where most of the carbon sinks, in the form of trees, pastures, and other permaculture, will be located. It is also where what we hope will be decreasing amounts of fossil fuels—petroleum, coal, and natural gas—will be extracted.

Consumer goods and services require *inputs,* the natural resources or raw materials needed in the production process. Once their useful life is over (and that life is becoming shorter and shorter for everything from computers to clothing), they are thrown away. Acquiring a new item, even an automobile, does not mean that it will be kept for several years. People are constantly trading or selling one thing to make a profit or to have something "newer and better."

The consumption that occurs in the process of producing commodities ultimately affects the environment. For instance, fertilizers and seeds are inputs that are consumed in the production of a crop. Electrical power and computers are inputs that are consumed in the process of producing goods or services in an industrial firm or in an educational institution. These inputs often are included in the calculation of costs of production. The costs of other elements consumed in the course of production, such as the quality of water, soil, and air, often are ignored in such calculations. Economists refer to these costs as *externalities.* Sociologists examine consumption in terms of its totality—inputs and externalities. Environmental degradation associated with acid rain, impure water, loss of biodiversity (indigenous plants and animals), toxic-waste dumps, and soil erosion is a by-product of consumption that ultimately affects the quality of life that consumption supposedly enhances.

Figure 10.1 Energy Consumption per Person

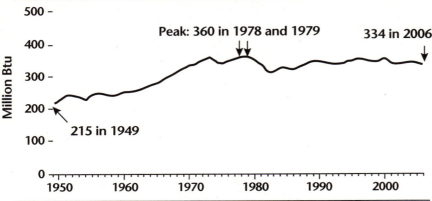

SOURCE: Energy Information Administration/Annual Energy Review 2006.

Per capita energy consumption in the United States has increased greatly since World War II, although it peaked in the 1970s right before the first large increase in petroleum prices, went down, and then up again as prices for energy decreased. (See Figure 10.1.) Currently the United States consumes approximately a quarter of the world's energy but accounts for less than 5 percent of the world's population. Until quite recently, there were few signs that the public would support a decline in level of consumption, which must be the first step in first slowing, and then reducing, worldwide growth in greenhouse gas production. Increasing resource efficiency and decreasing the use of resources, particularly nonrenewable resources, could maintain a stable standard of living. Yet as a society, we have not made this a priority. Instead, we depend on relatively cheap foreign sources of energy and subsidize the development of petroleum extraction in the United States, with severe environmental impacts for rural areas from Alaska to Louisiana. The sustainability of this level of resource use seems to be officially questioned only when the sources of cheap energy are jeopardized, as during the oil embargo in the 1970s, the Gulf War in the early 1990s, and the current concern over international terrorism centered in the Middle East. However, the official stance of the U.S. government has been to seek increased production through drilling in environmentally fragile areas rather than to reduce consumption or to increase fuel efficiency. Rural areas are particularly dependent on private transportation, and the rural poor drive older, less reliable vehicles that get very low gas mileage. Lack of public transportation in rural areas further hinders the rural poor, whose employment depends on showing up regularly and on time and whose transportation sources are unreliable and costly to operate.

A related uncertainty is the safe and environmentally sound disposal of the waste derived from consumption. The refuse created by production and domestic consumption must go somewhere, and that somewhere is often a rural landfill or incinerator. Rural Americans often have to discard their garbage in their own backyards. When the trash collectors pick up garbage in the cities and the suburbs, few of their residents could tell you its final destination. Rural communities are homes for most waste dumps, euphemistically termed sanitary landfills, including those that contain toxic materials or nuclear waste. Most rural people know exactly where refuse, theirs and that of others, is dumped.

Most environmental degradation is considered to be the externalized by-product of our production and marketing processes. The price of the commodities produced and consumed usually does not include the cost of correcting the environmental degradation caused by use or disposal of those products. For example, the price of the farm commodity produced does not include the costs of cleaning up the waterways or the inestimable health costs of a water table polluted by pesticides that have percolated down from surface applications. These costs are borne by the public sector or the individuals, disproportionately the rural poor, who suffer the health consequences.

The consequences of these trends of production and consumption are of particular importance to rural people. First, their sense of material satisfaction now depends upon high levels of consumption, and rural people do not differ greatly from city dwellers in their consumption levels. Second, rural people account for only less than one-fifth of the U.S. population but they live in 97 percent of the land area. That lower population density relative to urban areas makes it politically attractive for decision makers (politicians and technicians) to locate dumps for solid, toxic, and nuclear waste in rural areas.

In general, the less densely populated the rural area, the stronger the inclination to select it as a waste site. From the technician's point of view, the fewer the number of people directly affected, the smaller the social impact. From the politician's point of view, the smaller and more dispersed the population, the less the likelihood of effective political organization in opposition to that particular site. NIMBY ("not in my backyard") opposition may appear anywhere, but all other things being equal, politicians would prefer to have only a few people angry with them.

The increased commodification of leisure activities also creates environmental dilemmas. The number of visitors to the U.S. national parks each year has reached the point that the parks may no longer be able to maintain the pristine environment they were designated to protect. The proliferation of off-road vehicles for use in leisure activities threatens environmental damage that may take centuries to repair. Rural residents find themselves affected as consumers, yet they are also affected as residents of the land they enjoy using for recreation. Communities find they must carefully weigh the economic benefits of tourism and recreation against the environmental costs.

Financial Capital

High levels of consumption in the United States have meant a very low rate of savings, which has implications for those who withdraw from the labor force, either voluntarily or involuntarily. They have little cushion when financial needs suddenly arise. Emergency expenses must be taken from current disposable income, leaving many households with few alternatives. Furthermore, the rate of debt in the United States is extremely high. Rural areas do have less debt per capita than urban areas. A large amount of that debt is on credit cards or with relatives, but the relatives of the rural poor are also poor, putting them into the hands of predatory lenders. This has disastrous consequences.

Alice Smith lives in a small, persistently poor rural community with her four children. After a difficult divorce from an abusive husband, she struggled to provide for her family with income from her job in a local textile factory. Active in her church, she participated in Habitat for Humanity and worked hard to help build her new home, which she financed with a low-income loan. The loan was figured based on her income and what she needed for food, utilities, child care, car expenses, and some spending money for the children. Soon after she moved in, Alice received a phone call offering her the opportunity to refinance her mortgage to pay off her debts. At that point, she had only one credit card, paying off the balance due each month. She wasn't interested. But then the textile factory closed. She began working part-time jobs, waiting tables in several restaurants, but the hours made it difficult to spend time with her children, and tips were undependable. Alice maxed out her credit card and got several more from the many offers that frequently arrived in the mail, using one card to pay off another.

When the same person called again, offering her the opportunity to consolidate her debts with her mortgage if she would refinance the house with them, she gratefully agreed. The new loan paid off the low-interest loan on her house and her credit cards, but then, instead of paying 2 percent interest with $200 monthly house payments, she was paying 10 percent interest and $325 a month for house payments. Gradually Alice fell behind in her house payments, and she eventually lost her house.

Karen and Ed Adams also had high credit card debt and a substantially higher house payment than Alma. They were baby-boom professionals living in a rural community near a metropolitan area, and their two children were now in college. Ed was an engineer with Enron Corporation, and Karen had just become a partner with the Arthur Andersen accounting firm. The dramatic growth in the stock market during the 1990s greatly increased their paper net worth. They began to anticipate early retirement with an affluent lifestyle once their children graduated from college. They used debt to finance the things they would "need" when they retired: a boat, a remodeled home, and new furniture. In 2002, with the stock market in free fall, both their companies went into bankruptcy. Their "savings" were represented by a partnership in Arthur Andersen and Enron stock. They had no liquid savings (money in the bank) that they could fall back on. Karen was able to get part-time accounting work with several local businesses, and Ed looked for job openings in electrical engineering. They also lost their house and are now renting a small apartment.

Low rates of savings can occur at all income levels, putting both the rich and the poor at risk. As we see in Chapter 7, Financial Capital, low rates of savings reverberate in the community because there is less available capital to lend to new businesses that might improve economic conditions. Rural residents and rural communities are caught in a vicious circle.

Built Capital

The U.S. National Academy of Sciences recently addressed the issues of sustainable consumption. It found that the first step toward sustainable consumption is to recognize that consumption patterns inevitably will change in the future, if only by the force of environmental circumstances, such as global warming. A changed approach to built capital can make a huge difference.

If human communities were to deploy all of the ecotechnologies that are already available from innovative businesses (such as energy efficiency, pollution controls, waste management, recycling, cradle-to-grave products, and zero-emissions industry), we could enjoy twice as much material welfare while consuming only half as many natural resources and causing only half as much pollution and waste. Decisions to transform built capital, made by rural entrepreneurs and local governments, could improve both natural and financial capital.

Cultural Capital

In 2007, the Mauna Loa observation station in Hawaii recorded 385 parts per million (ppm) of carbon dioxide in the atmosphere. The Fourth Assessment Report of the Intergovernmental Panel on Climate Change states that the atmospheric mixing of CO_2 gas increased globally by about 100 ppm (36 percent) over the past 250 years, from a range of 275 to 2,385 ppm in the preindustrial era (AD 1000–1750) (2007, 137). Current concentrations are at their highest levels in at least 650,000 years, at approximately 385 ppm by volume in the earth's atmosphere. CO_2 is the principal, but by no means the only, greenhouse gas. The potentially devastating impacts of human-induced global climate change over the present century reminds us of the limits to human beings' alteration of our home, the earth. However, changing our rate of alteration will require a major change in cultural capital. Rather than viewing ever-increasing consumption of "stuff" as a route to personal fulfillment, as a source of status among our friends and acquaintances, and as the mechanism by which we keep our economy healthy, we must begin to cultivate a new ethic built around lessening our ecological footprint on the land.

Distinctions that once differentiated between rural and urban residents have given way to variations based on wealth. Rural communities once valued individuals for what they produced; now, as in urban areas, individuals are valued for what they consume. Different amounts of disposable income limit what any individual and household can consume. Consuming, in terms of purchasing goods, increasingly is looked upon as leisure, with entire families going together to the mall for an afternoon. A family's income, however, limits what family members can buy and how far the parents can drive to buy it. There are different versions of consumption items for different economic groups, and venues range from Saks Fifth Avenue to Dollar Stores; high-end stores cluster in urban areas, whereas Dollar Stores and outlet malls are a rural phenomenon. Yet there are still some rural residents who work hard not to be caught up in a mentality of constant consumption (see Box 10.4).

Box 10.4 Is It Possible to Stop Wasteful Habits?

Janie Lee, a member of In Praise of Mountain Women in Eubank, Kentucky, regards recycling as a way of life. For her, buying secondhand items is economical and an easy way to decrease the accumulation of waste in landfills.

"I have issues with mindset and recycling," she says. "As a mountain woman who has not had much, I have learned many ways to recycle that people do not admire in our general society. I have used many clothing centers in my life, and over time I have realized that I am recycling someone else's clothing that is good enough for me, but it is stuff that might otherwise go to a landfill."

Janie points out that what people throw away is not always trash; people often discard items simply because they are tired of them. Many Americans, in Janie's eyes, are too concerned with "keeping up with the Joneses," spending money on faddish items in order to compete with their peers. They buy new things and discard their old, out-of-style goods. Even if these items are donated to a clothing store or secondhand shop, the store may not keep all of the donations because it does not have room for them, as Janie illustrates:

"What happens to the things we have when we get rid of them? They may be given to places that throw them away, case in point: Goodwill Industries. I am a curious person, so one day I looked in their trash bins, and what did I find? Many good things. One year when I first started looking in their trash, I got so many stuffed animals that after I took them home, washed them and let them dry, I had enough to give every child on my son's preschool bus one and still had more for my son. The bus driver told me that one of the children loved their toy so much, it was as if he had never gotten any new toys before. . . . Many mountain people are very poor."

Janie contacted the president of Goodwill Industries in Kentucky to let him know that there were items being thrown away at the Goodwill that were not "nasty." He urged her to find a nonprofit organization that would take items discarded by Goodwill. Unfortunately, she could not. Such places as Goodwill often cannot keep up with all the donations they receive. The public donated an estimated 975,000 tons of goods in 2002, and charities such as Goodwill face big challenges as more and more of their donated items end up in landfills. Electronic

continues

Box 10.4 *continued*

waste—old cellular phones, computers, and televisions, for example—is steadily increasing, and there are big costs involved with the handling and disposal of such items because they contain hazardous materials, such as the lead found in computer monitors and television screens.

Recycling, for Janie, is personal and necessary. However, Janie recognizes that she often is guilty of adding to landfills herself, which frustrates her.

"Something else I see myself doing is rather than taking my throwaways and recycling them into crafts or useful objects, I throw them away. . . . So many things, like plastic bottles, toilet paper rings or paper towel rings, or egg boxes could be painted and reused but I don't have the time, so I just throw them away. I am not a person that likes to waste things like this. Sometimes I do recycle some of my plastic bottles for spray bottles and things, but I know I waste even more. How do we stop all of this?"

Source

Lee, Selma Juanita (Janie). 2003. "Public Policy Priorities for 2003."

What we consume greatly determines not only our material well-being but also our cultural identity. For example, food preparation has been a significant part of the role women have played as homemakers. However, cooking a frozen dinner in a microwave oven is a profound change in the way we consume food compared with the way we ate just a few decades ago. Our language and culture change as a result of this alteration in consumption patterns; for example, the verb "to microwave" did not exist in the 1960s.

More important, however, the nature of a homemaker's role has changed from when Susan's great-grandmother cooked meals for a threshing crew. Her great-grandmother was concerned with filling the stomachs of hungry workers engaged in hard physical labor, whereas Susan is concerned about nutrition and controlling calories. Susan's great-grandmother was known throughout the county for pie crusts made flaky by a generous use of lard; Susan, on the other hand, includes low-fat yogurt in her children's lunches. Although their meals may differ, these women were and are viewed by their peers as excellent providers of good food for their families. The definition of good food and the amount of time spent preparing it have changed dramatically: More of Susan's food-preparation time goes into planning meals, and most of her great-grandmother's time went into cooking them.

An expensive pair of athletic shoes endorsed by a professional basketball star will not necessarily improve a person's basketball game any more than a much less expensive pair will. Wearing them may bring their user higher status even if not a higher vertical jump. What we consume can become a statement of who we are or want to be, whether in our eyes or in the eyes of others. The group identity provided by consumption makes us painfully conscious of not having or not being able to acquire the symbols that show we are "in style." This is particularly true of young people, who are changing rapidly and whose sense of self is still developing. Both Eric and Jake needed to feel they were part of the "in" group.

For those whose jobs are not inherently satisfying, being able to provide consumer goods and services for their families becomes a reason for working. Increased consumption can give meaning to work. Sociological studies show that an increasing number of people work because of what their earnings allow them to consume rather than because of what they produce. How can this mentality be changed? There is no one way. Inequalities must be reduced. We need to focus on making work more meaningful and perhaps changing the way we organize our communities, firms, governments, civil society, and even families. Social movements (an aspect of civil society) undoubtedly will play an important role in directly changing cultural capital and in influencing governments to encourage us to view the earth as a partner, rather than exploiting it for our short-term benefit.

Political Capital

As we finish the first decade of the twenty-first century, policies are in place to support and expand the current rate and forms of consumption. Bigger is better, and tax breaks to large energy users reinforce that value. Norman Myers (2000) suggests three policy initiatives that could promote the transition to sustainable consumption:

1. Abandon gross national product (GNP) as an indicator of economic well-being. As an indicator, it suggests that we do not need to take account of sustainability. In the United States, per capita GNP rose by 49 percent between 1976 and 1998, whereas

per capita genuine progress (the economy's output with environmental and social costs subtracted and added weight given to
education, health, and the like) declined by 30 percent.

2. Ensure that prices reflect all environmental and social costs. For
   example, U.S. society ultimately pays at least $6 to burn a gallon
   of gasoline (through pollution, road accidents, traffic congestion,
   and so on). Pricing gasoline realistically would curtail the excessive car culture and open up market demand for improved public
   transportation. Similar considerations would apply to the prices
   of other products.

3. Stop subsidies that encourage environmental ignorance. Such subsidies support fossil fuels ten to fifteen times more than clean and
   renewable sources of energy such as solar energy or wind power.
   There are many other subsidies that promote the car culture, overly
   intensive agriculture, wasteful use of water, over logging of forests,
   and over harvesting of marine fisheries. They induce massive dis-
   tortions in our economy and do great harm to the environment.

These are radical proposals. They have strong implications for rural
areas. In general, rural legislators have resisted much milder policy changes,
in part because the political capital of those who profit from the current
forms of consumption is much greater than those of other citizens.

Chapter Summary

What we consume has changed as dramatically as the way goods and services are produced. Expanded earnings, increased presence of women in
the workforce, and the technical capacity to produce more varied products have both increased and changed the character of what we consume.
These changes have made a person's level of income a more distinguishing
quality than his or her urban or rural residence, thereby influencing one's
self-identity; what matters is not where people live but how much income
they make. Regardless, rural residents are more likely to be poor than urban ones, particularly in the South and in the Great Plains.

Several economic and social factors have contributed to the change in
consumption patterns. Globalization encourages consolidation of both retail and service firms. Changes in the labor force have increased the number of jobholders per family, stimulating the growth of the service and
informal sectors of the rural economy. The poor in rural areas are more

likely to be working than in urban areas. Mass advertising has led to the standardization of products. More recently, advertising has been targeted at market niches. The rural poor have a difficult time ignoring this advertising, especially teenagers who want to keep up with the latest fads.

The way we produce goods and services is linked with the way these commodities are consumed, where they are consumed, and why they are consumed. The life cycle of a commodity or service is much more than the points of production and purchase. The final resting places for many commodities are landfills and toxic incinerators located in rural areas. As concern for the environment acquires greater importance, increases in our societal consumption patterns and the consequent concerns about resources, the environment, and waste disposal will become national political issues. These issues, though, already are personal and family issues for rural people and their communities.

Global warming offers an opportunity to rethink these outcomes—to redesign the market, civil society, and government in such a way as to transform our relation with the earth, with our fellow humans, and with technology.

KEY TERMS

Central-place theory proposes that population centers, whether small crossroads communities or large cities, are geographically organized into hierarchical retail and public-service markets.

Commodification is the transformation of a good or service that previously has been available outside the market as a result of community or individual effort into a good or service that is available in the market for a price.

Conspicuous consumption refers to purchases made for social rather than biological needs.

Economies of scale occur when a greater volume of business can occur at one particular site, since volume is a way to spread some costs (of transportation, land and buildings, equipment, and labor) over a larger number of products.

Externalities include the social costs of production not borne by the company producing the goods. These might include the contamination of the soil, air, or water when waste products are released to the environment.

Inputs include the natural resources or raw materials needed in the production process.

References

Cotterill, Ronald W. 2001. "Neoclassical Explanations of Vertical Organization and Performance of Food Industries." *Agribusiness: An International Journal* 17:33–57.

Duncan, Greg J., and P. Lindsey Chase-Lansdale. 2002. *For Better or Worse: Welfare Reform and the Well-being of Children and Families.* New York: Russell Sage Foundation.

Goldman, Robert, and David D. Dickens. 1983. "The Selling of Rural America." *Rural Sociology* 48, no. 4:585–606.

Intergovernmental Panel on Climate Change. 2007. "Change in Atmospheric Constituents and in Radiative Forcing." In *Climate Change 2007: The Physical Science Basis. Contribution of Working Group I to the Fourth Assessment Report of the Intergovernmental Panel on Climate Change,* ed. S. Solomon, D. Qin, M. Manning, Z. Chen, M. Marquis, K. B. Averyt, M. Tignor, and H. L. Miller. New York and Cambridge, U.K.: Cambridge University Press. Also online; available: http://ipcc-wg1.ucar.edu/wg1/Report/AR4WG1_Pub_Ch02.pdf; accessed September 1, 2007.

Lawrence, Barbara Kent, Steven Bingler, Barbara M. Diamond, Bobbie Hill, Jerry L. Hoffman, Craig B. Howley, Stacy Mitchell, David Rudolph, and Elliot Washor. 2002. *Dollars and Sense: The Cost Effectiveness of Small Schools.* Cincinnati, Ohio: KnowledgeWorks Foundation. Also online; available: www.goodsmallschools.org/resources/dollars_sense1.pdf; accessed July 18, 2007.

Mahter, Mark, and Dia Adams. 2007. "The Crossover in Female-Male College Enrollment Rates." *Population Reference Bureau.* Online; available: www.prb.org/Articles/2007/CrossoverinFemaleMaleCollegeEnrollmentRates.aspx?p=1.

Meyers, Norman. 2000. "Sustainable Consumption." *Science* 287:2419.

Pollan, Michael. 2006. *The Omnivore's Dilemma.* New York: Penguin Press.

Stone, Kenneth E. 1995. *Competing with the Retail Giants: How to Survive in the New Retail Landscape.* New York: Wiley.

Veblen, Thorstein. [1899] 1967. *The Theory of the Leisure Class.* New York: Funk & Wagnalls.

11

GOVERNANCE

Arthur Crocket had been a waterman all his life, as had his father, grand-father, great-grandfather, and even his great-great-grandfather, along the rocky coast of Cornwall, England. The blue crabs that he caught in the Chesapeake Bay of Virginia had a good market. But blue crabs were getting harder and harder to find. What with pollution and increased fishing equipment in the bay, the catch was decreasing. It became easy to cut corners—take in a few undersized crabs at the end of the day, as he threw overboard the remains of his lunch, including plastic water bottles and aluminum cans. The sea would always take care of them. Each Sunday at his evangelical Christian church he prayed along with the entire congregation for the crabs to come back, as all of the Tangier Island community depended on the crabs for their livelihoods.

Art and his congregation were not the only ones concerned about the decreasing availability of blue crabs. When it became clear that government alone could not clean up the Bay, Tom Stoner of the Chesapeake Bay Foundation (CBF) was part of a volunteer monitoring team to mark the progress of bay restoration. To him, the decline in crab harvests indicated decline in water quality and over harvesting of crabs. The CBF supported the Virginia Marine Resources Commission (VMRC) regulations on blue crab harvesting, although they were not involved in their implementation. They were alarmed that the laws were blatantly ignored. Data used by the CBF and the VMRC came from the scientists at the Virginia Institute of Marine Science (VIMS), part of the state-supported William and Mary University.

The conflict came to a head when strict regulations were put in place in 1994; a shed owned by the CBF was burned. At that point, Art's pastor contacted the Au Sable Institute of Environmental Studies (ASIES), which states its mission as "the integration of knowledge of the Creation with biblical principles for the purpose of bringing the Christian community and the general public to a better understanding of the Creator and the stewardship of God's Creation. All of its programs and activities are structured to allow, and are conducted for, promotion of Christian environmental stewardship." Susan Drake Emmerich learned about the conflict through ASIES and chose Tangier Island to gather ethnographic data for her dissertation on faith-based approaches to conservation. She arrived in 1997 and became involved in the churches on the island, attending services and teaching Sunday school classes. Working with the Tangier Island watermen through the two churches on the island, she helped them write a stewardship covenant that acknowledged the biblical base of obeying civil law, no matter how unjust the law seemed to be, and the biblical mandate to be good stewards of the land and sea. Faith-based stewardship meant obedience to God.

As they negotiated the covenant and began what became the Tangier Island Watermen Community Stewardship 2020 Initiative, the mistrusted and threatening outsiders representing the Virginia Marine Resources Commission, the Chesapeake Bay Foundation, and the scientists of Virginia Institute of Marine Sciences gradually joined in the discussions and learned to respect and understand the community's distinctly biblical approach to the situation. The community formed the Tangier Waterman's Stewardship for the Chesapeake (TaSC) and, a few years later, joined with the CBF in implementing fishery and wetland projects.

The 2020 Initiative formed two subcommittees, Sustainable Economic Development and Preserving Waterman Culture Subcommittee and the Fishery Stewardship Subcommittee, which conducted a survey. Much to the surprise of the organizers, who thought of Tangier Island as a very patriarchal society where men made all the decisions, the survey revealed that the watermen would accept the assistance of their wives in working with government, environmentalists, and scientists to maintain the watermen way of life. As a result, watermen's wives created the advocacy group Families Actively Involved in Improving Tangier's Heritage (FAIITH). They collected scientific and regulatory information to aid them in their representation of watermen's interest at VMRC meetings. And they took an active role in planning economic alternatives for the island.

These activities gained momentum, and the Tangier Town Council endorsed TaSC, providing a community-based mechanism for participation of those concerned about environmental stewardship but uncomfortable with its faith-based orientation. FAIITH works with the local school district to deliver conservation education in the school. Conservation is now part of Tangier Island lifestyle. Even the oldest watermen carry back their garbage in a bag, rather than dumping it in the ocean. And the economic diversification into tourism is blossoming, mainly run by Tangier Island women.

What Is Governance?

The watermen and Tangier Island residents did not participate in a key decision that threatened their livelihood and way of life. By mobilizing around their cultural capital—their religious values and local knowledge of the natural resource—they were able to become part of the dialogue around the implementation of those decisions. But for the disorganized watermen to defend their market interests, they had to join with state and civil society groups around shared desired future conditions. Once they escaped from their victim mentality, they were able to identify the core values that allowed them to negotiate their local knowledge with scientific knowledge and regulatory regimes. The people of Tangier Island utilized local institutions, first civil society (the two local churches) and later the state (town government), to make alliances that could support their market activities into the future. That ability to form internal and external alliances to inform decisions at the state level and to make decisions at the local level is what governance is about. By broadening the base of participation (increasing bonding social capital) and reaching out to others who shared their vision of the future of the region, transformational change took place at the individual, organizational, and community level.

The Rural Policy Research Institute has identified three major components of governance (Stark 2007):

- Collaboration
- Crossing sectors (market, state, and civil society)
- Crossing political boundaries (jurisdictions) and recognizing regions
- Sustained citizen engagement

- Welcoming new voices, especially underrepresented individuals and youth
- Visioning a different future
- Leveraging regional resources, which include multiple capitals from multiple sources to reach mutual ends
- Analyzing the region's competitive advantages (focus on strengths, identify clusters)
- Strengthening competencies of local elected officials
- Engaging key intermediaries
- Investing local capital

Governance is particularly important in rural areas, where governments are small, elected government officials serve part time with small budgets, and few professional staff are available to find the necessary information to make sound decisions or to implement decisions when they are made. At the same time, there is devolution of responsibility with a large portion of accompanying stresses and a very small portion of accompanying resources. And in rural areas, everyone knows where the mayor lives, and she may spend much of her time quieting barking dogs or containing a burst waterline, always absorbing the blame when expectations—that may be set on big-city standards of public services—are not met.

Yet even in light of the huge burdens, elected officials often do not seek collaboration with local market or civil society organizations—and vice versa. Very often the elected officials view the other groups as somehow undemocratic, as they are not formally elected, while civil society groups see elected officials as bean counters who just want to keep things the way they are. The Tangier Island Town Council previously had worked very hard to keep the separation of church and state intact on the island, where 87 percent professed Christianity (and 13 percent did not). It was only when there was the common goal of building a better future by increasing all the community capitals that local government felt comfortable allying with the two churches in town.

Although there are many ways that communities can benefit from collaboration with other entities, most state and federal funding is distributed through narrow, programmatic silos that discourage collaboration across jurisdictions or sectors. For example, small communities with limited Internet connectivity cannot allow local private businesses to have broadband access through the schools, which receive federal support for installation and maintenance.

Governance means moving beyond the usual way of doing things, and focusing on ends, not the rules that limit the means that are used. Often the rules and the means become ends in themselves, rather than means to an end. Governance means broader community participation and more flexibility on the part of state, market, and civil society groups. (See the discussion in Chapter 1.)

Governance provides an avenue for citizen participation beyond voting for local officials. Governance provides a flexible structure by which communities can respond to challenges and opportunities. And governance offers an arena where issues of responsibilities are explored.

A number of conditions militate against governance and reinforce segmentation, fragmentation, and intergovernmental and interorganizational battles over turf. Yet, as we have seen in the case of Tangier Island, it is possible for rural communities to move beyond the confines of jurisdiction and sector when they have a vision of an alternative future.

First we discuss the structures of local governments. Then we discuss some of the challenges that local governments face and ways that moving from government to governance can overcome those challenges. We then give examples of collaboration, sustaining resident involvement, and leveraging regional resources.

ORGANIZATION AND FUNCTIONS OF LOCAL GOVERNMENTS

What do local governments do? And how flexible can they be in the way they do it? What is needed to move from government to governance? In most places in the United States, local governments control taxation. The ability to tax enables a government to raise the resources needed to set an agenda and implement policies to accomplish that agenda. Planning and zoning, which determine land use, is a power that some local governments can exercise. Governance means that the resources raised through taxes can be combined with those raised by other entities, including other jurisdictions, such as the school district; civil society, such as the CBF; and market groups, such as the watermen's association and the A&N Electric Cooperative on Tangier Island.

This section explores the powers shared by local governments, the types of local governments found in rural areas, and who does the work of local governments.

Power of Local Governments

The U.S. system divides power, including the power to tax, between two levels of government. As provided by the Tenth Amendment to the U.S. Constitution: "The powers not delegated to the United States by the Constitution, nor prohibited by it to the States, are reserved to the States, respectively, or to the people." Which powers are reserved only for the states often is in question, and the resulting flexibility enables the balance of power to shift back and forth between the two levels. This form of government is referred to as *federalism*.

Local governments are not mentioned in the U.S. Constitution. They are, in fact, created by each state, which makes for a great deal of variation across the country. Local governments derive their power either from grants of authority in state constitutions, which are known as "home-rule provisions," or by general laws or statutes passed by state legislatures.

In theory, local governments provide the mechanism by which participation, needs, and responsibility are linked. They can allow for direct citizen participation in government, or they can provide representative government, in which local citizens elect officials to act on their behalf. New England town meetings are among the more famous examples of direct citizen participation. Annual town meetings enable all citizens to participate in setting the agenda as well as in making decisions. The number of townships in the United States decreased from 16,691 in 1989 to 16,629 in 2002; however, many localities still conduct their business through town meetings.

Under representative government, local residents elect a group of people (to a town council, city commission, school board, or board of supervisors) who then make decisions. These decisions relate to (1) what services will be provided, (2) who will be hired to provide them, (3) how the revenue will be raised to pay for those services, and (4) how land under their authority can be used.

When communities are small, as they are in rural areas, a higher percentage of residents can play an active role in this process. Wide participation should allow services to be tailored to the unique needs of the local population. Having the power to tax enables local governments to ensure that the community accepts responsibility for raising revenue needed for the services that the community values most. Theory often falls short of reality, however. Elite groups in communities can block the participation of certain categories of residents. Local resources simply may not be available to respond to local needs, at which point other levels of government often become involved.

Types of Rural Governments

Rural governments are as diverse as rural economies. As shown in Table 11.1, the many forms of government can be sorted into two types: general-purpose and special-purpose governments. *General-purpose governments* are, as their name implies, governments created to respond to the general needs of a county, city, or town. They usually have the power to raise revenue and determine its use. State governments may restrict use of certain types of taxes or place ceilings on tax levels, as happened when taxpayers revolted in states such as California, which in 1978 limited property taxes to no more than 1 percent of the property's "full cash value," defined in terms of the assessed valuation. For people owning a California property two years prior to enactment of Proposition 13, " . . . [t]he 'full cash value' means the county assessor's valuation of real property as shown on the 1975–76 tax bill" (California, State of, n.d.). These people received an immediate reduction in their property tax bill on homes, businesses, and farms estimated by the Howard Jarvis Taxpayers Association (Jarvis was the intellectual and political author of Proposition 13) to have been 57 percent for the state as a whole (Fox 2007). People buying a home after 1975,

Table 11.1 Number of Local Government Units, 2002, 1987, and 1962

Type of Government	2002	1987	1962
Total local governments	87,849	83,186	91,185
General-purpose governments			
County	3,034	3,041	3,043
Municipal	19,431	19,200	17,997
Township	16,506	16,691	17,144
Special-purpose governments			
School district	13,522	14,721	34,678
Special district	35,356	29,532	18,323

SOURCE: U.S. Census of Governments, 2002. "Government Finance." Online; available; http://www.census.gov/govs/cog/2002COGprelim_report.pdf.

whether the home was newly constructed or purchased from a prior owner, were to pay the assessed value based on its current full cash value. An annual inflationary adjustment of the assessed valuation is allowed that equals the percentage change in the Consumer Price Index or an increase of 2 percent, whichever is less. If the home declines in value, the assessed valuation "may be reduced to reflect substantial damage, destruction, or other factors causing a decline in value" (California, State of, n.d.). No percentage limit was placed on the decline. These property-tax restrictions greatly reduced all local governments' ability to meet the needs of citizens and had serious repercussions on such special-purpose governments as school districts.

Special-purpose governments are created to respond to specific community needs, such as schools (see Chapter 4, Human Capital), water supply, or medical services. These special districts usually can raise revenue to cover their costs, generally through fees or property taxes. Their freedom to tax often is severely restricted by state governments, but they also can raise revenue by user fees, as do water districts.

Other special tax concessions in the name of economic development, such as tax increment financing (TIF), can limit governments' ability to support the services they offer. *Tax increment financing* is a tool used by municipalities to reduce or eliminate blighting conditions, foster improvement, and enhance the tax base of every district that extends into the area. TIF provides for redevelopment that would not occur without the support of public investments. This tool allows a city to capture the increase in state and local property and sales taxes that result from a redevelopment, which also contributes to the TIF fund. The city is required to prepare a redevelopment plan for each district that identifies uses for the TIF fund. However, the redirection of the taxes means that special-purpose governments, such as school or hospital districts, can lose funding during the period the TIF is in place.

The relative importance of any one type of rural government varies by region of the country and from state to state. In some states, small municipalities are the most common type of general-purpose government. In the West and throughout much of the South, counties provide most local governmental services; villages and towns often are not incorporated. In the West, where counties are much larger than in other regions of the country, county government can be essentially regional in character. In the states across the Great Plains, small municipalities and counties vie for political prominence, often providing complementary services. In New England and across the northern tier of states, townships are the most important general-purpose government. Differences in political traditions and state law are reflected in the diversity in local governance. The differences can also influence the flexibility that local governments have to collaborate with other jurisdictions and market and civil society groups. Because Virginia limits the role of town and county governments, civil society took the lead role in negotiating with other levels of government in the case of the Tangier Island watermen. Yet the visible support for the 2020 planning effort by the town was critical in moving it forward.

CHALLENGES FACED BY LOCAL GOVERNMENTS

Fiscal Stress

Many rural governments suffer from what is called *fiscal stress,* which occurs when available revenues decrease and the need for services increases. When jobs are lost to plant closure, for example, property tax revenue declines, but demand increases for community services such as job training, welfare, and housing.

Some services also require a certain minimum number of users before it becomes cost-effective to provide them. When a community's population starts to decline, the number of users may drop below that minimum level. Fixed costs then must be shared by a smaller number of remaining residents. At some point, local governments must decide to eliminate a service, allow it to be provided by a higher level of government, or arrange for it to be provided privately. For instance, townships in various Midwestern states transferred the upkeep of township roads to county governments when farms were consolidated and the number of farmers declined. Acute fiscal stress frequently triggers decisions in which local governments give up providing services. County governments with new responsibility for more roads likely would close the roads least traveled to limit their fiscal exposure.

Most rural governments are funded by a combination of local, state, and federal funds. In general, rural communities rely upon local sources of revenue for about 65 percent of their budget. That percentage has been increasing since 1977, more sharply since the onset of federal cutbacks in response to tax cuts and to fund U.S. involvement in the wars in Afghanistan and Iraq. Local governments typically rely on property taxes, often supplemented by a local sales tax. Business taxes, user charges, and miscellaneous revenues such as fines and fees bring in lesser amounts. Very few rural counties or towns levy income taxes.

Types of taxes can be contrasted based on the most affected taxpayers' ability to pay. *Progressive taxes* place a disproportionate share of the tax burden on those most able to pay: the wealthy. *Regressive taxes* do the reverse, placing a disproportionate amount of the tax burden on middle-income and lower-income taxpayers. Local taxes tend not to be progressive. Sales taxes are the most regressive of all. In contrast, real property taxes are more capricious than regressive. They are only loosely related to the ability to pay. For instance, elderly people who own their own home or small farm and are on a limited fixed income will pay a higher proportion of their income in property taxes than will a prosperous tenant farmer or wealthy banker. Because federal funds are derived primarily from income taxes, they generally are progressive, although tax loopholes may allow wealthy individuals or corporations with good lawyers to sharply reduce their tax burden. State funds come from a mixture of progressive and regressive tax sources.

Locally generated taxes depend on local economic activity. The 1980s were a particularly difficult period for rural governments: Farm values declined, the energy economy collapsed, timber and mining activity dwindled, and a nationwide recession occurred, with an attendant decline in retail trade. As a result, the base for property taxes (real property values) and the base for sales taxes (retail trade) decreased sharply. The fiscal capacity of local governments declined at the same time that federal and state governments shifted the burden of particular services to local governments. Local governments suffered acute fiscal stress throughout the 1980s and into the twenty-first century. Only with the eight-year expansion that coincided with the Clinton administration was fiscal stress lifted. The economic downturn in the third quarter of 2001 and the costs of security measures mandated by the U.S. Department of Homeland Security (2002) significantly impaired the budgets of state and local governments. Many state governments, in order to have symmetry with federal income tax forms, implemented the tax reductions that were in the Bush administration's federal tax-cut package of 2001. They experienced significant loss of revenue through a de facto tax cut (Sawicky 2002), which will continue if the tax cuts to high-income entities are made permanent.

Although property taxes have been the major source of local government revenue, they became increasingly unpopular in the 1970s and 1980s. Consequently, some rural areas have significantly reduced their reliance on property taxes. Very rural areas (counties with fewer than 2,500 urban residents) still collect almost 60 percent of local revenues from property taxes, however.

Efforts at raising additional local non–property tax revenues have proved difficult. Several factors hamper rural governments, including a lack of staff and leadership to adopt and administer creative financing, the relatively low incomes in some rural areas, shrinking retail sectors in smaller communities, and restrictions by state government on non–property tax sources (Reeder 1990).

In general, current mechanisms for funding local community needs have not proven effective, especially for rural communities faced with a declining economy. The tax burden on rural residents increases as the health of the local economy decreases. The inequity of such a system has become obvious in the financing of schools. Judges in past court decisions in Kentucky and Texas have invalidated state financing strategies, pointing to the tremendous gap between per-pupil expenditures in suburban and rural areas. Courts are insisting that states allocate state educational funds in such a way as to ensure that rural and suburban children alike have access to a high-quality education.

More Responsibility, Less Money

In 1981, President Ronald Reagan and his administration made large-scale reductions in federal assistance to state and local governments a major policy objective, supporting the Omnibus Budget Reconciliation Act of 1981. Under this "new federalism," federal support of local communities declined. The Budget Reconciliation Act also converted seventy-seven categorical grants to nine new block grants, eliminating sixty programs. Cuts in local services were dramatic, and the states were forced to adjust to declining federal support. In 1987, general-revenue sharing was eliminated with equally dramatic results. Some rural governments depended on general-revenue sharing for as much as 15 percent of their general-fund budgets.

Except for a period in the second half of the 1990s, state aid has not compensated for the decline in federal assistance. Following the passage of the Personal Responsibility and Work Opportunity Reconciliation Act (PRWORA) in 1996, which ended "welfare as we know/knew it," state governments were flush with money because of a growing economy. State legislatures added funds for job training, transportation subsidies, child care, and child health insurance to the federal block grants for welfare and child care. The economy slowed down in 2001, and between 2002 and 2005, state and local governments' spending on social services (child care, child welfare services, employment services, low-income energy assistance, and services for disabled and homeless persons) and cash assistance to low-income persons declined in real terms for the first time since the early 1980s. (Cash assistance provided by state and local governments actually began declining in 1996, mirroring the decline in numbers of people on the federal welfare rolls due to PRWORA.) On the other hand, nonfederal spending on health for low-income people (the bulk of which is the state's share of Medicaid) has grown at an accelerating rate since 1983—from less than $2,000 per poor person to more than $7,000 per poor person, measured in constant dollars (Gais, Bac, and Dadayan 2007). This growth is due primarily to the rapid growth in the cost of health care throughout society.

The decline in federal responsibility for rural development has led to increased state efforts to promote economic development (Brace 2002). Federal funds for programs with a primarily rural community- or economic-development focus (administered by the U.S. Department of Agriculture, the Environmental Protection Agency, and the Department of Health and Human Services) declined about 8 percent (plus inflation) between fiscal year 2003 and fiscal year 2007 and, if the Bush administration's 2008 budget were adopted, would decline 28 percent from fiscal year 2003 (National Rural Network 2007, 6–7). Today most states have an economic development program, but unless such programs explicitly include a rural development component, rural communities generally receive much less than their share of state funds. Urban business interests often dominate state economic development programs. In addition, many state economic development programs focus on recruitment of industry, which is more appropriate for metropolitan cities and regional trade centers than for smaller rural communities.

When viewed from a national perspective, state industrial policies tend to be a zero-sum game. One state can raid other states for industrial firms, but these efforts do not necessarily increase total industrial capacity or expand net employment opportunities in the nation. They simply move jobs from one state to another. Rather than taking the initiative by adopting policies that encourage new job development and discourage industrial raiding across state borders, the federal government is virtually abandoning economic development.

Multiple Government Structures

The very organization of local government in rural areas presents special problems for the effective delivery of services. The multiple general-purpose and special-purpose governments that serve a single community can lead to conflict. Additionally, the types of services needed also are becoming increasingly complex and sometimes highly technical. The capacity of local officials to deal with these issues is limited. Several examples illustrate the character of these problems.

In an effort to encourage regional cooperation, federal and later state governments created regional government districts. The Area Redevelopment Act of 1965 created a series of regional or multicounty districts through which federally supported area development efforts could be focused. In addition, states have also created multicounty strategies through which to deliver a wide range of services: regional planning; solid waste disposal; health, mental health, and aging services; and so forth. In general, these districts have been created to distribute federal or state aid to local communities and to implement the program and planning activities required to receive the funds. These regional governments, in many states known as councils of governments, when adequately staffed can provide smaller communities with needed technical expertise and with the knowledge necessary for getting grants, hiring consultants, and generally supplying information about links to outside resources, whether human, financial, social, environmental, or even political. However, they often are not linked with civil society and often depend on a small group of market actors to provide the services they support.

On the other hand, combined with local governments, these regional agencies create an enormously complex structure to meet the needs of communities. One obvious problem is that conflict is created when local and regional agencies are both addressing the same need. Multiple and overlapping agencies also lead to fragmented efforts that may not necessarily respond to the needs of the entire community. To promote economic growth, for example, a general-purpose government may decide to float TIF bonds on behalf of industries or businesses that that government would like to attract. Any increase in tax collections within the TIF district during the life of the bonds goes toward paying off the bonds for the newly arrived firm(s). The local government that initiates the TIF district essentially commits all other local governments collecting taxes within that district to forgo any increase in tax receipts during the same period.

The logic is that had the new commercial or industrial firm not been enticed to come, the various general- and special-purpose governments would not have had those taxes to spend because the tax base would not have grown. The rub comes, however, when the new firms generate need for greater public services. School districts depend heavily on property-tax revenues for their operation, yet they do not participate in the decisions made by general-purpose governments. The decision to lower or waive the property taxes charged to local industry helps promote local economic development, but it can be harmful to local schools.

For example, the city commission of Manhattan, Kansas, used tax increment financing to pay for the city's share of costs to build a downtown mall. This method of financing assumes that the development of a mall will result in increased valuation of the property being developed. The increased revenues expected from the higher valuation then can be used to pay off the bonds needed to finance the construction of the mall. Two or three years after the mall was completed, citizens realized that tax increment financing limited their short-term ability to expand school budgets or upgrade streets in response to new needs because the increased tax revenue already had been committed to the bonds used to construct the mall. One local government, the city commission, had made a decision that affected another local government, the schools.

Staffing Rural Governments

Citizen-officials, who receive only symbolic remuneration and thus must have another source of income, often lead small governments. The town mayor (paid for by local taxes) might also be the city postmaster (paid for by the federal government) and local fire chief (not paid at all). In contrast to their urban counterparts, rural governments are highly dependent on citizen volunteers as opposed to paid elected and appointed officials.

Despite the limited time they can devote to their duties, rural officials face many issues similar to those faced by larger governments. Professional networks and associations can be helpful, but officials in rural areas are less likely to participate in such groups than are those from urban areas. Advisory councils and technical assistance available through state agencies often provide information that aids policy decisions. They may also offer training that will improve public management. For example, small municipalities in Pennsylvania receive training and technical assistance in everything from financial investments to rural development. Assistance providers include the State Department of Community Affairs, the Association of Township Supervisors, the Cooperative Extension Service, borough associations, universities and colleges, private consultants, neighboring municipalities, the Pennsylvania Economic League, and others.

Small city councils rely primarily on the advice and expertise of the few people who hold paid management and consulting positions in the local government. They include such people as the town clerk, the city attorney, the county engineer, and the city treasurer. These individuals are extremely valuable to the community, but they can exercise inordinate control over the decision-making process.

City or county attorneys and engineers, for example, can act as gatekeepers to the community. Because they often have exclusive control of technical expertise, these officials can limit the information that is shared about an issue or determine which outside resources are sought. These officials also can spend more time on local affairs than elected officials because they have paid positions in the local government. Thus, paid technical staff can exercise a substantial amount of political control over inexperienced or part-time elected officials.

Providing Public Services: An Example of Collaboration

Rural governments face a common problem: providing adequate levels of public services with limited resources. The problem is common to all rural communities, whether they are experiencing growth or decline. Communities with growing populations must provide services for more people, despite the fact that tax revenue rarely keeps up with the increased demand. Declining rural communities grapple with the problem of providing continued services in the face of an eroding tax base and waning support from the state and federal governments. Poor communities have little tax base with which to provide any services, yet these communities include people whose need for assistance is great.

The problem of losing local funding and services is widespread. Richard Rathge suggests that success in saving rural, remote counties depends on "cooperative ventures that nurture and promote collaboration among differing levels of governments or organizations" (2002, 18). However, this cooperation, although important, often depends upon federal mandates. Can such inter-jurisdictional, cross-sector collaboration occur as a result of bottom-up organizing, rather than state or federal requirements?

Rural areas are particularly challenged in providing drinking water that meets the standards of the federal Clean Water Act. Provision of water in rural areas is often highly fragmented, with arrangements that made perfect sense during the settlement period still in place. The planning process of the Northwest Missouri Water Partnership (Chapter 8) demonstrates how such a participatory process can work to provide a key service using existing assets with dynamic collaboration.

The effort began in early 2005, with county commissioners from five rural counties coming together because of an impending water crisis in an area of the state that had grown in population and income over the past decade, to form a multicounty water system in northeast Missouri. The Missouri Department of Natural Resources (DNR), concerned about the quality and accessibility of water in the region, attended the group's March meeting, and in July group members met with the DNR in Jefferson City. They were told they could get state help for their project *if* they included all twelve northeastern counties and came up with a locally driven regional plan.

The expanded group of county commissioners and concerned citizens took them up on the challenge. With the assistance of Missouri Cooperative Extension and Northwest Missouri State University in Maryville, they held a well-attended regional conference on drinking water in November, supported by the DNR. The expanded network, which now included market and civil society actors as well as diverse state jurisdictions, continued to meet. After numerous monthly meetings, they came up with a mission: The Water Partnership for Northwest Missouri is a coalition of local and regional stakeholders working to identify solutions for a long-term, affordable, high-quality water supply for the citizens of northwest Missouri. The stakeholders determined that water was the basis for achieving many of their regional goals and that the coalition around water helped them solidify their regional identity. With that mission, the planning, supported by another DNR grant, began. First, group members mapped the assets in the region's eighty-three water districts to provision, treat, and distribute water, and, based on these assets, developed seven alternative scenarios by November 2006. Extension organized twelve town hall meetings around the region, in which more than two hundred people participated. Only one of the scenarios, the one that utilized the maximum number of existing local resources, was approved.

To gain the participation necessary for true governance, it was necessary to increase human capital by increasing local knowledge about the water. Thus the group instituted a number of efforts to share information with citizens about the current available water supply by county, the real cost of water, the economic impact of water, and possible regional approaches to meet water needs. As a result of the information sharing, participation in the partnership increased, as citizens identified specific areas lacking water.

The DNR is supporting a study of feasibility of the chosen plan, which will determine the routes of the regional water mains, the costs, and alternative financing mechanisms, including involving private investors. All the water boards will remain in place as part of the partnership, and Missouri Cooperative Extension is offering board training on laws and regulations, duties and responsibilities, ethics, operation and maintenance, rate setting, public education and customer service, and system vulnerability and emergency response. Moving from government to governance in the provision of community services depends on investing in human, social, political, financial, and built capital, as well as natural capital, the basic resource. But most important of all, it requires a change in cultural capital: a sense of regional identity and a belief that cooperation is better than each community going it alone.

The partnership illustrates a number of the key principles of effective rural governance. It crosses sectors, starting with the state (county government), but forming a civil society organization (the Water Partnership of Northwest Missouri). Market actors have yet to be involved but certainly will come in as investors and financers.

SUSTAINED CITIZEN ENGAGEMENT

The Bayview Citizens for Social Justice (BCSJ), led by the group's president, Alice Coles, headed up the movement to better this community in Virginia. BCSJ is made up of people in the community who became active in preserving the area and improving the infrastructure.

Bayview is a town on the eastern shore of Virginia that was founded by freed slaves and, in the past, was dependent on the fishing and farming industries for work. The town once thrived, but when those industries dried up, the town plummeted into extreme poverty and remained that way for more than a hundred years. As of the 1990s, Bayview residents, who were descendants of the town's original founders, were living in tarpaper shacks, most without running water, indoor plumbing, or adequate heating. The streets were made of dirt; the seats and floors of outdoor privies were covered in dried sewage that had seeped up through the ground during the spring's heavy rains. Residents were cleaning their clothing in water mixed with sewage—all the water in town was contaminated, with wells in desperate need of replacement. Most people had no idea what it meant to "flush" a toilet. Some residents shared a toilet—sometimes six to one toilet, and bathing in a bucket was a usual routine. Jobs in this town were not stable, mostly seasonal work or out of town. Annual household income was $10,000, and many residents depended on seasonal crop or shellfish processing jobs that brought in only $45 to $50 a month. These jobs often were an hour or more away from town.

In 1994, the Virginia Department of Corrections wanted to put a maximum-security prison near the town's limits. Although the prison would have meant 425 jobs, it would have demolished several of the area homes, which were part of the cultural landscape. The BCSJ formed out of an effort to fight the prison. The group was successful, and the prison was not put near the town, but BCSJ's motivation to improve the community continued. The group decided to turn its focus toward the community's struggle with poverty and substandard housing, winning a $20,000 grant from the Environmental Protection Agency (EPA) to create a community-based plan to eliminate the substandard housing. This grant paid for technical consultants to help the group and residents come up with a plan for remaking the town into what it once was, with retail stores, churches, a post office, privately owned homes, rental units, and cottage industries. Fifty to one hundred affordable homes were to be built.

During this turn in focus, the state chapter of the NAACP paid the town a visit and members were mortified with what they saw, declaring the town a disaster and calling the residents victims of a "modern-day apartheid system." The county administrator took great offense to these statements, saying that the town had problems, but there was not an apartheid system in place. A few months after these statements were made, the governor visited Bayview, and he said the conditions were "deplorable and need attention immediately." It was then that the ball really got rolling.

The BCSJ continued in its mission to revitalize the town and the economy. It worked to form coalitions with local and state businesses, solicited the participation of more than a hundred area residents, and won grants and loans from the U.S. Department of Agriculture (USDA) Rural Development and the Virginia Department of Housing and Community Development.

During the planning process of rebuilding the town, the EPA and the local nature conservancy teamed up with the BCSJ and held ten workshops throughout the year. Many of the workshops were organized as picnics, concerts, and fish fries, which encouraged a sense of community for participants. Storytelling was used at these gatherings to gain a sense of history and culture, which inspired participants. During the workshops, design ideas were generated, and it was decided that clustered housing was the best for Bayview, and an open space was preserved along the edge of town. The group was able to purchase 158 acres of land, and upon this land affordable rental apartments, single-family homes, and critical infrastructure are being built. The rent for the units will be fixed, accounting for no more than a third of the resident's income. New, deeper wells were dug so that homes had clean water for drinking and washing.

The next step in development is to work toward creating business development for the townspeople, now that they are living in safe conditions with good physical infrastructure. The community is working to construct a child care center, community center, and laundry facility to serve area residents.

LEVERAGING REGIONAL RESOURCES

In 1987, a fire destroyed a very popular antiques store in Abbeville, South Carolina, which was a huge tourist attraction. The town recognized a big loss of tourism when this happened. This loss of revenue was deeply impacting the community, and residents knew they had to take action. The community decided to contact the South Carolina Department of Parks, Recreation, and Tourism (SCPRT) for assistance. In the town's past, the economy had been a mix of agriculture, manufacturing, and tourism, but the agricultural base was diminishing and this caused a revenue shift. Manufacturing in the area, although stable, did not provide enough wealth for the community's Main Street businesses to survive without additional income. Tourism could offer this source of new money if the town created attractions that would draw people to the area. The loss of the antiques store hit the town hard, and residents had to find another way to get people to come to Abbeville.

Joan Davis from SCPRT began working with local residents on resource development, which began with asking them what they saw as the town's appeal and what had changed to cause a decrease in numbers in the town. It was obvious that the answer to this was the antiques shops in the area.

The SCPRT served as a "friendly government shopper," as its representatives looked for new ideas and researched opportunities for technical assistance and funding to support local initiatives. They brought in expert staff from other agencies and organizations to formulate the community's tourism plan, which included an assessment with residents of their natural, cultural, and historic resources. Together, they worked on ways to develop these resources into new products to create the attractions needed to bring visitors into the community. The SCPRT was able to show residents how to capitalize on the resources they already had in the community.

Abbeville's leaders invited the entire county to participate in their regional tourism plan, which gave residents a real sense of ownership over the project. They were able to bring ideas to the table and give their input, making this a community effort. The energy and support of the members of the community were obvious to the SCPRT, and it helped to make the project a success.

In 1991, planning of the project began, which included the preservation of cultural resources, while still generating more tourist dollars. Each rural community was to develop and implement a comprehensive cultural plan to reflect its diversity, and this plan would become an integral part of the community's economic development strategy. Each community was able to tell part of its regional story by showcasing its own particular cultural, natural, or historic resources. This involved a four-step process: organize, inventory, develop, and promote. The idea behind this was that each area would become a living museum that told a story of the development of the South from the beginning to the present day. This plan addressed the economic and social history covering agriculture (especially cotton), the Revolutionary War, textile manufacturing, the Civil War, education, water power, courthouse towns, and community development. The South Carolina Arts Commission gave the organized group a grant to develop a demonstration project to show the connection between economic development and cultural development. In 1996, the South Carolina Heritage Corridor was designated by Congress as a National Heritage Access area—one of only twenty in the United States.

The Heritage Corridor, as the project is called, extends 240 miles and includes fourteen counties across the state. Many of the communities in the project resembled Abbeville, in that the economy was declining because of population loss and a loss of economic base. Federal programs also have been reduced in recent years, so towns often have to take things into their own hands to make change. The hope with this project is that heritage tourism will lead to economic development by offering small towns and rural areas a strategy to capitalize on the economic value of their various resources. It also provides an opportunity to link economically depressed rural areas, abundant in potential historic attractions, with the management skills and infrastructure of their urban neighbors.

Heritage tourism promotes cluster sites where towns group together to improve their economic situation. Discovery Centers are located in each of the four regions along the corridor, and these will be welcome centers for visitors that offer information about the region. The centers provide interpretive themes unique to each region as well as continuing themes throughout the entire corridor. The four regions in the Heritage Corridor include the Mountain Lake Region, the Freshwater Coast Region (which includes Abbeville), the Rivers, Rails, and Crossroads region, and the Lowcountry Region. The region that encompasses Abbeville studies the communities' impact on politics in South Carolina and the nation, including the area's effect on the state's agricultural history. Local historians claim that the Confederacy was born and died in the county of Abbeville, and according to them, the first secession papers were read aloud on a hilltop in the county in 1860. All of this lends to the political-history focus that is visited in this region of the corridor. Block grants and contributions were used to build the Freshwater Coast Discovery Center, which was completed in 2001.

Recreation activities are available along the corridor as well, such as kayaking along the Edisto River, which is a service available in Abbeville. The focus throughout all the regions is oral history—telling the stories of the past in each region. Everyone involved in the effort believes it is a truly successful venture because it is a grassroots effort, with everyday people trying to make a living and to keep their town economically prosperous.

In 2001, more than 4 million tourists visited heritage sites in South Carolina, accounting for 17.2 million visitor days. Heritage visitors spend $833 million in South Carolina annually and bring in more than $48 million in local and state taxes. A recent SCPRT study showed that heritage visitors coming to the state to attend festivals, museums, cultural events, and historic sites spend over 60 percent more than other visitors. This brings in an additional 700,000 visitors to the state. The study concluded that the corridor will bring in 1,200 direct jobs and up to 3,000 temporary or part-time jobs related to tourism. In Abbeville alone there are several historic sites, some of which might have been overlooked without the corridor project in place, such as the 1908 opera house.

For sociologists, the larger issue is how the flexible networks of market, state, and civil society can stimulate healthy local societies. No one questions the need for clean water or adequate food. Ill or malnourished children cannot learn effectively and thus cannot develop the skills they eventually will need to support themselves and their families. Although governance can be motivated by a collective desire for economic development, often, as is the case of Tangier Island and northwest Missouri, economic development can be a by-product of the collaborations initiated around more concrete, immediate issues.

Chapter Summary

Governance involves the mobilization of civil society, participatory forms, public-private partnerships, and nested administrative structures. It entails a shift away from state bureaucracies and formal institutions as the locus of coordination and decision making, and its emergence raises important questions regarding the performance of alternative organizational configurations compared to government-centered local development. Governance is more than government, although governments at all levels play a vital role in making and implementing decisions.

Governance can provide flexible structures by which community members participate in local decisions, find innovative ways to provide services and community facilities, and link local resources to local needs.

Governance includes the many forms of local government found in rural areas. General-purpose governments are those created to respond to the general needs of a county, city, or town. Special-purpose governments are those created to respond to specific community needs, such as schooling, water supply, or medical services. Part-time officials and citizen volunteers often staff the governments of rural communities.

For this reason, successful rural communities not only engage local governments but also selectively link with other local governments and higher levels of government. Often such linkages, an important part of governance, are catalyzed by civil society groups or by market firms that recognize the need for systemic change.

Because of their limited resources, most rural governments find it difficult to provide adequate levels of public services when acting on their own. By mandating certain services, state and federal governments can require that local resources be directed to services that may not be needed. Multiple general-purpose and special-purpose governments can lead to conflicted or fragmented responses to local community needs. Or they can overcome the natural protection of turf to collaborate to provide synergy and efficiency. Finally, most rural governments face fiscal stress that arises from a limited tax base despite increased demand for local services. Governance, widening decision-making and responsibility to multiple jurisdictions and including market and civil society groups, can help rural governments provide services and increase public involvement.

KEY TERMS

Federalism is a system of government in which separate states or provinces are united by a central authority while retaining certain powers, including the power to tax.

Fiscal stress in rural communities arises when a limited tax base is faced with an increased need for services.

General-purpose governments are governments created to respond to the general needs of a county, city, or town.

Progressive taxes place a larger share of the tax burden on wealthier citizens and firms. The percent of income paid as income tax, for example, increases as a person's income increases.

Regressive taxes place a disproportionate share of the tax burden on those less able to pay. Consumer sales taxes become a decreasing share of people's income as their income increases. Wealthier people tend to save and invest a higher proportion of their incomes than do poor people.

Special-purpose governments are created to respond to specific community needs, such as schools or water.

Tax increment financing (TIF) is financing based on increased taxes in a particular area. For example, a city may rezone a given area and use the expected increased (or "incremental") real estate taxes to pay for new infrastructure, such as roads and sewers.

REFERENCES

Au Sable Institute for Environmental Studies. "Our Mission." Online, available: www.ausable.org/au.ourmission.cfm; accessed September 9, 2007.

Brace, Paul. 2002. "Mapping Economic Development Policy Change in the American States." *The Review of Policy Research* 19:161–178.

California, State of, Legislative Counsel. N.d. "California Constitution: Article 13A. [Taxation Limitation]." *Official California Legislative Information.*

Online; available: www.leginfo.ca.gov/cgi-bin/waisgate?waisdocid= 3482755718+20+0+0&waisaction=retrieve; accessed September 9, 2007.

Fox, Joel. 2007. "Proposition 13: A Look Back." Howard Jarvis Taxpayers Association. Online; available: www.hjta.org/content/ARC000024B_ Prop13.htm; accessed September 9, 2007.

Gais, Thomas, Subo Bac, and Lucy Dadayan. 2007. "The End of Post-Reform Growth in Social Services: Social Welfare Spending by State and Local Governments, 1977–2005." The Nelson A. Rockefeller Institute of Government, State University of New York, August 9. Online; available: www.rockinst.org/assets/F4E87BAF-B424-4AD0-821D -24C5F7B54105.pdf; accessed September 8, 2007.

National Rural Network. 2007. "Why Rural Matters III: The Rural Impact of the Administration's FY08 Budget Proposal." Washington, D.C.: National Rural Network, March. Online; available: www.rupri.org/ Forms/NRNBudget3.pdf; accessed September 8, 2007.

Office of Homeland Security. 2002. *National Strategy for Homeland Security.* Washington, D.C.: U.S. Government Printing Office. Online; available: www.whitehouse.gov/homeland/book/nat_strat_hls.pdf; accessed September 9, 2007.

Rathge, Richard. 2002. "The Changing Population Profile of the Great Plains." Unpublished paper.

Reeder, Robert J. 1990. "Introduction." *Local Revenue Diversification, Rural Economies* (March):1–6. Washington, D.C.: Advisory Commission on Intergovernmental Relations.

Sawicky, Max B. 2002. "U.S. Cities Face Fiscal Crunch: Federal and State Policies Exacerbate Local Governments' Budget Shortfalls." *EPI Issue Brief,* no. 181 (June 13). Washington, D.C.: Economic Policy Institute. Online; available: www.epi.org/content.cfm/issuebriefs_ib181; accessed September 9, 2007.

Stark, Nancy. 2007. "Eight Principles for Effective Rural Governance—And How Communities Put Them into Practice." Lincoln, Neb.: RUPRI Center for Rural Entrepreneurship. Online; available: www.rupri.org/ coreprogramviewer.php?id=33; accessed September 9, 2007.

U.S. Census of Governments. 2002. "Government Finance." Online; available: www.census.gov/govs/cog/2002COGprelim_report.pdf; accessed September 9, 2007.

12

GENERATING COMMUNITY CHANGE

Elma is a quiet town in Howard County in northeast Iowa. Although incomes are low, so are rents. A lot of widows live in town, but most folks are married and most married-couple families have at least two wage earners. Almost half the working population commutes over half an hour each way. Through Iowa State University Extension, local leaders learned of the Horizons Program of the Northwest Areas Foundation, designed to help rural communities reduce poverty. After a group attended an introductory seminar—realizing the large time commitment coupled with the opportunities—they took it back to the community, and the community signed on. Horizons is an eighteen-month program with five required segments of participation. Communities must meet the thresholds for each segment within defined time frames in order to move forward as part of Horizons. Each threshold is connected to skills and achievement that help strengthen a community. In addition to participation in the introductory seminar, the segments include:

- Community conversation and action planning focused on poverty. This segment requires twelve hours during a two-month period and the involvement of a minimum of thirty people or 2 percent of the population. The goal is for the community to learn what poverty looks like and what they can do about it. Momentum grows as the community builds skills, involves more people, and becomes increasingly strategic.

- Leadership building using LeadershipPlenty training. At least twenty-five people give thirty to forty hours of time. This is a popular segment because it is practical and assumes every community member can provide leadership.
- Community visioning and planning focused on leadership growth and poverty reduction, involving 15 percent or more of the community.
- Idea implementation.

Iowa State University Extension provides the community with support, coaching, and additional resources as they put their plans into action. The Northwest Area Foundation will coordinate grants of up to $10,000 to each community that successfully completes all components of the program.

During the community conversation using a specially designed study circle guide focused on building thriving communities, the community committed to making sure that those who had less access to community assets were considered in each action. They took stock of their assets that could be used to enhance prosperity for all the citizens, including a look at all the community capitals. They found out in their conversations that the community had lots of assets that could lead to increased prosperity for all, and that they could recombine their current assets, which included their community foundation, to reach their goals.

Although many people were eager to work, and a number of jobs in manufacturing and in the local nursing home were available, several of the thirty-one employers in the commuting area operated multiple shifts. No child care was available that served all shifts. A two-phase, three-year plan to build an early childhood center onto the community's school was developed from a study circle action plan. Using the social and political capital of the study circle group, citizens were able to mobilize financial capital: $50,000 of the $92,000 project was awarded through a U.S. Department of Agriculture rural development grant; $10,000 from a Department of Education charter school grant; $10,000 would be raised from community fund drives; and the remaining $22,000 would come from the school. Phase I would create thirty slots; Phase II would create twenty more slots (fifty total). As they assessed the built capital in the community, citizens located an available building worth moving onto the site, allowing the child care center to be up and running in a year.

In the course of their conversations, they discovered that 70 percent of the youth in town received free and reduced-price lunches. Many children came to school without the necessary supplies, so book bags filled with school supplies were to be provided for all youth. Free-will donations were accepted based on ability to pay. By making school supplies available to all, families with fewer financial resources would not be stigmatized.

The study circle revealed a strong appreciation for families and healthy recreation in Elma, but also a lack of affordable activities for families. Remembering fondly the way the community used to work together, study circle participants started offering free music and movies in the park every other week during the summer. This venue also provided a place to meet newcomers and to welcome them.

To provide safe and free fun for youth, the community applied for and received a $45,200 federal grant from the Land and Water Conservation Fund for a park improvement project. Local matching funds for the grant came from a number of civil society groups, including the Howard County Community Foundation, the Elma Area Community Foundation, BRIDGE (Building Relationships In the Development of a Greater Elma Area), and the Fox Memorial Fund for Park Improvements; a business; concession sales; and from the City of Elma.

The Horizons program expanded with interested volunteers as the community moved into the next stages of the project. The steering committee and study circle participants were amazed at the strong response. People who had never participated before came forward and volunteered. Half of the thirty-two members of the study circle had never stepped forward on a community project before.

Impact was felt outside the study circle as well. Individuals who had a very negative attitude toward their community became very positive and vocal about all Elma had to offer—including council members, school administration, and residents. As one study circle member said, "Horizons has opened eyes to the possibilities."

Community development is occurring in Elma because of the community's ability to identify its assets—including levels of bridging and bonding social capital—and to invest them in themselves. They are able to mobilize many sectors of the community to work together to make things happen. Elma has a history of self-investment and community participation, as shown by the presence and activities of the BRIDGE organization and the community foundation. Mobilizing local networks and forming new external linkages were relatively easy to achieve. Economic development is one of the results of the study circles, but not the major motivation for the project.

In many other communities, taking charge of change seems almost hopeless. New people move to town with great dreams for community improvement, but their dreams never materialize. Or local residents concerned about a declining economic base seek to attract industry, with ever-decreasing likelihood of success. What makes the difference between towns that develop and change in the face of globalization, climate change, and shifting rules and regulations of market and the state, and those that seem unable to respond effectively? What are the components of community development, and what makes it happen?

This chapter centers on different theories of community development, which stem from the political and economic contexts in which they originated. All of them assume that human agency can overcome broader trends that impact places, but they are very different on the appropriate *source* of the agency and the degree to which they take a linear or systemic approach. The assumptions behind them are followed by illustrations of how they can be and have been implemented in terms of which capitals are invested in and the impact of those investments on other community capitals and the community's triple bottom line: healthy ecosystem, vital economy, and social inclusion, which together constitute quality of life.

COMMUNITY AND DEVELOPMENT

The word "community" comes from the Greek word for "fellowship." Fellowship involves interaction, so *community development* implies that the quality of interaction among the people living in a locality improves over time. Such interaction both depends on and contributes to enhanced quality of life for each member of the community: better housing, better education, enhanced recreational and cultural opportunities, and so on. Central to the concept of community development is the idea of collective agency. *Collective agency* is the ability of a group of people—in this case those living in the same community—to solve common problems together. For community development—and collective agency—to occur, people in a community must believe that working together can make a difference and organize to collectively address their shared needs. Existing cultural capital often instills a victim mentality in the entire community—that things happen to them and nothing can be done but endure them and resent them. There is a focus on deficits and what is not there.

Community development is much broader than economic development. Indeed, one could argue that economic development could be antithetical to community development for two reasons: Economic development does not necessarily involve collective agency, and economic development may not result in an improvement of the quality of life. For instance, the high rates of economic growth in boomtowns have a negative impact on community development. The incomes of some members of the community may increase, but as crime rates increase, schools become overcrowded, housing prices soar, and neighborliness declines, the quality of life for the majority of the residents may deteriorate. This is particularly true when economic growth in the community is triggered by an absentee firm, whether it is an oil or coal company, a national meatpacker, a recreational conglomerate, or a transnational manufacturing company.

When we look at community development, we will focus on what local people do to improve the overall quality of life of the community. In the difficult economic times of the 1990s and 2000s, economic development was and is seen as the dominant means for community betterment. But bringing in jobs is not enough, and bringing the wrong type of jobs may decrease the community's quality of life. We will now examine approaches taken by community members and leaders to improve their collective well-being and how these approaches relate to collective agency. Richard Florida's work on creative economics—which encourages innovation by attracting high-quality human capital—has refocused attention on quality of life, achieved by combining talent, technology, and tolerance in new ways. In these cases, the goal is to identify and enhance assets in a systemic way, rather than singularly solve a particular problem.

MODELS OF COMMUNITY DEVELOPMENT

Three major approaches to community development have been laid out by James Christenson (1989): technical assistance, conflict models, and self-help models. To this we add the appreciative inquiry approach. Each of the approaches identifies a different role for the change agent, a different orientation to task versus process, different clientele, a different image of the individual, a different conception of the basis of change, a different core problem to be addressed, and a different action goal.

Current community development theory and practice is confronting the limitations of the practical, problem-solving approach that has long dominated development work in the North and the South. After World War II, when much reconstruction had to occur in Europe and Asia, it was easy to believe that the solution lay in the transfer of technology and money from developed areas to those seeking to develop. The goal was modernization, which embraced technological solutions to human problems. The developer provided technical assistance, which included financing technology, installing technology, and teaching people to use technology. The secret of a good community development professional, then, was to be a good diagnostician. Unfortunately, the key problem was generally found to be whatever technological fix the technical expert offered. Solving one problem always reveals another, and thus dependency on outside experts was built into the model. But becoming "modern"—to produce more and to consume more—required changing technology and mindsets.

Technical Assistance Model

In situations of low levels of community participation, community leaders often seek technical assistance that brings in resources. It can involve attraction of an outside firm, often by hiring an industrial recruiter, or by finding an expert to solve a particular problem.

The *technical assistance model* takes a problem-solving approach:

- identify community need or problem
- analyze causes
- find solution, often from the outside
- implement the solution

The basic assumption is: provide what is not there and fix what is not working.

The technical assistance model stresses the task that is to be performed. A few local leaders might decide that the community needs child care. After talking among themselves in private, they call in technical experts to assess the local situation and to find the most efficient way to build and run a child care center. The construction of the center might require receiving government grants or finding a private investor. The consultant and the local leaders would determine the method of funding, and the site would be chosen based on objective criteria determined by experts in child care centers. The success or failure of the project would be judged on the presence or absence of a child care center building at the end of a prescribed period. The combination administrator–child development specialist would be chosen on technical criteria. If a capable administrator was found, the project would continue. However, if the hired director proved inefficient or dishonest, it would be up to the town leaders (if publicly owned) or the board of directors (if privately owned), not to users of the child care center or its employees, to correct the situation. Limited community oversight then could lead to limited success.

It is assumed in this approach that answers to community problems can be reached scientifically. The problems themselves are phrased in technical terms that require expert advice regarding choices among a variety of technically feasible options. This approach requires that local residents, if they desire to participate in decisions, assimilate and absorb a great deal of information concerning complex legal and scientific issues. This greatly decreases motivation to participate. A common response is to assume that there is only one technically appropriate choice and that the experts should be left alone to make it.

Another assumption of the technical assistance approach is that development should be evaluated based on the achievement of predetermined measurable goals. Not only is the achievement of the goal important, but so is the efficiency with which it is achieved. Cost-benefit analysis, a technical tool developed by economists to determine a project's ratio of costs to benefits to the public, is a particularly appropriate tool for a technical assistance approach. Local citizens are defined as consumers of development, not participants in it. For example, success of a child care center could be determined by whether it makes a profit, whether local workers use it, how well the children do in school, or whether there is an increase in labor force participation and regularity and promptness of workforce attendance. If the community of Elma is to evaluate the success of the endeavor, all of these would be important: Financial capital, human capital, and social capital would all increase because of the presence of the child care center. It would not be administered to maximize a single goal, such as a profit, but to optimize the creation of multiple community capitals. The technical assistance approach does not lend itself to such complex measures of success.

Government bureaucracies are the most frequent employers of the technical assistance approach. This approach often works to the advantage of the power structure because of its agenda-setting ability (see Chapter 6, Political Capital). The power structure is frequently able to prevent a particular problem from reaching the level of public discussion or, in other cases, to prevent certain technically feasible solutions to a publicly defined problem from being considered realistic options.

An illustration of how politics and the technical assistance approach relate to each other is in industrial recruitment. Successful growth machines are able to define industrial recruitment as an essential economic development objective, especially in communities experiencing a loss of services or population. This is done by identifying industrial recruitment as the only technically feasible alternative for generating new employment through influential organizations such as the city's chamber of commerce or community development office. It may in fact be true, for example, that in a declining community where the elderly make up a high proportion of the population, transfer payments (including such things as Social Security, Medicare, and Medicaid payments, as well as private pensions and health insurance payments) are a large portion of community income. A program for the development of locally owned services used by retirees would keep that money circulating in the community and perhaps could generate more employment and greater employment stability and income than would a potential new factory. But in most cases, industrial recruitment wins out because the elderly income multiplier does not even get on the agenda. Furthermore, companies considering a move do not want it public until the decision is final. They also prefer to deal with a single person who represents the entire community. All of these facts militate against broad community participation in efforts to recruit industry.

Implementing the Technical Assistance Model.   In the pure technical assistance approach, a local entity, either a local government or a private entity such as a chamber of commerce, calls upon an outside expert either to develop and assess the effectiveness and efficiency of alternative solutions to a particular problem or to design the most efficient way to perform a certain task, that is, to implement a predetermined solution to a predetermined problem. In the latter instance, which represents the vast majority of technical assistance consultancies, the expert does not question the task assigned or how it was determined that the particular problem was important. The expert merely develops a plan to implement the solution.

At times, local experts, such as planners, can deliver technical assistance. They generally receive their orders from local or regional government officials and are involved in defining how to perform a particular task efficiently. Defining what the task should be is reserved for the politicians. Mark Lapping, Thomas Daniel, and John Keller (1989) outline the steps planners should undertake for effective economic development. In the technical assistance approach, an individual with technical competence is called upon to complete each step in the process. It is a linear and iterative process:

1. gather information and data
2. identify the problem
3. analyze the problem
4. develop goals and objectives
5. identify alternative solutions
6. select a solution
7. implement the solution
8. enforce the plan
9. monitor the effort and give feedback
10. readjust the solution

The Conflict Approach

Criticism of the technical assistance model and its accompanying dependency began in the global South in the late 1960s. Scholars and activists questioned the causal assumptions behind the modernization model, although they did not question the modernization goal. From revolutionary movements to liberation theology, redistribution, not just growing the pie, seemed necessary. In community development, it meant organizing excluded people to analyze their own problems and situation of oppression to solve those problems. A major organizing tool is the confrontation of those seen blocking the agreed-upon solution to the problem.

Using a *conflict approach,* a group of local people outside the local power structure comes together to discuss their problems and needs, which could include child care. For example, if the local elites proposed a golf course as an economic development project, the group seeking empowerment would mount a counterproposal—a child care center—that also would create jobs and provide a way for parents to participate in the labor force and their children to receive good care and educational opportunities—especially those families who could not afford golf clubs, lessons, or greens fees. Instead of either calling in outside experts or working in an informal fashion with local elites to mobilize local resources, the conflict-oriented group would identify a potential site and then approach the city council and the local landowner to demand that the land be donated or purchased. The organizer would focus on building strong groups to make these demands, stressing as an important issue the lack of child care facilities, particularly for the less-well-to-do members of the community. Emphasis would be on the responsibility of those with power within the community—the city council and local landowners—to act responsibly in response to the needs of the community. In another conflict model scenario, once the golf course was established, the group would demand access to the course for youth, minorities, and the elderly, with subsidized transportation and public equipment, so that the principle of communitywide access to collective resources would be enforced.

The conflict approach to community development has urban origins in the United States. The approach was codified by Saul Alinsky, who began as a community organizer in the 1930s in a Polish neighborhood of Chicago known as Back of the Yards. By working with the residents in the working-class community to identify their grievances, the organizers helped them make specific demands of the city government. This methodology has been expanded to black organizing in Chicago; Rochester, New York; Boston; Kansas City, Kansas; and Kansas City, Missouri. It has been the basis of organization of the United Farm Workers, since Cesar Chavez trained with Alinsky's group. The Association of Community Organizations for Reform Now, founded by Wade Rathke in 1970 based on Alinsky's organizing principles, has worked hard to implement and refine the conflict methodology. Many community organizers around the country continue to use and modify the approach, including the Land Stewardship Project, which organizes farmers in Minnesota, and the Industrial Areas Foundation in the *colonias* along the Mexico-Texas border.

Alinsky says that the world and hence any community is "an arena of power politics moved primarily by perceived immediate self-interests" (1971, 12). Whereas the technical assistance approach views the existing power structure as having the interests of the community at heart, the conflict approach is deeply suspicious of those who have formal community power.

The conflict approach assumes that power is never given away; it always has to be taken: "Change means movement. Movement means friction" (Alinsky 1971, 21), and friction causes heat. The goal of a conflict approach is to build a people's organization to allow those without power to gain it through direct action. Since organizations of the powerless do not have access to significant monetary resources, they must rely on their numbers. Their numerical strength is realized only through organizational strength.

Such organizations must be democratic and participatory. Alinsky believed that downtrodden people (whom he called the Have Nots, as opposed to the wealthy Haves and the Have Some, Want Mores, or the middle class) acquire dignity through participation. Experiencing denial of participation is central to their being Have Nots. He saw democracy and participation instrumentally: as means, not ends. The overall ends of community organizing should be such things as equality, justice, or freedom. But in an open society such as the United States, undemocratic organization by the Have Nots can negate those ends. Alinsky also emphasized the learning process. Organizing should be accompanied by a conscious effort to broaden horizons. Such education then helps prevent the Have Nots—once they become Have Some, Want Mores—from acting in their immediate narrow self-interest.

Implementation of the Conflict Model.   Because of the control exercised by the existing power structure, an outside organizer going into the community generally catalyzes the conflict approach. The following steps generally are followed to build a permanent, multi-issue community organization to achieve its local members' interests and link with other like-minded groups across the state and nation:

1. Community entry by an outside organizer, usually at the request of the local group wanting change:
    —Appraise the local leadership, looking at both formal and informal institutions in the community.
    —Analyze the community power structure. Who has power and what are their vulnerabilities and strengths?
    —Analyze the situation and the territory. In particular, what seem to be the major objective problems, what conflicts would attempts at solution lead to, and which conflicts are winnable?
2. Begin building a people's organization or coalition:
    —Stimulate those outside the power structure to voice their grievances. Both the creation of an organizing committee of community leaders and canvassing residents in their homes are effective.
    —Synthesize the grievances into a statement of the problem. An effective strategy for this has been neighborhood house meetings. For the conflict approach to be effective, it must concentrate on a single issue at a time, although the organization cannot be a single-issue organization. Crucial in this process is that the issue picked for the organization to focus on be winnable.

—Link the problem to organizations—working with existing organizations of the disenfranchised, creating new ones, and forming alliances with potential sympathizers. The organizing process must provide opportunities to express anger and overcome fear.

3. Engage in direct action:

—Demonstrate the value of the power of a large number of people working together to makes gains from the traditional power structure through direct action. In particular, to retain legitimacy, people's organizations need to produce a stable supply of what public administration expert Sherry Arnstein terms "deliverables": wins that are quickly achieved and yield visible benefits wrested from political and economic institutions.

4. Formalize the people's organization:

—Develop a permanent organizational structure, with dues and a structure that involves members in policy, financing, and achievement of group goals and community improvements.

In rural areas, particularly in the Midwest, where conflict with one's neighbors is viewed as disruptive and unmannerly, the most effective use of conflict organizations appears to be in mobilizing against the outside, particularly in efforts to stop nuclear waste dumps, power lines, school consolidation, polluting industries, and the like.

An example of such an organization is Save Our Cumberland Mountains (SOCM, pronounced "sock 'em"). SOCM was established in 1972 as a dues-paying, membership-based group that employs professional organizers. The organization is centered in the Cumberland Plateau region of eastern Tennessee and in 2002 had a membership of two thousand individuals in chapters that are county or community based.

The SOCM chapter is the primary political unit of the organization. It is a nonprofit Tennessee grassroots citizens' organization working on a local level for environmental, social, and economic justice in areas such as forestry, strip-mining, toxic waste issues, tax reform, and dismantling racism. The various chapter groups send representatives to the larger SOCM board or to various issue-driven steering committees, such as the legislative committee, which largely lobbies state legislators in Nashville. The SOCM board and the various committees hold a great deal of power in the organization and plan many of the group's political activities. To qualify for staff assistance, the chapter groups have to show that they have been actively working on an issue that they have identified themselves, in response to some problem originating in their local community. The staff organizer works as a "coach" for the local "teams." SOCM's recent successes include winning a ten-year battle to protect Fall Creek Falls State Park from devastation from acidic mine drainage by getting a federal designation of sixty-one thousand acres as lands unsuitable for mining; members also have hosted their first workshop to combat racism.

Kentuckians for the Commonwealth (KFTC), an organization with a similar organizational structure, succeeded after many battles in stopping the strip-mining of land without allowing the surface owner any rights or say in the matter, a practice springing from the *broadform mineral deed,* whereby land purchasers in the early 1900s were able to buy up hundreds of thousands of acres of mineral rights. KFTC was instrumental in getting legislation approved to set up Universal Service Funds as well as in getting the land around the historic Pine Mountain Settlement school declared off-limits to strip-mining. In 2006, KFTC had its twenty-fifth anniversary.

All of these instances involved confronting an outside public or private entity to stop a project or policy deemed detrimental to the inhabitants of the local community. Organizers from outside the local community and support from the parent organization are important elements in a local chapter's success against such outside forces.

Self-Help Model

The *self-help model* emphasizes process: people within the community working together to arrive at group decisions and taking actions to improve their community. Internationally, it arose when the response of elites to the conflict model became extremely effective—even lethal. That coincided with the fiscal crisis of the state under neoliberal policies, which meant cutting back on programs that addressed safety nets and redistribution of existing resources.

The self-help process builds civic capacity for collective action to move toward a shared vision for the future of the community. Like the conflict model, it aims at systemic change. The community is not so much mobilized to complete a particular project as to institutionalize a process of change based on building community institutions and strengthening community relationships to work toward desired future conditions. Elma's new free entertainment efforts contain major elements of self-help community development because putting them into place involved reinforcing patterns of community interaction, cooperation, and decision making. The change agents acted as facilitators for community input rather than sources of infinite knowledge about poverty reduction. They helped the community connect with sources of technical knowledge related to the actions they were considering, as well as assessing the costs and benefits of various alternatives.

It took awhile to instigate the child care project in Elma due to the number of meetings required to obtain everyone's input, form the appropriate committees, and respond to each committee's reports and suggestions. Yet once the child care center was established, it easily became part of the public agenda in terms of local participation in running it and in convincing city government to participate in its construction and maintenance.

A number of assumptions about the nature of rural communities are behind the self-help model (discussed by Littrell and Hobbs 1989). When assumptions about the structure of the community are wrong, self-help as a strategy is difficult to implement. These assumptions include: (1) that community members have a similarity of interest and that community development involves building consensus, (2) that generalized participation and democratic decision making within the community are necessary and possible, and (3) that the community has a degree of autonomy such that community actors can in fact influence the community's destiny.

A central assumption in the self-help model of community development is that communities are homogeneous and based on consensus. In fact, despite the norm of "we're all just folks" endorsed in many rural communities, most communities have increasing disparities in income and access to other resources. Thus, development efforts, which depend on existing local leaders as a basis for community organizing, may systematically bias development efforts away from the problems of the least-advantaged citizens. That bias, in turn, can give rise to increased inequalities and increasing poverty or to conflict-based community development activities. In fact, interests within communities can conflict, as we saw in Chapter 6, Political Capital.

Participation and democratic decision making are essential to the self-help model of development. The self-help approach assumes that it is indeed possible to motivate a broad-based band of community members to participate in community affairs. However, if community residents are uninterested and unmotivated and do not want to become involved, participation will not take place. Some groups of local residents will not see the community as relevant to their welfare, as happens, for example, with some farmers who feel their well-being depends almost entirely on government programs. Thus, these farmers may simply bypass the community and be actively involved only in their commodity organizations, which focus on the national and not on the community level. If in a particular community no farmers are active participants in efforts to solve community problems, broad-based community participation can be said not to exist, for one important segment of the community is uninvolved.

The time commitment mandated by the self-help approach may cause many to drop out, which threatens the processual aspects of this approach. Even if the stated objectives of the community development effort are reached, the effort cannot be said to have been successful if participation in the process was minimal. The approach cannot be used to solve another community problem because no new means of interaction and quality of interaction were enhanced. In a word, the process was not institutionalized, and from the self-help point of view, the effort was not successful. One obstacle to effective use of the self-help approach in small towns is the fact that people know each other in too many roles. Thus, the risk of taking a public stance, which sometimes is necessary for effective discussion, may result in public disagreement with a boss, a customer, or a colleague. This risk is seen as too great in many small towns.

Furthermore, different segments of the community have different levels of participatory skills. Higher education and professional employment give a disproportionate voice to the more privileged segment of any community, in part because they have experience with participation. And as we saw in Chapter 3, Cultural Capital and Legacy, middle-class youth are raised with verbal and discussion skills, whereas obedience—until a situation involving confrontation arises—is part of working-class socialization patterns.

Finally, self-help models of development assume a significant degree of community autonomy. Yet as we have shown in earlier chapters, rural communities are highly involved in regional, national, and even international networks that have enormous impacts on them. Being dependent on the global economy, however, does not mean that it is useless for communities to undertake self-help activities. But it does make it important that the global economic trends are understood. Part of the process of the self-help model therefore includes community education on the community's place in the global economy and the current trends within it.

The case of Ivanhoe, Virginia, illustrates this point. The first effort of the Ivanhoe Civic League following its founding in the mid–1980s was to gain control of a shell building from the county government in the hope that the community would be able to attract an industry to occupy the building. Following major efforts to obtain an industry, the Civic League concluded that adult education and youth programs would be more beneficial to the community. The Ivanhoe Civic League continues to work to make Ivanhoe a better place for all of its citizens. The education program consists of community-based Adult Basic Education/General Education Development (ABE/GED). The Ivanhoe Civic League's education program offers college classes, youth tutorials that include guidance on college and careers, professional development workshops, and computer and adult literacy classes. In 1993, a vocational component rehabilitated a historic structure in Ivanhoe to provide office and education facilities for the Ivanhoe Civic League, which is now used as a base for colleges to bring students to learn about the capitals in this hard rock–mining area.

The citizens of Ivanhoe decided that the assets of their community— their culture and the beautiful setting—should be shared by those who share their vision of a positive future for the community. In the mid–1990s, the Ivanhoe Civic League inaugurated Volunteers for Communities, now a separate organization, which is currently training seventeen communities throughout the region to host volunteers. Community service and celebration continue to play a major role for the Ivanhoe Civic League. They host an annual all-community Christmas party, a Thanksgiving prayer service, and a weeklong Jubilee festival, as well as many other community events. They built bonding social capital to help determine the vision and built bridging social capital to mobilize resources to be locally invested for an Ivanhoe where young people and elders prospered together.

Implementing the Self-Help Approach.   The self-help approach can be implemented in many ways. One of the most common set of steps of implementation, stressed by such existing community development entities as cooperative extension services, is the social action process. The approach involves a number of steps—*visioning*, determining desired future conditions and long-term goals, using broad-based participation, determining the assets in the community, analyzing alternative ways of using those assets to move toward the collective vision, choosing specific projects that move the community toward the desired future, generating communitywide commitment, planning the implementation phase, actually implementing the plan, and finally evaluating. This process focuses on social capital and generally does not address political and cultural capitals.

As a result, this approach often places heavy reliance on agenda-setting by the existing power structure: The power structure has veto power over any proposal brought to it by the initiators.

Recognizing the cozy relationship with traditional community leaders, which this approach represents, and seeing the need for more rapid change as resource-based communities experience serious problems of out-migration, unemployment, and decline of services, cooperative extension approaches have been modified to incorporate broad community participation in the problem-identification phase rather than waiting until the organizing-to-sell phase. Strategic planning methodologies, *futuring* exercises, whereby a representative group from a community is asked to establish priorities based on a strategic plan and the community's mission, and empowerment approaches all involve either a careful selection of representatives from a broad spectrum of organizations and occupations or an open town meeting approach to problem selection.

The Appreciative Inquiry Approach

The *appreciative inquiry (AI) approach* builds first on existing community capitals:

- Discover assets and what is working best
- Dream about how what is working could work even better
- Design how to build on current assets and what works to get to desired future conditions

Basic Assumption: Build On What Is There and What Is Working. AI began as a tool for the transformation of business leadership to build more effective organizations based on discovering the positive core of the enterprise and building assets around it. First used as a community development tool in the global South, beginning in Nepal, it contains many of the elements of the self-help approach but focuses on strengths, rather than needs. AI focuses attention on what works rather than on problems or needs. Although the first three models are aimed at correcting deficiencies by discovering community deficits, AI engages community partners in conversations to learn about the factors that contribute to success. Appreciative inquiry demands that the change agents approach community development as co-learners to co-construct both expert "know-what" knowledge and the wisdom that emerges from locally specific tacit, or "know-how," knowledge.

AI requires a different form of fact-finding than the other models. Identifying the assets, at times using the Community Capitals Framework, it attempts to build transformative change by taking into the future what works best in the present and what has worked for community well-being in the past.

AI emphasizes the importance of learning from others by emphasizing:

- the power of storytelling
- the need to recognize the wisdom of others
- the importance of curiosity in our quest for doing better
- the value of hearing stories
- the primacy of conversations and dialogue

These tools are used in six iterative stages:

1. Define: Decide what to focus on.
2. Discover: Discover what is working well to identify the community's positive core.
3. Dream: Envision what might be; shared images for a preferred future.
4. Design: Find innovative ways to create that future; provocative proposition about what the community can be.
5. Delivery: Implement the design and sustain the change.
6. Debrief: Reflect on and celebrate the work together, including sharing measurement of the changes (positive and negative) in community capitals and progress toward the community's desired future.

Step 6 then can trigger a new set of discoveries and innovative adaptations to achieve positive change.

Appreciative inquiry requires a new sort of change agent: the coach. One of the duties of the coach is to make sure that diverse community participants are included in the 6-D process. If, as in Elma, the goal is to increase prosperity, it is critical to include not only those who are doing well economically but also those who are not. In organizations, the CEO can require all employees to attend "AI summits" and to interview one another prior to that summit. Participation in communities requires moral suasion rather than executive fiat. An open call for participation will recruit those who always come to civic endeavors. Brenda Schmitt, the extension educator trained to be the coach in Elma, worked hard to be sure to include a wide range of Elma's residents, including single mothers, widows and widowers, business leaders, elder care workers, and construction workers. As a result, sixteen out of the thirty-two in the core study circle group were new participants—and their insights were particularly important in finding the positive core.

Although AI assumes that most of the assets for change will come from the inside and that the energy for change will be generated from within, a number of experiences show how coaches and facilitators can act as brokers to identify assets and passions within the community and link them with appropriate collaborators to achieve entrepreneurial visions (Sirolli 1999) or community visions (Rubin 2001). Part of the power of the process is to turn individual bridging social capital into community-level social capital by including the community team in discussions with those with personal connections to other key resources, such as human capital (technical expertise) or financial capital.

To learn more about AI, visit: http://appreciativeinquiry.cwru.edu/.

Implementing AI.   Around the United States and in the global South, AI is being implemented in a dynamic approach to planning, strategizing, and monitoring change processes using approaches that are:

- asset-based
- framed by the appreciative inquiry approach to work with people and change
- situated in the Community Capitals Framework

The Community Capitals Framework (CCF) allows community members to see the whole system and how the various capitals interact with one another. Appreciative inquiry shapes the process of engaging community members with one another for discussion, planning, implementation, and monitoring. The community capitals represent the things we have to work with; appreciative inquiry defines how we will work with them.

In analyzing the HomeTown Competitiveness (HTC) program, designed to build entrepreneurial communities through retaining youth and wealth and creating entrepreneurs and leadership, in Nebraska the North Central Regional Center for Rural Development used the CCF to identify three key asset transformations (Emery and Flora 2006). First, sustainable change often began when a new approach from outside the community, "know-what knowledge," was joined with local wisdom, "know-how knowledge," to create a new social practice. Tribal colleges have mobilized expert and local knowledge in a range of endeavors, such as the development of wind power at Turtle Mountain Community College in North Dakota.

The second asset transformation occurred when the HTC program began to show results. Our data indicated the subsequent expansion of assets in human capital as more people were aware of the new approach, and the assets in social capital brought new people together around the new practice. At this point in the change process, there was a dramatic change in cultural capital indicating that accepted ways of getting things done now included the new practice and that people's vision of the possible included a proactive healthy community. Residents discussed how the programs helped people find their identity, empowered them to continue their education, and encouraged them to seek a new destiny, thus building human capital. They focus on individuals and supporting change for their participants with an implicit assumption that the growth of individual cultural, social, and human capital assets eventually will impact all the capitals at the community level. For example, the collection includes a number of practices that help young people prepare to succeed in college by focusing on academic and social skills, as well as cultural identity.

Finally, in the HTC study we found evidence that the resources supporting the social practice increased to include a diversity of financial capital assets once the cultural capital had expanded to include the idea that the community can and will take charge of its future. New cultural capital resources include the belief that the community is responsible for its future and that it has the resources to take action in regard to that belief. In these examples, we find the practice attracting financial capital from diverse resources. For example, the tribal college construction program at Sitting Bull Community College in North Dakota and an incubator, farmers' market, and rural health center in Hawaii all include the introduction of "know-what" knowledge linked with traditional cultural practices, leading to new cultural assets related to empowerment, self-sufficiency, and community agency. Each of the projects also has accessed financial resources beyond grant or college start-up funding.

Not only does mapping of assets provide a picture of current assets and how those assets might be improved, it can yield a historical record of changes over time, represented by spiraling up and spiraling down of the different community capitals, helping community members understand what capital investments are critical at different points in the community development process.

The Horizons program in Elma contributed to an upward spiral in the community (see Figure 12.1). The study circle process, initiated by bridging social capital, created bonding social capital as local wisdom was combined with professional expertise. The first projects were aimed at increasing human capital by focusing on early childhood education and success of community schoolchildren by planning the child care center and the book bag program. Investment was made in built capital for the child care center, which utilized political capital, financial capital, social capital, and existing built capital. This success enhanced cultural capital, as the community's belief in its ability to bring about positive change collectively increased. Natural capital was enhanced as the team's focus on healthy outdoor activity (also inspired by the Northeast Iowa Food and Fitness Initiative) led to park improvements. Mobilizing the resources to get these things done increased political capital at the local, county, state, and federal levels. Finally, once child care was in place, financial capital increased for working families, for regional businesses that had a more reliable supply of workers, and for the community itself through the jobs the

Figure 12.1 Upward Spiral: Increasing Prosperity through Investing in Community Capitals

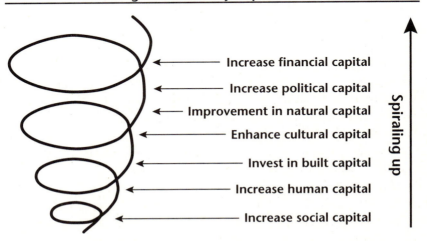

Increase financial capital

Increase political capital

Improvement in natural capital

Enhance cultural capital

Invest in built capital

Increase human capital

Increase social capital

Spiraling up

SOURCE: Emery and Flora 2006, 22

child care center generated. (See Traill and Brown 2005 on child care as economic development.)

Factors in Effective Change

We now will examine two important factors in all four models in community development—linkages with the outside and the planning/visioning process—to see differences and similarities among the models.

Linkages for Community Change

None of the models of community development that we have presented deny the need to obtain outside resources for community development to take place. In the technical assistance and conflict approaches, an outside person or group of people is central to the process. In both cases, an objective of the effort often is to obtain resources from the outside. The self-help and AI approaches emphasize reliance on local resources. However, as will be seen, the ability to mobilize local resources often is proof to those who control outside resources that the self-help effort is serious. Thus, there is a complementarity between mobilizing local resources and the ability to obtain resources from outside the community. Creating strategic partnerships is necessary in all cases (Blakely and Bradshaw 2002). This is particularly true under conditions of very limited outside resources because those who control such resources are especially keen to ensure that their funds are well spent. What better place to spend them than on a project that has shown it can obtain resources?

Financial capital from the outside is becoming more and more scarce as both federal and state governments deal with mammoth deficits by cutting funding for social programs, including those that benefit rural communities. As endowments of most foundations declined with the stock market, so did possibilities of grants from both private and public sources in the first half of the decade. Private- and public-sector groups are starting state and regional venture capital funds, which can be an important input into community development (see Chapter 7, Financial Capital).

However, these linkages to the outside through investment can be risky in terms of the collective agency of a community. There is an old saying: "He who pays the piper calls the tune." This means that the source of funding, whether the federal government or a multinational corporation, can impose a large number of conditions on the delivery of capital resources. Sometimes those conditions actually cost the community more than they gain. For example, a number of studies have shown that the tax abatements, infrastructure construction, and other financial incentives poured into attracting industry in the 1980s did not even pay back the local public investment, much less create wealth in the local community.

Another important type of outside linkage is less hierarchical and therefore less risky in terms of loss of collective agency: More and more communities are forming horizontal linkages with other communities that have faced and dealt with similar problems of their own. This type of lateral learning by community groups tends to foster rather than impede collective agency. Community groups analyze their own situation and consider alternative ways to confront it. Often a community member knows of another community that has faced a similar problem. Citizen-to-citizen exchanges take place as the group that has tried a solution explains both the process and the outcome to the other community.

For example, when Lexington, Nebraska, became the site of a large IBP meatpacking plant, community officials met with leaders from Denison, Iowa, where IBP began as Iowa Beef Packers, and from Garden City, Kansas, where IBP's largest processing plant is located, to learn of the problems and discuss potential solutions. As part of the general move toward consolidation in the food industry, IBP was purchased by Tyson Foods Inc. in 2001. Because the communities already had links, they were better able to work together to understand the implications of the change in ownership. The acquisition by communities of information relevant to their needs through lateral learning and technical assistance can strengthen their ability to maintain collective agency when they enter into joint ventures or other means of obtaining capital from the outside to improve their own quality of life.

Planning versus Visioning as Strategies for Implementing Change

Increasingly, communities are recognizing that planning is a key part of development. Planning may serve any of the types of community development, but the approach to planning differs significantly according to the model of community development being pursued.

Planning is an integral part of the technical assistance model of community development. Under this model, the primary concern is with the final product, the plan, which then can be used as a map that displays the explicit tasks that must be performed. Professional planners charged with developing community planning documents may consult with the community when necessary either by talking to designated leaders, conducting surveys, or presenting results to community meetings. Community members are involved in the process not as active participants in the decision-making process but as passive providers of information on which such decisions are made.

Planners then develop an overall strategy and plan of action. The plan usually consists of a baseline projection, a projection of the desired level of economic activity, and a description of ways of bringing the two projections closer together.

Once written, the plan and its implementing components then can be used to prioritize activities and eliminate options or tasks that are not included in it. In such circumstances, the plan can be used to reinforce the notion of calling on technical rather than political solutions to problems. For example, if the plan calls for a golf course, under the technical assistance model there is little need to get broad community input into the series of decisions that goes into its construction and operation.

The increasing complexity of the decisions communities are forced to make gives a great deal of power to the city engineers or administrators who are closest to the source of technical information. Their clear expertise in understanding the arcane language of, for example, zoning and taxing alternatives aids this process. Just as the city or county attorney in the past was able to dismiss a call for change by saying the proposed change was not legal (forcing the person or group who wanted change to hire a lawyer to get an alternate opinion, which the person or group then had to take to a higher authority), now the city engineer can dismiss any change in community resource management by saying, "It doesn't fit the plan." At this point, the conflict model of community development becomes appropriate, for groups may mobilize to seek other experts to support an alternative action. But most often, the first "technical" judgment goes unquestioned. The technical assistance approach depends on human capital (often from the outside or a few inside experts), built capital, and financial capital for incremental improvements that do not challenge the current political, social, or financial capital.

The conflict model of social change relies more on cultural capital. The conflict is almost always justified by a shared vision of the future of the community, often based on an idealization of what once existed (a more inclusive and environmentally sound community), either in the current location or in ancestral memory. This feeds a vision of the future that can be justified by the past, showing such a community *could* exist, even if it does not at this place at this time. The conflict model builds first on cultural capital to mobilize the other capitals for systemic change.

Since, by definition, the conflict model is used by those who do not have power, the relationship between goals and means is less obvious than in either of the other two models. The tactical plan for implementation of goals depends heavily on the response of the powerful opposition to the prior actions of the group practicing the conflict approach. Tactics may change from day to day. Alinsky emphasized the importance of the element of surprise in responding to those who are in power. This need for flexibility, quick response, and surprise, coupled with the fact that initially the community organizer (who usually is from the outside) must be a catalyst for building an organization, are tendencies that militate toward a narrowing of decision making to a small group of people or sometimes to a single leader. However, the long-term survival and effectiveness of the organization in achieving its goals depend on broad and deep support from within the disadvantaged group. That support is best maintained through broad and active participation. So long as the organization commands few resources, participation, if not democratic decision making, is central to maintaining support for the organization. Numbers are a substitute for financial resources. Thus, there is a permanent tension in the organization or movement between democracy and centralization of control. As the organization becomes more successful in gaining resources, participation and democracy may decline unless democratic decision-making processes were explicitly attended to in the organizational phase. Thus, in addition to goal setting, the strategy for organizing is a central part of the planning process for a group using the conflict approach.

The self-help model does not challenge the status quo but generally is based on a vision of desired future conditions and the cultural belief that it is important that change be locally driven. There is also a general understanding that local communities cannot control their destiny, only influence, and thus the self-help model contains elements of flexibility, based more on a vision than a static plan. Practitioners of self-help community development favor a different version of the planning process. When conducted in a highly participatory way, planning not only allows for development of a collective vision of community but also provides mutually agreed-upon signposts to help achieve it. For example, the commitment and incorporation phases of the social action approach are, respectively, the goal-setting and implementation-design phases of that planning process. But, unlike in the technical assistance model, they are imbedded within a participatory approach. Community members who participate in the social action or similar processes have some role in shaping the goals and means of implementing those goals (although as was discussed earlier, community opinion leaders may have already channeled the social action process toward certain problems and away from others). In most participatory approaches that use the self-help model, there is broad participation in determining the basic questions to be asked. The downside of the self-help approach to planning is that it is clearly more time-consuming than is the technical assistance approach.

APPROACHES TO ECONOMIC DEVELOPMENT

The four approaches discussed above are based on community development, rather than simply economic development. But as rural communities continue to be buffeted by global forces, economic development can obscure a more holistic approach. Different people have different ideas as to what economic development entails. Some see economic development as identical with an increase in community income. Others view it in terms of an expansion in the number of jobs. Still others would say that economic development involves an increase in population. The relationship between community development and economic development depends on the kind of economic development that is pursued. Approaches to economic development vary based on how broadly or narrowly economic development is defined and how success is measured. The firm recruitment approach generally has one goal: job creation. Self-development often seeks to reduce poverty, increase local firm efficiency, increase community economic diversity, and increase the assets of local residents.

Firm Recruitment

One approach to economic development that stems from the technical assistance model is the *firm recruitment model*. It assumes that private-sector firms have considerable geographic mobility as they seek more-favorable locations. Early tactics aimed at firm recruitment during the growth years of the 1950s through the 1970s were very straightforward, involving such things as the construction of industrial sites and proactive industrial recruiting by more sophisticated cities. It was assumed that any particular locality had a series of advantages to offer and that firms would somehow find them, although by the 1970s it had become clear that despite the favorable climate for domestic industrial growth, a community had to develop a sophisticated approach to firm recruitment if it was to be successful. Planners and social scientists carried out studies to see where firms located and what they looked for when they chose new sites.

By the economic downturn of the 1980s, states and localities had begun to realize that only a few firms moved each year and that those that did usually went overseas for cheaper labor and more lax pollution controls. Competition for the few firms serious about relocating in the United States became intense. States began instituting a wide variety of inducements for firms, including grants, loans, loan guarantees, tax incentives, targeted industrial revenue bond financing, tax increment financing, and state enterprise zones. When one state or locality offered an incentive, others felt obliged to do so.

Less publicized but also prevalent during the 1980s were changes on the state and federal levels that weakened organized labor. Communities used low wages as a bargaining chip in attracting firms. In fact, in a number of high-growth areas where public infrastructural investments and favorable tax structures attracted industries, the jobs that were generated paid so poorly and the working conditions were so bad that immigrant workers had to be recruited to fill them. Meatpacking plants in Kansas and Nebraska are examples of this kind of industrial recruitment. Political scientist Peter Eisenger (1988) refers to these attempts to locally reduce the cost of land, labor, capital, infrastructure, and taxes as supply-side development.

The firm recruitment approach to economic development is most compatible with the technical assistance approach to community development. Local governments hire economic development professionals to obtain grants for built capital, to develop local tax incentive packages, and to recruit new firms. These activities required little grassroots participation. In fact, they are antithetical to broad-based community involvement. Getting grants requires technical knowledge of bureaucracies and procedures or particularistic political connections. Negotiations with firms that might move to the community are best carried out in secret. The firms insist on such secrecy so that communities competing for their branch plants can be played off against each other and so that their present workforce can be kept in the dark about the potential move. Firms considering a move prefer to deal with only one person who can speak for the entire community. Such approaches discourage broad community participation.

Self-Development

In contrast to this supply-based approach to economic development is what Eisenger refers to as a demand-oriented approach, which includes the search for new markets and new products to fit those markets. Instead of simply offering incentives to any firm willing to move, public-private partnerships are formed that help determine what firms will be underwritten by the public as those with the most potential for success—and positive community impact.

One type of demand-side approach that has been effective in rural communities is *self-development.* This involves public-sector groups, usually a city or county government, working with private-sector groups of individuals within a community to establish a locally controlled enterprise. A national inventory of self-development projects by rural sociologists Jan Flora, Gary Green, Frederick Schmidt, and Cornelia Flora identified a number of types of self-development efforts and mechanisms through which they worked. Key to each of them was local investment of time and capital, coupled with a sound management structure and good links to outside resources of both capital and information. Although the short-term impact on the number of jobs created may not be as great as attracting a branch plant of a major multinational corporation, communities involved in self-development have found that the risk is lower and the gains more consistent than even successful industrial recruitment. Furthermore, self-development communities were more successful in attracting branch plants than were non-self-development communities. The choice to emphasize self-development did not preclude firm recruitment, although it did make the communities less likely to offer extreme tax benefits or public investments in infrastructure.

Self-development involves sustained local economic development activities. It encourages broad-based participation, involving newcomers, women, and minorities. It depends on and encourages the development of community organizations. Self-development contributes to community development and tends to encourage participation. It gives community members a feeling of control over the economic life of their communities. In short, it promotes collective agency. It is most consistent with the self-help form of community development, although it can be compatible with the conflict approach.

Successful self-development models reorganize and mobilize local assets (Kretzmann and McKnight 1993; Green and Haines 2002; Feikema,

Segalavich, and Jeffries 1997). Local communities and organizations that conduct asset-mapping exercises realize the power of local assets as a mobilizing tool to bring people together, as illustrated by Elma's experience.

Asset mapping is a process of discovery, of learning what is there. If carried out properly, this process will result in new patterns of interaction among community members. Discovery is most effective when it revolves around an issue.

Mapping assets, however, is not enough. There has to be commitment on the part of local people to figure out ways of recombining the assets to address the issue under discussion. The Heartland Center for Leadership Development, the Nebraska Community Foundation, and the Nebraska Cooperative Extension have been engaged in important issue-oriented asset mapping as a basis for community action.

Asset mapping is important because it allows communities to move beyond a victim mentality and recognize that by working together locally, changes can be made. It means putting faith in local people to evolve a people's program (Alinsky 1946, 56). Asset mapping works best when communities begin by addressing pieces of issues that can be quickly alleviated. However, early success should be a learning experience on addressing the more complex aspects of the issue, such as unequal power within the community or long-term disinvestment in the community by public and private sectors.

Focusing on assets does not mean that a community is unaware of the impact of major social forces, including economic concentration, increasing competition, and changes in government programs. Some see an *asset-based approach* as ignoring such issues. Although this can happen, mobilizing local resources in new ways is more likely to create a climate for successfully addressing more difficult structural issues by strengthening local social capital.

Chapter Summary

Community development is what people do to improve the overall quality of life in the community. Although community development often involves economic development, it implies far more. Central to the concept of community development is the concept of collective agency. Collective agency is the ability of a group of people to solve common problems together.

Contrasting three models of community development illustrates dramatically different approaches to community change. The self-help model focuses on the process by which people work together to arrive at group decisions and take action. It assumes that communities are homogeneous and consensus-based. The technical assistance model focuses on the task to be accomplished and uses outside expertise to help community members accomplish that task. This model assumes that answers can be arrived at objectively, using the scientific method. The conflict model focuses on the redistribution of power among community members. It assumes that power is never given but must be taken away. Each model gives rise to a different community development strategy.

Two factors are important to all three models of community development. The first is linkages. Communities need linkages to outside sources of information. These linkages can be with external agencies or they can be with other communities, enabling lateral learning to occur. The second factor is planning, which is a key part of development but will be approached differently depending on the model of community development being followed.

Economic development is one part of community development. Consequently, the type of economic development strategy pursued should match the community development model used. Two of the more common models are the firm recruitment model and the self-development model. For both community development and economic development, new collaborations must be formed inside and outside communities.

Key Terms

Appreciative Inquiry (AI) is a collective process through which members of a community of interest or place reflect on times when they implemented progressive participation, what was in place that made that happen, what an alternative future would look like building on the strengths of the community, and design and implement systemic change based on the community's positive core.

An *asset-based approach* to development is used by most community developers now, in contrast to the old *needs assessments*. Whereas a needs assessment focused on what was not in a community and developed a wish list of projects and programs, an asset-based approach links the various capitals existing in a community to see how they can be recombined to achieve a desired future condition.

The *broadform mineral deed* was used by land purchasers in the early 1900s to buy up hundreds of thousands of acres of mineral rights, leaving subsequent surface owners legally helpless to prevent destruction of their homes, yards, and gardens by strip-mining when this technology came into vogue in the middle of the century.

Collective agency is the ability of a group of people to solve common problems together.

Community development is what people do to improve the overall quality of the community.

The *conflict approach* of community development focuses on the redistribution of power among community groups or with the outside.

The *firm recruitment model* of economic development assumes that private-sector firms have considerable geographic mobility and seeks to engage community resources to attract those industries to the community.

Futuring is a process used by community developers and planners that brings together a small but representative group to assess the current environment, develop a strategic positioning plan, and establish priorities based on the assessment and consistent with the plan and the organization's or community's mission.

The *self-development model* of economic development uses public-sector groups working with private-sector groups to establish locally owned enterprises.

The *self-help model* of community development focuses on the process by which people work together to arrive at group decisions and take action.

The *technical assistance model* of community development focuses on the task to be accomplished and uses outside expertise to help community members accomplish that task.

Visioning is a process used by community developers and planners to work with a broad-based group of citizens to determine desired future conditions and long-term goals for what their community should be.

REFERENCES

Alinsky, Saul D. 1946. *Reveille for Radicals.* New York: Random House.

———. 1971. *Rules for Radicals.* New York: Vintage Books.

Arnstein, Sherry. 1972. "Maximum Feasible Manipulation." *Public Administration Review* 32 (September):377–492.

Blakeley, Edward J., and Ted K. Bradshaw. 2002. *Planning Local Economic Development: Theory and Practice.* Thousand Oaks, Calif.: Sage Publications.

Christenson, James A. 1989. "Themes of Community Development." In *Community Development in Perspective,* ed. James A. Christenson and Jerry W. Robinson Jr., 28–48. Ames: Iowa State University Press.

Eisenger, Peter K. 1988. *The Rise of the Entrepreneurial State: State and Local Economic Development Policy in the United States.* Madison: University of Wisconsin Press.

Emery, Mary, and Cornelia Butler Flora. 2006. "Spiraling-Up: Mapping Community Transformation with Community Capitals Framework." *Community Development: Journal of the Community Development Society* 37: 19–35.

Feikema, Robert J., Joanne H. Segalavich, and Susan H. Jeffries. 1997. "From Child Development to Community Development: One Agency's Journey." *Families in Society: The Journal of Contemporary Human Services* 78, no. 2:185–195.

Green, Gary Paul, and Anna Haines. 2002. *Asset Building and Community Development.* Thousand Oaks, Calif.: Sage Publications.

Kretzmann, John P., and John L. McKnight. 1993. *Building Communities from the Inside Out: A Path toward Finding and Mobilizing Community Assets.* Chicago: ACTA Publications.

Lapping, Mark B., Thomas L. Daniel, and John W. Keller. 1989. *Rural Planning and Development in the United States.* New York: Guilford.

Littrell, Donald W., and Darryl Hobbs. 1989. "The Self-Help Approach." In *Community Development in Perspective,* ed. James A. Christenson and Jerry W. Robinson Jr., 48–68. Ames: Iowa State University Press.

Rubin, Sarah. 2001. "Rural Community Colleges as a Catalyst for Community Change: The RCCI Experience." *Rural America* 16, no. 2: 12-19.

Sirolli, Ernesto. 1999. *Ripples on the Zambezi: Passion, Entrepreneurship, and the Rebirth of Local Economics.* Stony Creek, Conn.: New Society Publishers.

Traill, Saskia, and Brentt Brown. 2005. "Increasing the Supply of Quality, Accessible, Affordable Child Care: An Economic Development Strategy for the North Central Region." Policy brief, North Central Regional Center for Rural Development, April. Online; available: www.ncrcrd.iastate.edu/pubs/policybriefs.html; accessed September 9, 2007.

Walzer, N., S. C. Deller, H. Fossum, G. Green, J. Gruidl, S. Johnson, S. Kline, D. Patton, A. Schumaker, and M. Woods. 1995. "Community Visioning/Strategic Planning Programs: State of the Art." RRD 170. Ames, Iowa: North Central Regional Center for Rural Development. Online; available: www.iira.org/pubsnew/publications/RETAC_Other_147.pdf; accessed September 9, 2007.

APPENDIX

The videos designed to accompany the first edition of this book can be accessed online at www.learner.org/resources/series7.html#jump1, and they are available on DVD. The current organization of this book suggests the following links between the videos and the text, although they do not completely correspond. The videos were made in the early 1990s to go with the first edition of the book, which is quite different from its current form.

Book Chapter	Video
1. The Rural Landscape and the Importance of Place	*2. Economic Base* Illustrating the shifting economic base of rural communities, this video juxtaposes the history of four diverse rural areas—Irwin, Iowa; Mammoth Lakes, California; Eatonton, Georgia; and McDowell County, West Virginia—with their current economic transitions. *1. Who Cares?* Why is rural America important to us as a nation? What steps should be taken to respond to rural communities in crisis, and what does the future hold for these rural areas?
2. Natural capital	*7. The Town That's Been through the Mill* The people of Oakridge, an Oregon timber community whose mill is now closed, show their resilience. Mill workers, community leaders, and government officials share their perceptions of what led to the economic crisis in their community.

Book Chapter	Video
3. Cultural capital	***3. Just Folks*** This video highlights community values and beliefs, which contribute to the power of social institutions, such as churches and schools. Why changes need to be made within the parameters of social and cultural customs and standards is explored.
4. Human capital	***11. Capacity to Care*** This video examines how rural communities with limited resources are able to meet the needs of special populations. Communities in Virginia, Alabama, and Ohio are shown to provide such programs. ***4. Legacy*** Rural families discuss the "legacies" they hope to pass on to their children. What is deemed important—a business, land, education, the environment, or something else—depends on social class, gender, race, and ethnicity.
5. Social capital	***10. The Will to Grow*** Why does a community such as Caliente, Nevada, survive all odds while another with almost identical resources becomes a ghost town? The social infrastructure of these communities is examined for clues.
6. Political capital	***8. Hereby Notified and Called to Meet*** This video features a discussion of how public decisions are made in a variety of settings.
7. Financial capital	***5. Act Locally . . . and Invest*** Keeping and attracting investment in rural areas require creative approaches. The Penobscot Nation in Maine and a family-run shoe factory in Ohio demonstrate how rural people overcome problems stemming from a lack of capital.
8. Built capital	***9. The Basics*** The quality of everyday life depends on public services and community maintenance. Taken for granted in modern society, these services become expensive for the sparse population base of rural areas.

Book Chapter	Video
9. The Global Economy	*6. Think Globally* This video addresses strategies rural communities can use to adapt their labor force to the global economy. Southeast Asians move to Kansas to work in a factory and women in the Dominican Republic sew shoes for a manufacturer in Ohio.
10. Consumption in Rural America	*7. The Town That's Been through the Mill* As the dominant industry declines, levels of consumption of the ex–lumber workers is affected, and a new group of high-consumption individuals attracted by natural amenities shows the widening inequalities.
11. Governance	*8. Hereby Notified and Called to Meet* How do local governments work? This program shows how two local governments mediate conflict. Direct democracy in a town meeting in Fletcher, Vermont, is compared with the city council in Caliente, Nevada.
12. Generating Community Change	*12. Communities on the Move* Visionary leaders and innovative approaches can compensate for limited resources. This program visits a sheep and weaving cooperative in northern New Mexico; a melon collective in Texas; and the Appalachian Center for Economic Networks in southeast Ohio. *13. What's Next?* Sociologists discuss rural public-policy issues for the next decade, trying to articulate how rural Americans can take advantage of opportunities now and in the future.

INDEX